CAPTAIN AMERICA

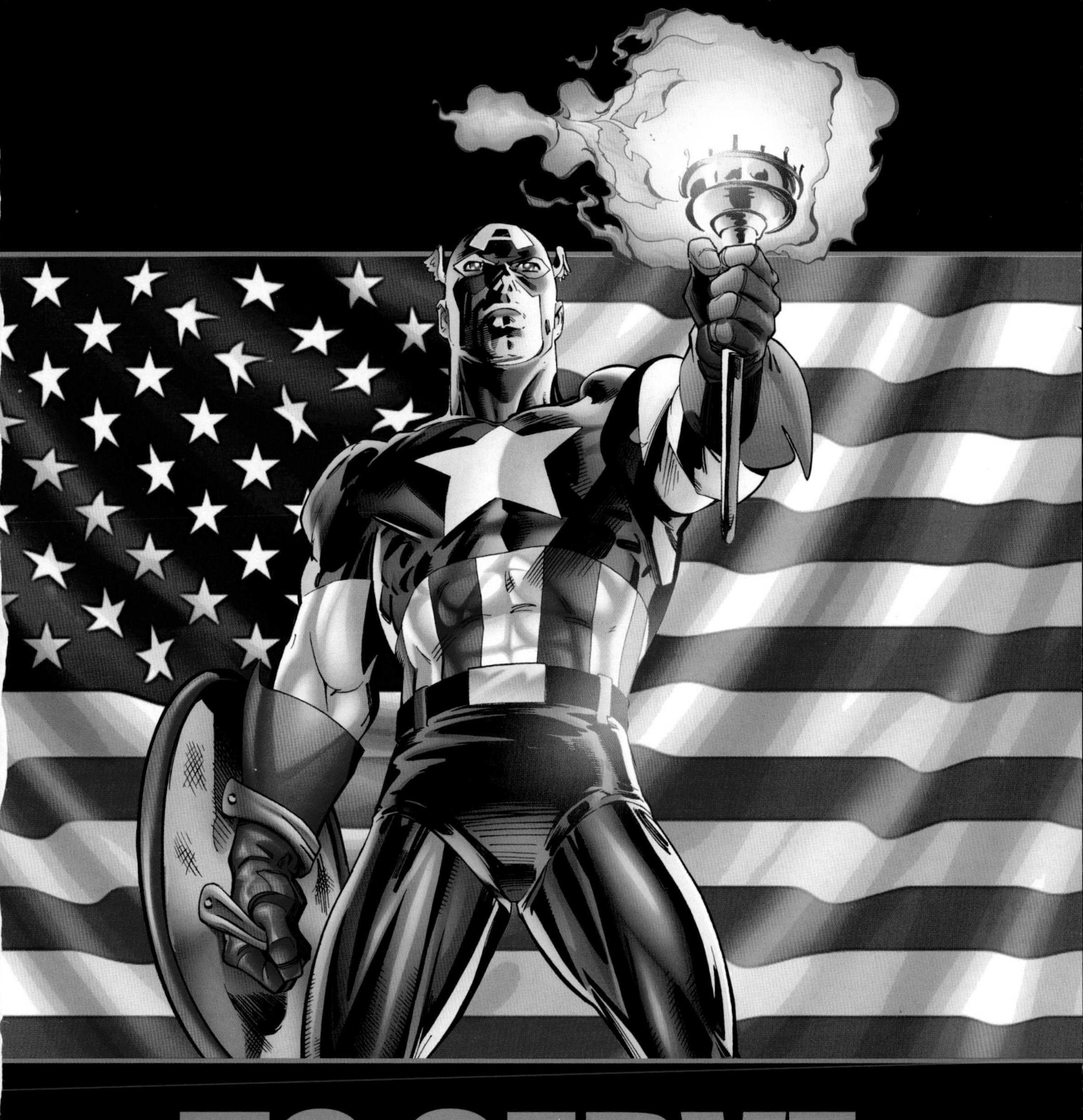

TO SERVE & PROTECT

CAPTAIN AMERICA

WRITER
MARK WAID

PENCILERS
RON GARNEY
WITH DALE EAGLESHAM & ANDY KUBERT

INKERS
BOB WIACEK
WITH SCOTT KOBLISH &
JESSE DELPERDANG

COLORISTS
JOE ROSAS
WITH DIGITAL CHAMELEON &
JASON WRIGHT

LETTERERS
JOHN COSTANZA
WITH TODD KLEIN

EDITOR
MATT IDELSON

FRONT COVER ARTISTS
RON GARNEY & BOB WIACEK

FRONT COVER COLORIST
ATOMIC PAINTBRUSH

CAPTAIN AMERICA: TO SERVE & PROTECT. Contains material originally published in magazine form as CAPTAIN AMERICA #1-7. First printing 2011. ISBN# 978-0-7851-5082-4. Published by MARVEL WORLDWIDE, INC., a subsidiary of MARVEL ENTERTAINMENT, LLC. OFFICE OF PUBLICATION: 135 West 50th Street, New York, NY 10020. Copyright © 1998 and 2011 Marvel Characters, Inc. All rights reserved. $24.99 per copy in the U.S. and $27.99 in Canada (GST #R127032852); Canadian Agreement #40668537. All characters featured in this issue and the distinctive names and likenesses thereof, and all related indicia are trademarks of Marvel Characters, Inc. No similarity between any of the names, characters, persons, and/or institutions in this magazine with those of any living or dead person or institution is intended, and any such similarity which may exist is purely coincidental. Printed in China. ALAN FINE, EVP - Office of the President, Marvel Worldwide, Inc. and EVP & CMO Marvel Characters B.V.; DAN BUCKLEY, Publisher & President - Print, Animation & Digital Divisions; JOE QUESADA, Chief Creative Officer; JIM SOKOLOWSKI, Chief Operating Officer; DAVID BOGART, SVP of Business Affairs & Talent Management; TOM BREVOORT, SVP of Publishing; C.B. CEBULSKI, SVP of Creator & Content Development; DAVID GABRIEL, SVP of Publishing Sales & Circulation; MICHAEL PASCIULLO, SVP of Brand Planning & Communications; JIM O'KEEFE, VP of Operations & Logistics; DAN CARR, Executive Director of Publishing Technology; JUSTIN F. GABRIE, Director of Publishing & Editorial Operations; SUSAN CRESPI, Editorial Operations Manager; ALEX MORALES, Publishing Operations Manager; STAN LEE, Chairman Emeritus. For information regarding advertising in Marvel Comics or on Marvel.com, please contact Ron Stern, VP of Business Development, at rstern@marvel.com. For Marvel subscription inquiries, please call 800-217-9158. Manufactured between 2/7/2011 and 3/16/2011 by R.R. DONNELLEY ASIA PRINTING SOLUTIONS, DONGGUAN, GUANGDONG, CHINA.

10 9 8 7 6 5 4 3 2 1

COLLECTION EDITOR
NELSON RIBEIRO

EDITORIAL ASSISTANTS
JAMES EMMETT & JOE HOCHSTEIN

ASSISTANT EDITOR
ALEX STARBUCK

EDITORS, SPECIAL PROJECTS
MARK D. BEAZLEY & JENNIFER GRÜNWALD

SENIOR EDITOR, SPECIAL PROJECTS
JEFF YOUNGQUIST

RESEARCH
JEPH YORK

PRODUCTION
RYAN DEVALL

SENIOR VICE PRESIDENT OF SALES
DAVID GABRIEL

EDITOR IN CHIEF
AXEL ALONSO

CHIEF CREATIVE OFFICER
JOE QUESADA

PUBLISHER
DAN BUCKLEY

EXECUTIVE PRODUCER
ALAN FINE

CAPTAIN AMERICA CREATED
BY JOE SIMON & JACK KIRBY

TO SERVE & PROTECT

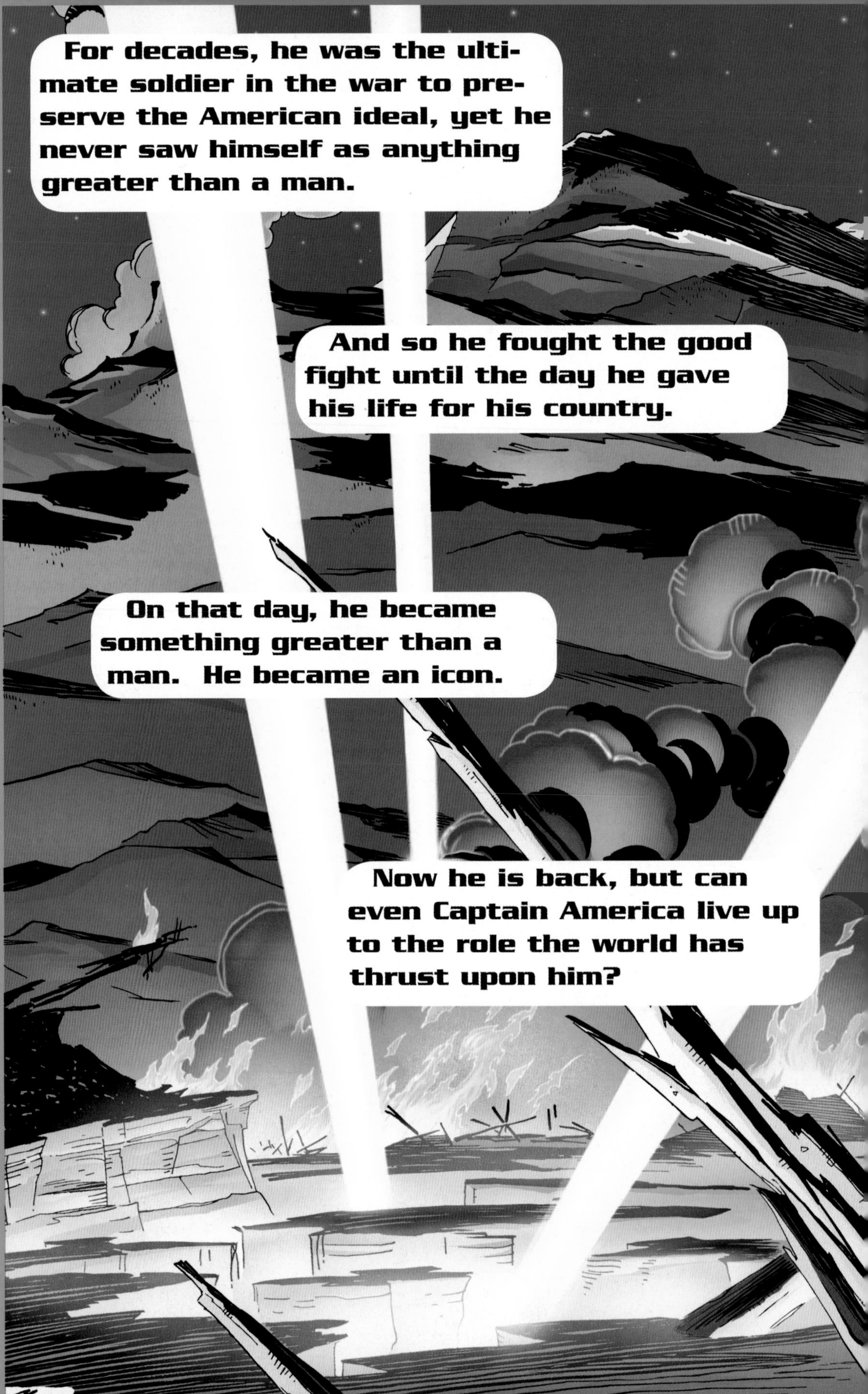
For decades, he was the ultimate soldier in the war to preserve the American ideal, yet he never saw himself as anything greater than a man.
And so he fought the good fight until the day he gave his life for his country.
On that day, he became something greater than a man. He became an icon.
Now he is back, but can even Captain America live up to the role the world has thrust upon him?

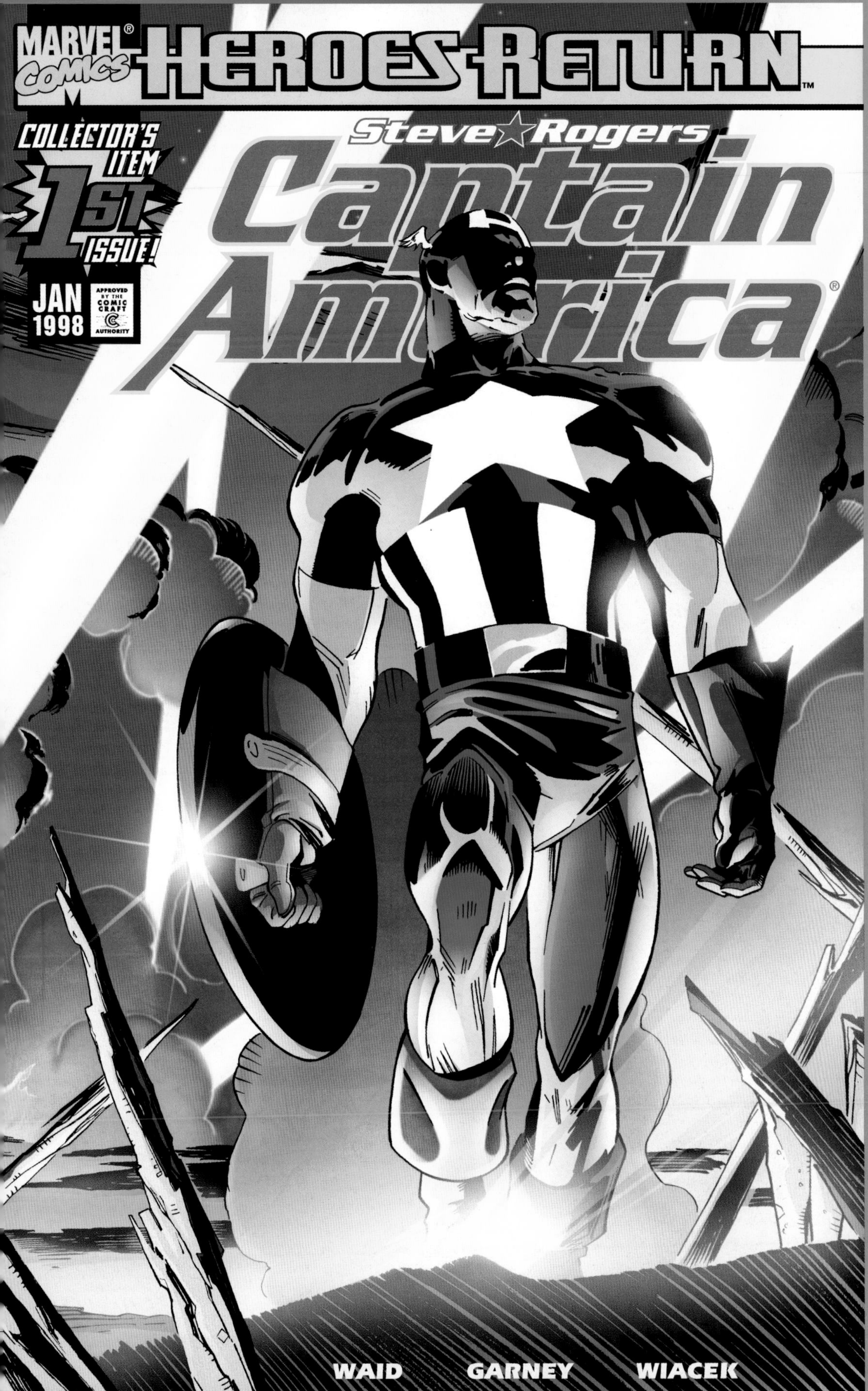
MARVEL COMICS
HEROES RETURN
COLLECTOR'S ITEM 1ST ISSUE!
JAN 1998
APPROVED BY THE COMIC CRAFT AUTHORITY
Steve Rogers
Captain America
WAID
GARNEY
WIACEK

STAN LEE Presents

THE RETURN OF

Steve ★ Rogers

Captain America

MARK WAID
writer

RON GARNEY
penciler

BOB WIACEK
inker

JOE ROSAS
colorist

DIGITAL CHAMELEON
separations

JOHN COSTANZA
letterer

MATT IDELSON
editor

BOB HARRAS
editor in chief

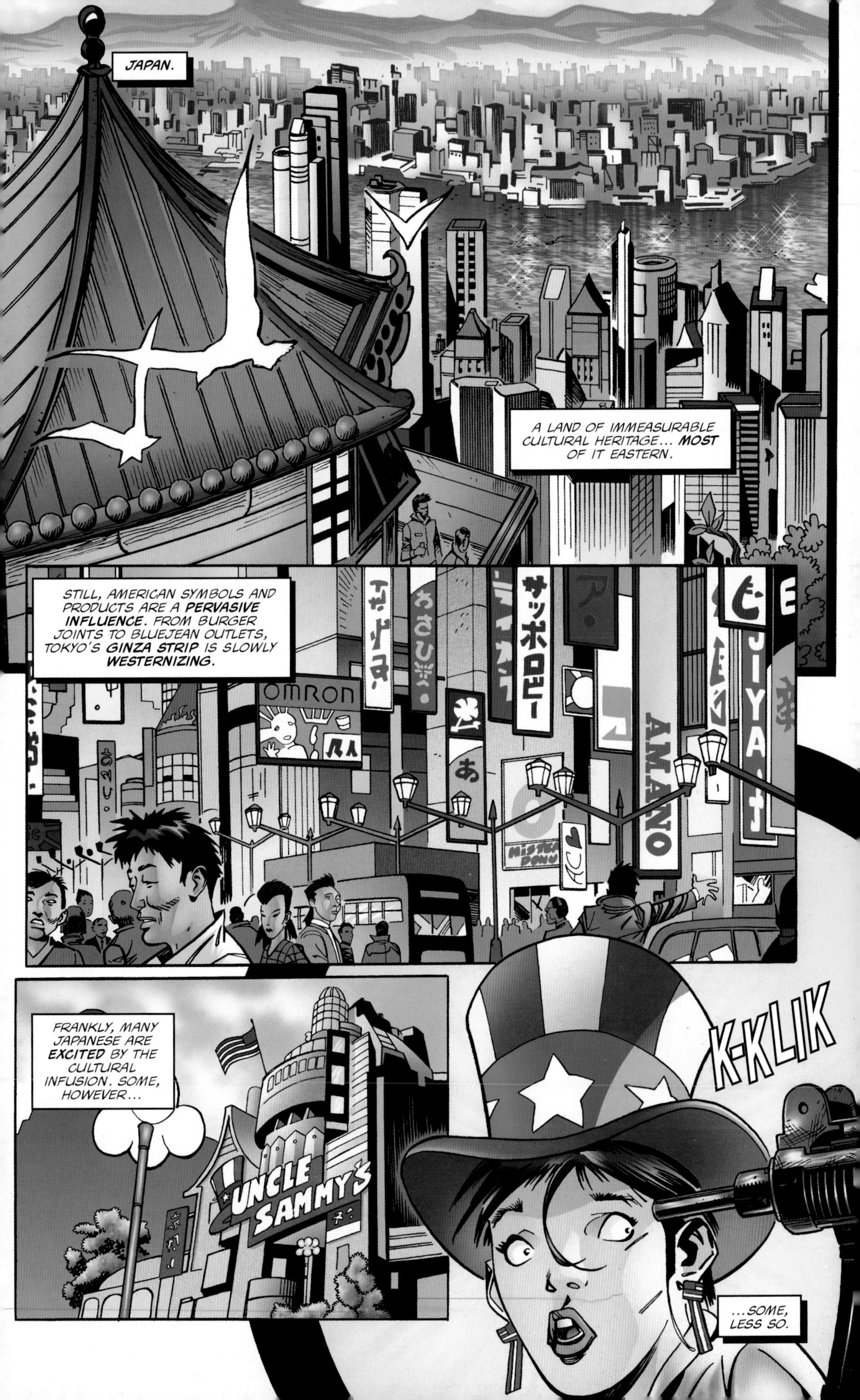
JAPAN.
A LAND OF IMMEASURABLE CULTURAL HERITAGE... MOST OF IT EASTERN.
STILL, AMERICAN SYMBOLS AND PRODUCTS ARE A PERVASIVE INFLUENCE. FROM BURGER JOINTS TO BLUEJEAN OUTLETS, TOKYO'S GINZA STRIP IS SLOWLY WESTERNIZING.
サッポロビー
OMRON
AMANO
FRANKLY, MANY JAPANESE ARE EXCITED BY THE CULTURAL INFUSION. SOME, HOWEVER...
UNCLE SAMMY'S
K-KLIK
...SOME, LESS SO.

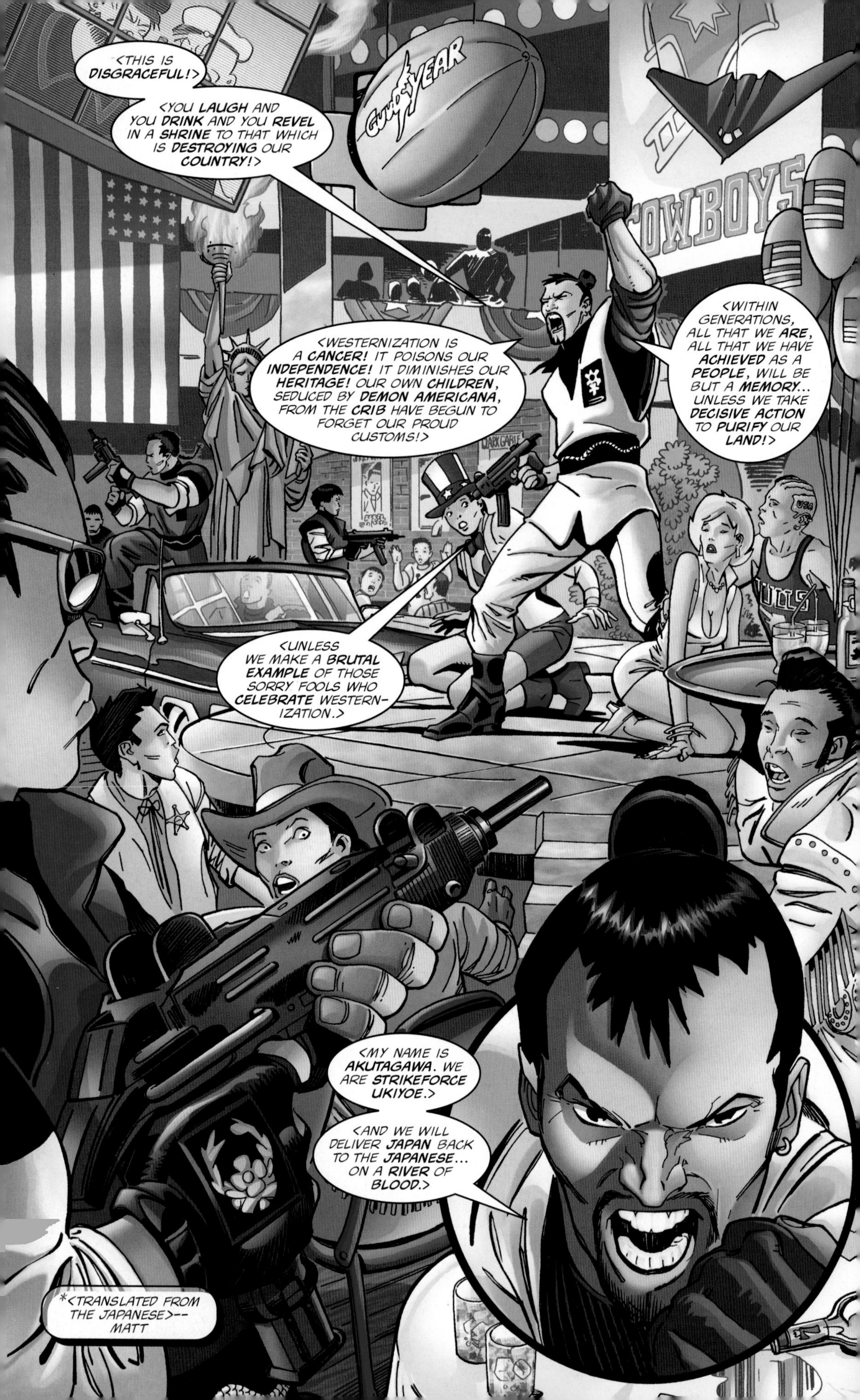

GOODYEAR
COWBOYS
<THIS IS DISGRACEFUL!>
<YOU LAUGH AND YOU DRINK AND YOU REVEL IN A SHRINE TO THAT WHICH IS DESTROYING OUR COUNTRY!>
<WESTERNIZATION IS A CANCER! IT POISONS OUR INDEPENDENCE! IT DIMINISHES OUR HERITAGE! OUR OWN CHILDREN, SEDUCED BY DEMON AMERICANA, FROM THE CRIB HAVE BEGUN TO FORGET OUR PROUD CUSTOMS!>
<WITHIN GENERATIONS, ALL THAT WE ARE, ALL THAT WE HAVE ACHIEVED AS A PEOPLE, WILL BE BUT A MEMORY... UNLESS WE TAKE DECISIVE ACTION TO PURIFY OUR LAND!>
<UNLESS WE MAKE A BRUTAL EXAMPLE OF THOSE SORRY FOOLS WHO CELEBRATE WESTERN-IZATION.>
<MY NAME IS AKUTAGAWA. WE ARE STRIKEFORCE UKIYOE.>
<AND WE WILL DELIVER JAPAN BACK TO THE JAPANESE... ON A RIVER OF BLOOD.>
*<TRANSLATED FROM THE JAPANESE>--MATT

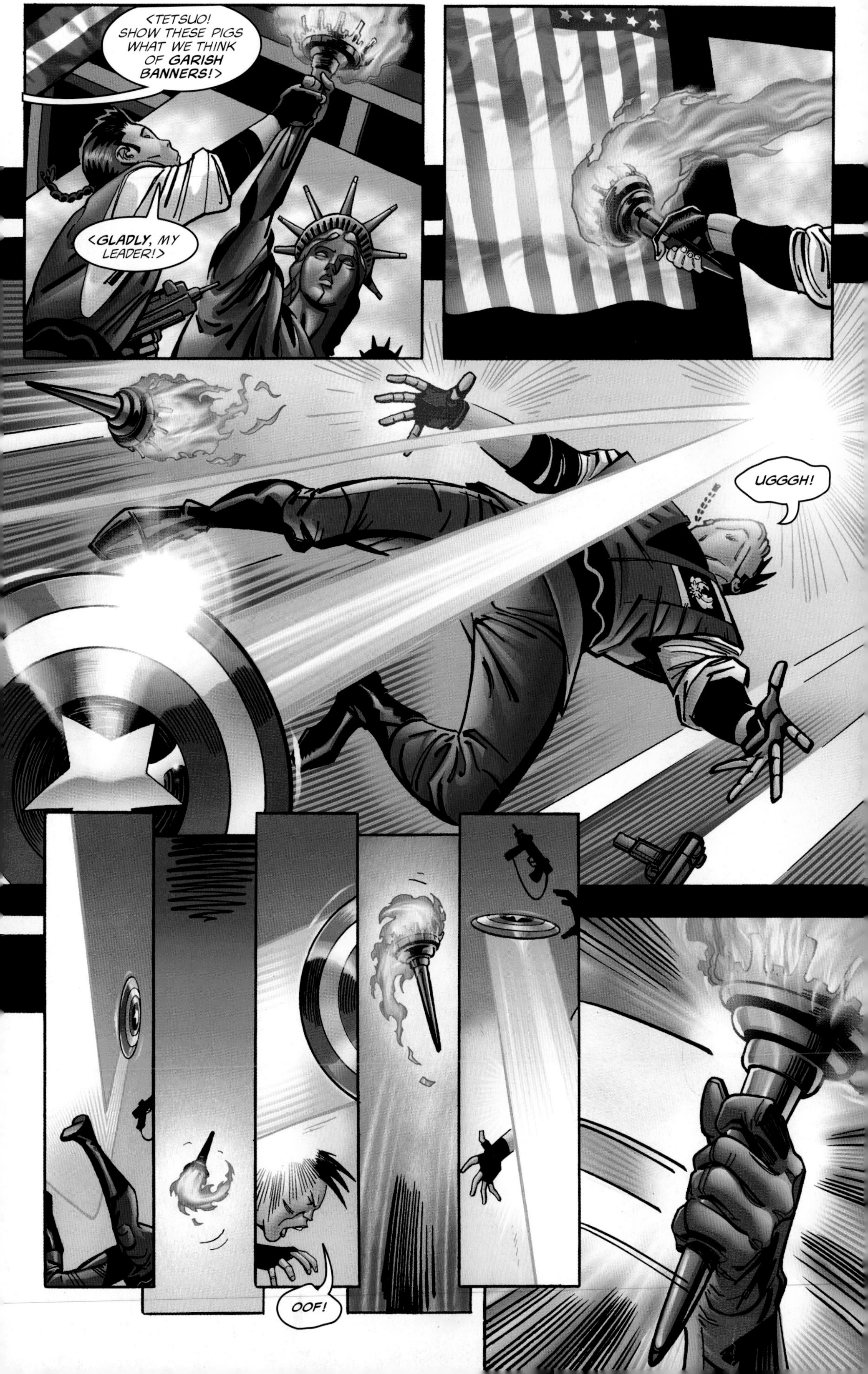
<TETSUO! SHOW THESE PIGS WHAT WE THINK OF **GARISH BANNERS!**>
<**GLADLY,** MY LEADER!>
UGGGH!
OOF!

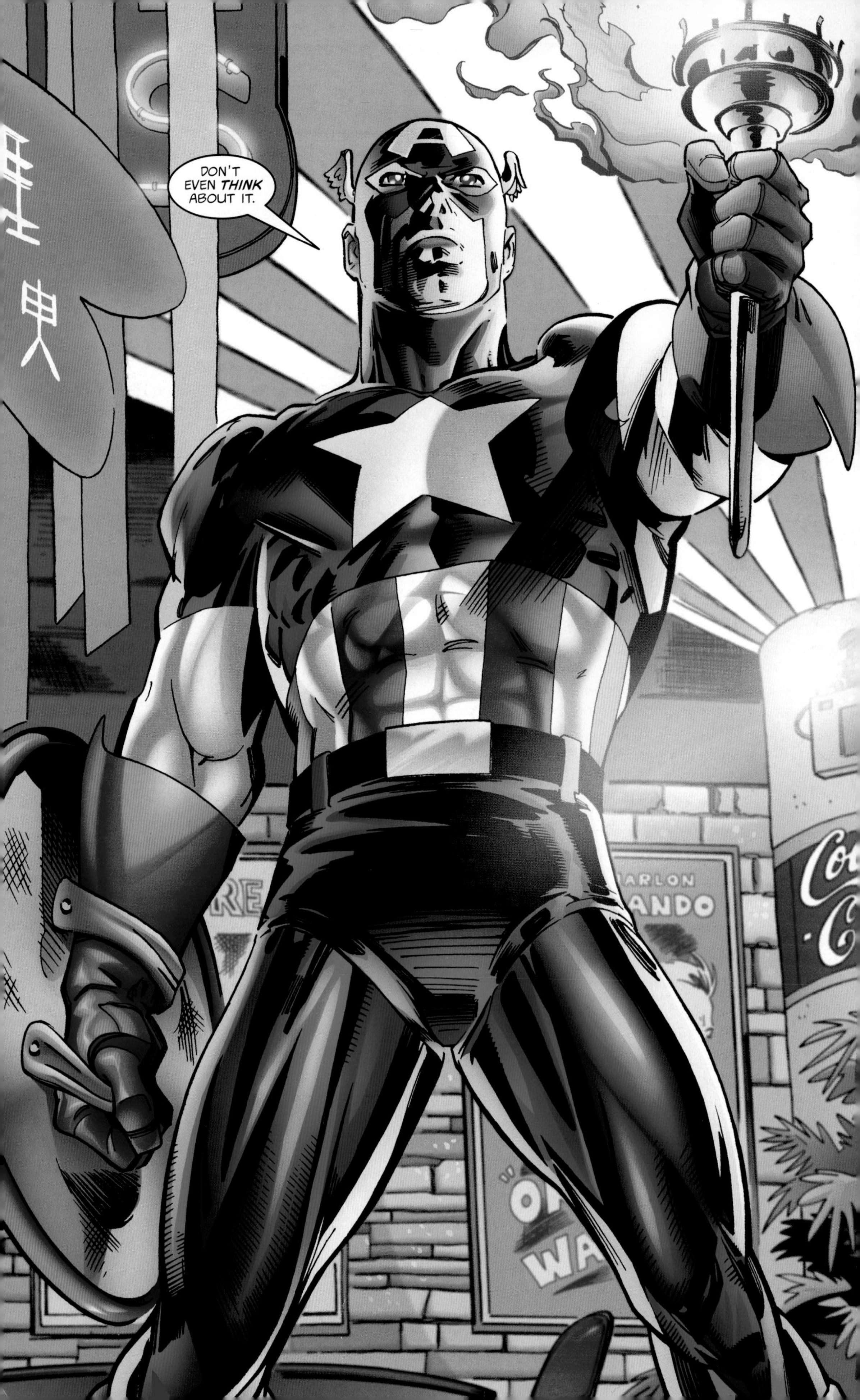
DON'T EVEN THINK ABOUT IT.

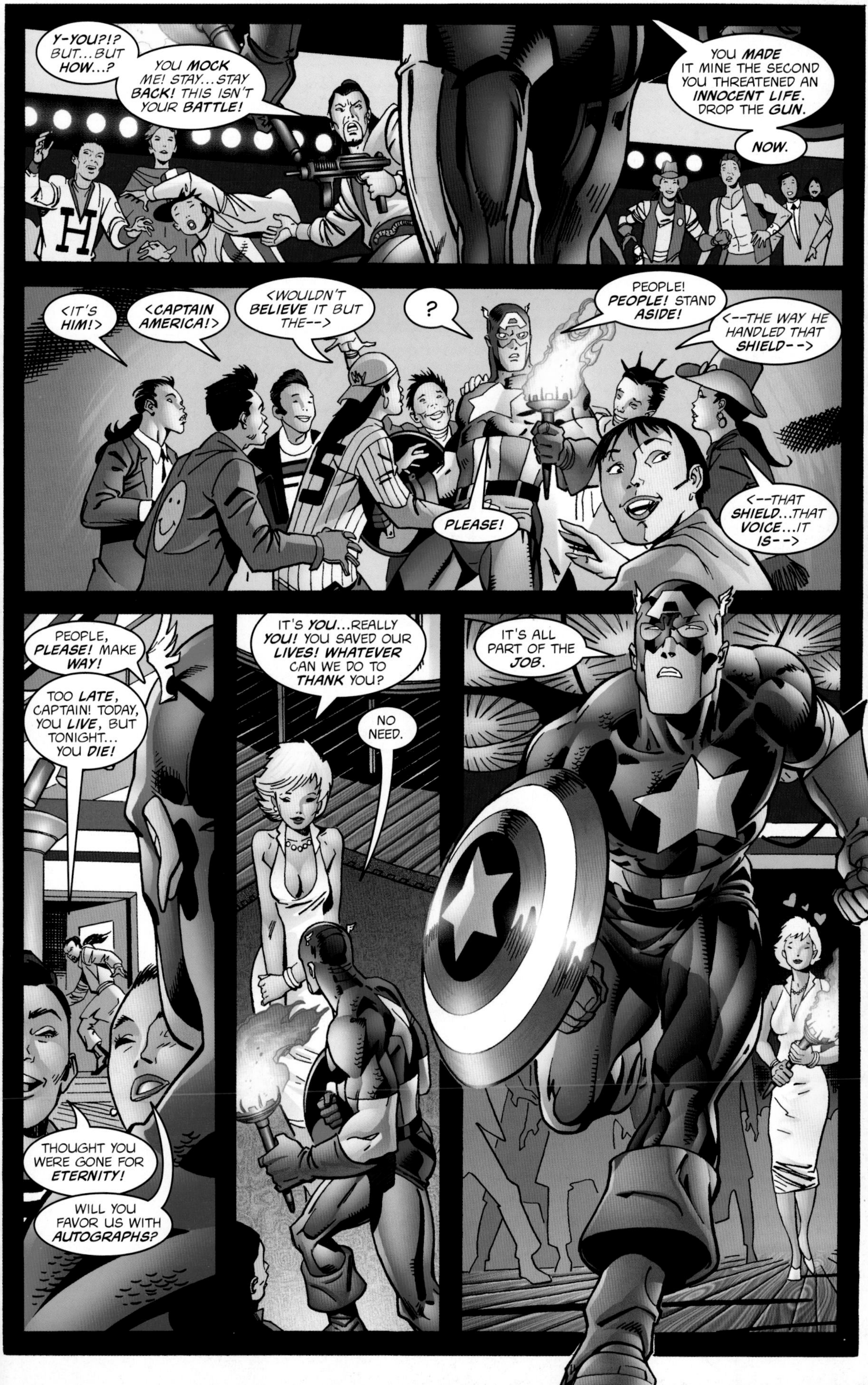

Y-YOU?!? BUT...BUT HOW...?
YOU MOCK ME! STAY...STAY BACK! THIS ISN'T YOUR BATTLE!
YOU MADE IT MINE THE SECOND YOU THREATENED AN INNOCENT LIFE. DROP THE GUN.
NOW.
<IT'S HIM!>
<CAPTAIN AMERICA!>
<WOULDN'T BELIEVE IT BUT THE-->
?
PEOPLE! PEOPLE! STAND ASIDE!
<--THE WAY HE HANDLED THAT SHIELD-->
PLEASE!
<--THAT SHIELD...THAT VOICE...IT IS-->
PEOPLE, PLEASE! MAKE WAY!
TOO LATE, CAPTAIN! TODAY, YOU LIVE, BUT TONIGHT... YOU DIE!
THOUGHT YOU WERE GONE FOR ETERNITY!
WILL YOU FAVOR US WITH AUTOGRAPHS?
IT'S YOU...REALLY YOU! YOU SAVED OUR LIVES! WHATEVER CAN WE DO TO THANK YOU?
NO NEED.
IT'S ALL PART OF THE JOB.

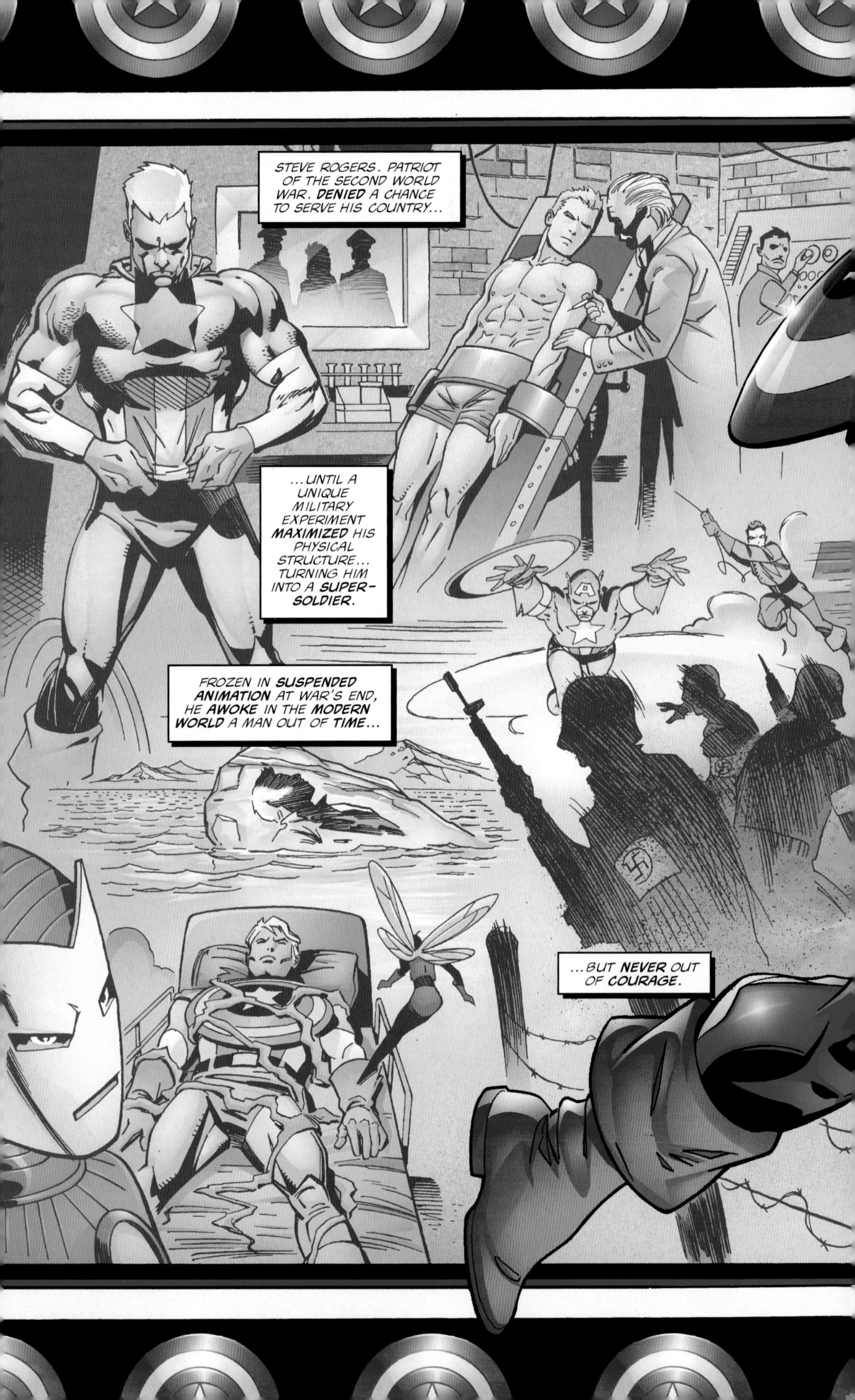
STEVE ROGERS. PATRIOT OF THE SECOND WORLD WAR. DENIED A CHANCE TO SERVE HIS COUNTRY...
...UNTIL A UNIQUE MILITARY EXPERIMENT MAXIMIZED HIS PHYSICAL STRUCTURE... TURNING HIM INTO A SUPER-SOLDIER.
FROZEN IN SUSPENDED ANIMATION AT WAR'S END, HE AWOKE IN THE MODERN WORLD A MAN OUT OF TIME...
...BUT NEVER OUT OF COURAGE.

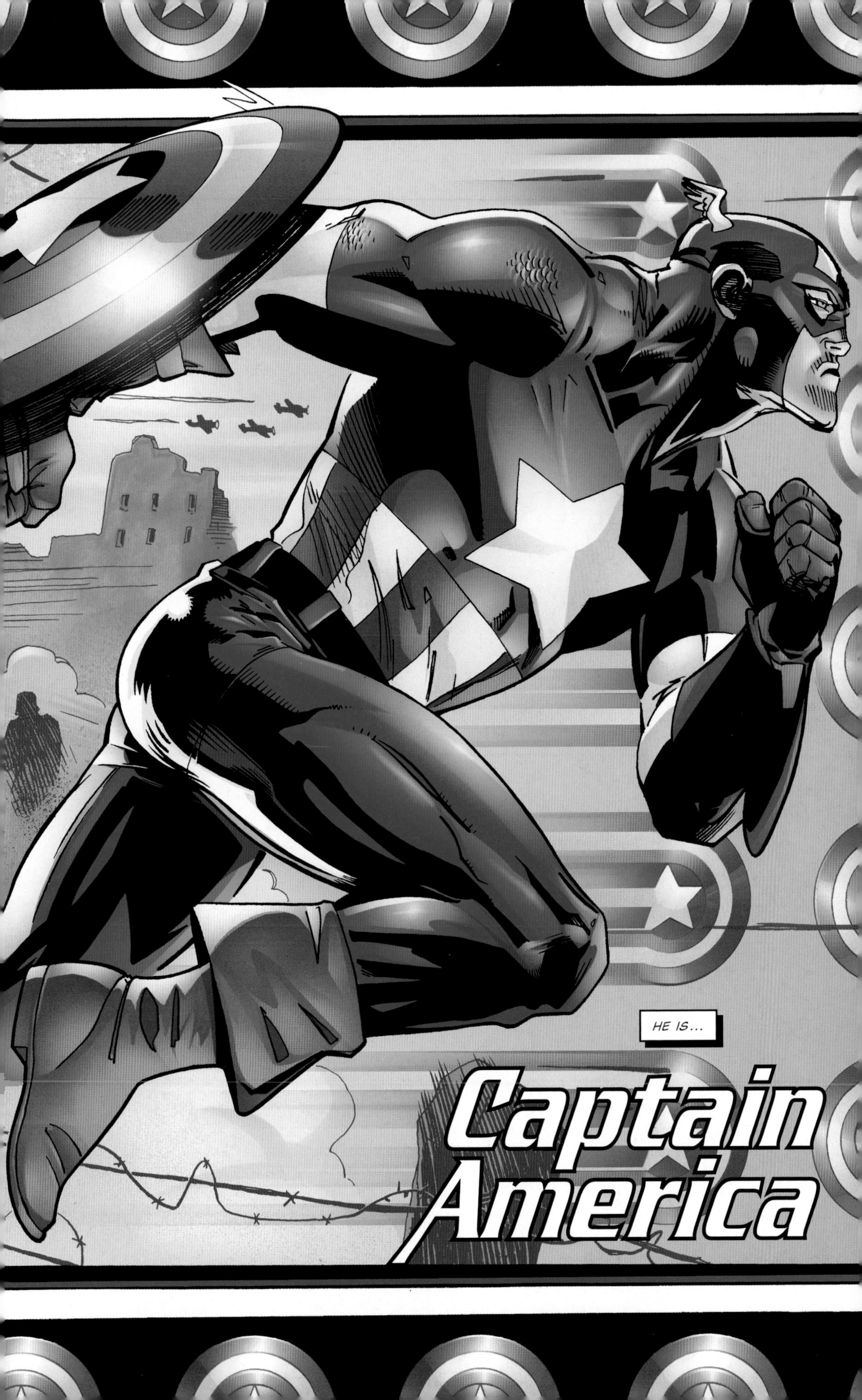
HE IS...
Captain America

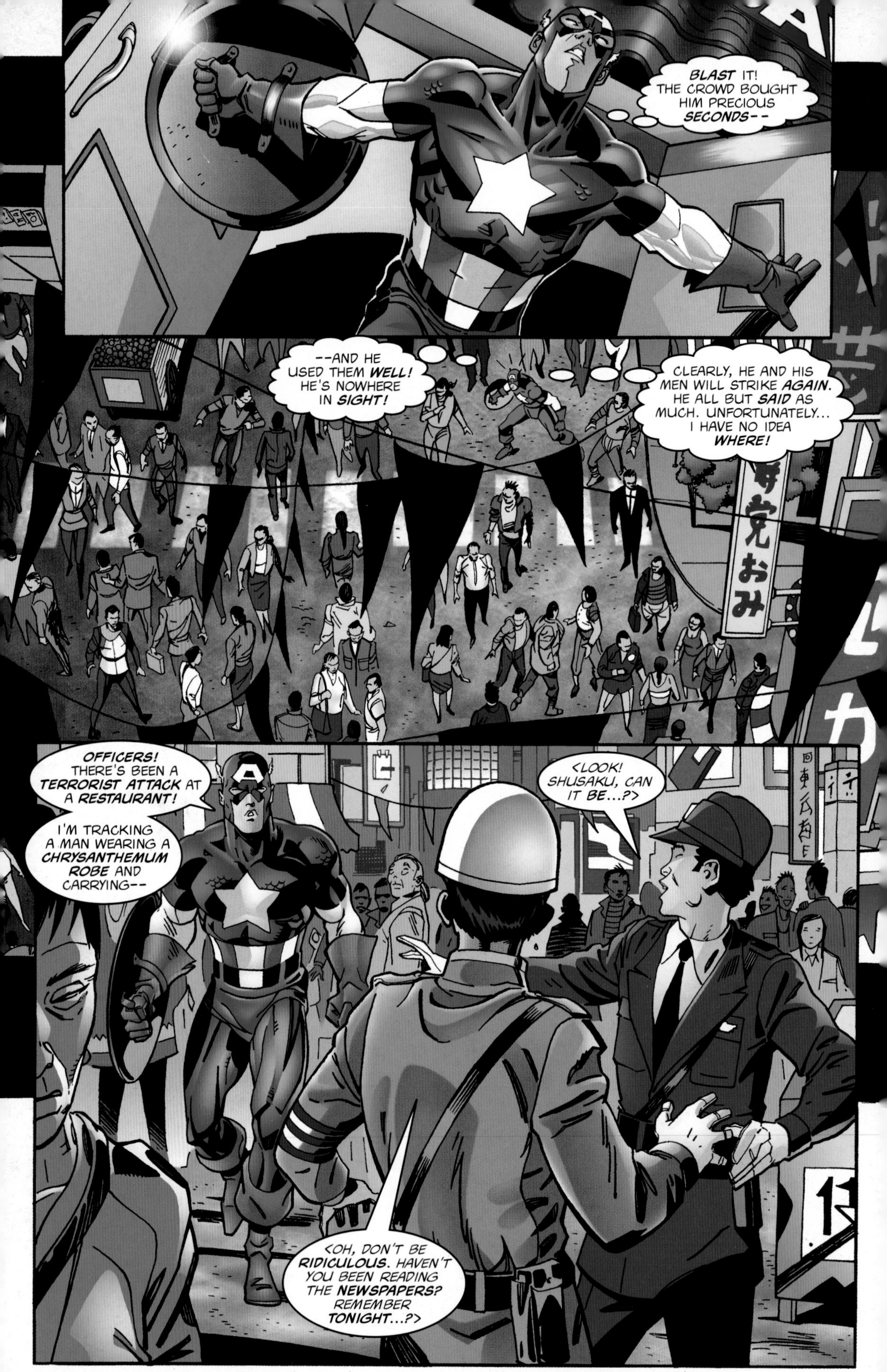
BLAST IT! THE CROWD BOUGHT HIM PRECIOUS SECONDS--
--AND HE USED THEM WELL! HE'S NOWHERE IN SIGHT!
CLEARLY, HE AND HIS MEN WILL STRIKE AGAIN. HE ALL BUT SAID AS MUCH. UNFORTUNATELY... I HAVE NO IDEA WHERE!
OFFICERS! THERE'S BEEN A TERRORIST ATTACK AT A RESTAURANT!
I'M TRACKING A MAN WEARING A CHRYSANTHEMUM ROBE AND CARRYING--
<LOOK! SHUSAKU, CAN IT BE...?>
<OH, DON'T BE RIDICULOUS. HAVEN'T YOU BEEN READING THE NEWSPAPERS? REMEMBER TONIGHT...?>

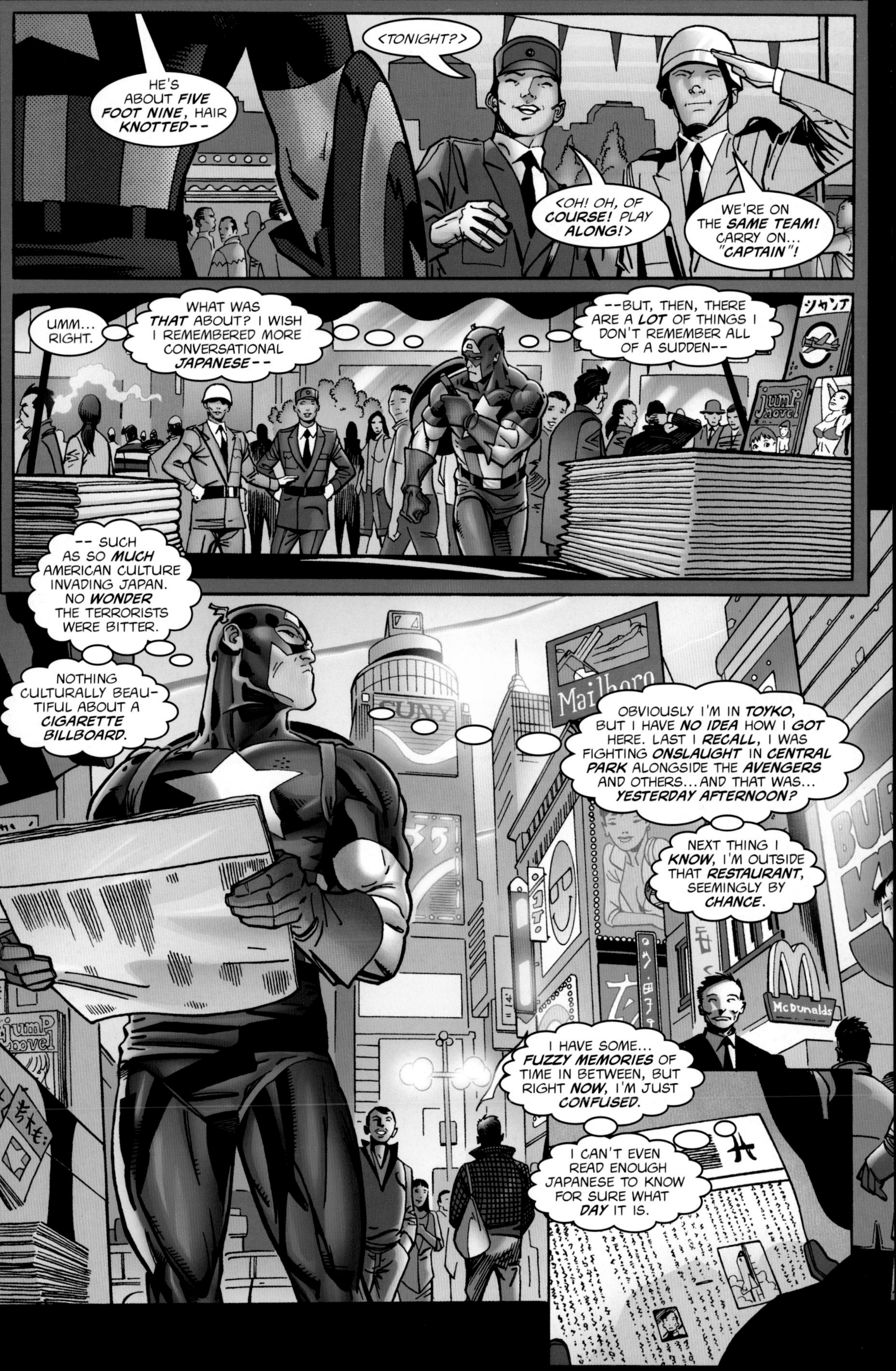
HE'S ABOUT FIVE FOOT NINE, HAIR KNOTTED--
<TONIGHT?>
<OH! OH, OF COURSE! PLAY ALONG!>
WE'RE ON THE SAME TEAM! CARRY ON... "CAPTAIN"!
UMM... RIGHT.
WHAT WAS THAT ABOUT? I WISH I REMEMBERED MORE CONVERSATIONAL JAPANESE--
--BUT, THEN, THERE ARE A LOT OF THINGS I DON'T REMEMBER ALL OF A SUDDEN--
-- SUCH AS SO MUCH AMERICAN CULTURE INVADING JAPAN. NO WONDER THE TERRORISTS WERE BITTER.
NOTHING CULTURALLY BEAUTIFUL ABOUT A CIGARETTE BILLBOARD.
OBVIOUSLY I'M IN TOYKO, BUT I HAVE NO IDEA HOW I GOT HERE. LAST I RECALL, I WAS FIGHTING ONSLAUGHT IN CENTRAL PARK ALONGSIDE THE AVENGERS AND OTHERS...AND THAT WAS... YESTERDAY AFTERNOON?
NEXT THING I KNOW, I'M OUTSIDE THAT RESTAURANT, SEEMINGLY BY CHANCE.
I HAVE SOME... FUZZY MEMORIES OF TIME IN BETWEEN, BUT RIGHT NOW, I'M JUST CONFUSED.
I CAN'T EVEN READ ENOUGH JAPANESE TO KNOW FOR SURE WHAT DAY IT IS.

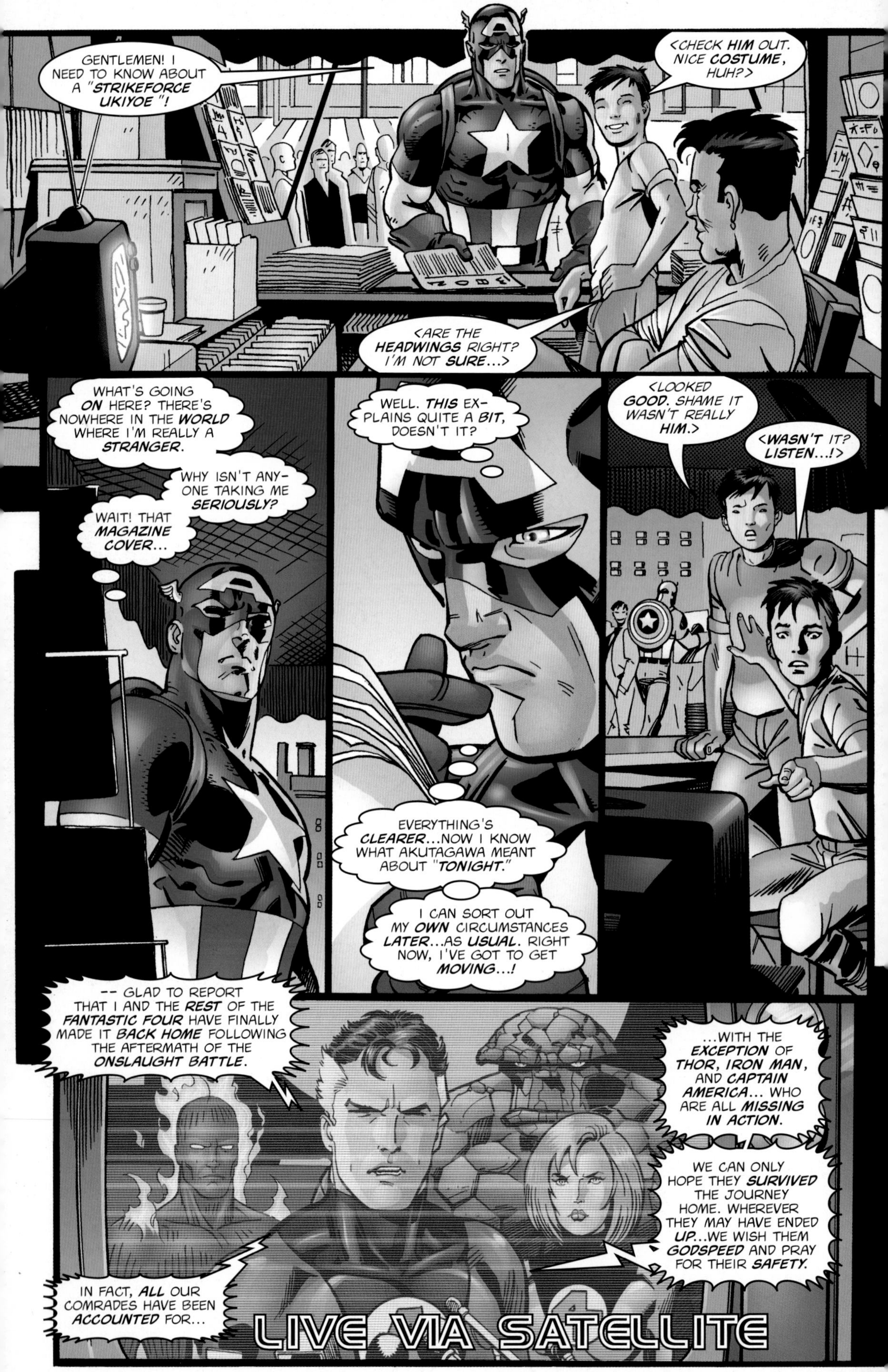
GENTLEMEN! I NEED TO KNOW ABOUT A "STRIKEFORCE UKIYOE"!
<CHECK HIM OUT. NICE COSTUME, HUH?>
<ARE THE HEADWINGS RIGHT? I'M NOT SURE...>
WHAT'S GOING ON HERE? THERE'S NOWHERE IN THE WORLD WHERE I'M REALLY A STRANGER.
WHY ISN'T ANYONE TAKING ME SERIOUSLY?
WAIT! THAT MAGAZINE COVER...
WELL. THIS EXPLAINS QUITE A BIT, DOESN'T IT?
EVERYTHING'S CLEARER...NOW I KNOW WHAT AKUTAGAWA MEANT ABOUT "TONIGHT."
I CAN SORT OUT MY OWN CIRCUMSTANCES LATER...AS USUAL. RIGHT NOW, I'VE GOT TO GET MOVING...!
<LOOKED GOOD. SHAME IT WASN'T REALLY HIM.>
<WASN'T IT? LISTEN...!>
-- GLAD TO REPORT THAT I AND THE REST OF THE FANTASTIC FOUR HAVE FINALLY MADE IT BACK HOME FOLLOWING THE AFTERMATH OF THE ONSLAUGHT BATTLE.
IN FACT, ALL OUR COMRADES HAVE BEEN ACCOUNTED FOR...
...WITH THE EXCEPTION OF THOR, IRON MAN, AND CAPTAIN AMERICA... WHO ARE ALL MISSING IN ACTION.
WE CAN ONLY HOPE THEY SURVIVED THE JOURNEY HOME. WHEREVER THEY MAY HAVE ENDED UP...WE WISH THEM GODSPEED AND PRAY FOR THEIR SAFETY.
LIVE VIA SATELLITE

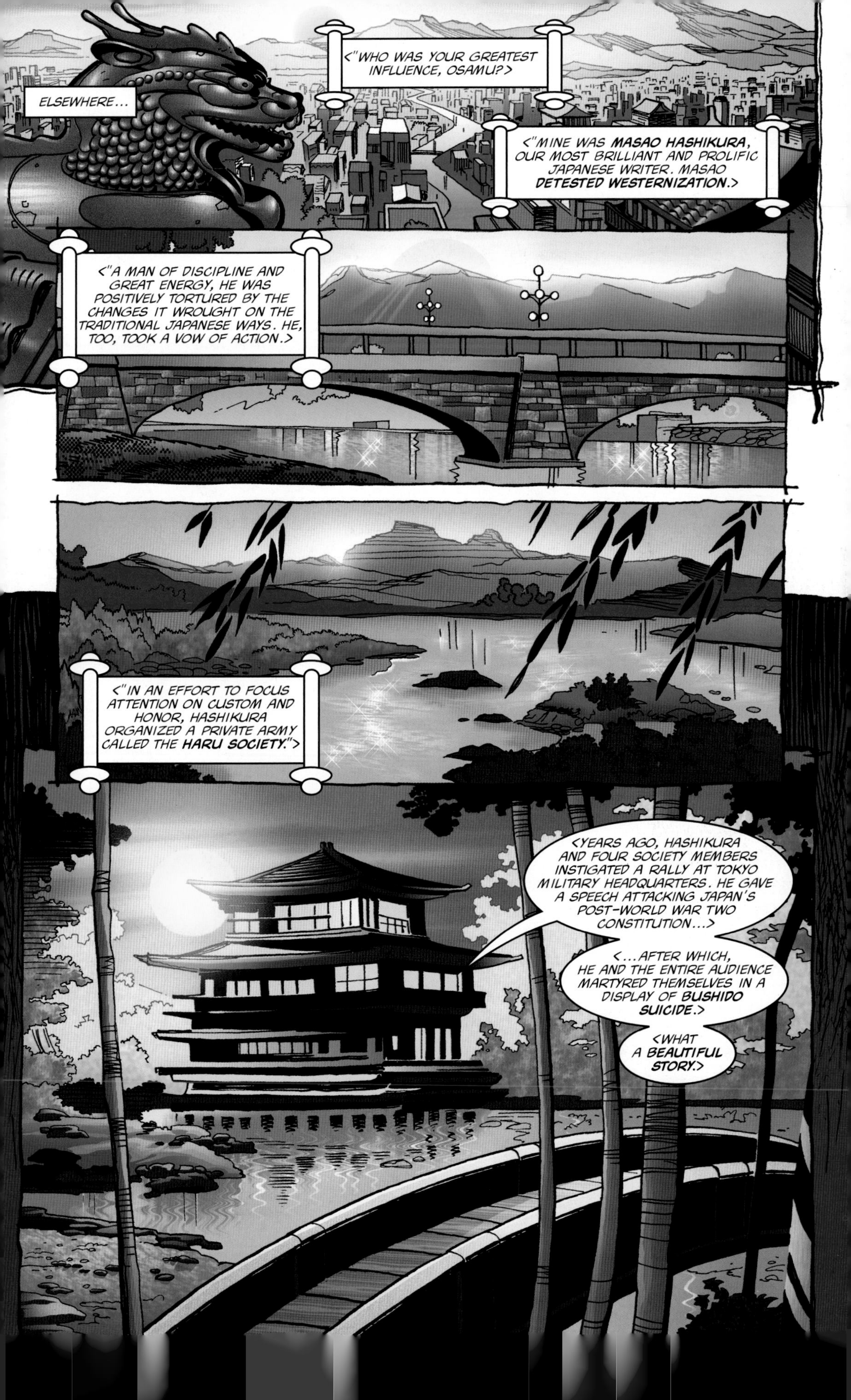
ELSEWHERE...
<"WHO WAS YOUR GREATEST INFLUENCE, OSAMU?>
<"MINE WAS **MASAO HASHIKURA**, OUR MOST BRILLIANT AND PROLIFIC JAPANESE WRITER. MASAO **DETESTED WESTERNIZATION**.>
<"A MAN OF DISCIPLINE AND GREAT ENERGY, HE WAS POSITIVELY TORTURED BY THE CHANGES IT WROUGHT ON THE TRADITIONAL JAPANESE WAYS. HE, TOO, TOOK A VOW OF ACTION.>
<"IN AN EFFORT TO FOCUS ATTENTION ON CUSTOM AND HONOR, HASHIKURA ORGANIZED A PRIVATE ARMY CALLED THE **HARU SOCIETY**.">
<YEARS AGO, HASHIKURA AND FOUR SOCIETY MEMBERS INSTIGATED A RALLY AT TOKYO MILITARY HEADQUARTERS. HE GAVE A SPEECH ATTACKING JAPAN'S POST-WORLD WAR TWO CONSTITUTION...>
<...AFTER WHICH, HE AND THE ENTIRE AUDIENCE MARTYRED THEMSELVES IN A DISPLAY OF **BUSHIDO SUICIDE**.>
<WHAT A **BEAUTIFUL** STORY.>

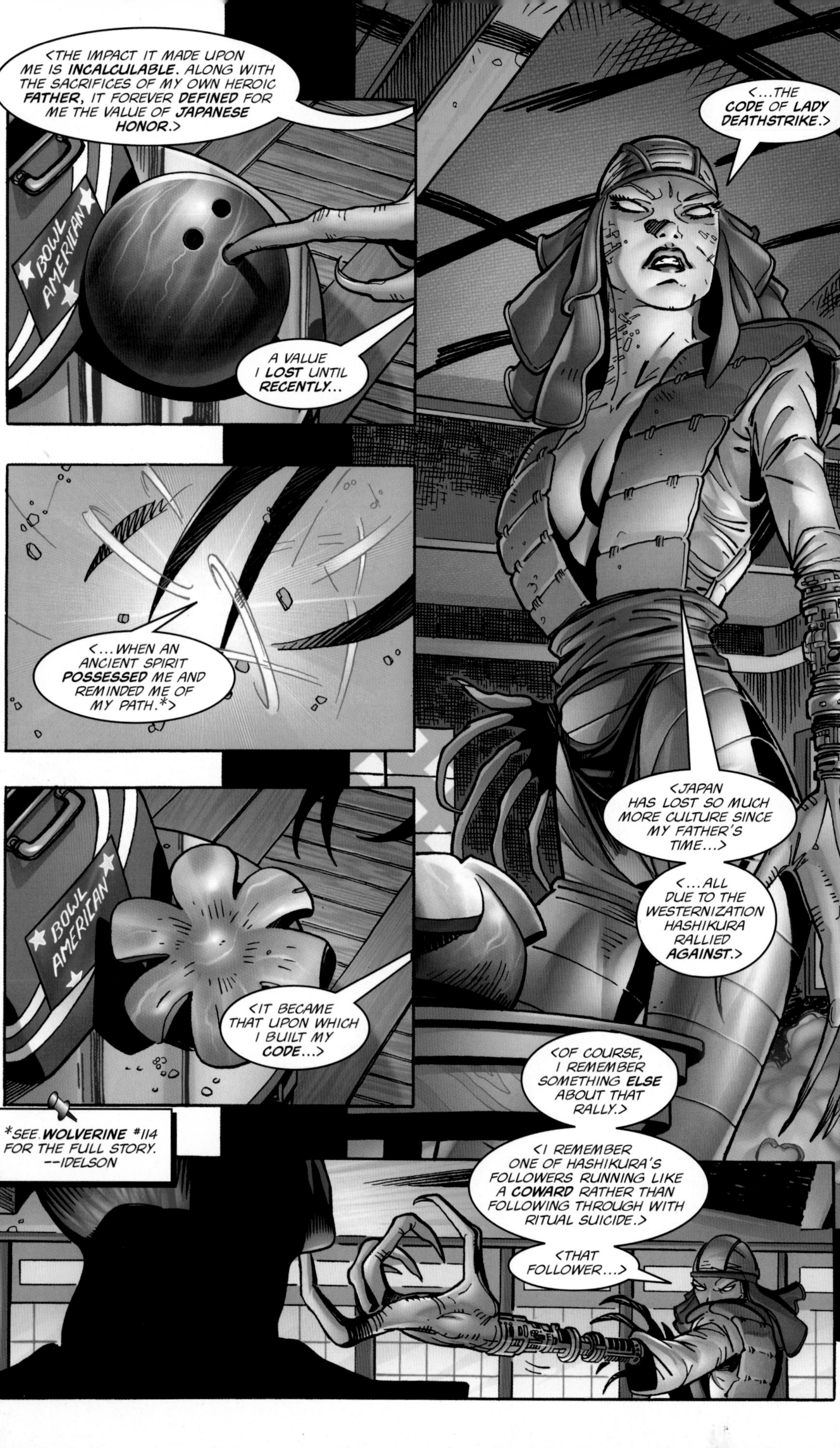

<THE IMPACT IT MADE UPON ME IS INCALCULABLE. ALONG WITH THE SACRIFICES OF MY OWN HEROIC FATHER, IT FOREVER DEFINED FOR ME THE VALUE OF JAPANESE HONOR.>
BOWL AMERICAN
A VALUE I LOST UNTIL RECENTLY...
<...THE CODE OF LADY DEATHSTRIKE.>
<...WHEN AN ANCIENT SPIRIT POSSESSED ME AND REMINDED ME OF MY PATH.*>
BOWL AMERICAN
<IT BECAME THAT UPON WHICH I BUILT MY CODE...>
<JAPAN HAS LOST SO MUCH MORE CULTURE SINCE MY FATHER'S TIME...>
<...ALL DUE TO THE WESTERNIZATION HASHIKURA RALLIED AGAINST.>
<OF COURSE, I REMEMBER SOMETHING ELSE ABOUT THAT RALLY.>
*SEE WOLVERINE #114 FOR THE FULL STORY. --IDELSON
<I REMEMBER ONE OF HASHIKURA'S FOLLOWERS RUNNING LIKE A COWARD RATHER THAN FOLLOWING THROUGH WITH RITUAL SUICIDE.>
<THAT FOLLOWER...>

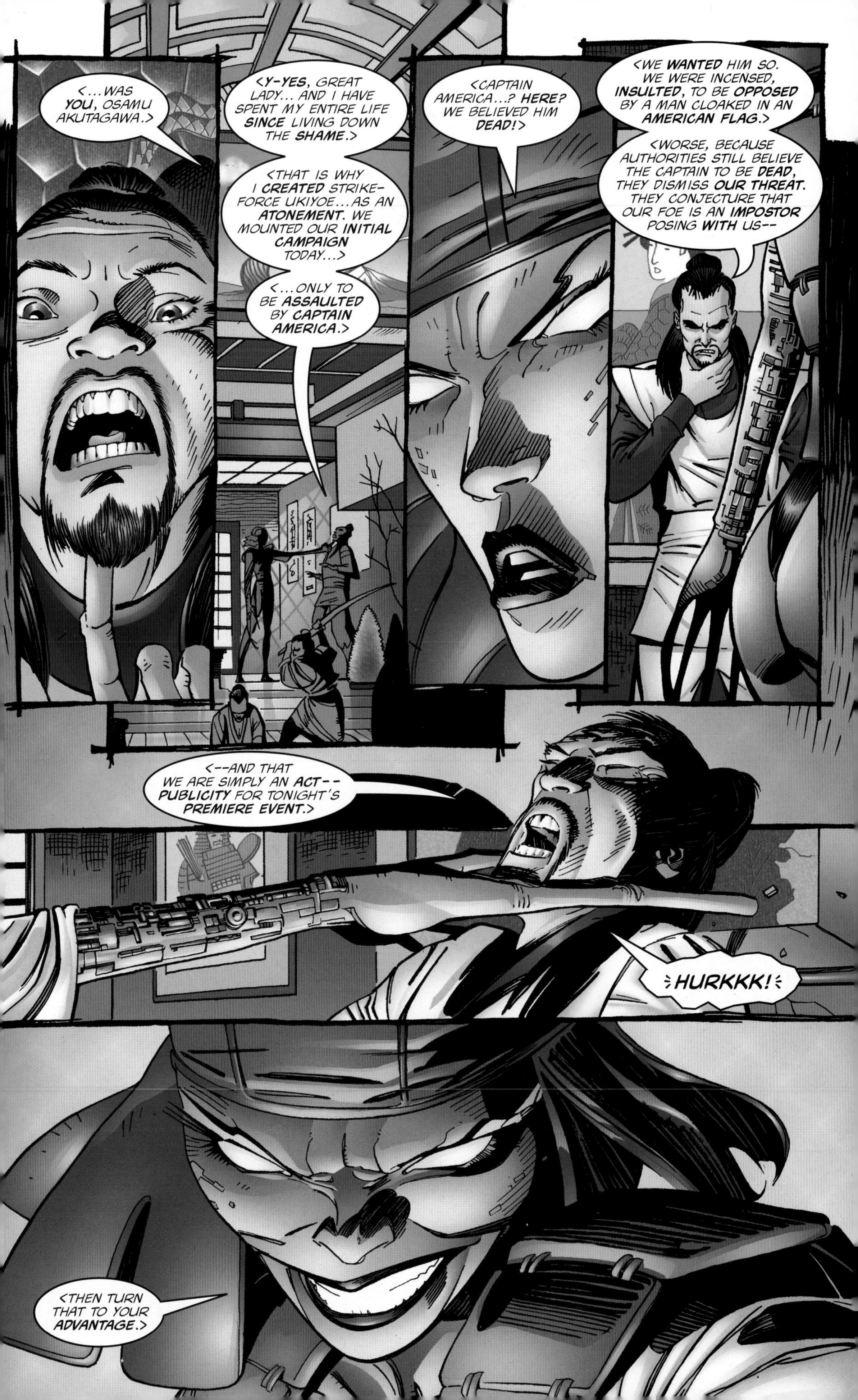
<...WAS YOU, OSAMU AKUTAGAWA.>
<Y-YES, GREAT LADY... AND I HAVE SPENT MY ENTIRE LIFE SINCE LIVING DOWN THE SHAME.>
<THAT IS WHY I CREATED STRIKE-FORCE UKIYOE...AS AN ATONEMENT. WE MOUNTED OUR INITIAL CAMPAIGN TODAY...>
<...ONLY TO BE ASSAULTED BY CAPTAIN AMERICA.>
<CAPTAIN AMERICA...? HERE? WE BELIEVED HIM DEAD!>
<WE WANTED HIM SO. WE WERE INCENSED, INSULTED, TO BE OPPOSED BY A MAN CLOAKED IN AN AMERICAN FLAG.>
<WORSE, BECAUSE AUTHORITIES STILL BELIEVE THE CAPTAIN TO BE DEAD, THEY DISMISS OUR THREAT. THEY CONJECTURE THAT OUR FOE IS AN IMPOSTOR POSING WITH US--
<--AND THAT WE ARE SIMPLY AN ACT-- PUBLICITY FOR TONIGHT'S PREMIERE EVENT.>
HURKKK!
<THEN TURN THAT TO YOUR ADVANTAGE.>

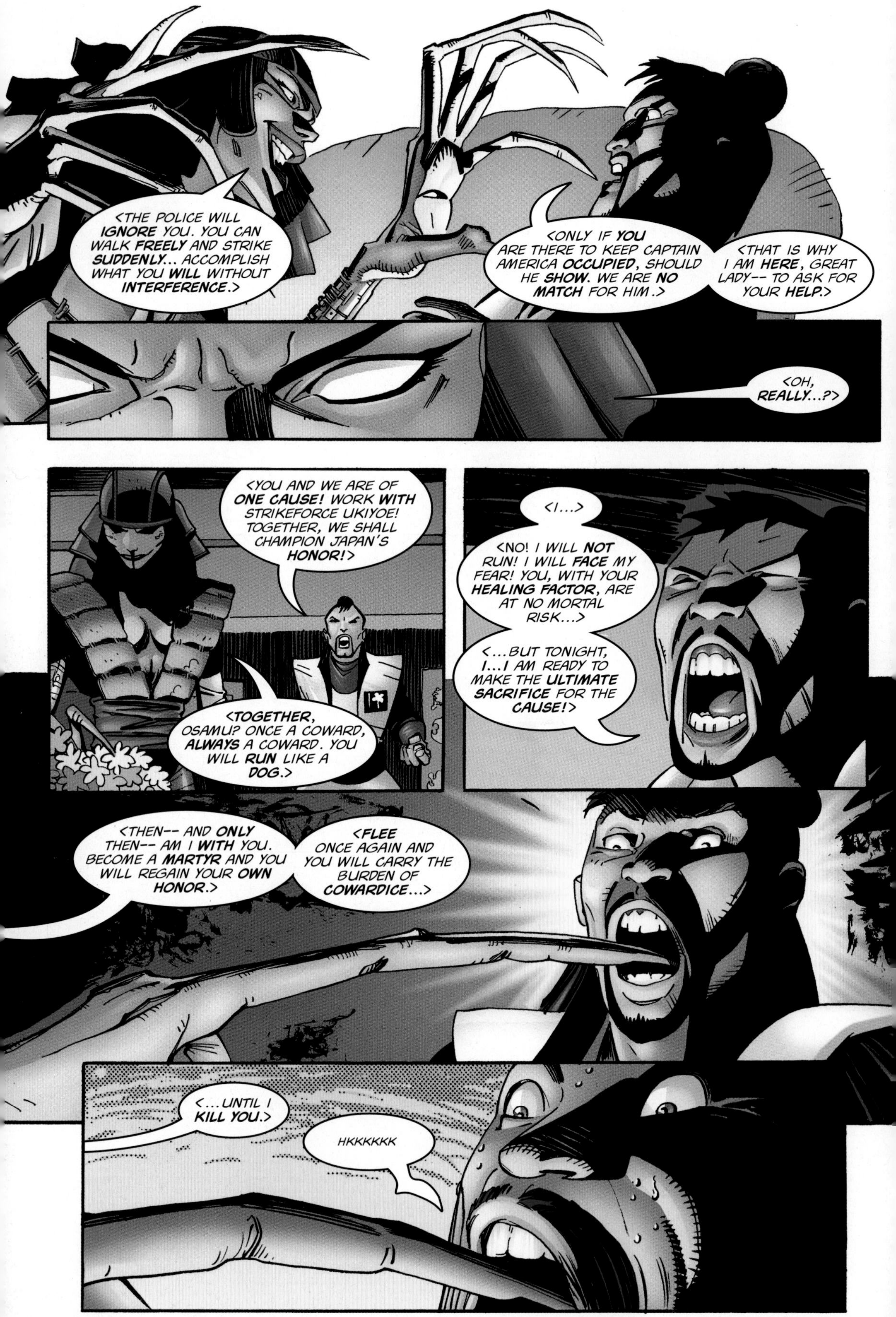
<THE POLICE WILL IGNORE YOU. YOU CAN WALK FREELY AND STRIKE SUDDENLY... ACCOMPLISH WHAT YOU WILL WITHOUT INTERFERENCE.>
<ONLY IF YOU ARE THERE TO KEEP CAPTAIN AMERICA OCCUPIED, SHOULD HE SHOW. WE ARE NO MATCH FOR HIM.>
<THAT IS WHY I AM HERE, GREAT LADY-- TO ASK FOR YOUR HELP.>
<OH, REALLY...?>
<YOU AND WE ARE OF ONE CAUSE! WORK WITH STRIKEFORCE UKIYOE! TOGETHER, WE SHALL CHAMPION JAPAN'S HONOR!>
<TOGETHER, OSAMU? ONCE A COWARD, ALWAYS A COWARD. YOU WILL RUN LIKE A DOG.>
<I...>
<NO! I WILL NOT RUN! I WILL FACE MY FEAR! YOU, WITH YOUR HEALING FACTOR, ARE AT NO MORTAL RISK...>
<...BUT TONIGHT, I...I AM READY TO MAKE THE ULTIMATE SACRIFICE FOR THE CAUSE!>
<THEN-- AND ONLY THEN-- AM I WITH YOU. BECOME A MARTYR AND YOU WILL REGAIN YOUR OWN HONOR.>
<FLEE ONCE AGAIN AND YOU WILL CARRY THE BURDEN OF COWARDICE...>
<...UNTIL I KILL YOU.>
HKKKKKK

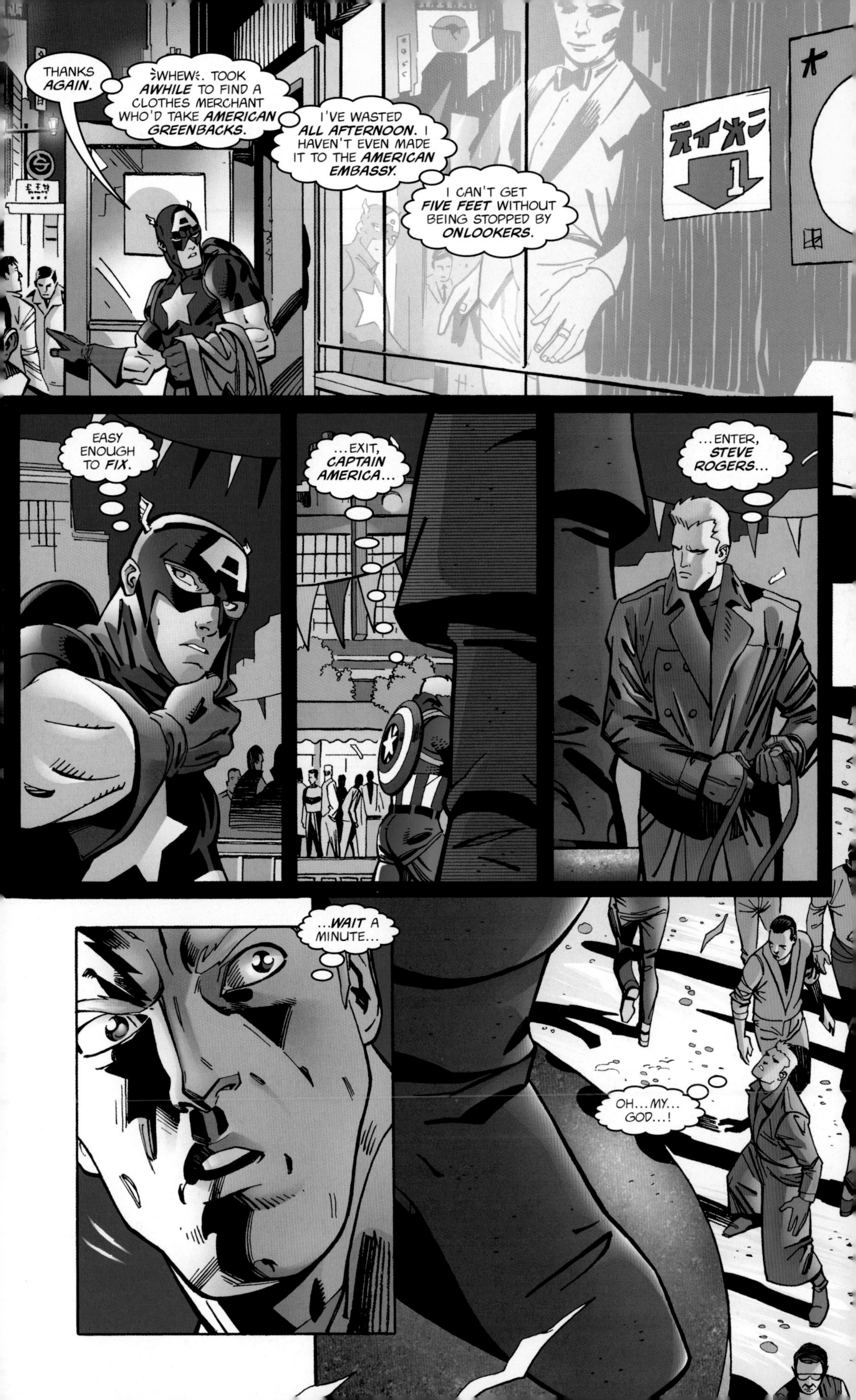
THANKS AGAIN.
WHEW. TOOK AWHILE TO FIND A CLOTHES MERCHANT WHO'D TAKE AMERICAN GREENBACKS.
I'VE WASTED ALL AFTERNOON. I HAVEN'T EVEN MADE IT TO THE AMERICAN EMBASSY.
I CAN'T GET FIVE FEET WITHOUT BEING STOPPED BY ONLOOKERS.
EASY ENOUGH TO FIX.
...EXIT, CAPTAIN AMERICA...
...ENTER, STEVE ROGERS...
...WAIT A MINUTE...
OH...MY... GOD...!

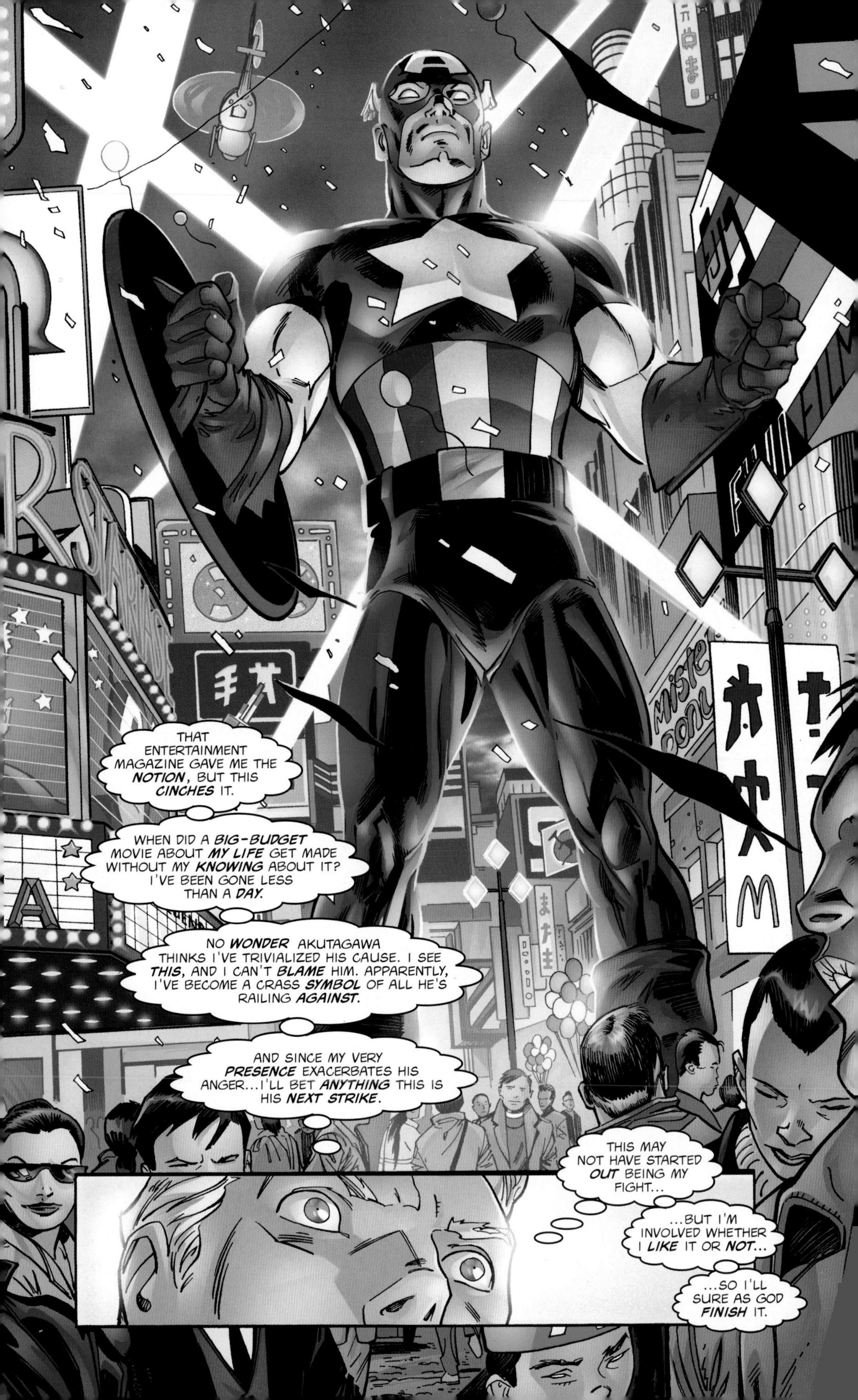
THAT ENTERTAINMENT MAGAZINE GAVE ME THE NOTION, BUT THIS CINCHES IT.
WHEN DID A BIG-BUDGET MOVIE ABOUT MY LIFE GET MADE WITHOUT MY KNOWING ABOUT IT? I'VE BEEN GONE LESS THAN A DAY.
NO WONDER AKUTAGAWA THINKS I'VE TRIVIALIZED HIS CAUSE. I SEE THIS, AND I CAN'T BLAME HIM. APPARENTLY, I'VE BECOME A CRASS SYMBOL OF ALL HE'S RAILING AGAINST.
AND SINCE MY VERY PRESENCE EXACERBATES HIS ANGER...I'LL BET ANYTHING THIS IS HIS NEXT STRIKE.
THIS MAY NOT HAVE STARTED OUT BEING MY FIGHT...
...BUT I'M INVOLVED WHETHER I LIKE IT OR NOT...
...SO I'LL SURE AS GOD FINISH IT.

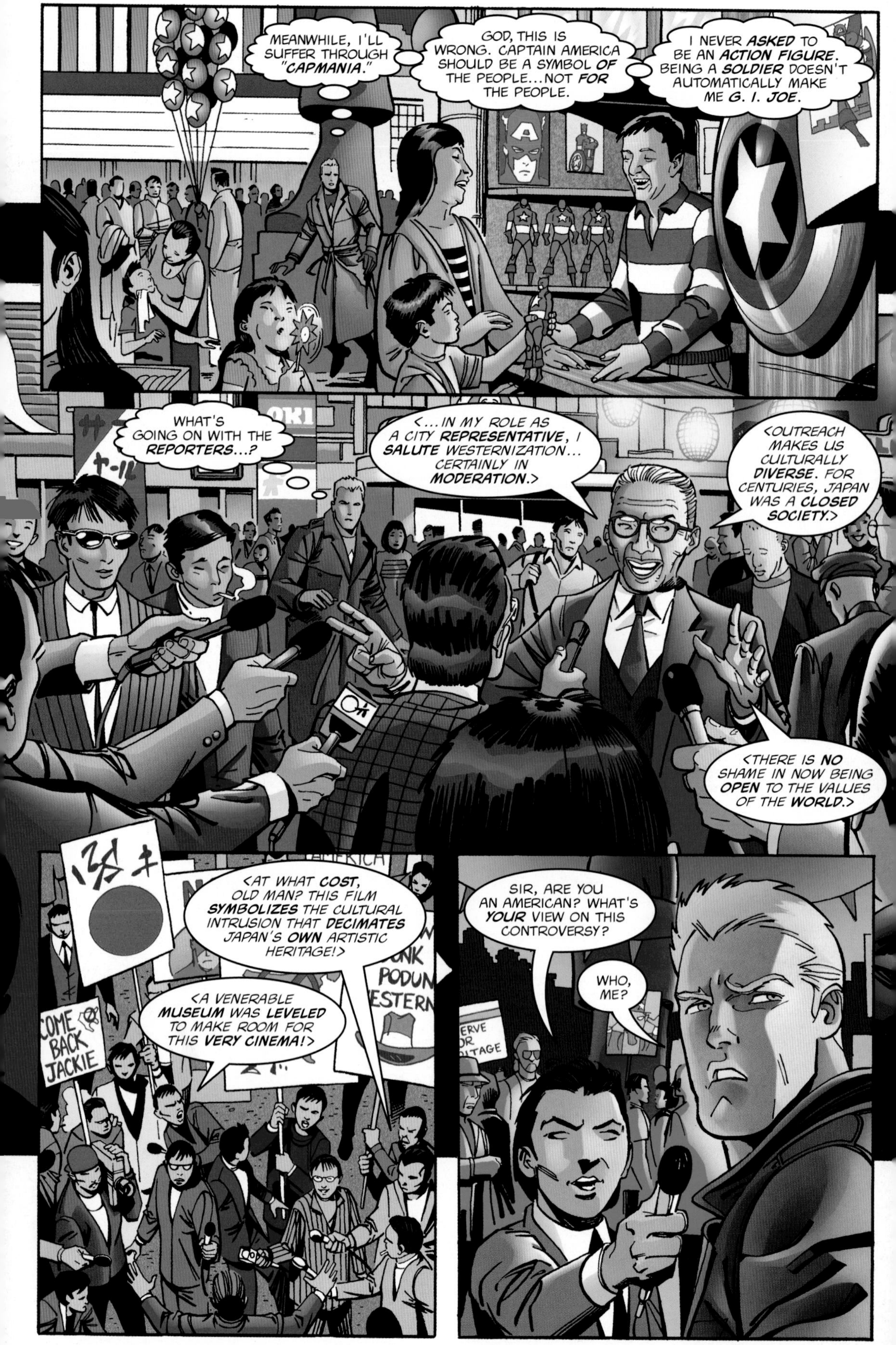

MEANWHILE, I'LL SUFFER THROUGH "CAPMANIA."
GOD, THIS IS WRONG. CAPTAIN AMERICA SHOULD BE A SYMBOL OF THE PEOPLE...NOT FOR THE PEOPLE.
I NEVER ASKED TO BE AN ACTION FIGURE. BEING A SOLDIER DOESN'T AUTOMATICALLY MAKE ME G. I. JOE.
WHAT'S GOING ON WITH THE REPORTERS...?
<...IN MY ROLE AS A CITY REPRESENTATIVE, I SALUTE WESTERNIZATION... CERTAINLY IN MODERATION.>
<OUTREACH MAKES US CULTURALLY DIVERSE. FOR CENTURIES, JAPAN WAS A CLOSED SOCIETY.>
<THERE IS NO SHAME IN NOW BEING OPEN TO THE VALUES OF THE WORLD.>
<AT WHAT COST, OLD MAN? THIS FILM SYMBOLIZES THE CULTURAL INTRUSION THAT DECIMATES JAPAN'S OWN ARTISTIC HERITAGE!>
<A VENERABLE MUSEUM WAS LEVELED TO MAKE ROOM FOR THIS VERY CINEMA!>
COME BACK JACKIE
SIR, ARE YOU AN AMERICAN? WHAT'S YOUR VIEW ON THIS CONTROVERSY?
WHO, ME?

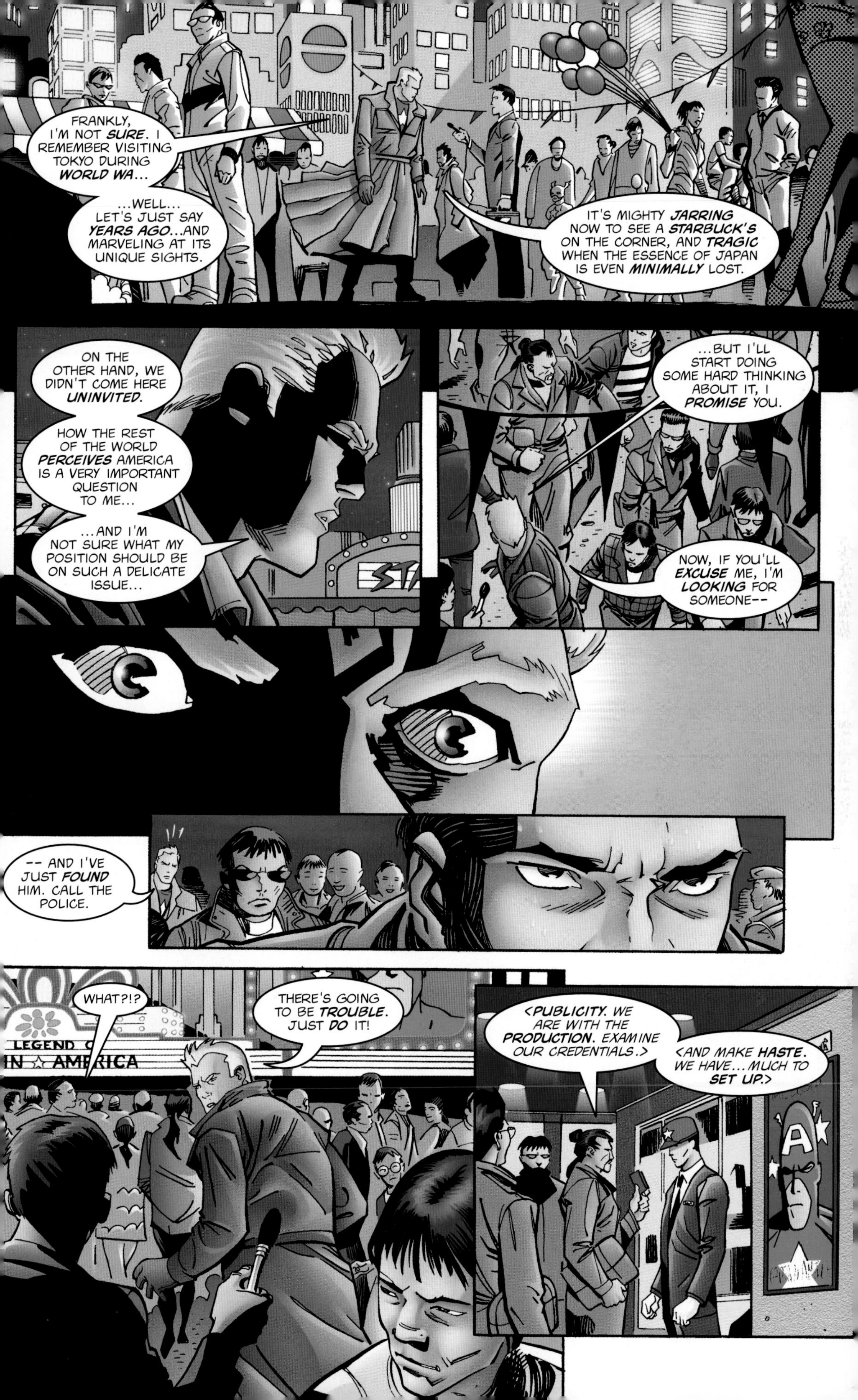
FRANKLY, I'M NOT SURE. I REMEMBER VISITING TOKYO DURING WORLD WA...
...WELL... LET'S JUST SAY YEARS AGO...AND MARVELING AT ITS UNIQUE SIGHTS.
IT'S MIGHTY JARRING NOW TO SEE A STARBUCK'S ON THE CORNER, AND TRAGIC WHEN THE ESSENCE OF JAPAN IS EVEN MINIMALLY LOST.
ON THE OTHER HAND, WE DIDN'T COME HERE UNINVITED.
HOW THE REST OF THE WORLD PERCEIVES AMERICA IS A VERY IMPORTANT QUESTION TO ME...
...AND I'M NOT SURE WHAT MY POSITION SHOULD BE ON SUCH A DELICATE ISSUE...
...BUT I'LL START DOING SOME HARD THINKING ABOUT IT, I PROMISE YOU.
NOW, IF YOU'LL EXCUSE ME, I'M LOOKING FOR SOMEONE--
-- AND I'VE JUST FOUND HIM. CALL THE POLICE.
WHAT?!?
THERE'S GOING TO BE TROUBLE. JUST DO IT!
<PUBLICITY. WE ARE WITH THE PRODUCTION. EXAMINE OUR CREDENTIALS.>
<AND MAKE HASTE. WE HAVE...MUCH TO SET UP.>

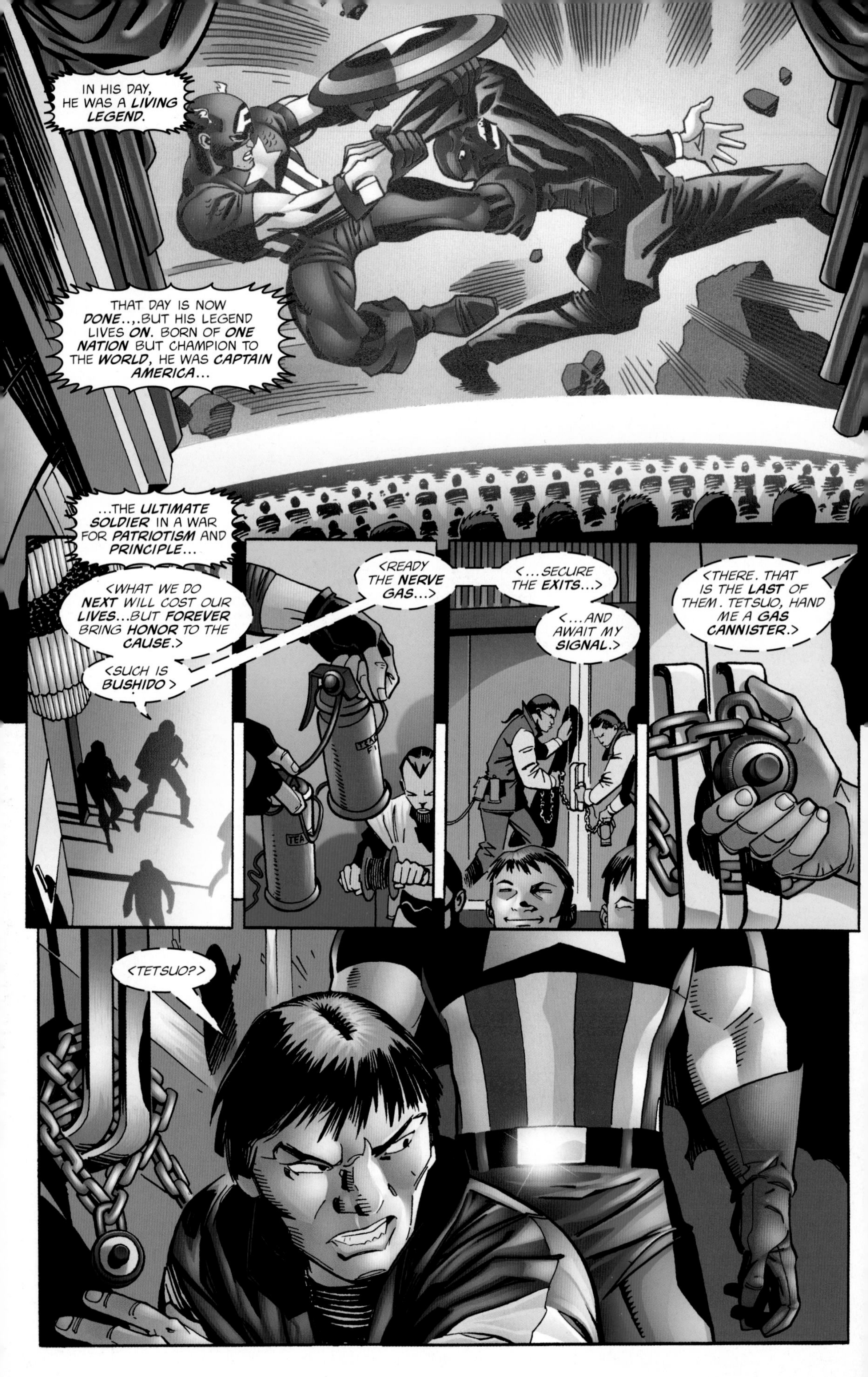

IN HIS DAY, HE WAS A LIVING LEGEND.
THAT DAY IS NOW DONE...,BUT HIS LEGEND LIVES ON. BORN OF ONE NATION BUT CHAMPION TO THE WORLD, HE WAS CAPTAIN AMERICA...
...THE ULTIMATE SOLDIER IN A WAR FOR PATRIOTISM AND PRINCIPLE...
<WHAT WE DO NEXT WILL COST OUR LIVES...BUT FOREVER BRING HONOR TO THE CAUSE.>
<SUCH IS BUSHIDO>
<READY THE NERVE GAS...>
<...SECURE THE EXITS...>
<...AND AWAIT MY SIGNAL.>
<THERE. THAT IS THE LAST OF THEM. TETSUO, HAND ME A GAS CANNISTER.>
<TETSUO?>

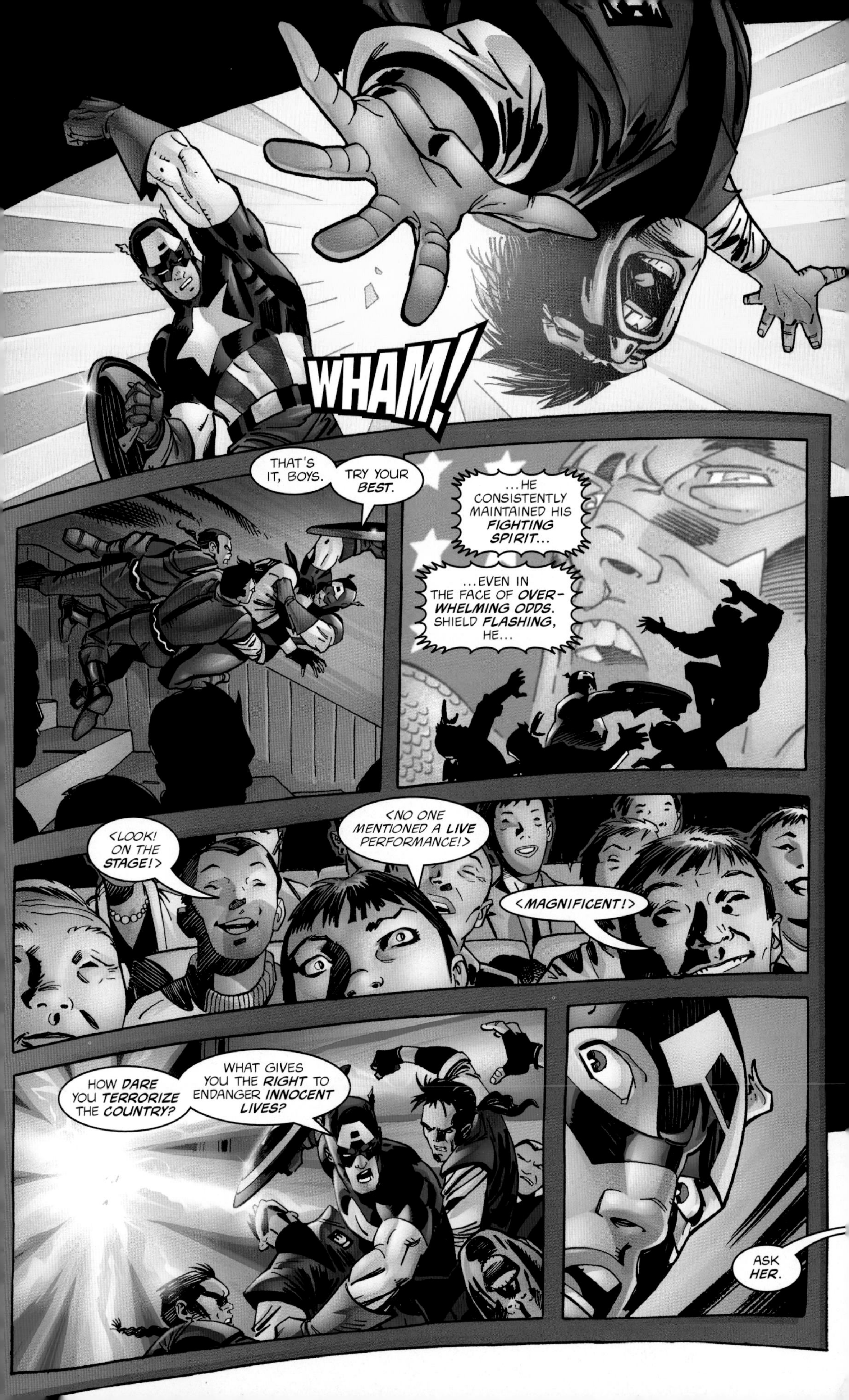

WHAM!
THAT'S IT, BOYS.
TRY YOUR BEST.
...HE CONSISTENTLY MAINTAINED HIS FIGHTING SPIRIT...
...EVEN IN THE FACE OF OVER-WHELMING ODDS. SHIELD FLASHING, HE...
<LOOK! ON THE STAGE!>
<NO ONE MENTIONED A LIVE PERFORMANCE!>
<MAGNIFICENT!>
HOW DARE YOU TERRORIZE THE COUNTRY?
WHAT GIVES YOU THE RIGHT TO ENDANGER INNOCENT LIVES?
ASK HER.

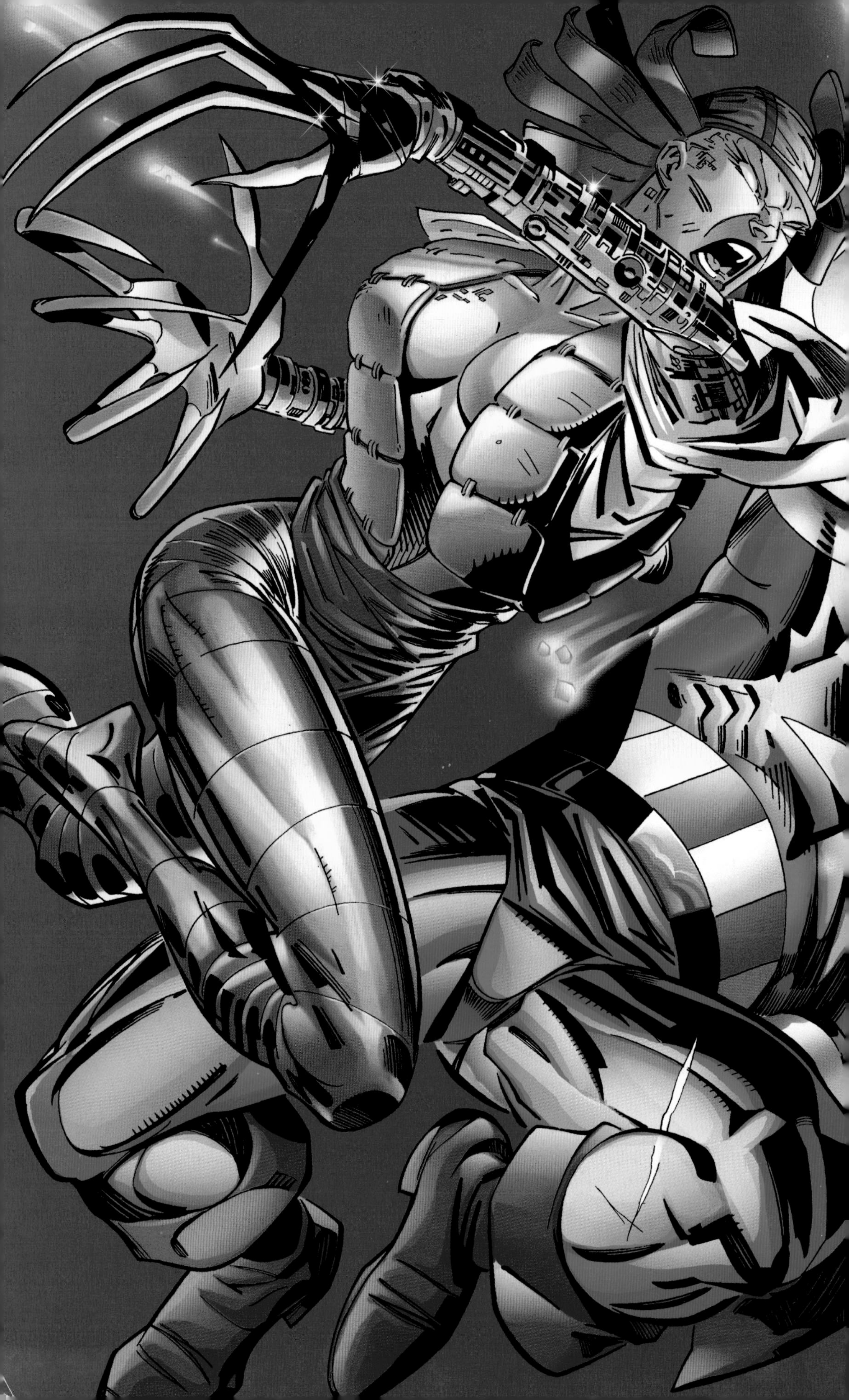

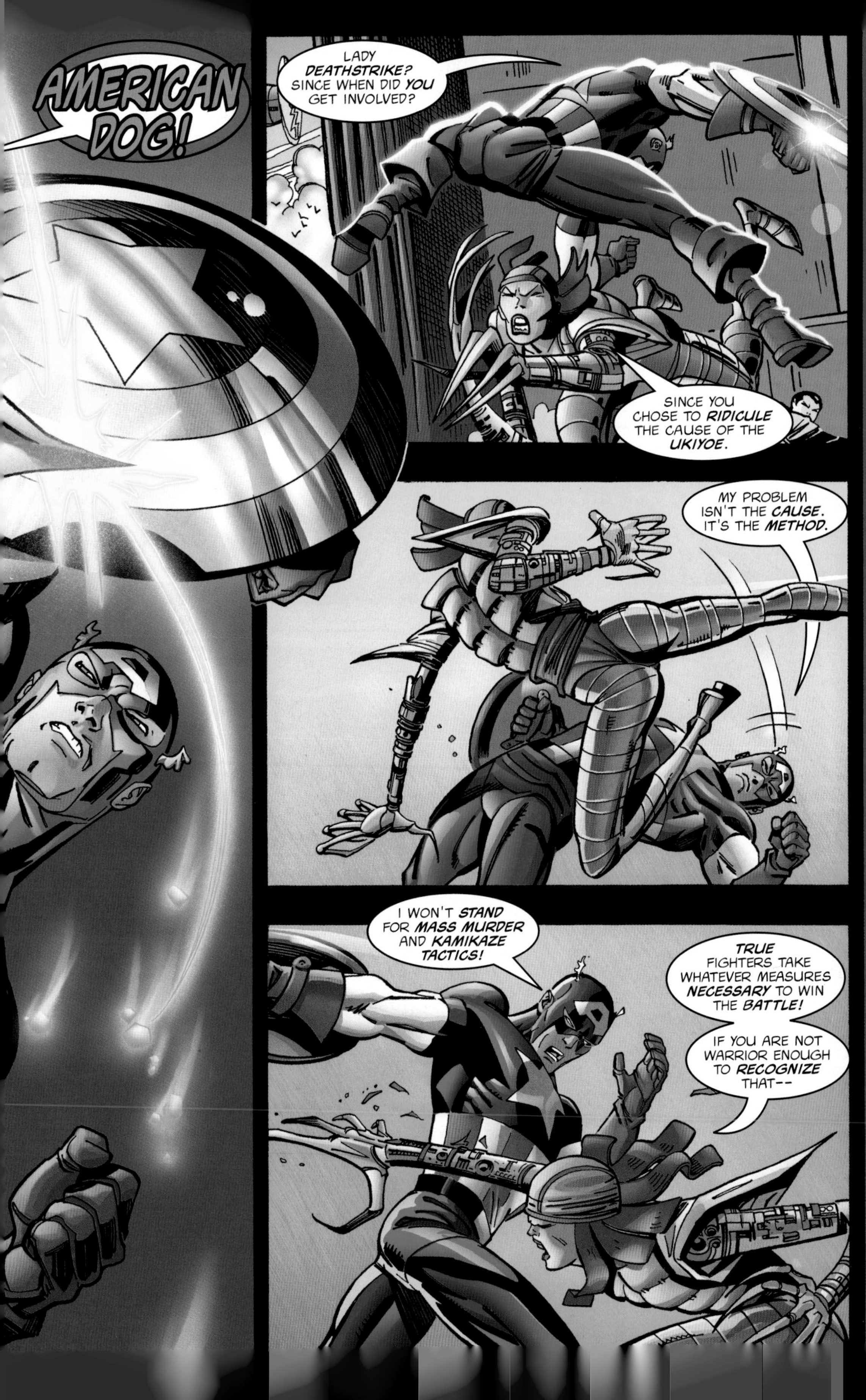
AMERICAN DOG!
LADY DEATHSTRIKE? SINCE WHEN DID YOU GET INVOLVED?
SINCE YOU CHOSE TO RIDICULE THE CAUSE OF THE UKIYOE.
MY PROBLEM ISN'T THE CAUSE. IT'S THE METHOD.
I WON'T STAND FOR MASS MURDER AND KAMIKAZE TACTICS!
TRUE FIGHTERS TAKE WHATEVER MEASURES NECESSARY TO WIN THE BATTLE!
IF YOU ARE NOT WARRIOR ENOUGH TO RECOGNIZE THAT--

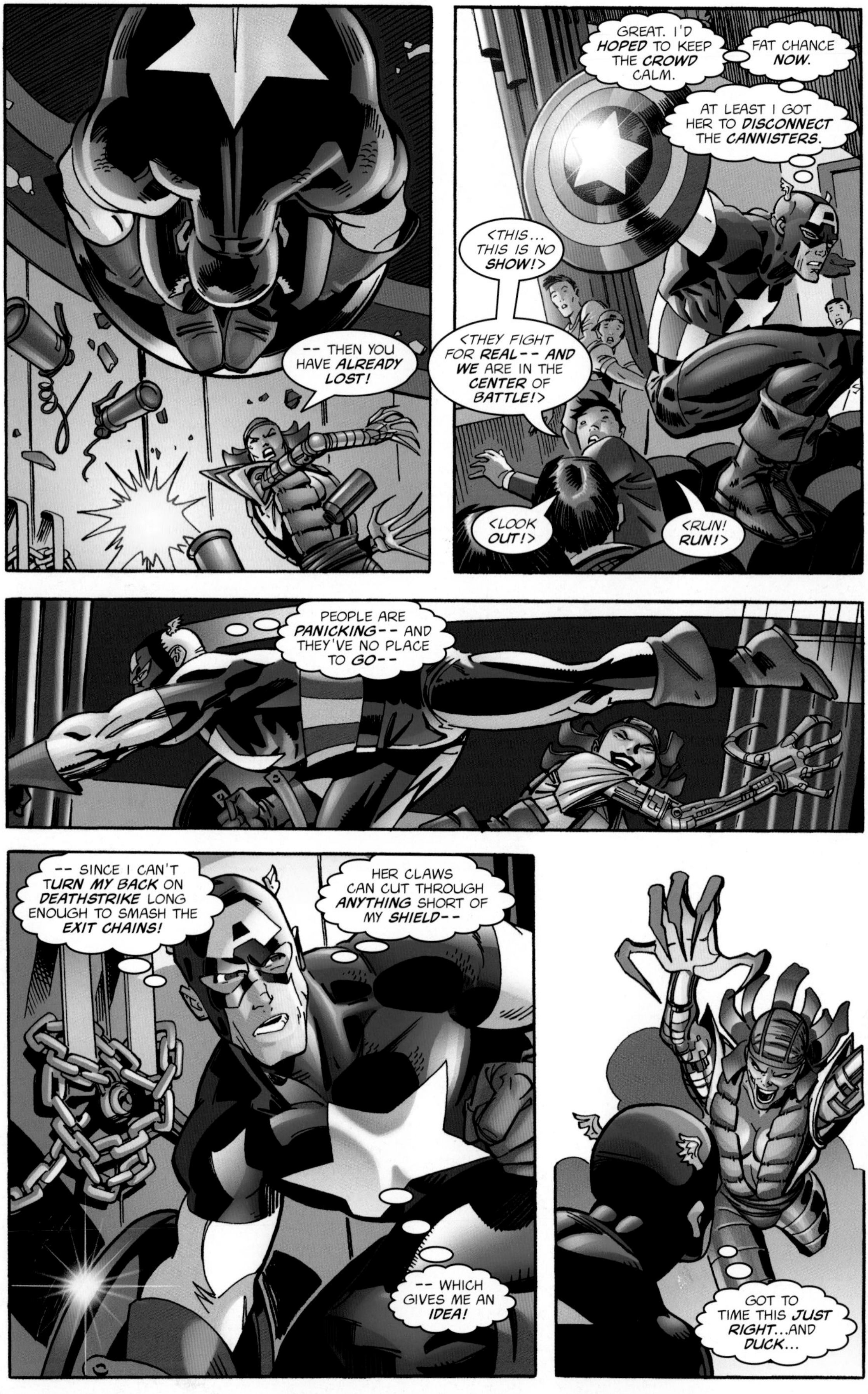
-- THEN YOU HAVE ALREADY LOST!
GREAT. I'D HOPED TO KEEP THE CROWD CALM.
FAT CHANCE NOW.
AT LEAST I GOT HER TO DISCONNECT THE CANNISTERS.
<THIS... THIS IS NO SHOW!>
<THEY FIGHT FOR REAL-- AND WE ARE IN THE CENTER OF BATTLE!>
<LOOK OUT!>
<RUN! RUN!>
PEOPLE ARE PANICKING-- AND THEY'VE NO PLACE TO GO--
-- SINCE I CAN'T TURN MY BACK ON DEATHSTRIKE LONG ENOUGH TO SMASH THE EXIT CHAINS!
HER CLAWS CAN CUT THROUGH ANYTHING SHORT OF MY SHIELD--
-- WHICH GIVES ME AN IDEA!
GOT TO TIME THIS JUST RIGHT...AND DUCK...

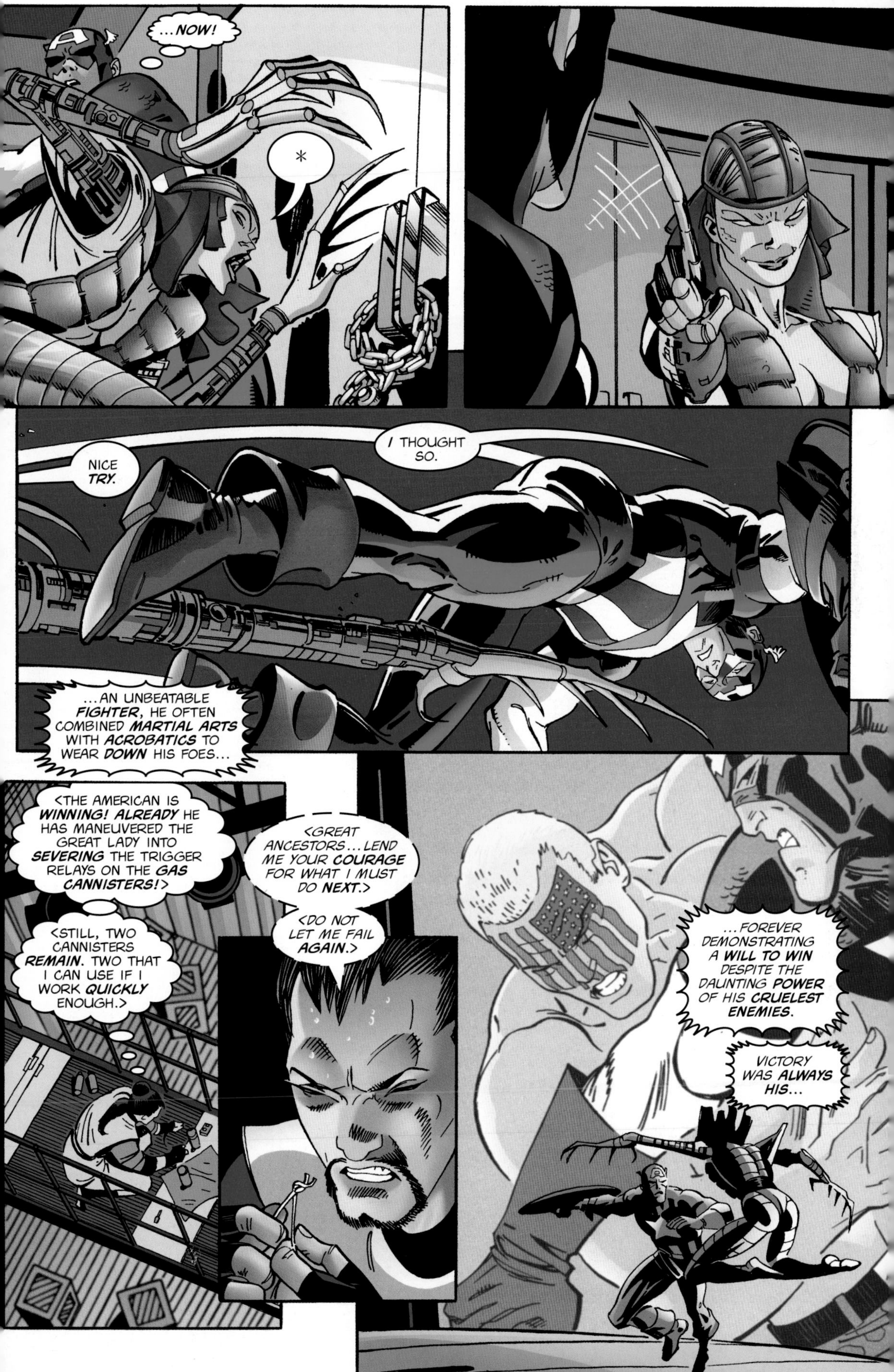
...NOW!
*
NICE TRY.
I THOUGHT SO.
...AN UNBEATABLE FIGHTER, HE OFTEN COMBINED MARTIAL ARTS WITH ACROBATICS TO WEAR DOWN HIS FOES...
<THE AMERICAN IS WINNING! ALREADY HE HAS MANEUVERED THE GREAT LADY INTO SEVERING THE TRIGGER RELAYS ON THE GAS CANNISTERS!>
<STILL, TWO CANNISTERS REMAIN. TWO THAT I CAN USE IF I WORK QUICKLY ENOUGH.>
<GREAT ANCESTORS... LEND ME YOUR COURAGE FOR WHAT I MUST DO NEXT.>
<DO NOT LET ME FAIL AGAIN.>
...FOREVER DEMONSTRATING A WILL TO WIN DESPITE THE DAUNTING POWER OF HIS CRUELEST ENEMIES.
VICTORY WAS ALWAYS HIS...

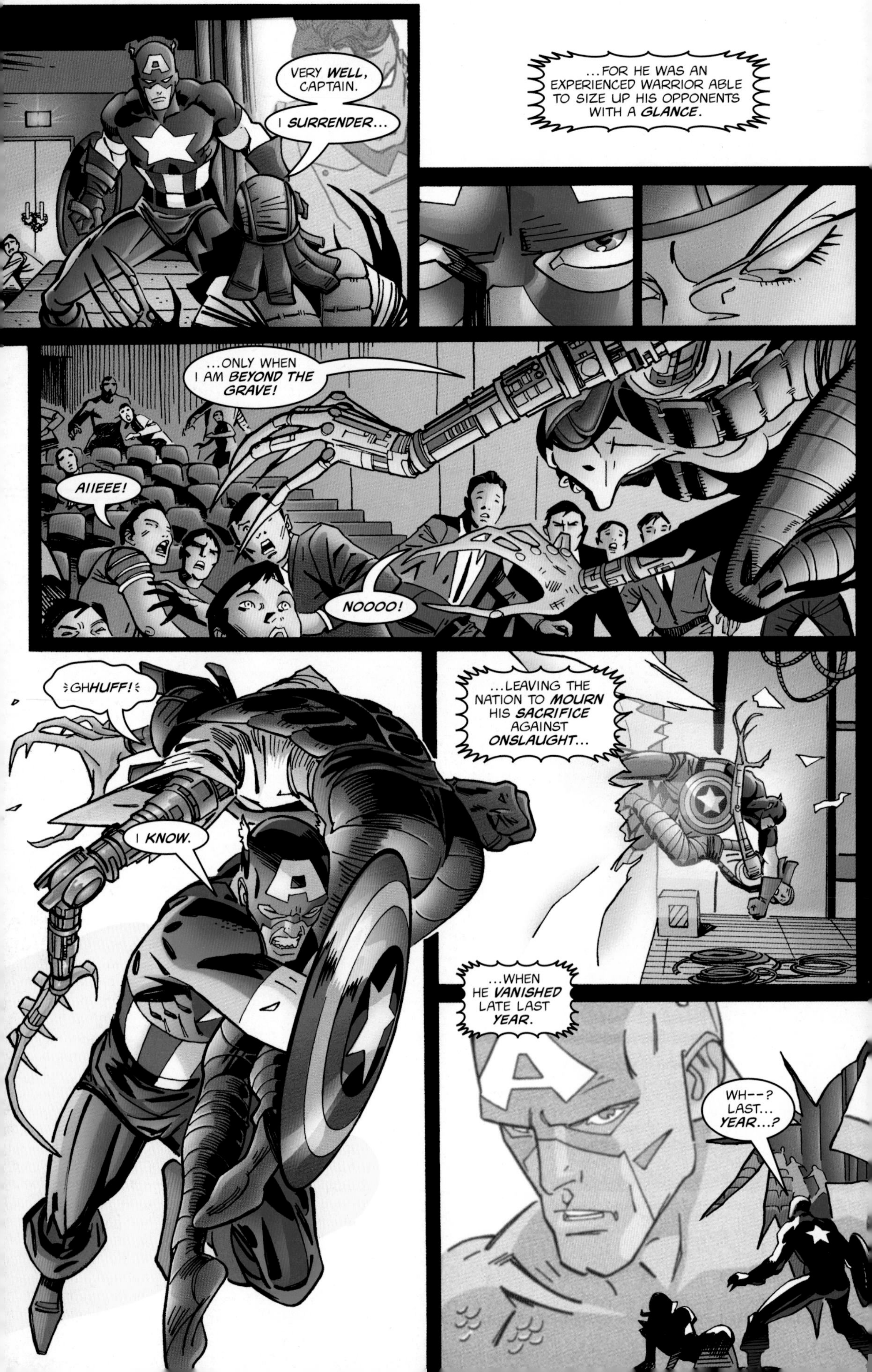
VERY WELL, CAPTAIN.
I SURRENDER...
...FOR HE WAS AN EXPERIENCED WARRIOR ABLE TO SIZE UP HIS OPPONENTS WITH A GLANCE.
...ONLY WHEN I AM BEYOND THE GRAVE!
AIIEEE!
NOOOO!
GHHUFF!
I KNOW.
...LEAVING THE NATION TO MOURN HIS SACRIFICE AGAINST ONSLAUGHT...
...WHEN HE VANISHED LATE LAST YEAR.
WH--? LAST... YEAR...?

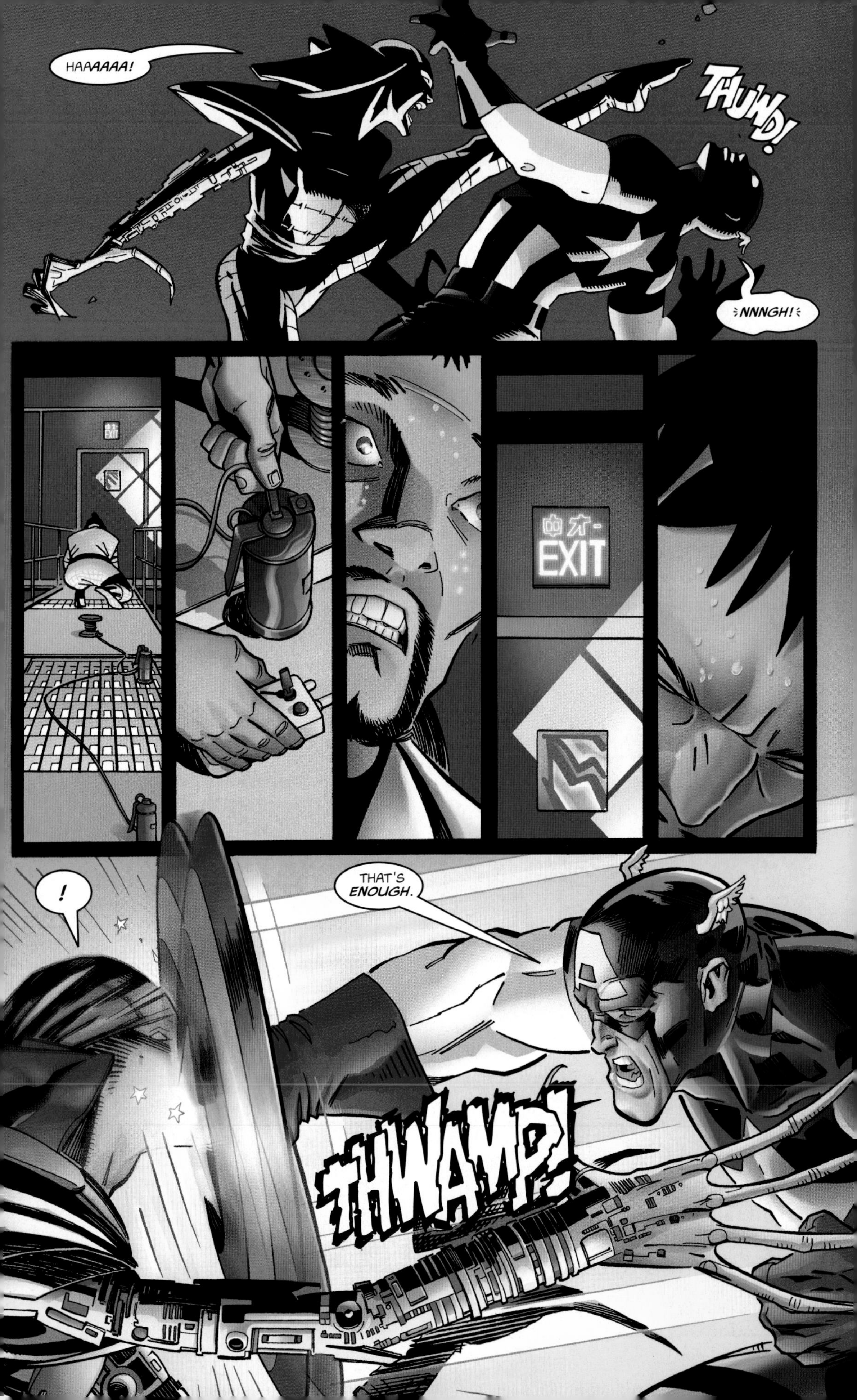
HAAAAAA!
THUWD!
NNNGH!
EXIT
!
THAT'S ENOUGH.
THWAMP!

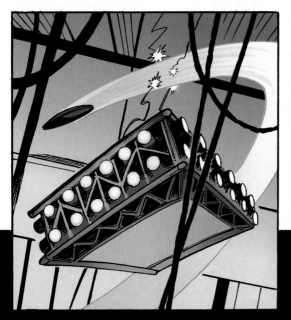

LET'S *FINISH* THIS.

KATHOOM

THE CROWD'S *INSANE* WITH *PANIC!* WHERE'S *AKUTAGAWA?*

TOO *LATE*, CAPTAIN!

TOO LATE.

IT ALL COMES DOWN TO *ME!* I HOLD A *DEADMAN SWITCH*. THE *INSTANT I RELEASE* IT, NERVE GAS *BILLOWS* THROUGH THE BUILDING--

-- POISONING ALL HERE TO SYMBOLIZE THE WAY *YOUR* PEOPLE HAVE POISONED OUR *CULTURE*.

WE WILL DIE *TOGETHER*, YOU AND I. THIS, I *SWEAR*.

WHAT *NOW*, CAPTAIN?

I HAVE HEARD IT SAID THAT YOU ALWAYS FIND A *WAY* TO *WIN*.

THIS TIME, YOU WILL *NOT*.

THERE *IS* NONE.

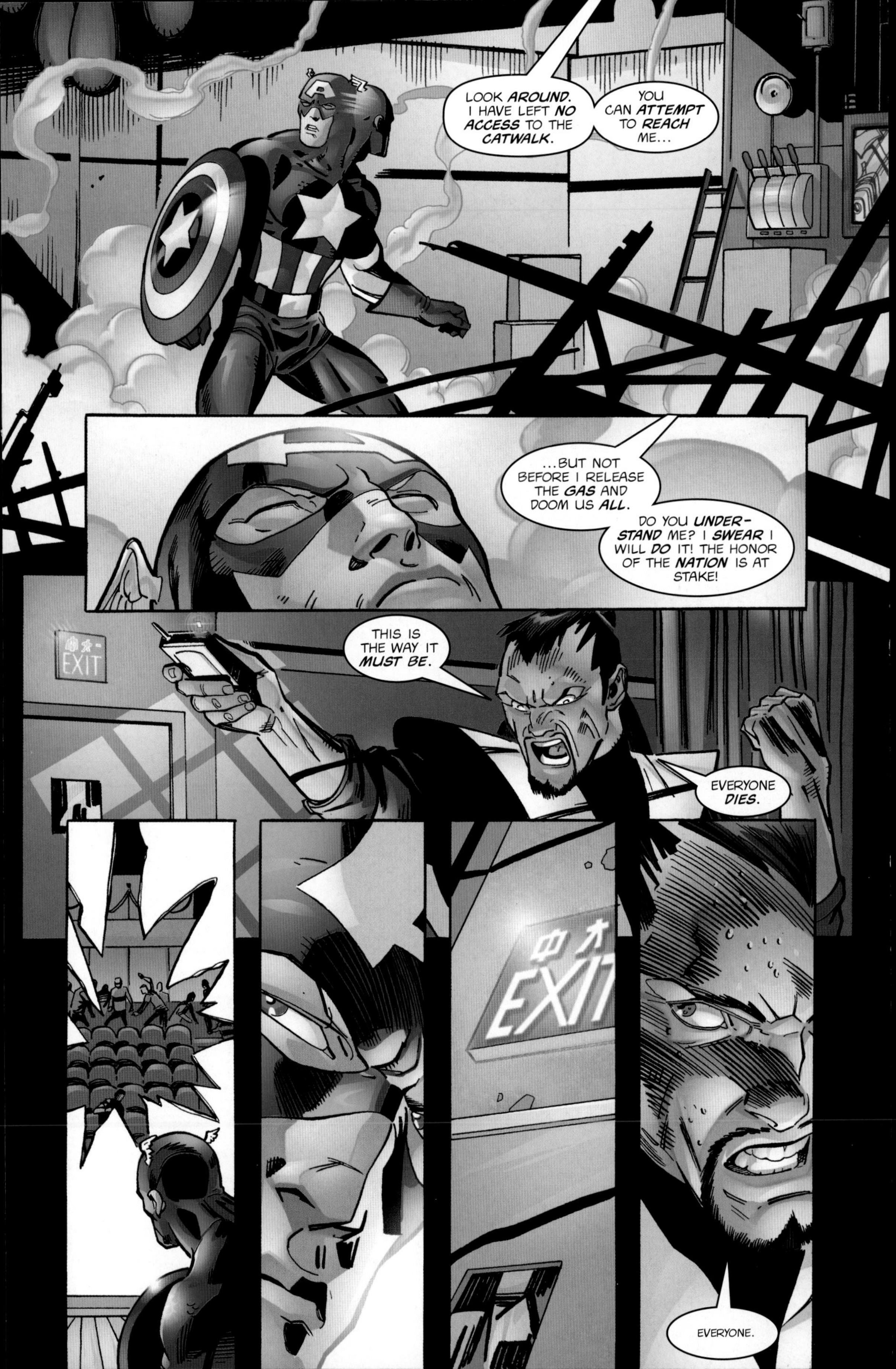
LOOK *AROUND*. I HAVE LEFT *NO ACCESS* TO THE *CATWALK*.
YOU CAN *ATTEMPT* TO *REACH* ME...
...BUT NOT BEFORE I RELEASE THE *GAS* AND DOOM US *ALL*.
DO YOU *UNDER-STAND* ME? I *SWEAR* I WILL *DO* IT! THE HONOR OF THE *NATION* IS AT STAKE!
EXIT
THIS IS THE WAY IT *MUST BE*.
EVERYONE *DIES*.
EXIT
EVERYONE.

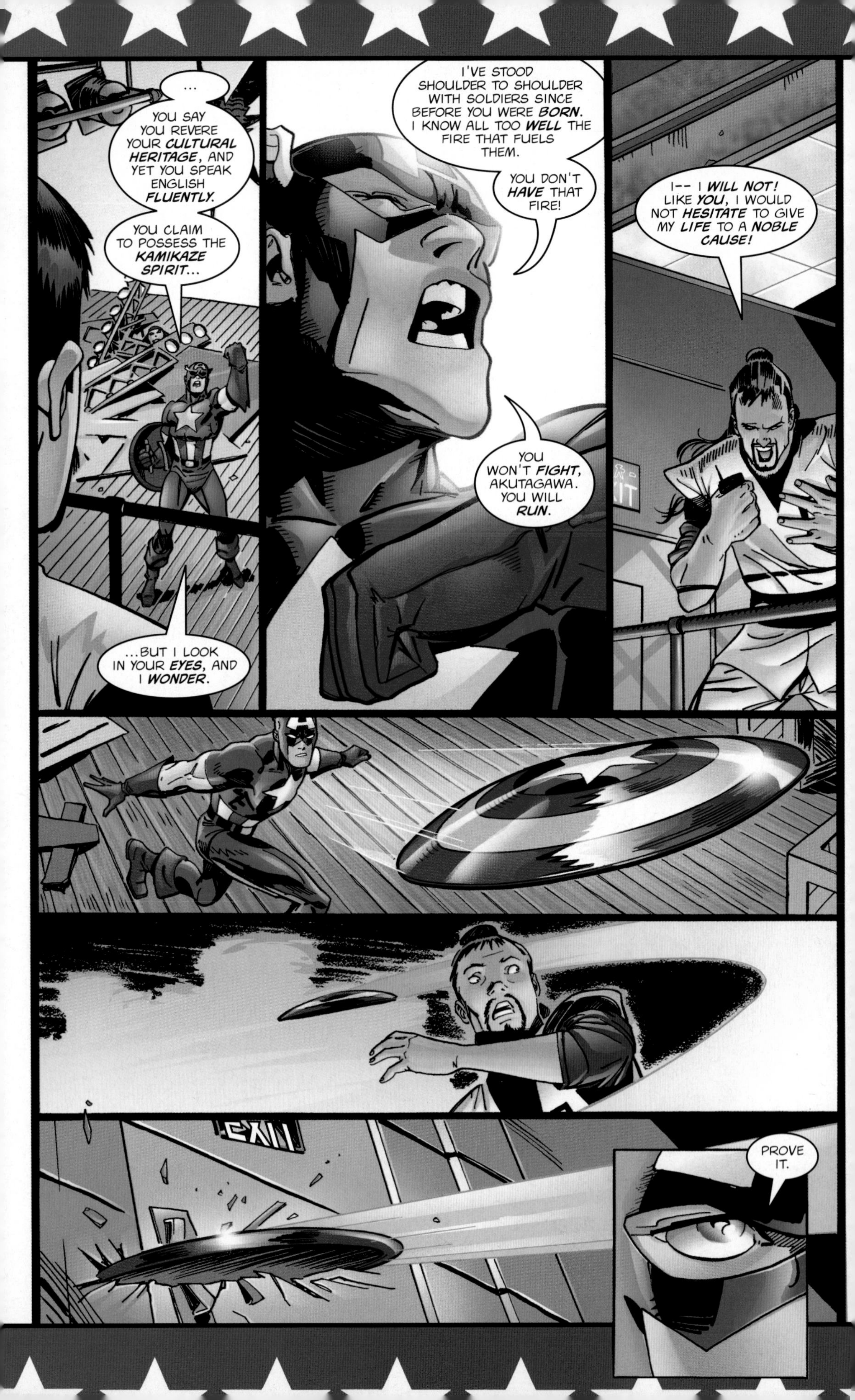
...
YOU SAY YOU REVERE YOUR CULTURAL HERITAGE, AND YET YOU SPEAK ENGLISH FLUENTLY.
YOU CLAIM TO POSSESS THE KAMIKAZE SPIRIT...
...BUT I LOOK IN YOUR EYES, AND I WONDER.
I'VE STOOD SHOULDER TO SHOULDER WITH SOLDIERS SINCE BEFORE YOU WERE BORN. I KNOW ALL TOO WELL THE FIRE THAT FUELS THEM.
YOU DON'T HAVE THAT FIRE!
YOU WON'T FIGHT, AKUTAGAWA. YOU WILL RUN.
I-- I WILL NOT! LIKE YOU, I WOULD NOT HESITATE TO GIVE MY LIFE TO A NOBLE CAUSE!
PROVE IT.

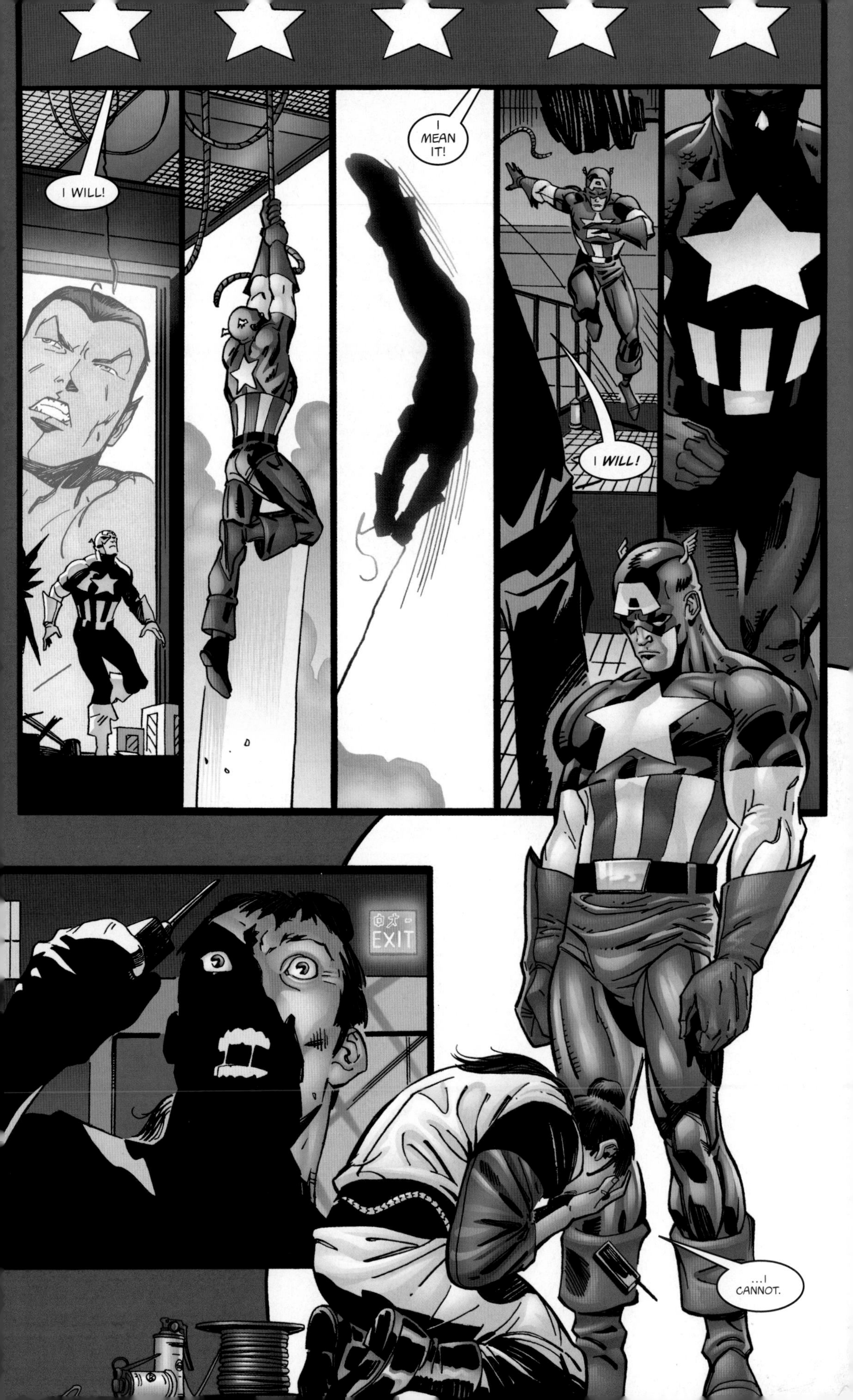
I WILL!
I MEAN IT!
I WILL!
EXIT
...I CANNOT.

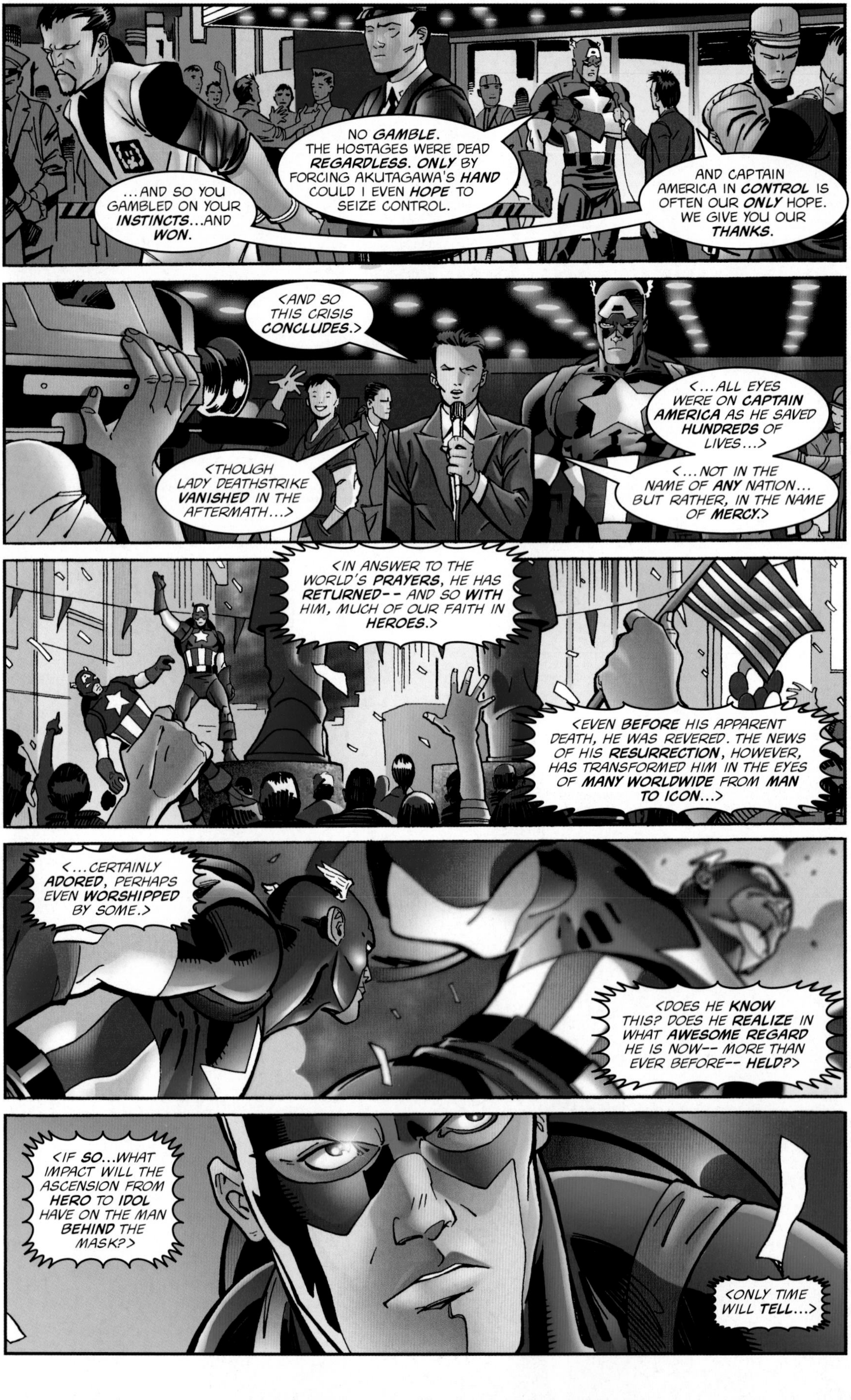
...AND SO YOU GAMBLED ON YOUR INSTINCTS...AND WON.
NO GAMBLE. THE HOSTAGES WERE DEAD REGARDLESS. ONLY BY FORCING AKUTAGAWA'S HAND COULD I EVEN HOPE TO SEIZE CONTROL.
AND CAPTAIN AMERICA IN CONTROL IS OFTEN OUR ONLY HOPE. WE GIVE YOU OUR THANKS.
<AND SO THIS CRISIS CONCLUDES.>
<THOUGH LADY DEATHSTRIKE VANISHED IN THE AFTERMATH...>
<...ALL EYES WERE ON CAPTAIN AMERICA AS HE SAVED HUNDREDS OF LIVES...>
<...NOT IN THE NAME OF ANY NATION... BUT RATHER, IN THE NAME OF MERCY.>
<IN ANSWER TO THE WORLD'S PRAYERS, HE HAS RETURNED-- AND SO WITH HIM, MUCH OF OUR FAITH IN HEROES.>
<EVEN BEFORE HIS APPARENT DEATH, HE WAS REVERED. THE NEWS OF HIS RESURRECTION, HOWEVER, HAS TRANSFORMED HIM IN THE EYES OF MANY WORLDWIDE FROM MAN TO ICON...>
<...CERTAINLY ADORED, PERHAPS EVEN WORSHIPPED BY SOME.>
<DOES HE KNOW THIS? DOES HE REALIZE IN WHAT AWESOME REGARD HE IS NOW-- MORE THAN EVER BEFORE-- HELD?>
<IF SO...WHAT IMPACT WILL THE ASCENSION FROM HERO TO IDOL HAVE ON THE MAN BEHIND THE MASK?>
<ONLY TIME WILL TELL...>

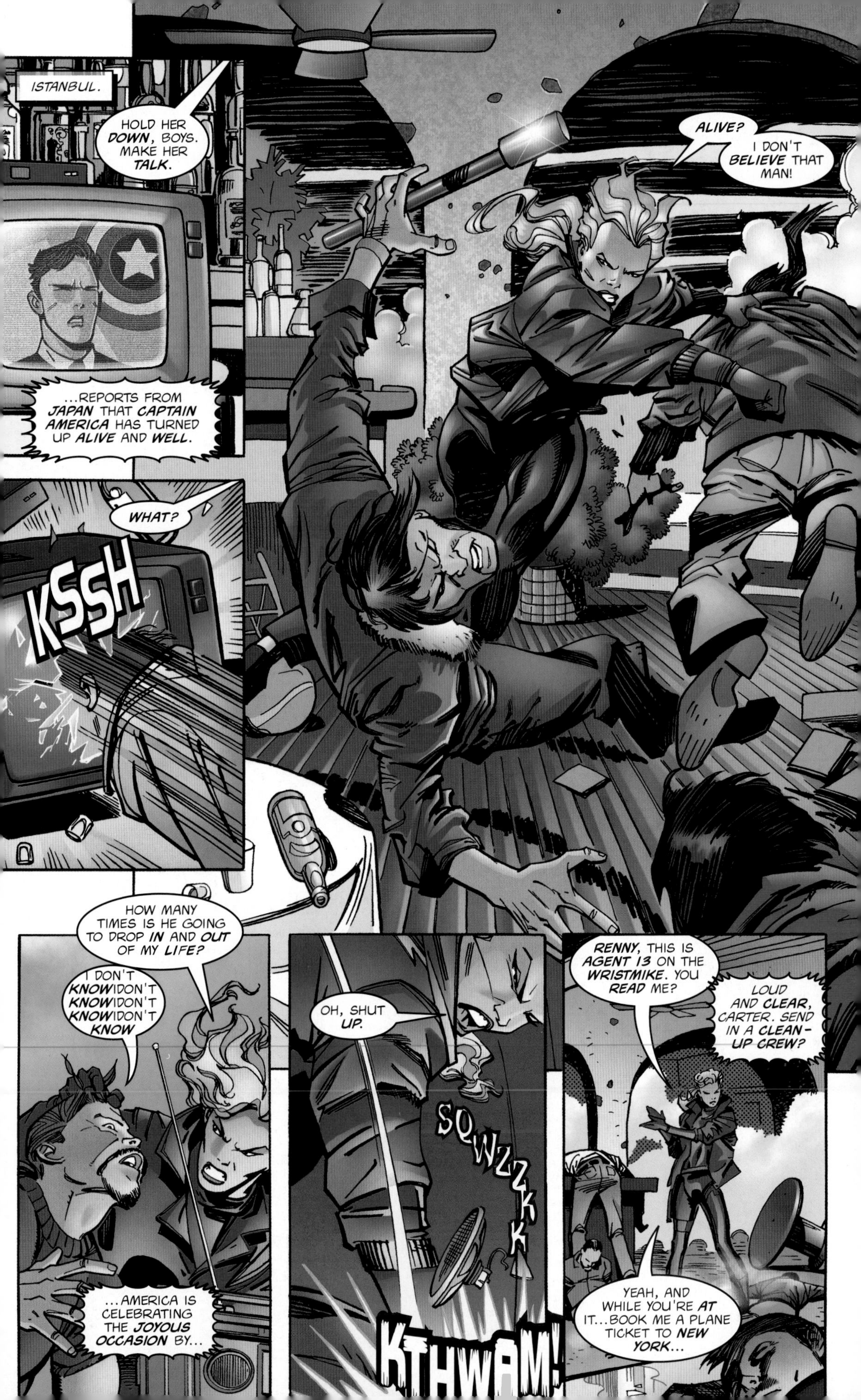
ISTANBUL.
HOLD HER DOWN, BOYS. MAKE HER TALK.
...REPORTS FROM JAPAN THAT CAPTAIN AMERICA HAS TURNED UP ALIVE AND WELL.
WHAT?
KSSH
ALIVE? I DON'T BELIEVE THAT MAN!
HOW MANY TIMES IS HE GOING TO DROP IN AND OUT OF MY LIFE?
I DON'T KNOWIDON'T KNOWIDON'T KNOWIDON'T KNOW
...AMERICA IS CELEBRATING THE JOYOUS OCCASION BY...
OH, SHUT UP.
SQWZZKK
KTHWAM!
RENNY, THIS IS AGENT 13 ON THE WRISTMIKE. YOU READ ME?
LOUD AND CLEAR, CARTER. SEND IN A CLEAN-UP CREW?
YEAH, AND WHILE YOU'RE AT IT...BOOK ME A PLANE TICKET TO NEW YORK...

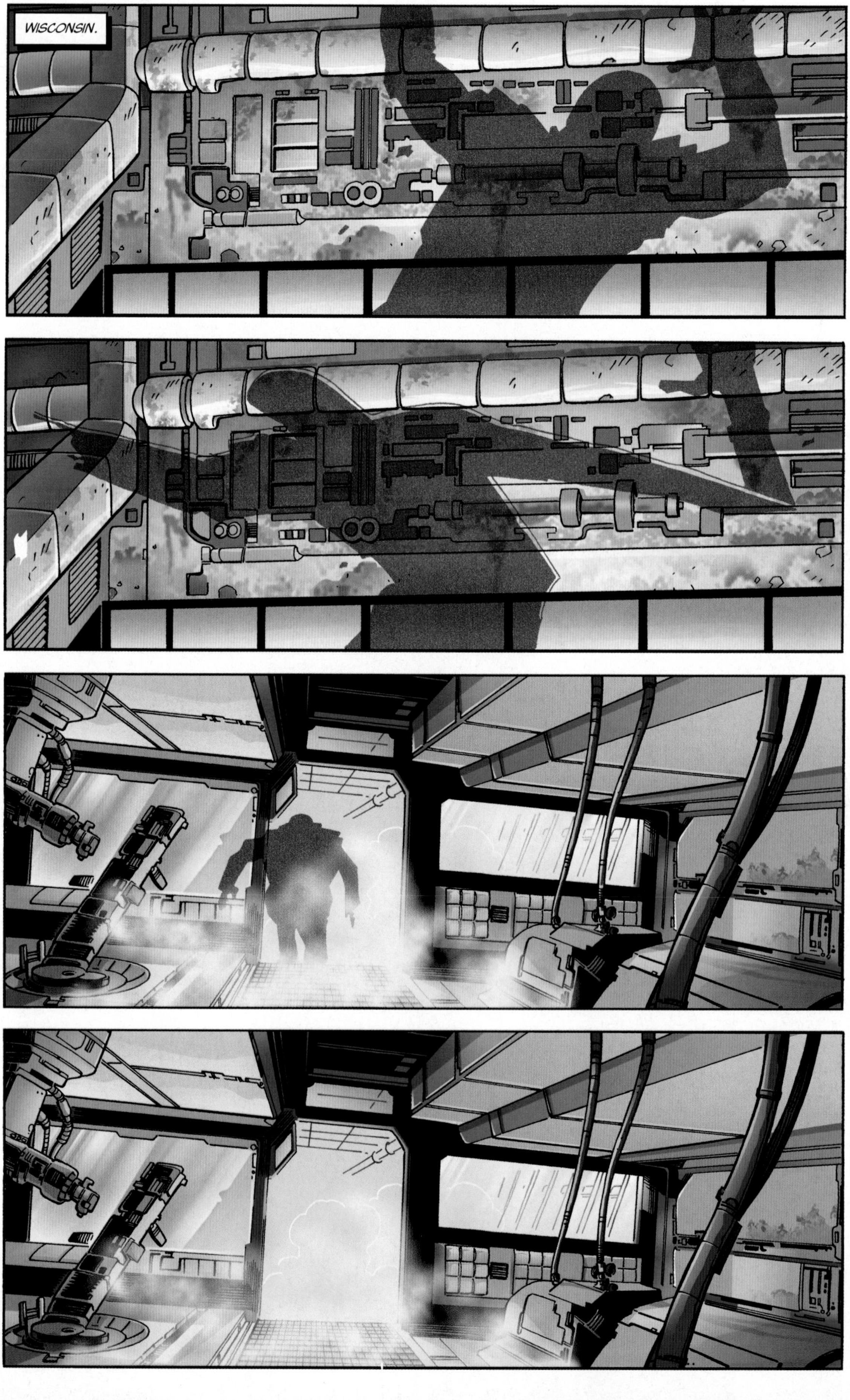
WISCONSIN.

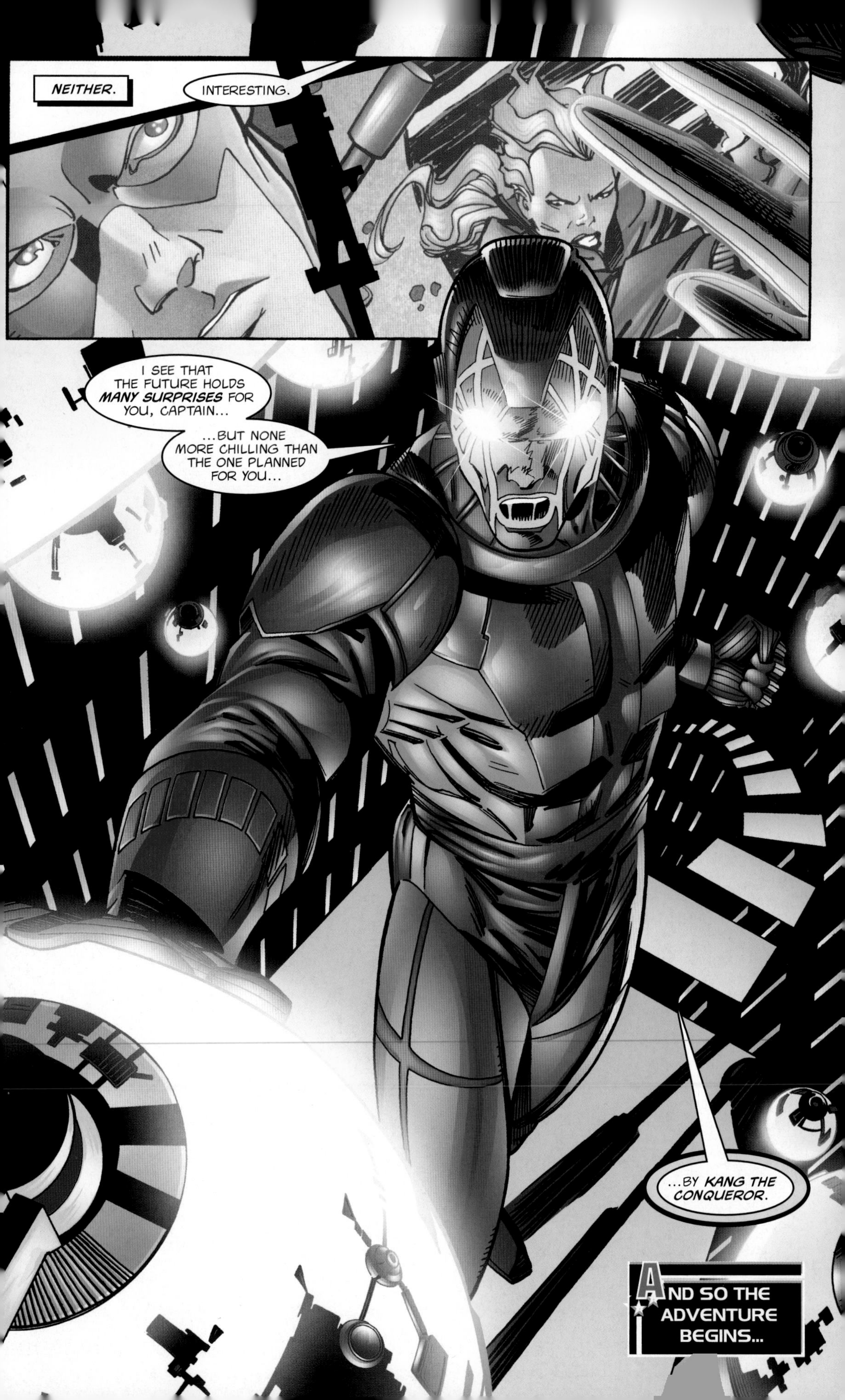
NEITHER.
INTERESTING.
I SEE THAT THE FUTURE HOLDS MANY SURPRISES FOR YOU, CAPTAIN...
...BUT NONE MORE CHILLING THAN THE ONE PLANNED FOR YOU...
...BY KANG THE CONQUEROR.
AND SO THE ADVENTURE BEGINS...

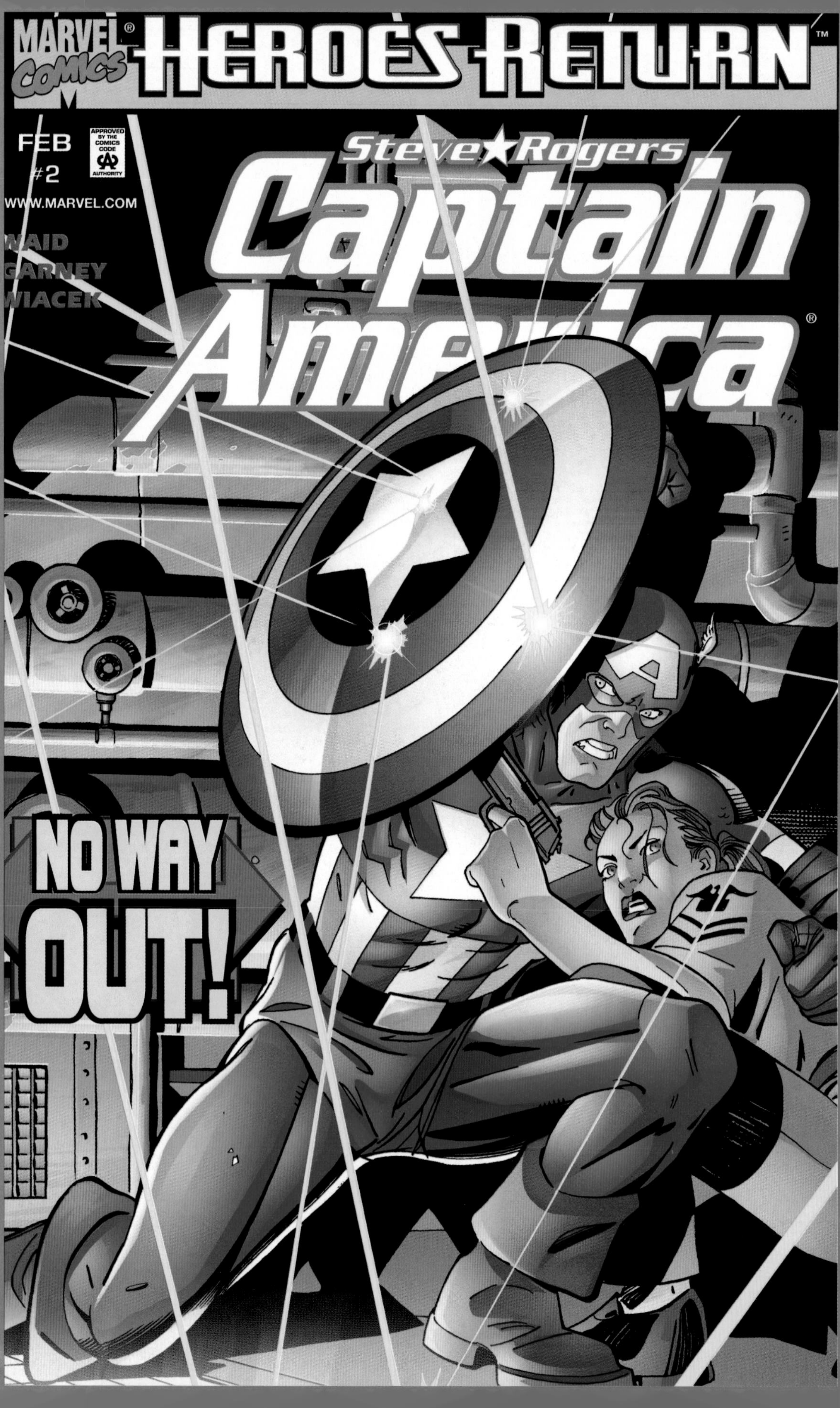
MARVEL® COMICS
HEROES RETURN™
FEB
#2
APPROVED BY THE COMICS CODE AUTHORITY
Steve★Rogers
Captain America®
WWW.MARVEL.COM
WAID
GARNEY
WIACEK
NO WAY OUT!

Stan Lee Presents

CAPTAIN AMERICA

in:

To SERVE And PROTECT

by

MARK WAID & RON GARNEY

BOB WIACEK - JOHN COSTANZA

JOE ROSAS - DIGITAL CHAMELEON

MATT IDELSON - BOB HARRAS

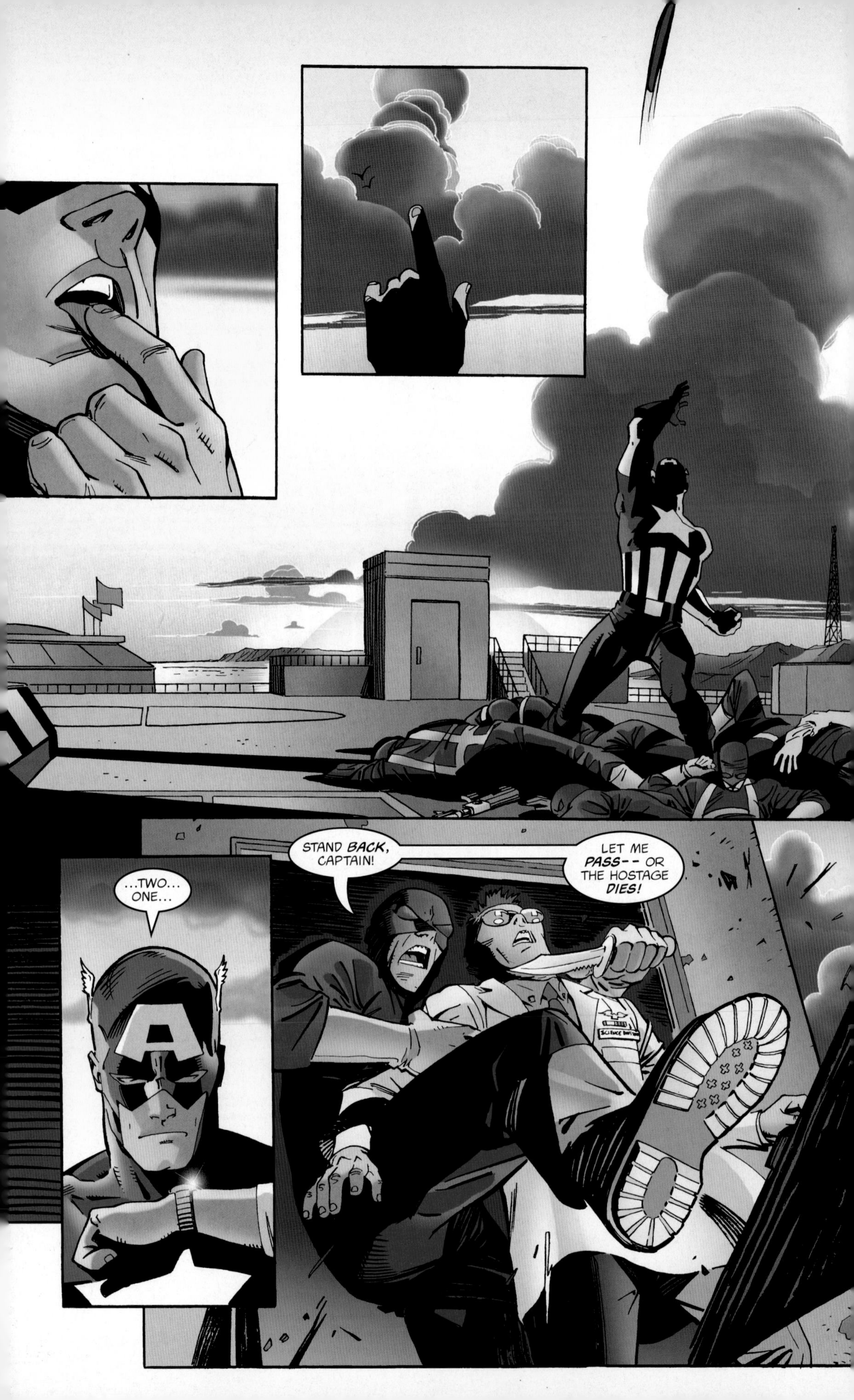
...TWO...
ONE...
STAND BACK, CAPTAIN!
LET ME PASS-- OR THE HOSTAGE DIES!

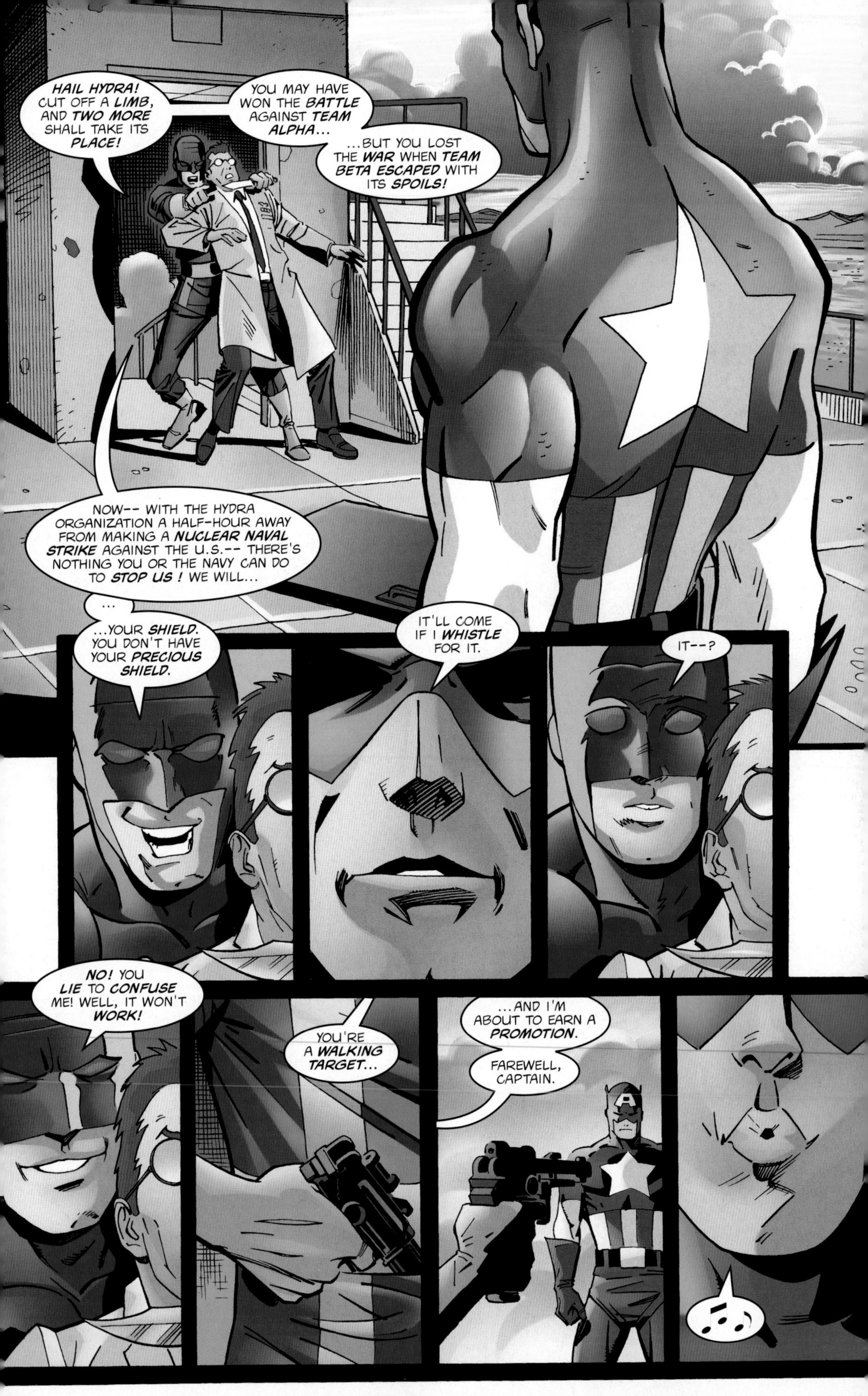

HAIL HYDRA! CUT OFF A LIMB, AND TWO MORE SHALL TAKE ITS PLACE!
YOU MAY HAVE WON THE BATTLE AGAINST TEAM ALPHA...
...BUT YOU LOST THE WAR WHEN TEAM BETA ESCAPED WITH ITS SPOILS!
NOW-- WITH THE HYDRA ORGANIZATION A HALF-HOUR AWAY FROM MAKING A NUCLEAR NAVAL STRIKE AGAINST THE U.S.-- THERE'S NOTHING YOU OR THE NAVY CAN DO TO STOP US ! WE WILL...
...
...YOUR SHIELD. YOU DON'T HAVE YOUR PRECIOUS SHIELD.
IT'LL COME IF I WHISTLE FOR IT.
IT--?
NO! YOU LIE TO CONFUSE ME! WELL, IT WON'T WORK!
YOU'RE A WALKING TARGET...
...AND I'M ABOUT TO EARN A PROMOTION.
FAREWELL, CAPTAIN.

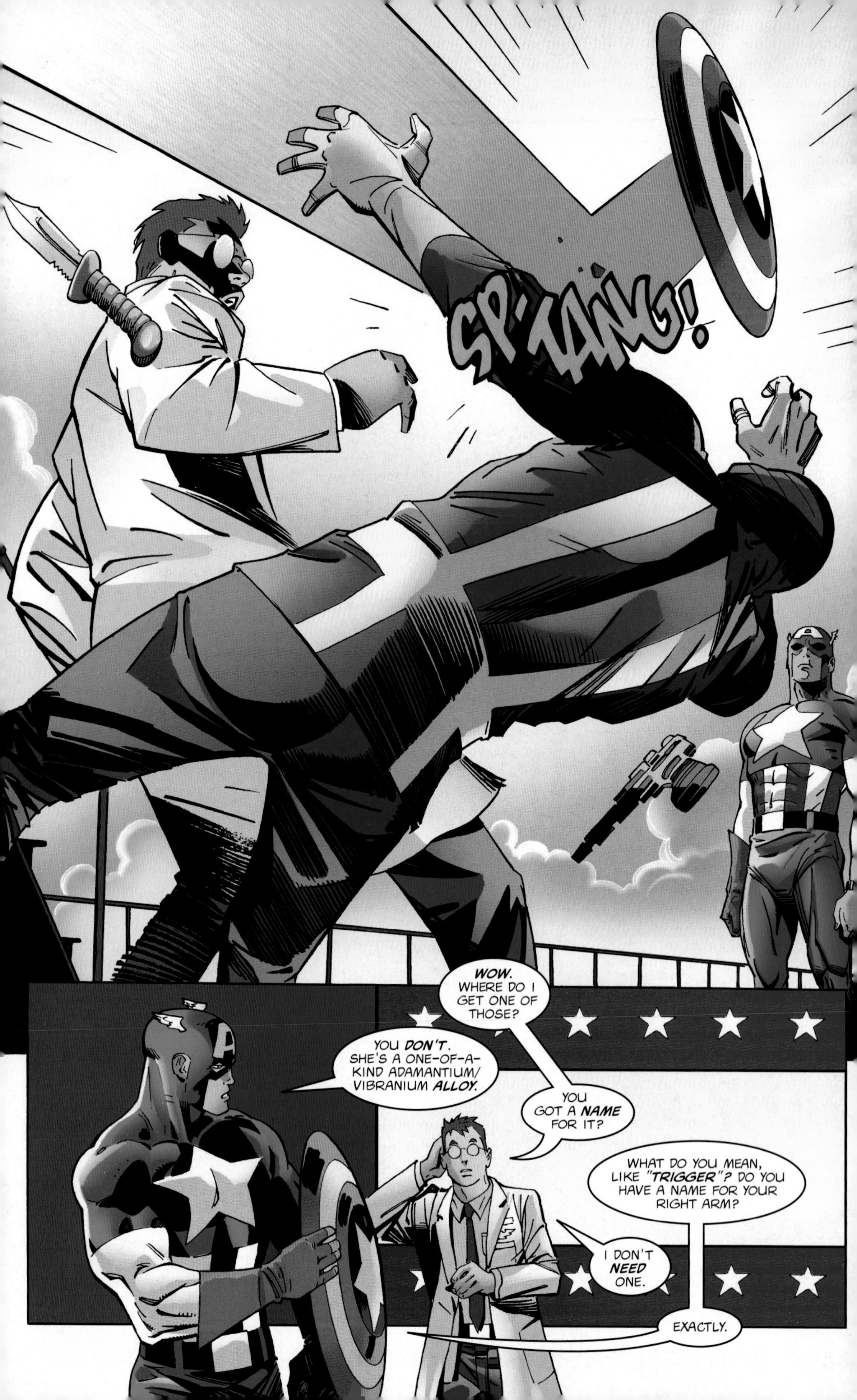
SP'TANG!
WOW. WHERE DO I GET ONE OF THOSE?
YOU DON'T. SHE'S A ONE-OF-A-KIND ADAMANTIUM/VIBRANIUM ALLOY.
YOU GOT A NAME FOR IT?
WHAT DO YOU MEAN, LIKE "TRIGGER"? DO YOU HAVE A NAME FOR YOUR RIGHT ARM?
I DON'T NEED ONE.
EXACTLY.

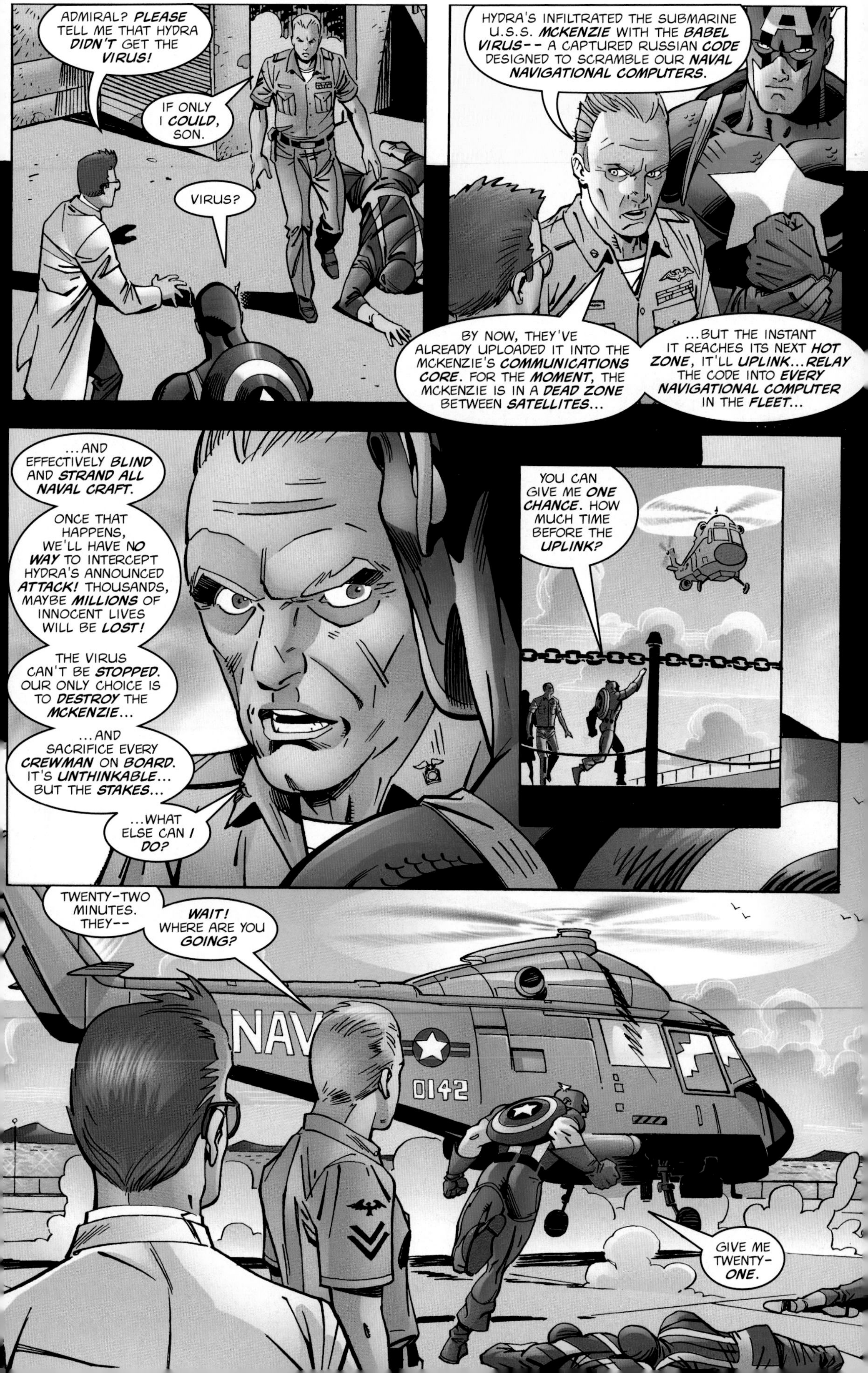
ADMIRAL? PLEASE TELL ME THAT HYDRA DIDN'T GET THE VIRUS!
IF ONLY I COULD, SON.
VIRUS?
HYDRA'S INFILTRATED THE SUBMARINE U.S.S. MCKENZIE WITH THE BABEL VIRUS-- A CAPTURED RUSSIAN CODE DESIGNED TO SCRAMBLE OUR NAVAL NAVIGATIONAL COMPUTERS.
BY NOW, THEY'VE ALREADY UPLOADED IT INTO THE MCKENZIE'S COMMUNICATIONS CORE. FOR THE MOMENT, THE MCKENZIE IS IN A DEAD ZONE BETWEEN SATELLITES...
...BUT THE INSTANT IT REACHES ITS NEXT HOT ZONE, IT'LL UPLINK...RELAY THE CODE INTO EVERY NAVIGATIONAL COMPUTER IN THE FLEET...
...AND EFFECTIVELY BLIND AND STRAND ALL NAVAL CRAFT.
ONCE THAT HAPPENS, WE'LL HAVE NO WAY TO INTERCEPT HYDRA'S ANNOUNCED ATTACK! THOUSANDS, MAYBE MILLIONS OF INNOCENT LIVES WILL BE LOST!
THE VIRUS CAN'T BE STOPPED. OUR ONLY CHOICE IS TO DESTROY THE MCKENZIE...
...AND SACRIFICE EVERY CREWMAN ON BOARD. IT'S UNTHINKABLE... BUT THE STAKES...
...WHAT ELSE CAN I DO?
YOU CAN GIVE ME ONE CHANCE. HOW MUCH TIME BEFORE THE UPLINK?
TWENTY-TWO MINUTES. THEY--
WAIT! WHERE ARE YOU GOING?
NAV
0142
GIVE ME TWENTY-ONE.

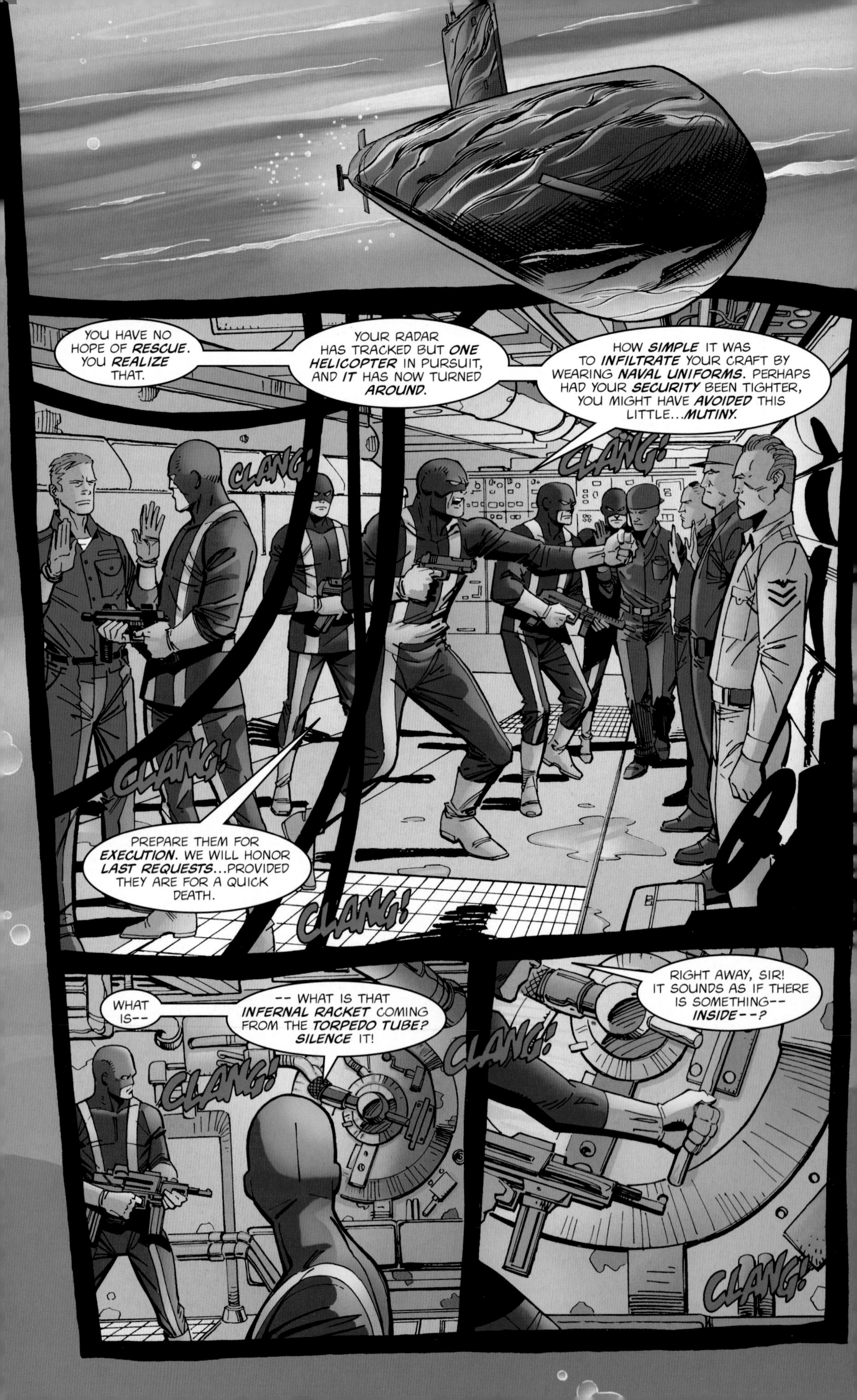

YOU HAVE NO HOPE OF RESCUE. YOU REALIZE THAT.
YOUR RADAR HAS TRACKED BUT ONE HELICOPTER IN PURSUIT, AND IT HAS NOW TURNED AROUND.
HOW SIMPLE IT WAS TO INFILTRATE YOUR CRAFT BY WEARING NAVAL UNIFORMS. PERHAPS HAD YOUR SECURITY BEEN TIGHTER, YOU MIGHT HAVE AVOIDED THIS LITTLE...MUTINY.
CLANG!
CLANG!
CLANG!
PREPARE THEM FOR EXECUTION. WE WILL HONOR LAST REQUESTS...PROVIDED THEY ARE FOR A QUICK DEATH.
CLANG!
WHAT IS--
-- WHAT IS THAT INFERNAL RACKET COMING FROM THE TORPEDO TUBE? SILENCE IT!
CLANG!
CLANG!
RIGHT AWAY, SIR! IT SOUNDS AS IF THERE IS SOMETHING-- INSIDE--?
CLANG!

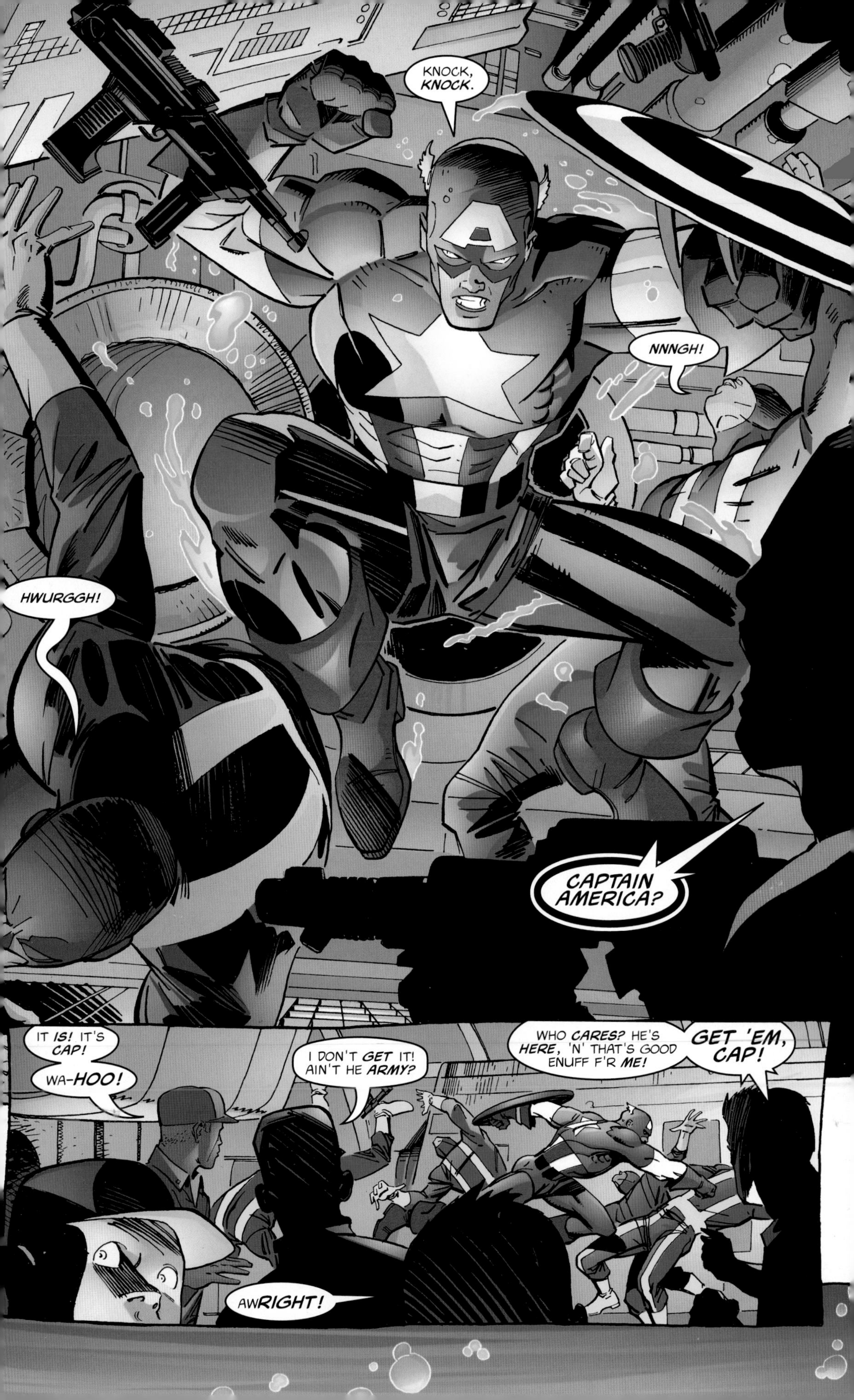
KNOCK, KNOCK.
NNNGH!
HWURGGH!
CAPTAIN AMERICA?
IT IS! IT'S CAP!
WA-HOO!
I DON'T GET IT! AIN'T HE ARMY?
WHO CARES? HE'S HERE, 'N' THAT'S GOOD ENUFF F'R ME!
GET 'EM, CAP!
AWRIGHT!

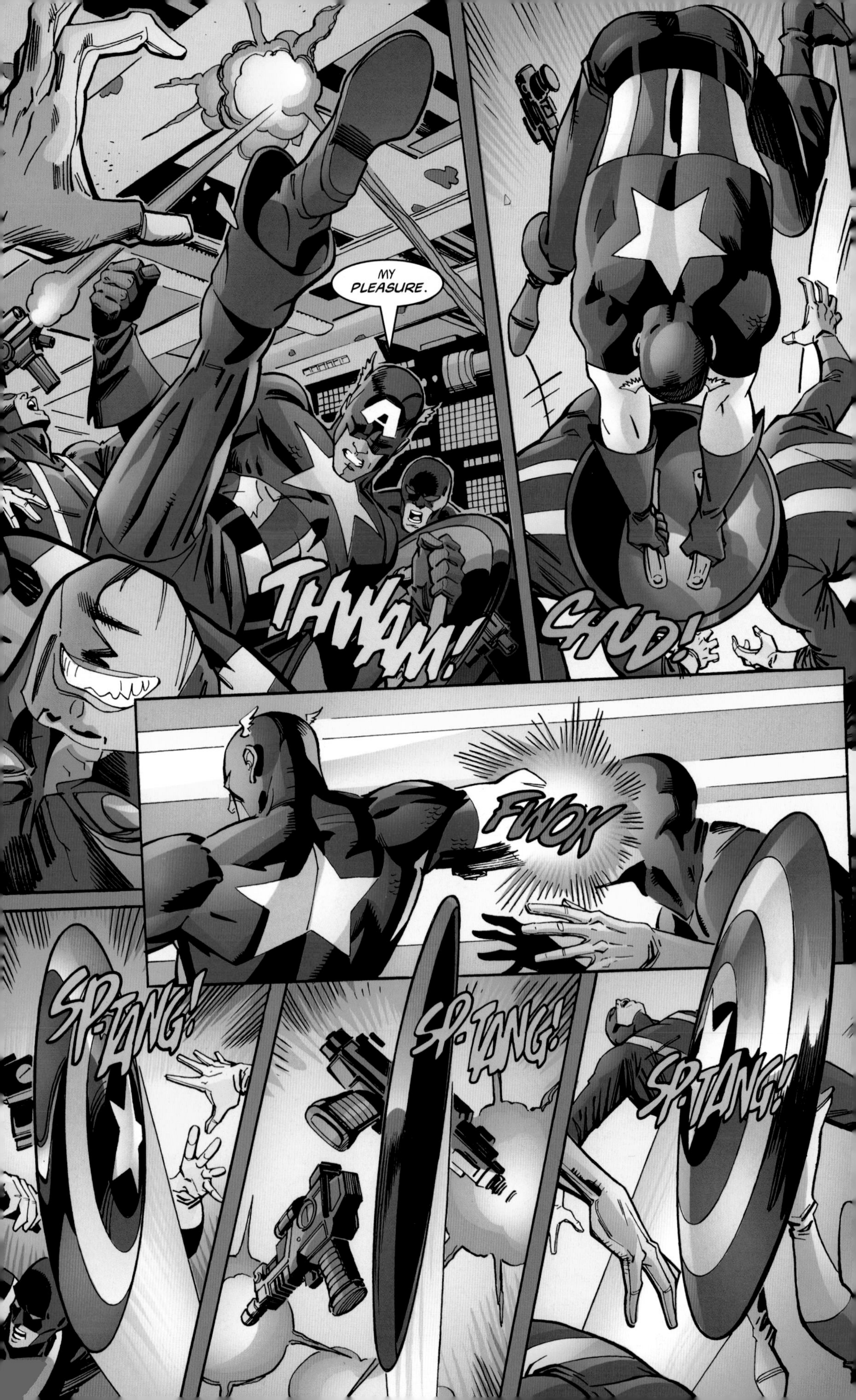

MY PLEASURE.
THWAM!
CHUD!
FWOK
SP-TANG!
SP-TANG!
SP-TANG!

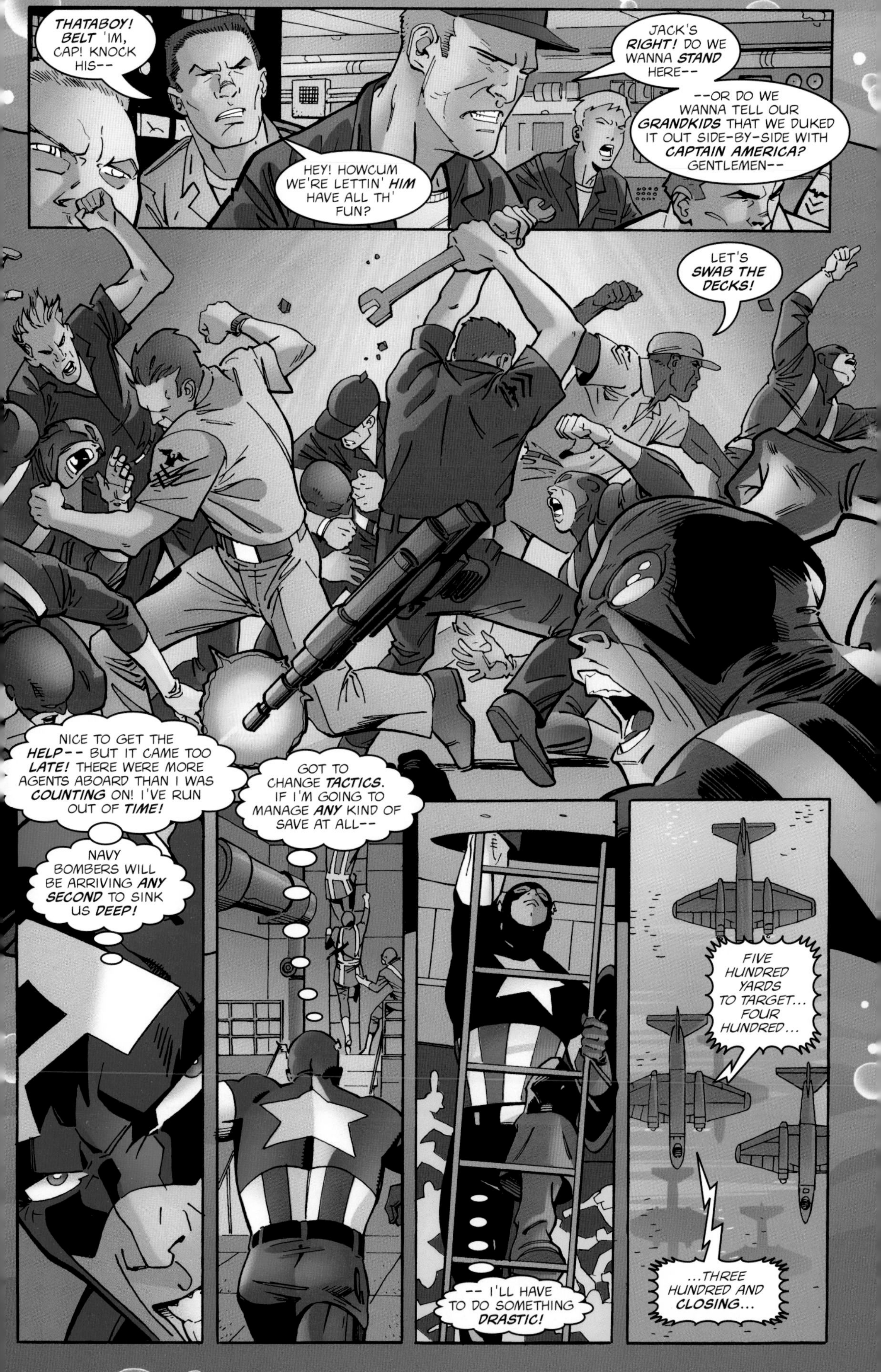
THATABOY! BELT 'IM, CAP! KNOCK HIS--
HEY! HOWCUM WE'RE LETTIN' HIM HAVE ALL TH' FUN?
JACK'S RIGHT! DO WE WANNA STAND HERE--
--OR DO WE WANNA TELL OUR GRANDKIDS THAT WE DUKED IT OUT SIDE-BY-SIDE WITH CAPTAIN AMERICA? GENTLEMEN--
LET'S SWAB THE DECKS!
NICE TO GET THE HELP-- BUT IT CAME TOO LATE! THERE WERE MORE AGENTS ABOARD THAN I WAS COUNTING ON! I'VE RUN OUT OF TIME!
NAVY BOMBERS WILL BE ARRIVING ANY SECOND TO SINK US DEEP!
GOT TO CHANGE TACTICS. IF I'M GOING TO MANAGE ANY KIND OF SAVE AT ALL--
-- I'LL HAVE TO DO SOMETHING DRASTIC!
FIVE HUNDRED YARDS TO TARGET... FOUR HUNDRED...
...THREE HUNDRED AND CLOSING...

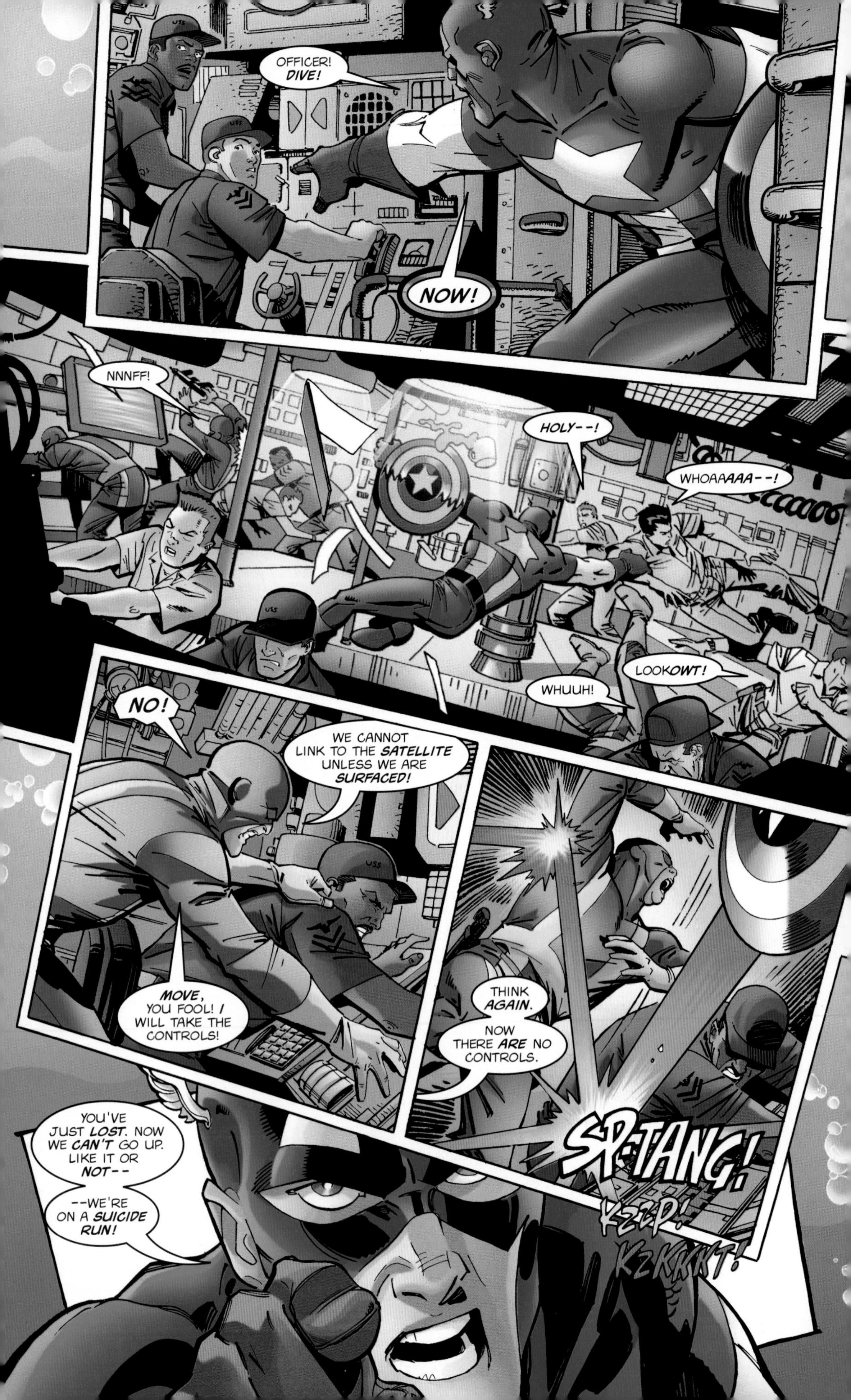

OFFICER! DIVE!
NOW!
NNNFF!
HOLY--!
WHOAAAAA--!
LOOKOWT!
WHUUH!
NO!
WE CANNOT LINK TO THE SATELLITE UNLESS WE ARE SURFACED!
MOVE, YOU FOOL! I WILL TAKE THE CONTROLS!
THINK AGAIN.
NOW THERE ARE NO CONTROLS.
SP-TANG!
KZZP!
KZKKKT!
YOU'VE JUST LOST. NOW WE CAN'T GO UP. LIKE IT OR NOT--
--WE'RE ON A SUICIDE RUN!

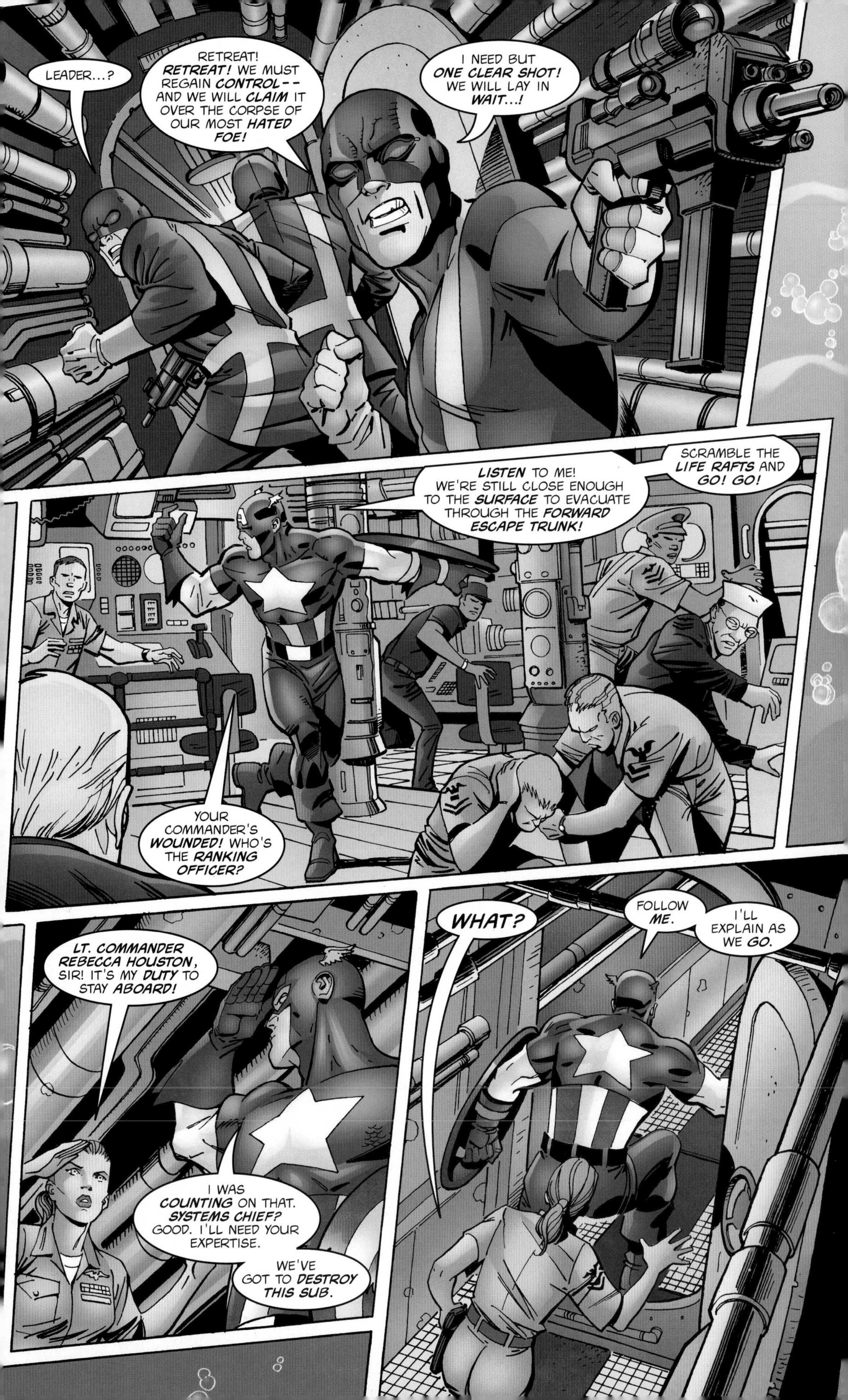
LEADER...?
RETREAT! RETREAT! WE MUST REGAIN CONTROL-- AND WE WILL CLAIM IT OVER THE CORPSE OF OUR MOST HATED FOE!
I NEED BUT ONE CLEAR SHOT! WE WILL LAY IN WAIT...!
LISTEN TO ME! WE'RE STILL CLOSE ENOUGH TO THE SURFACE TO EVACUATE THROUGH THE FORWARD ESCAPE TRUNK!
SCRAMBLE THE LIFE RAFTS AND GO! GO!
YOUR COMMANDER'S WOUNDED! WHO'S THE RANKING OFFICER?
LT. COMMANDER REBECCA HOUSTON, SIR! IT'S MY DUTY TO STAY ABOARD!
I WAS COUNTING ON THAT. SYSTEMS CHIEF? GOOD. I'LL NEED YOUR EXPERTISE.
WE'VE GOT TO DESTROY THIS SUB.
WHAT?
FOLLOW ME.
I'LL EXPLAIN AS WE GO.

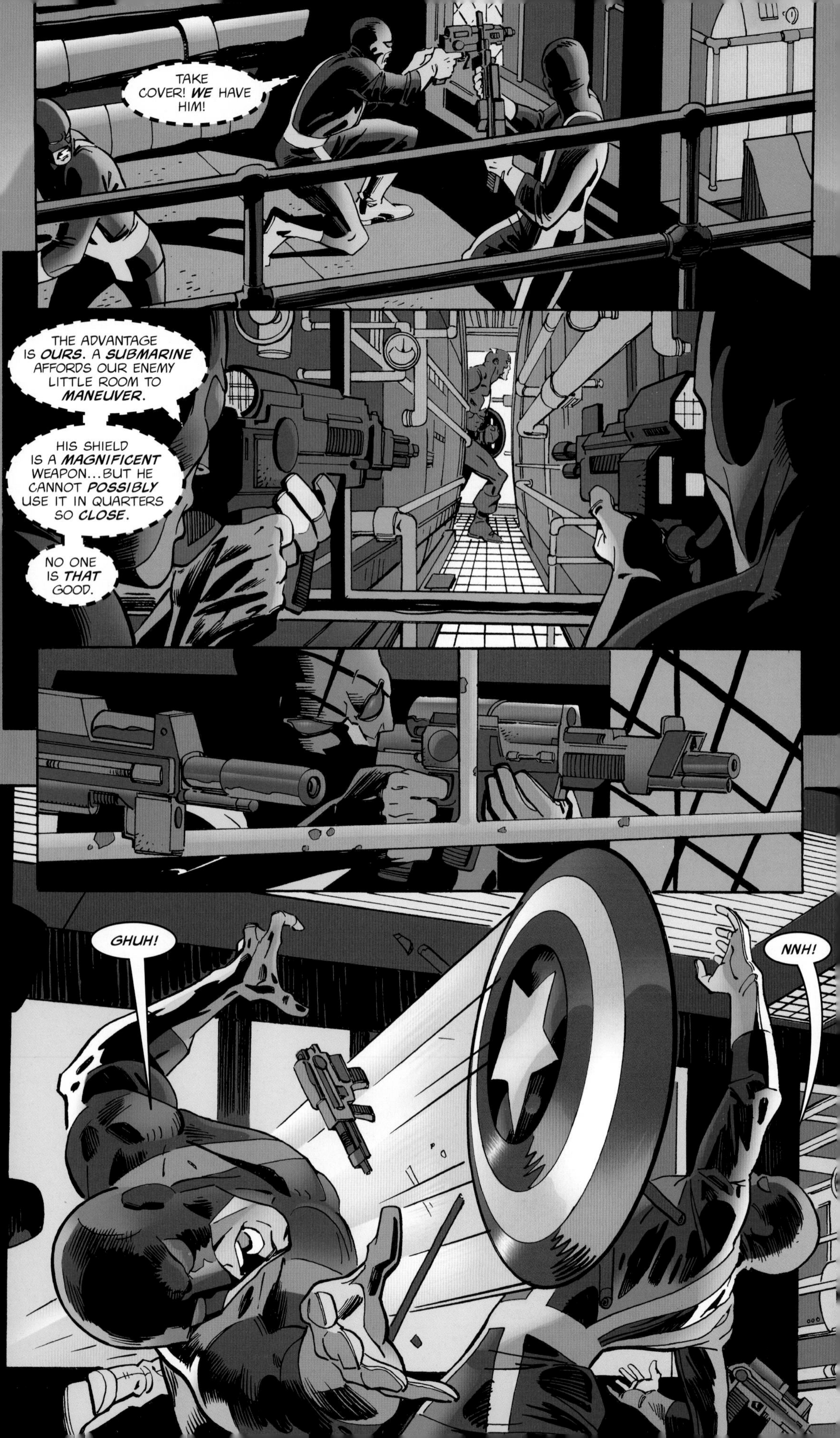
TAKE COVER! WE HAVE HIM!
THE ADVANTAGE IS OURS. A SUBMARINE AFFORDS OUR ENEMY LITTLE ROOM TO MANEUVER.
HIS SHIELD IS A MAGNIFICENT WEAPON...BUT HE CANNOT POSSIBLY USE IT IN QUARTERS SO CLOSE.
NO ONE IS THAT GOOD.
GHUH!
NNH!

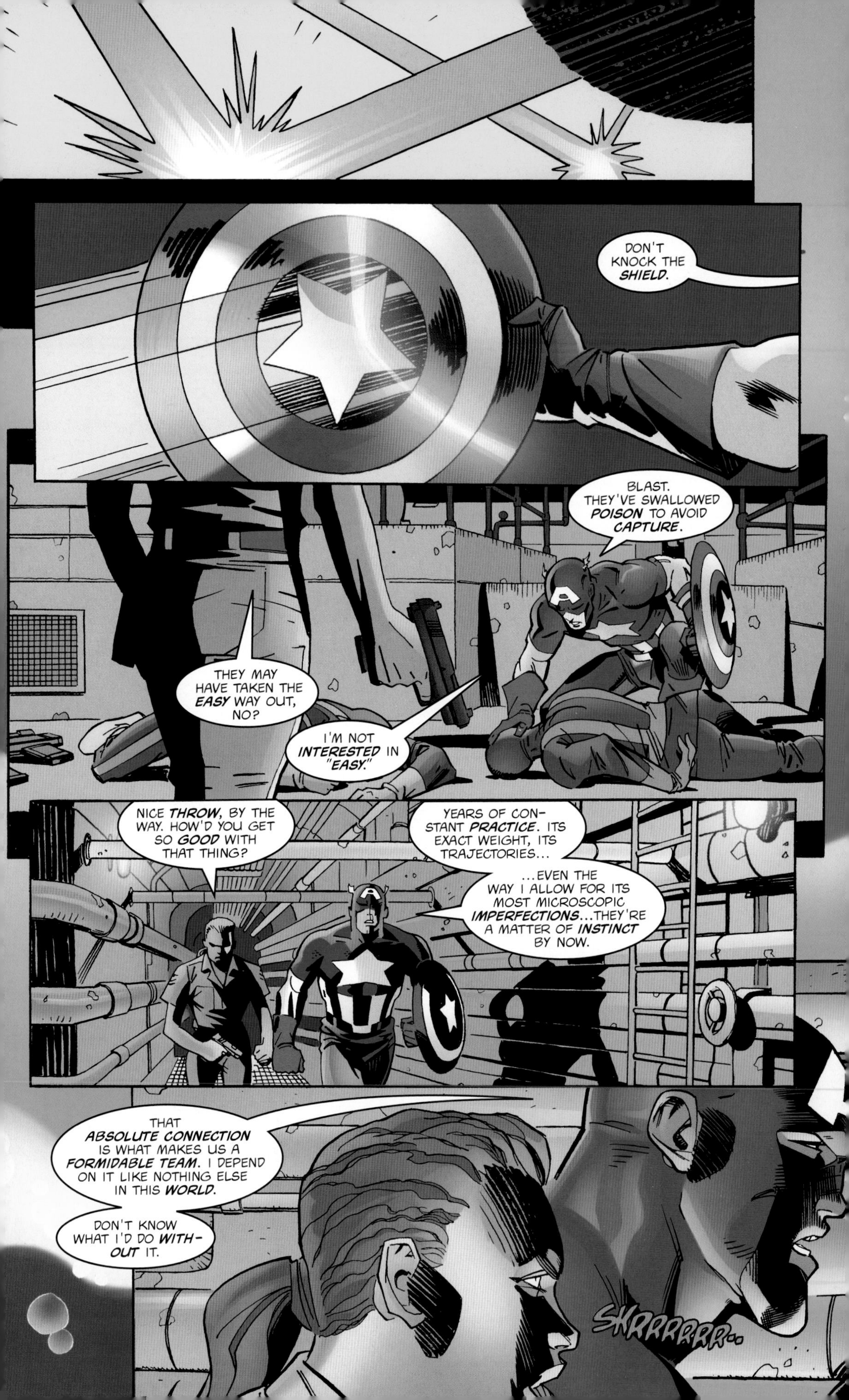
DON'T KNOCK THE SHIELD.
BLAST. THEY'VE SWALLOWED POISON TO AVOID CAPTURE.
THEY MAY HAVE TAKEN THE EASY WAY OUT, NO?
I'M NOT INTERESTED IN "EASY."
NICE THROW, BY THE WAY. HOW'D YOU GET SO GOOD WITH THAT THING?
YEARS OF CONSTANT PRACTICE. ITS EXACT WEIGHT, ITS TRAJECTORIES...
...EVEN THE WAY I ALLOW FOR ITS MOST MICROSCOPIC IMPERFECTIONS...THEY'RE A MATTER OF INSTINCT BY NOW.
THAT ABSOLUTE CONNECTION IS WHAT MAKES US A FORMIDABLE TEAM. I DEPEND ON IT LIKE NOTHING ELSE IN THIS WORLD.
DON'T KNOW WHAT I'D DO WITHOUT IT.
SKRRRRRRR..

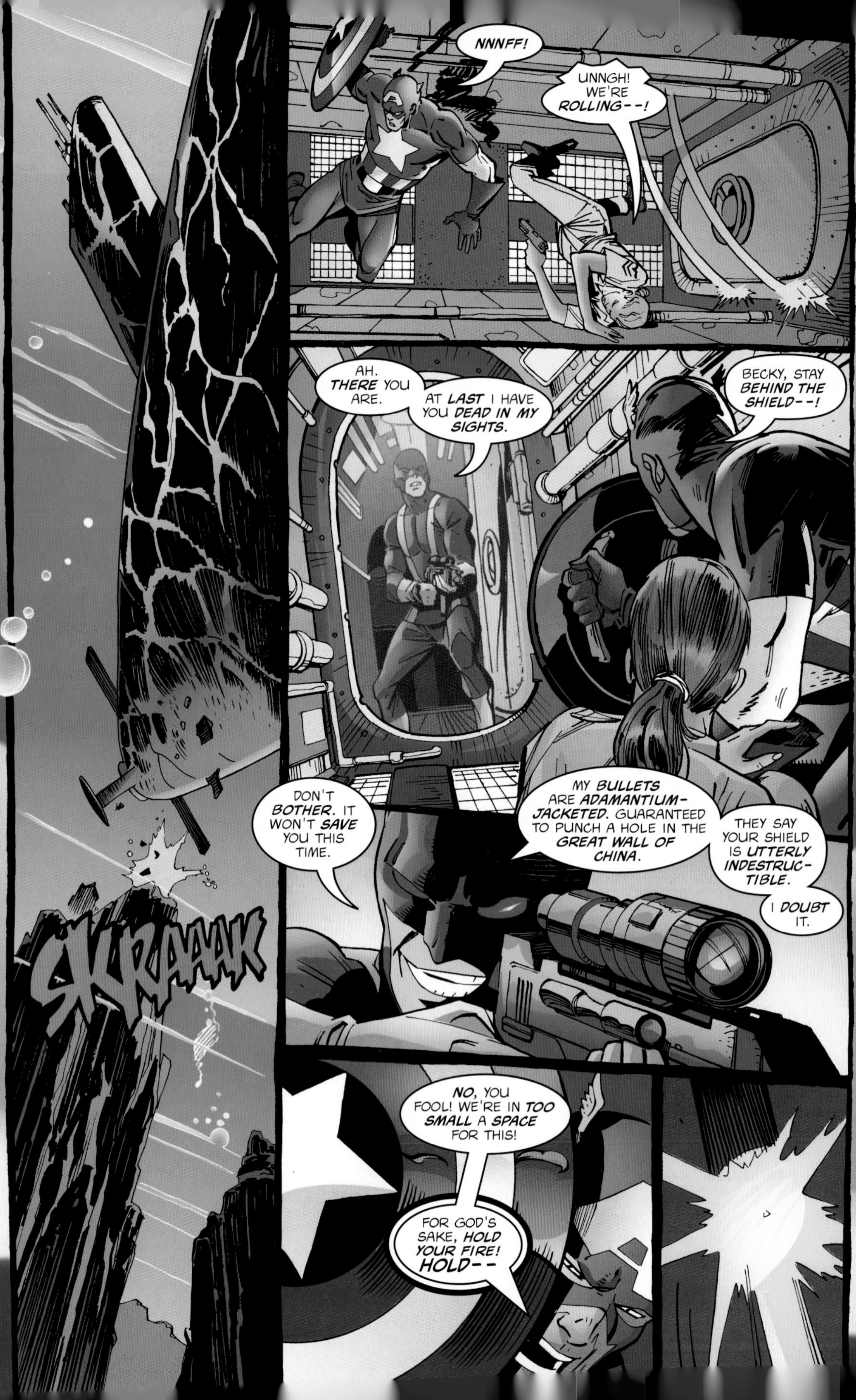
SKRAAAK
NNNFF!
UNNGH! WE'RE ROLLING--!
AH. THERE YOU ARE.
AT LAST I HAVE YOU DEAD IN MY SIGHTS.
BECKY, STAY BEHIND THE SHIELD--!
DON'T BOTHER. IT WON'T SAVE YOU THIS TIME.
MY BULLETS ARE ADAMANTIUM-JACKETED. GUARANTEED TO PUNCH A HOLE IN THE GREAT WALL OF CHINA.
THEY SAY YOUR SHIELD IS UTTERLY INDESTRUCTIBLE.
I DOUBT IT.
NO, YOU FOOL! WE'RE IN TOO SMALL A SPACE FOR THIS!
FOR GOD'S SAKE, HOLD YOUR FIRE! HOLD--

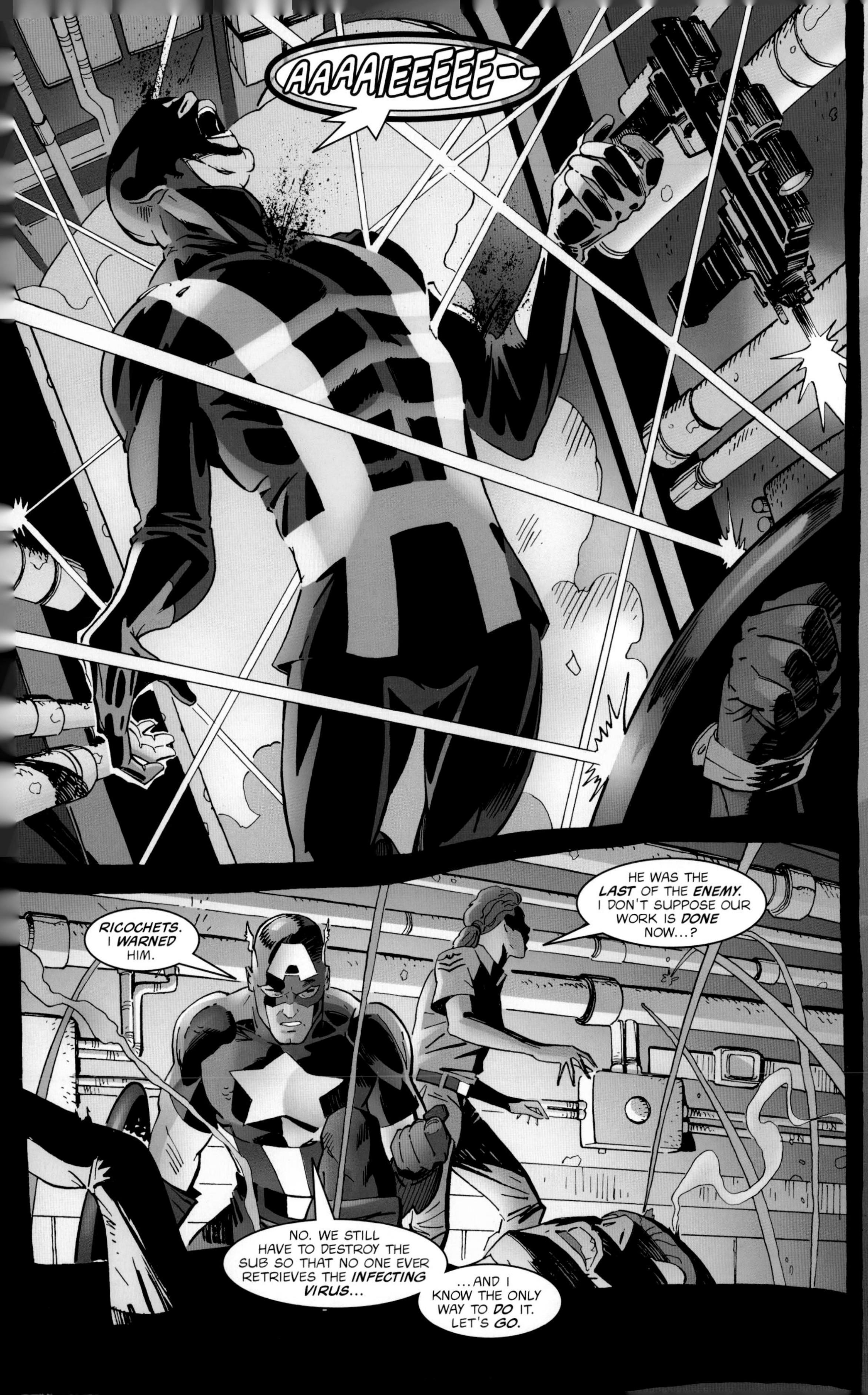
AAAAIEEEEEE--
RICOCHETS. I WARNED HIM.
HE WAS THE LAST OF THE ENEMY. I DON'T SUPPOSE OUR WORK IS DONE NOW...?
NO. WE STILL HAVE TO DESTROY THE SUB SO THAT NO ONE EVER RETRIEVES THE INFECTING VIRUS...
...AND I KNOW THE ONLY WAY TO DO IT. LET'S GO.

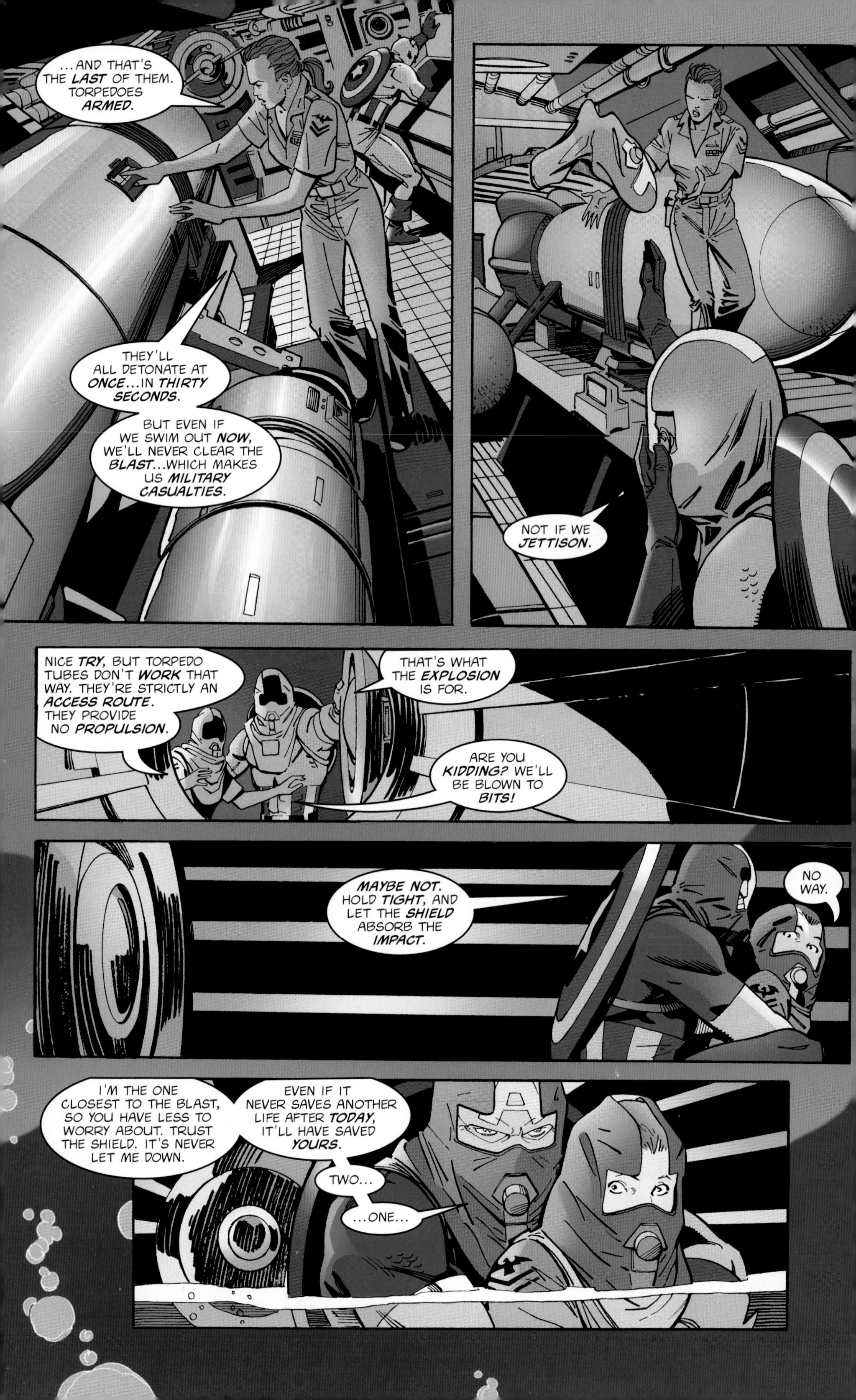
...AND THAT'S THE LAST OF THEM. TORPEDOES ARMED.
THEY'LL ALL DETONATE AT ONCE...IN THIRTY SECONDS.
BUT EVEN IF WE SWIM OUT NOW, WE'LL NEVER CLEAR THE BLAST...WHICH MAKES US MILITARY CASUALTIES.
NOT IF WE JETTISON.
NICE TRY, BUT TORPEDO TUBES DON'T WORK THAT WAY. THEY'RE STRICTLY AN ACCESS ROUTE. THEY PROVIDE NO PROPULSION.
THAT'S WHAT THE EXPLOSION IS FOR.
ARE YOU KIDDING? WE'LL BE BLOWN TO BITS!
MAYBE NOT. HOLD TIGHT, AND LET THE SHIELD ABSORB THE IMPACT.
NO WAY.
I'M THE ONE CLOSEST TO THE BLAST, SO YOU HAVE LESS TO WORRY ABOUT. TRUST THE SHIELD. IT'S NEVER LET ME DOWN.
EVEN IF IT NEVER SAVES ANOTHER LIFE AFTER TODAY, IT'LL HAVE SAVED YOURS.
TWO...
...ONE...

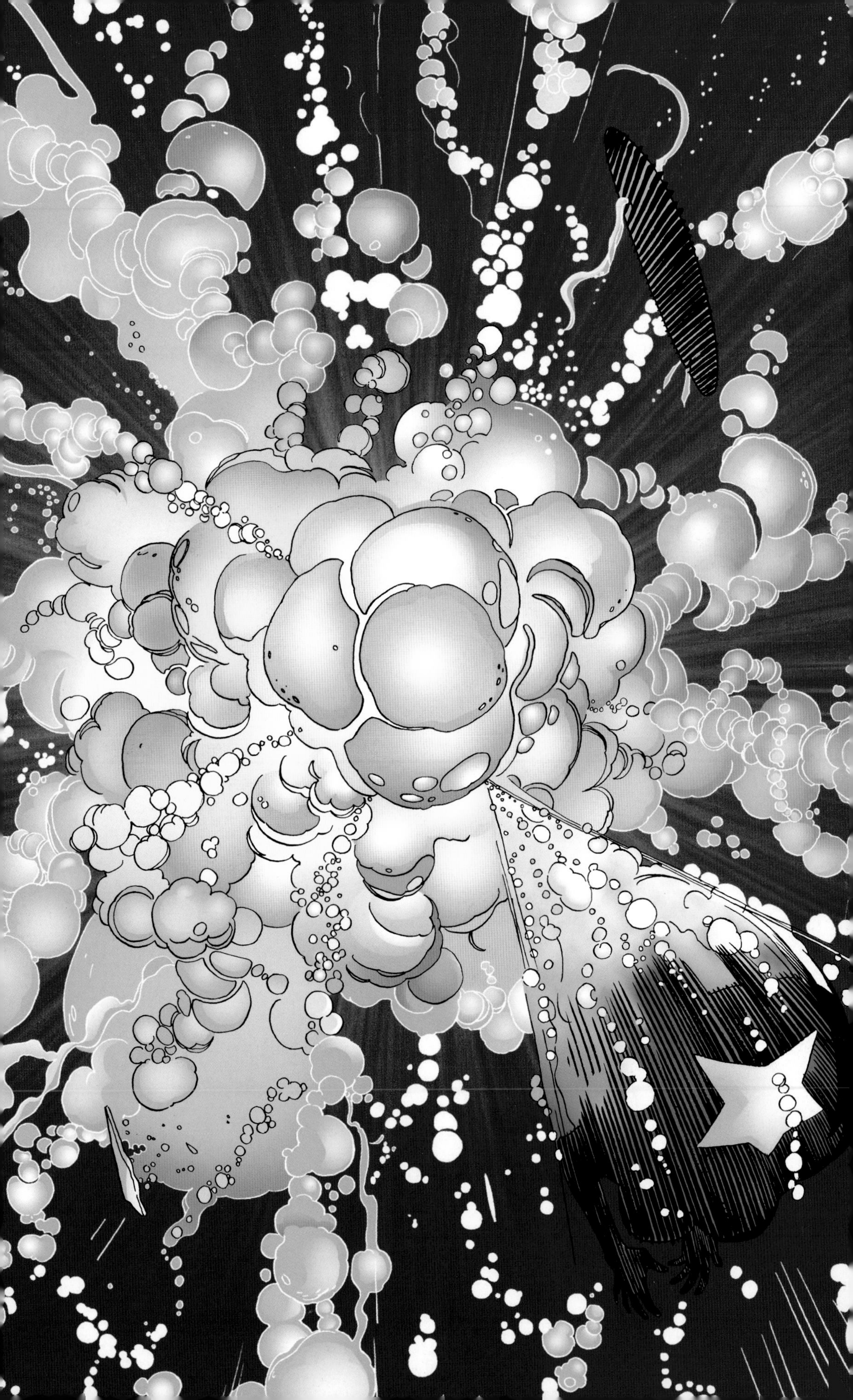

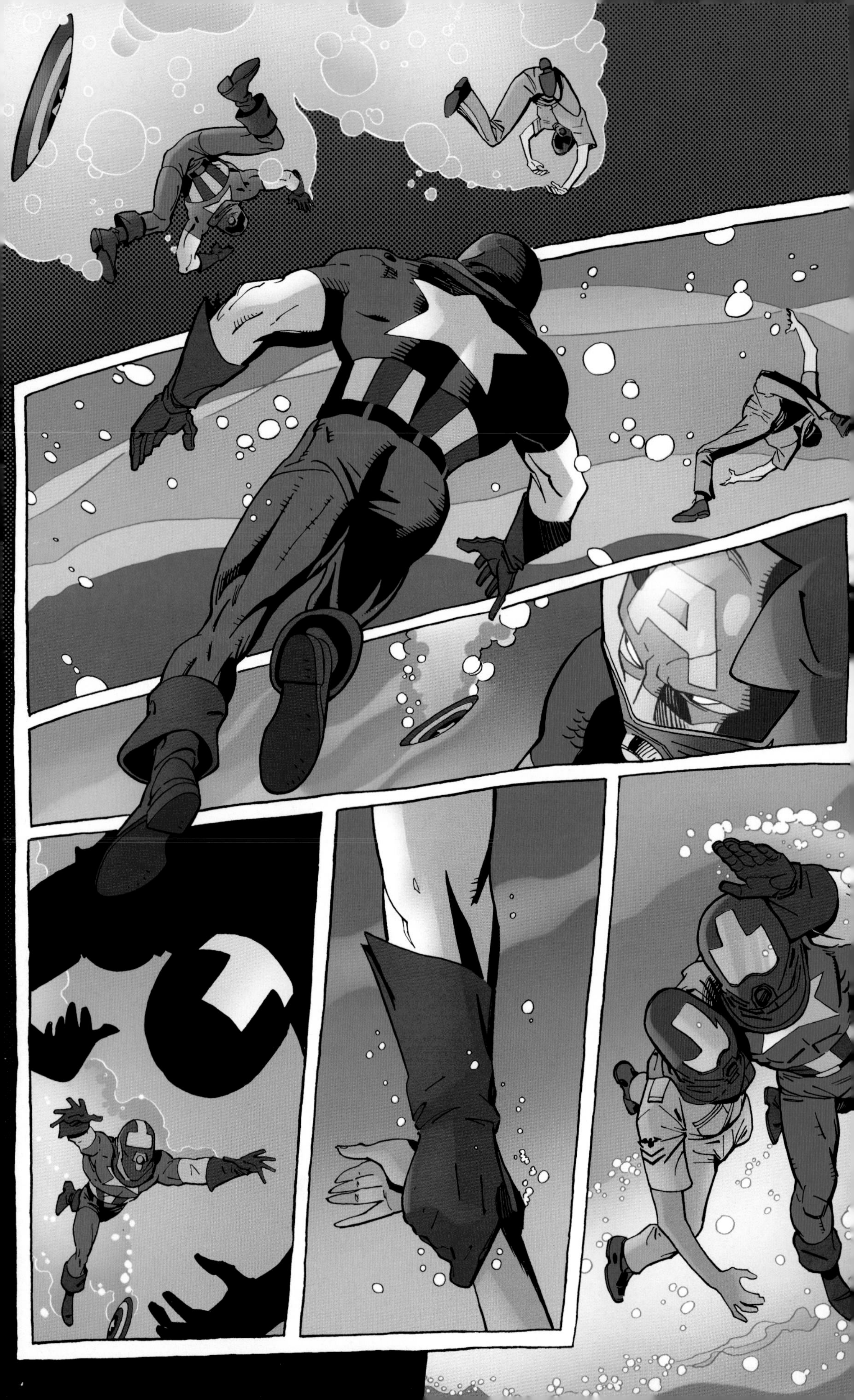

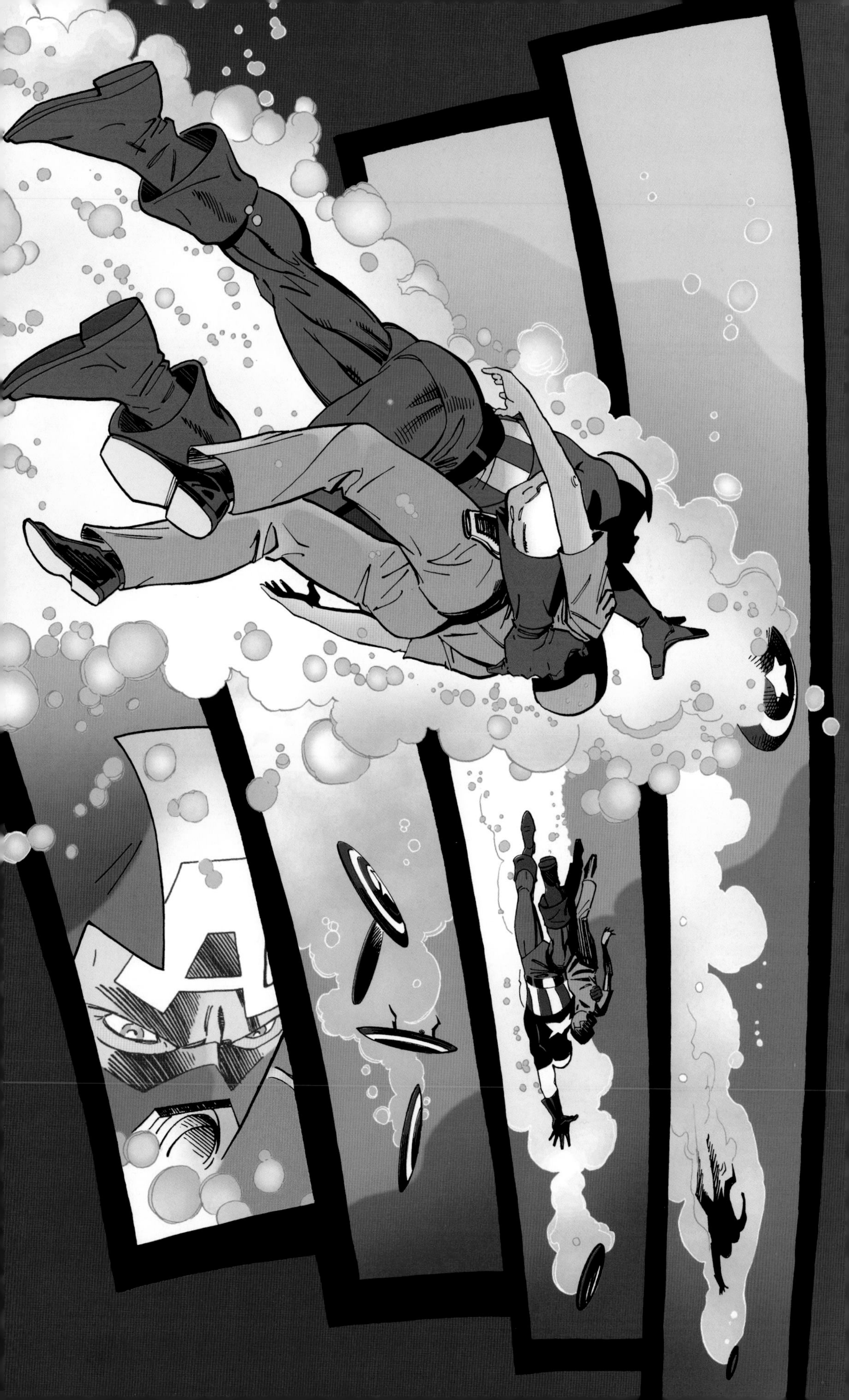

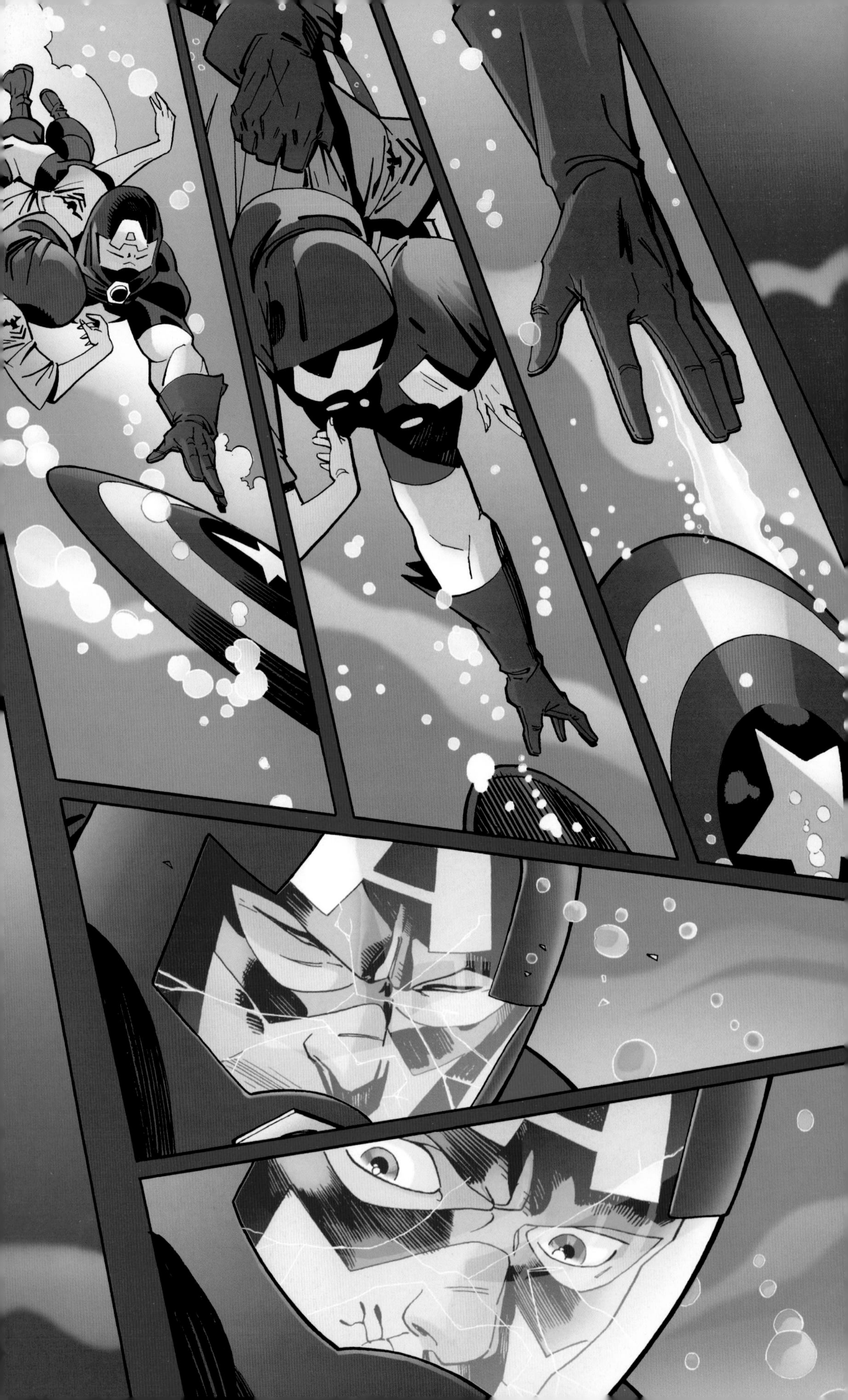

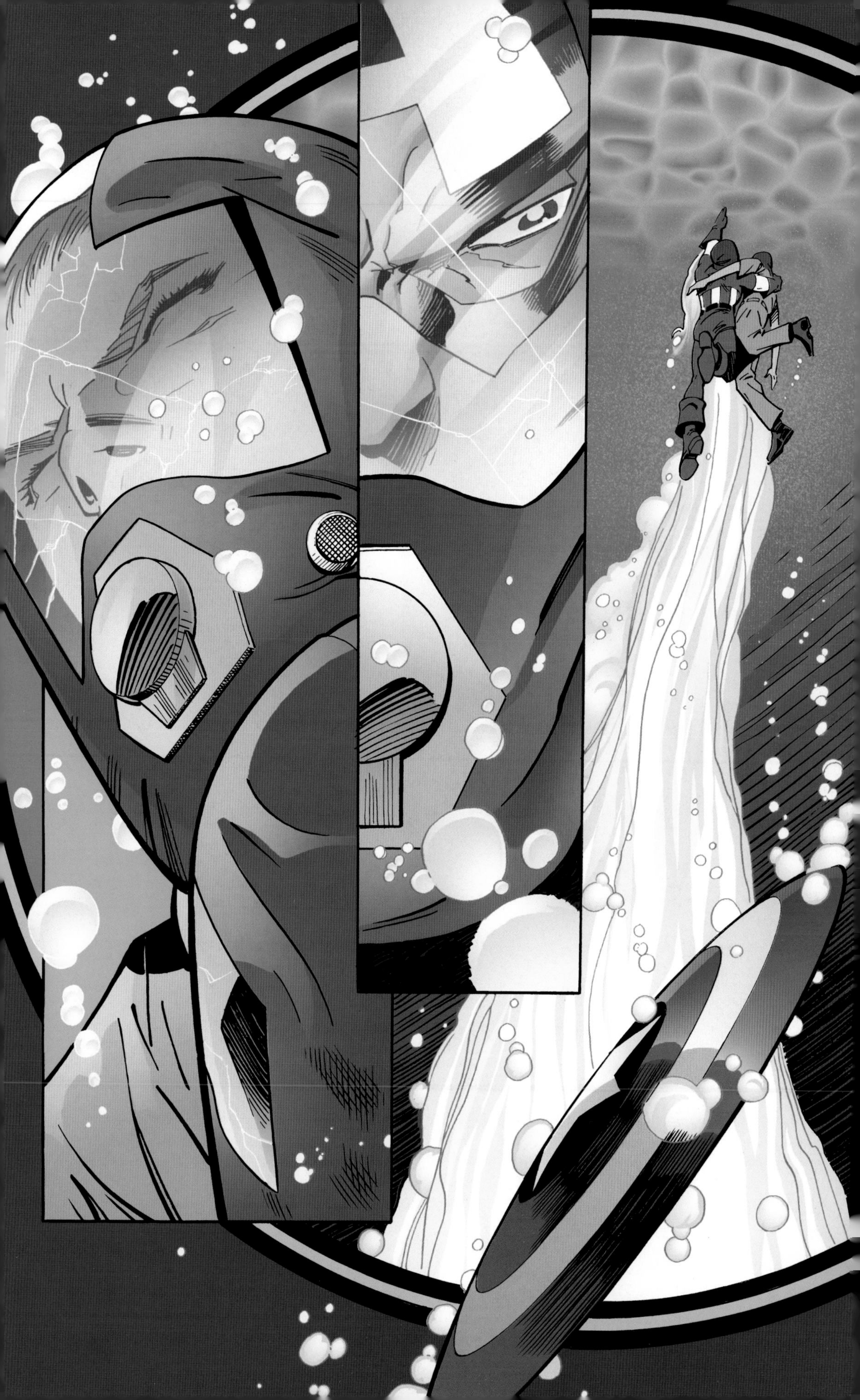

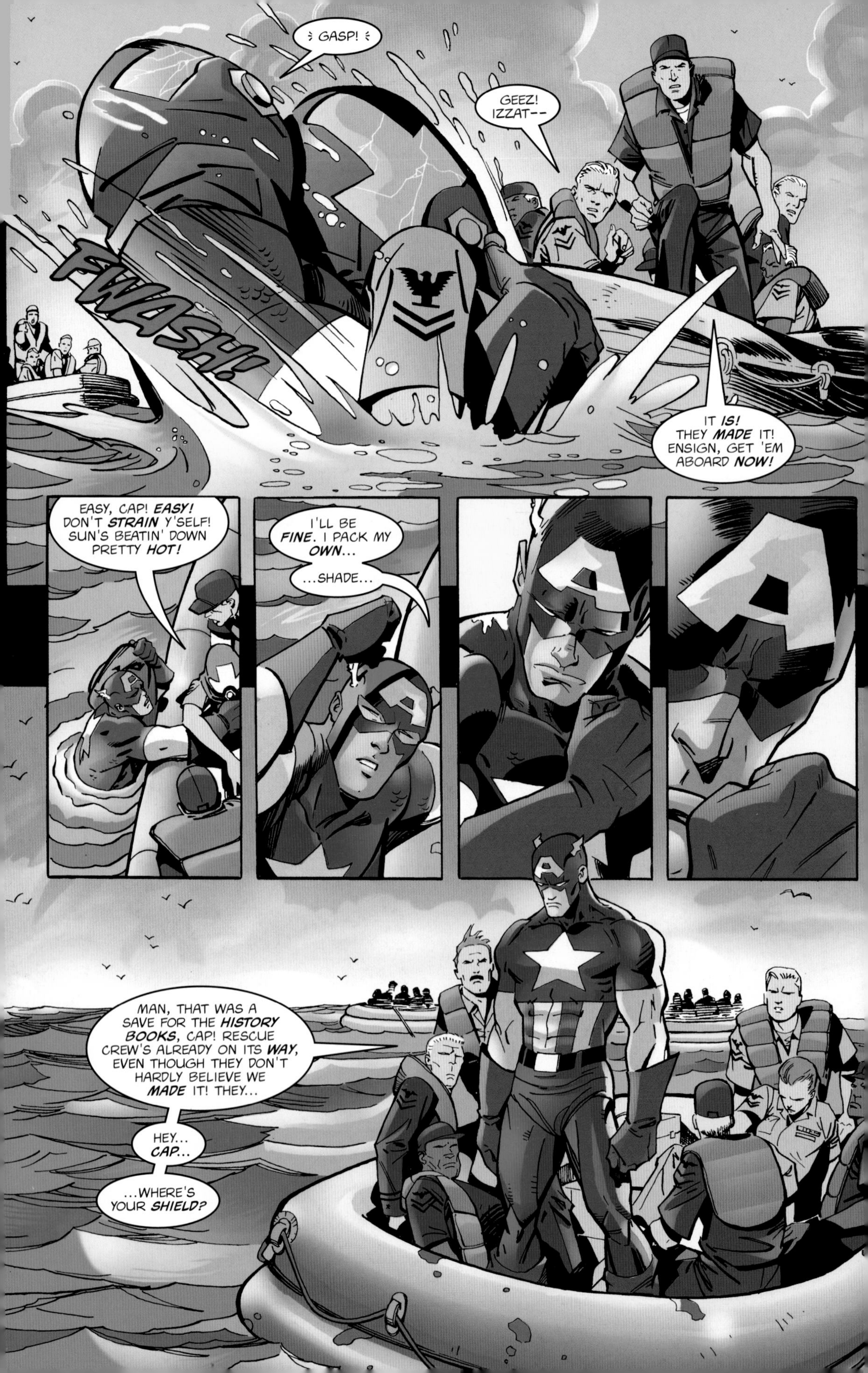
GASP!
FWASH!
GEEZ! IZZAT--
IT IS! THEY MADE IT! ENSIGN, GET 'EM ABOARD NOW!
EASY, CAP! EASY! DON'T STRAIN Y'SELF! SUN'S BEATIN' DOWN PRETTY HOT!
I'LL BE FINE. I PACK MY OWN...
...SHADE...
MAN, THAT WAS A SAVE FOR THE HISTORY BOOKS, CAP! RESCUE CREW'S ALREADY ON ITS WAY, EVEN THOUGH THEY DON'T HARDLY BELIEVE WE MADE IT! THEY...
HEY... CAP...
...WHERE'S YOUR SHIELD?

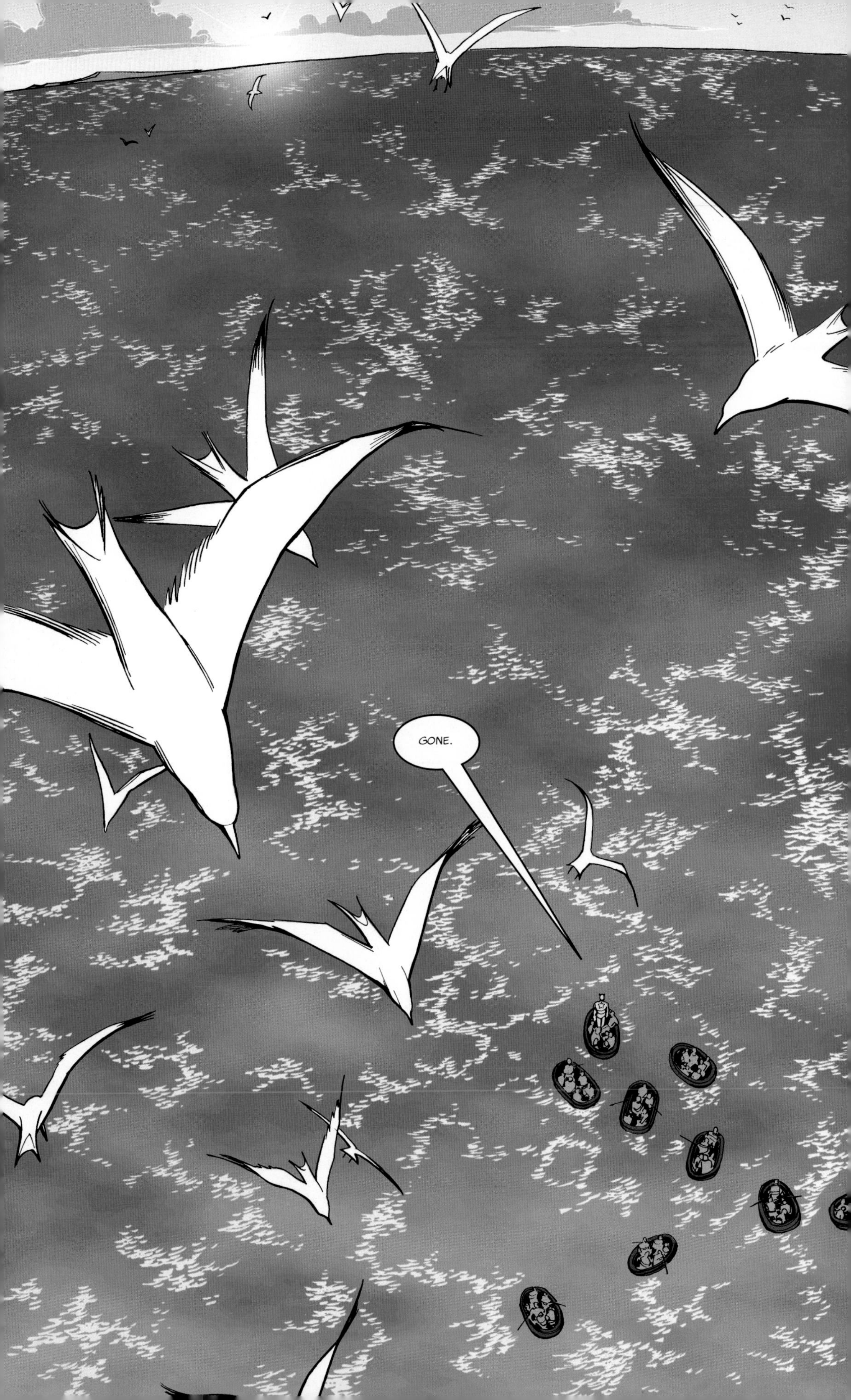
GONE.

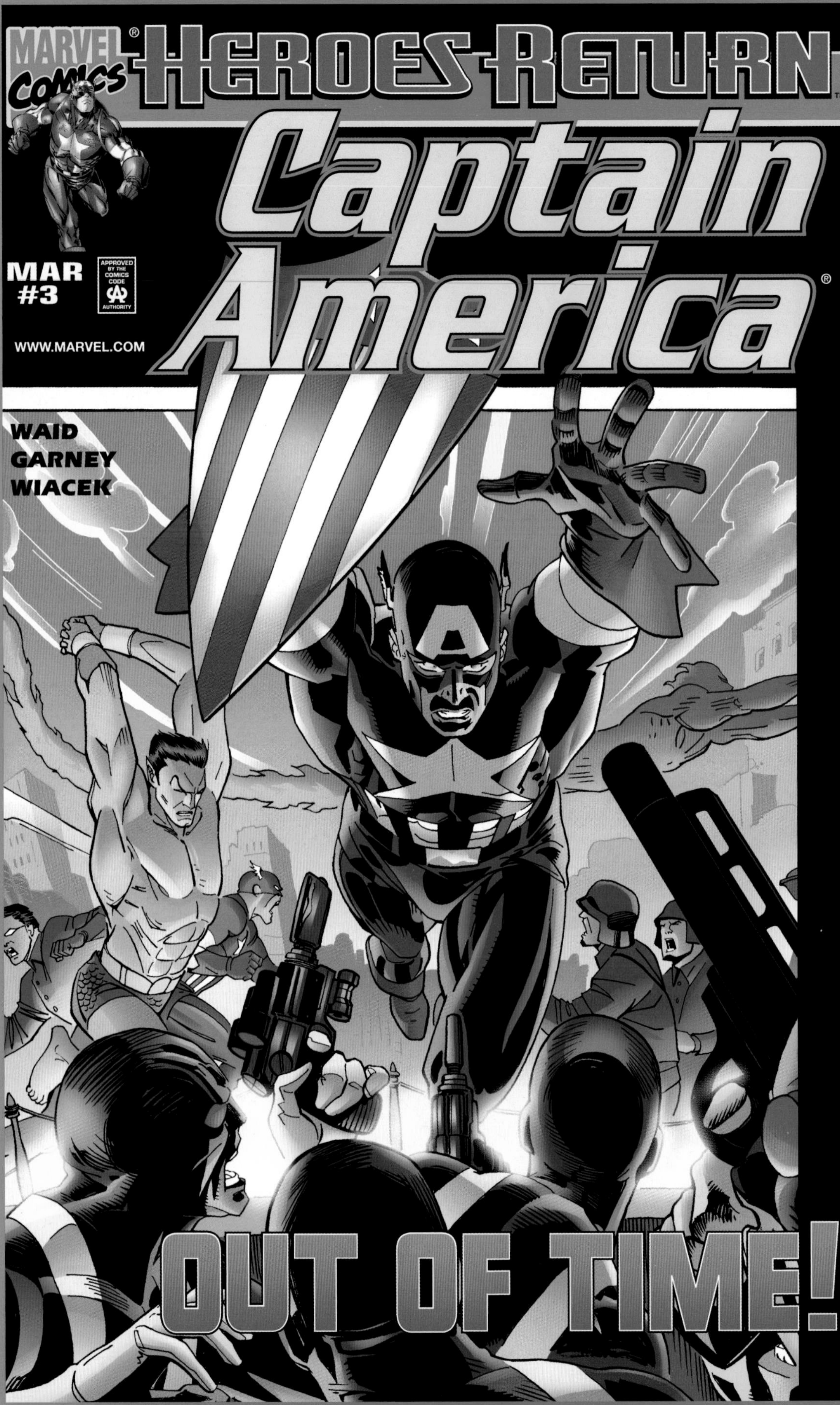
MARVEL® COMICS
HEROES RETURN™
Captain America®
MAR #3
APPROVED BY THE COMICS CODE AUTHORITY
WWW.MARVEL.COM
WAID
GARNEY
WIACEK
OUT OF TIME!

Stan Lee presents Captain America

Museum Piece

editor in chief MARK WAID AND RON GARNEY•storytellers BOB WIACEK•inker JOE ROSAS•colorist DIGITAL CHAMELEON•separations JOHN COSTANZA•letterer MATT IDELSON•editor BOB HARRAS•editor in chief

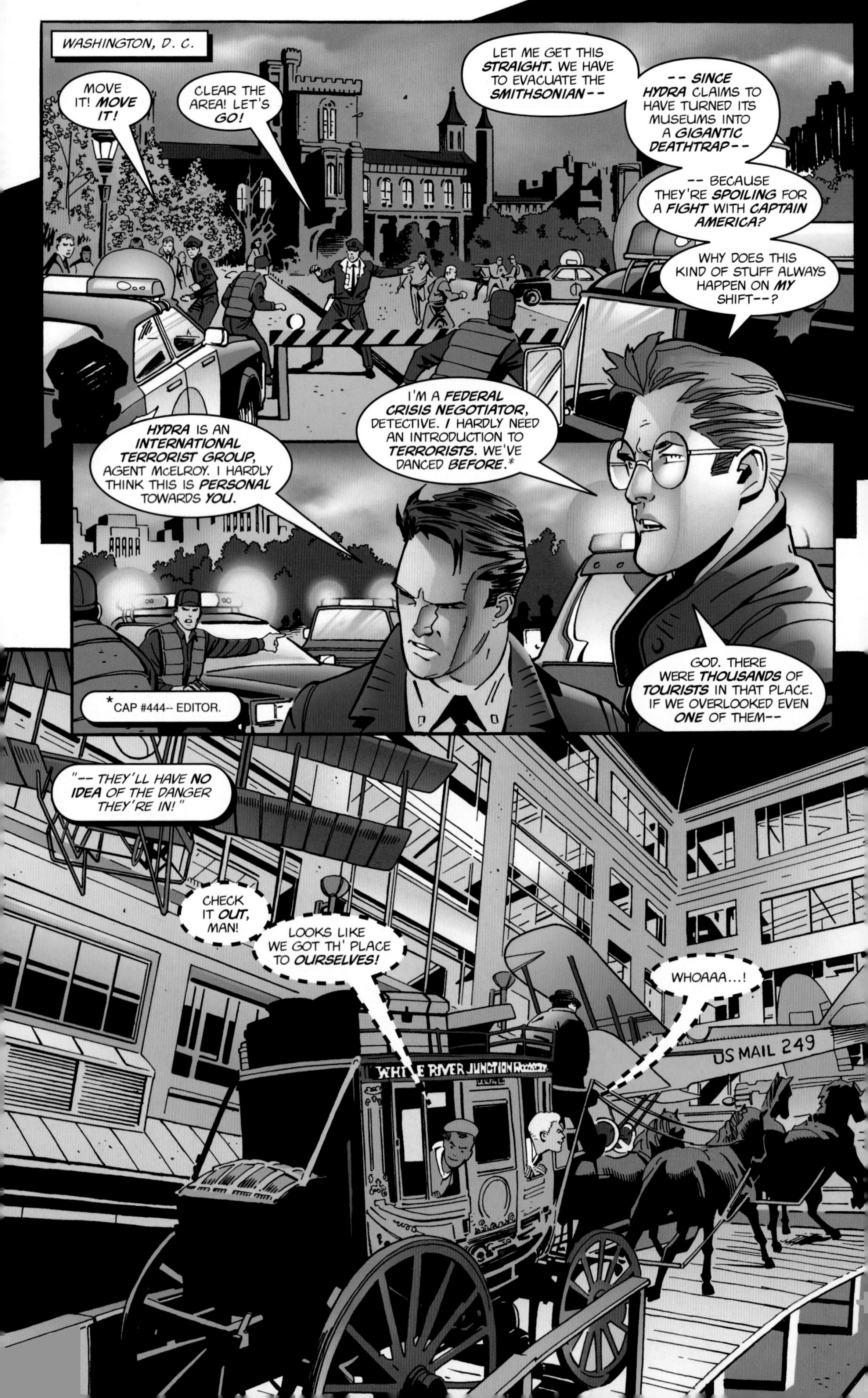

WASHINGTON, D. C.
MOVE IT! MOVE IT!
CLEAR THE AREA! LET'S GO!
LET ME GET THIS STRAIGHT. WE HAVE TO EVACUATE THE SMITHSONIAN--
-- SINCE HYDRA CLAIMS TO HAVE TURNED ITS MUSEUMS INTO A GIGANTIC DEATHTRAP--
-- BECAUSE THEY'RE SPOILING FOR A FIGHT WITH CAPTAIN AMERICA?
WHY DOES THIS KIND OF STUFF ALWAYS HAPPEN ON MY SHIFT--?
HYDRA IS AN INTERNATIONAL TERRORIST GROUP, AGENT McELROY. I HARDLY THINK THIS IS PERSONAL TOWARDS YOU.
I'M A FEDERAL CRISIS NEGOTIATOR, DETECTIVE. I HARDLY NEED AN INTRODUCTION TO TERRORISTS. WE'VE DANCED BEFORE.*
*CAP #444-- EDITOR.
GOD. THERE WERE THOUSANDS OF TOURISTS IN THAT PLACE. IF WE OVERLOOKED EVEN ONE OF THEM--
"-- THEY'LL HAVE NO IDEA OF THE DANGER THEY'RE IN!"
CHECK IT OUT, MAN!
LOOKS LIKE WE GOT TH' PLACE TO OURSELVES!
WHOAAA...!
US MAIL 249

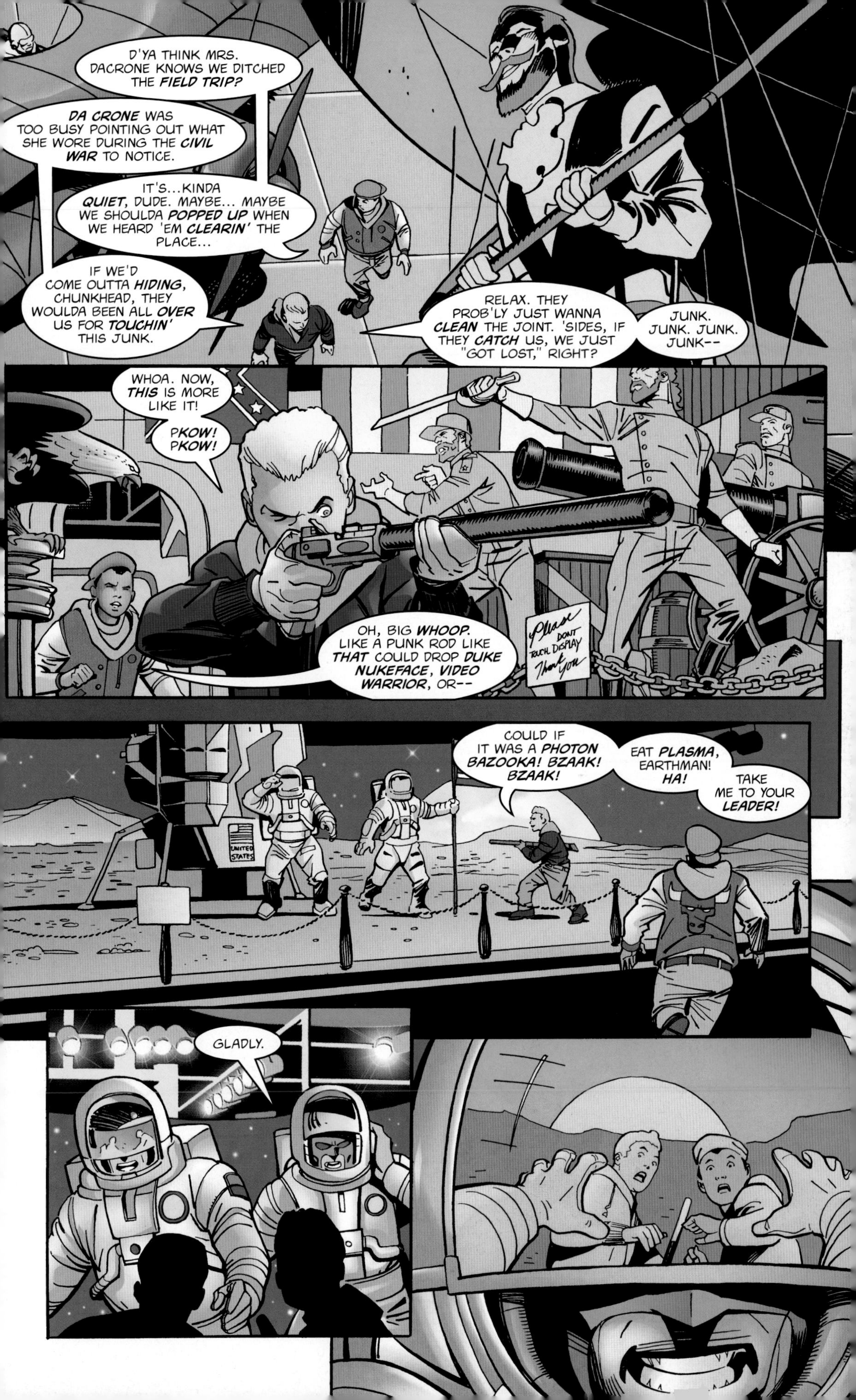
D'YA THINK MRS. DACRONE KNOWS WE DITCHED THE FIELD TRIP?
DA CRONE WAS TOO BUSY POINTING OUT WHAT SHE WORE DURING THE CIVIL WAR TO NOTICE.
IT'S...KINDA QUIET, DUDE. MAYBE... MAYBE WE SHOULDA POPPED UP WHEN WE HEARD 'EM CLEARIN' THE PLACE...
IF WE'D COME OUTTA HIDING, CHUNKHEAD, THEY WOULDA BEEN ALL OVER US FOR TOUCHIN' THIS JUNK.
RELAX. THEY PROB'LY JUST WANNA CLEAN THE JOINT. 'SIDES, IF THEY CATCH US, WE JUST "GOT LOST," RIGHT?
JUNK. JUNK. JUNK. JUNK--
WHOA. NOW, THIS IS MORE LIKE IT!
PKOW! PKOW!
OH, BIG WHOOP. LIKE A PUNK ROD LIKE THAT COULD DROP DUKE NUKEFACE, VIDEO WARRIOR, OR--
Please DONT TOUCH DISPLAY Thank You
COULD IF IT WAS A PHOTON BAZOOKA! BZAAK! BZAAK!
EAT PLASMA, EARTHMAN! HA!
TAKE ME TO YOUR LEADER!
UNITED STATES
GLADLY.

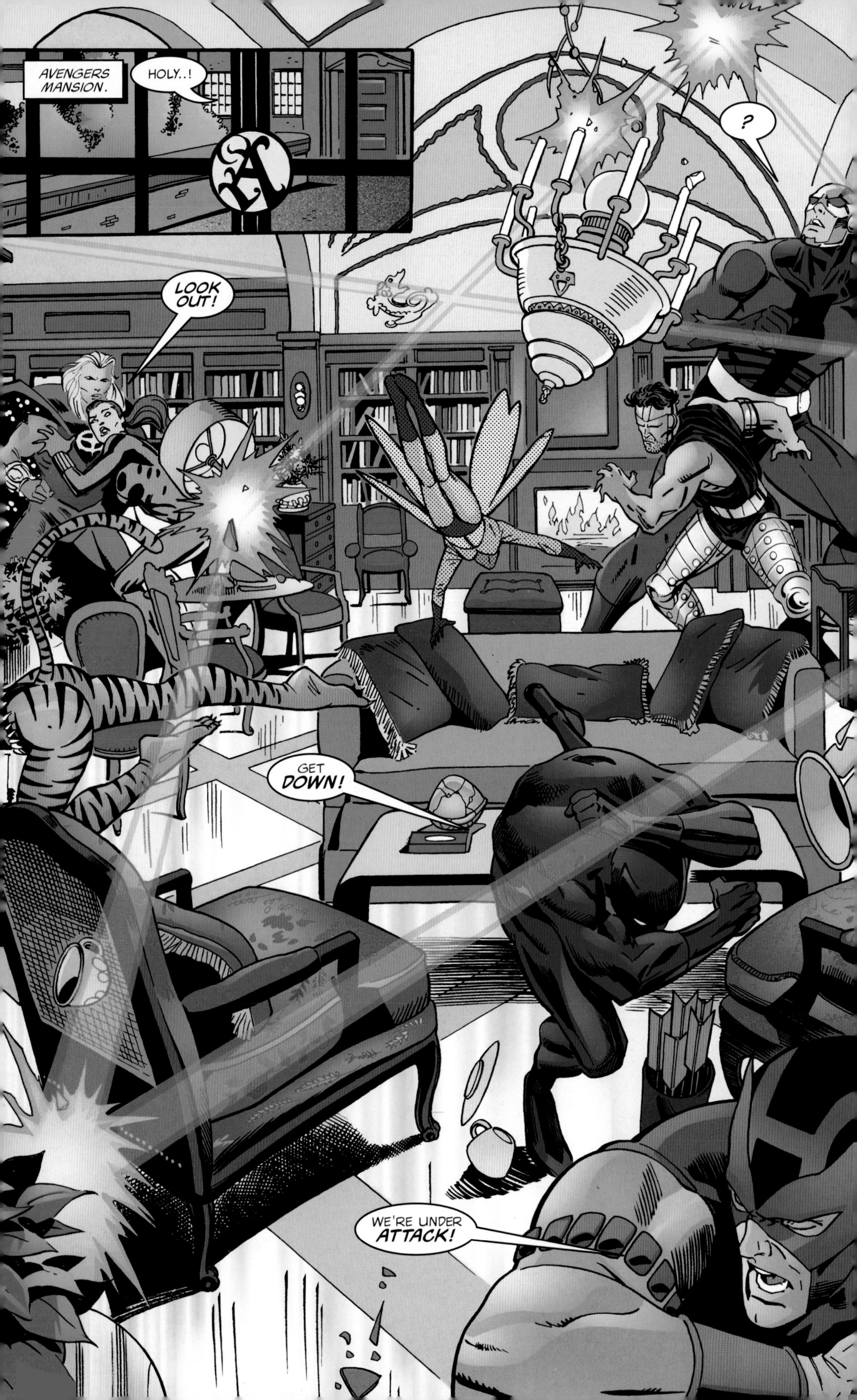
AVENGERS MANSION.
HOLY..!
?
LOOK OUT!
GET DOWN!
WE'RE UNDER ATTACK!

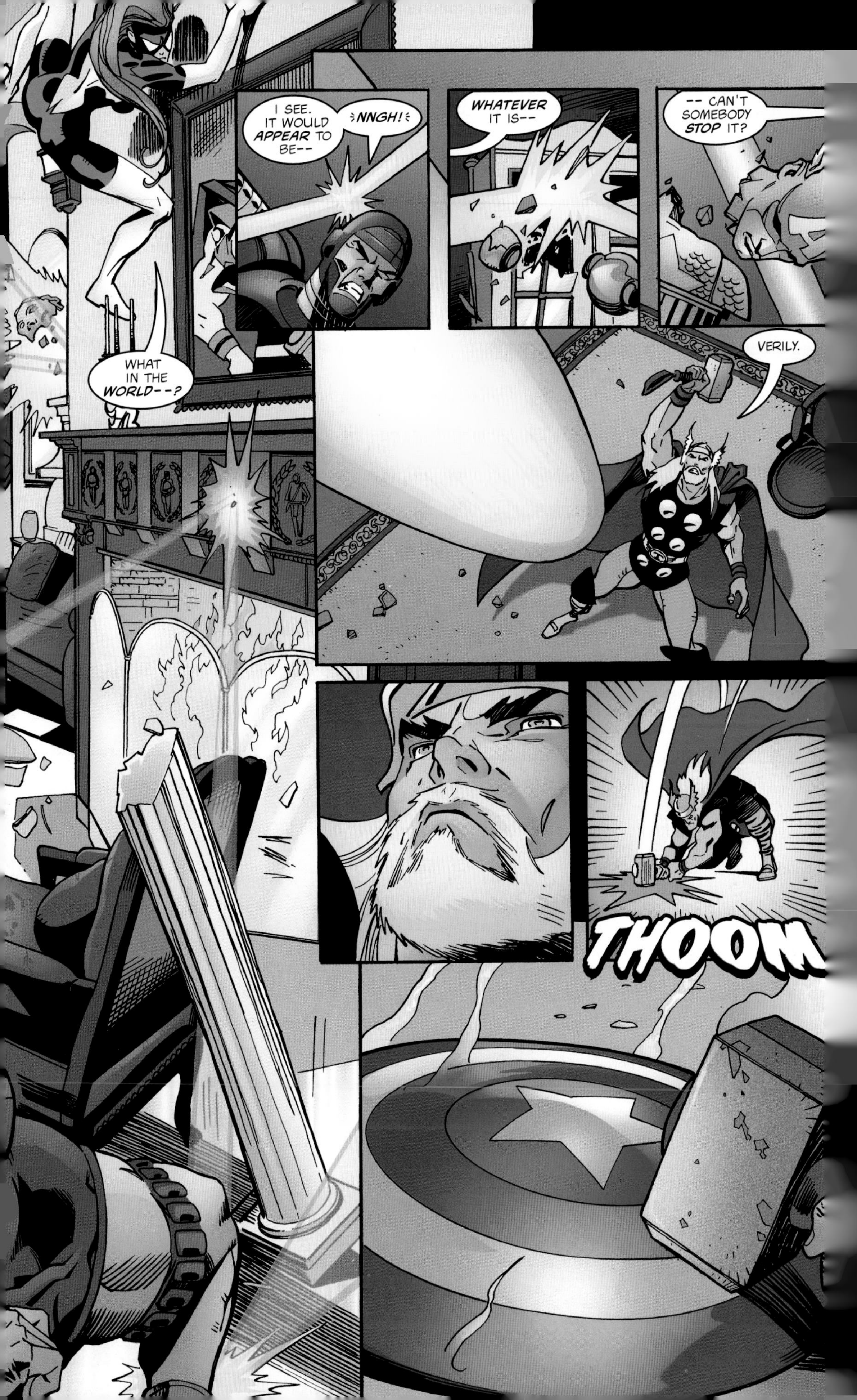
WHAT IN THE WORLD--?
I SEE. IT WOULD APPEAR TO BE--
NNGH!
WHATEVER IT IS--
-- CAN'T SOMEBODY STOP IT?
VERILY.
THOOM

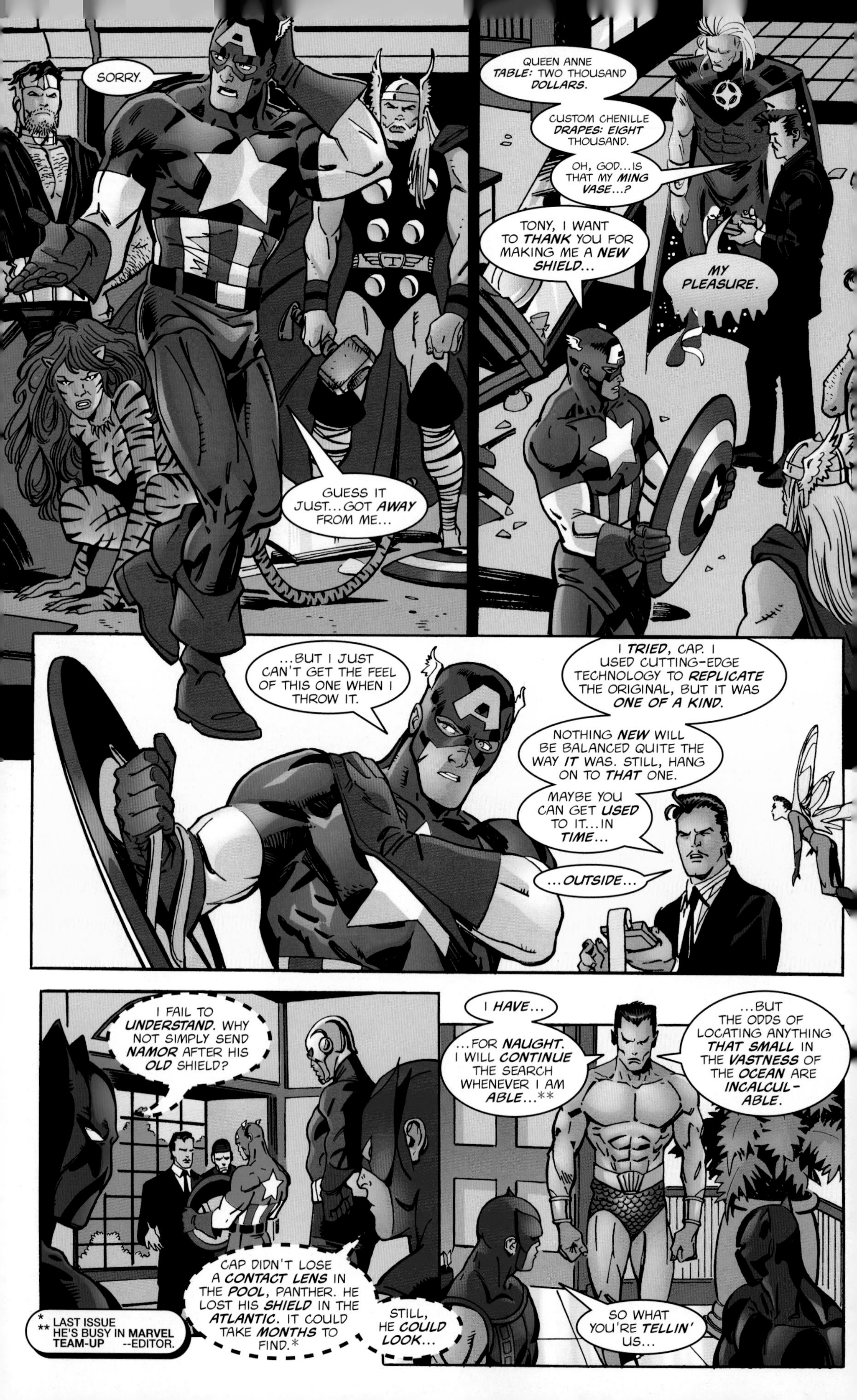
SORRY.
GUESS IT JUST...GOT AWAY FROM ME...
QUEEN ANNE TABLE: TWO THOUSAND DOLLARS.
CUSTOM CHENILLE DRAPES: EIGHT THOUSAND.
OH, GOD...IS THAT MY MING VASE...?
TONY, I WANT TO THANK YOU FOR MAKING ME A NEW SHIELD...
MY PLEASURE.
...BUT I JUST CAN'T GET THE FEEL OF THIS ONE WHEN I THROW IT.
I TRIED, CAP. I USED CUTTING-EDGE TECHNOLOGY TO REPLICATE THE ORIGINAL, BUT IT WAS ONE OF A KIND.
NOTHING NEW WILL BE BALANCED QUITE THE WAY IT WAS. STILL, HANG ON TO THAT ONE.
MAYBE YOU CAN GET USED TO IT...IN TIME...
...OUTSIDE...
I FAIL TO UNDERSTAND. WHY NOT SIMPLY SEND NAMOR AFTER HIS OLD SHIELD?
CAP DIDN'T LOSE A CONTACT LENS IN THE POOL, PANTHER. HE LOST HIS SHIELD IN THE ATLANTIC. IT COULD TAKE MONTHS TO FIND.*
STILL, HE COULD LOOK...
I HAVE...
...FOR NAUGHT. I WILL CONTINUE THE SEARCH WHENEVER I AM ABLE...**
...BUT THE ODDS OF LOCATING ANYTHING THAT SMALL IN THE VASTNESS OF THE OCEAN ARE INCALCULABLE.
SO WHAT YOU'RE TELLIN' US...
* LAST ISSUE
** HE'S BUSY IN MARVEL TEAM-UP --EDITOR.

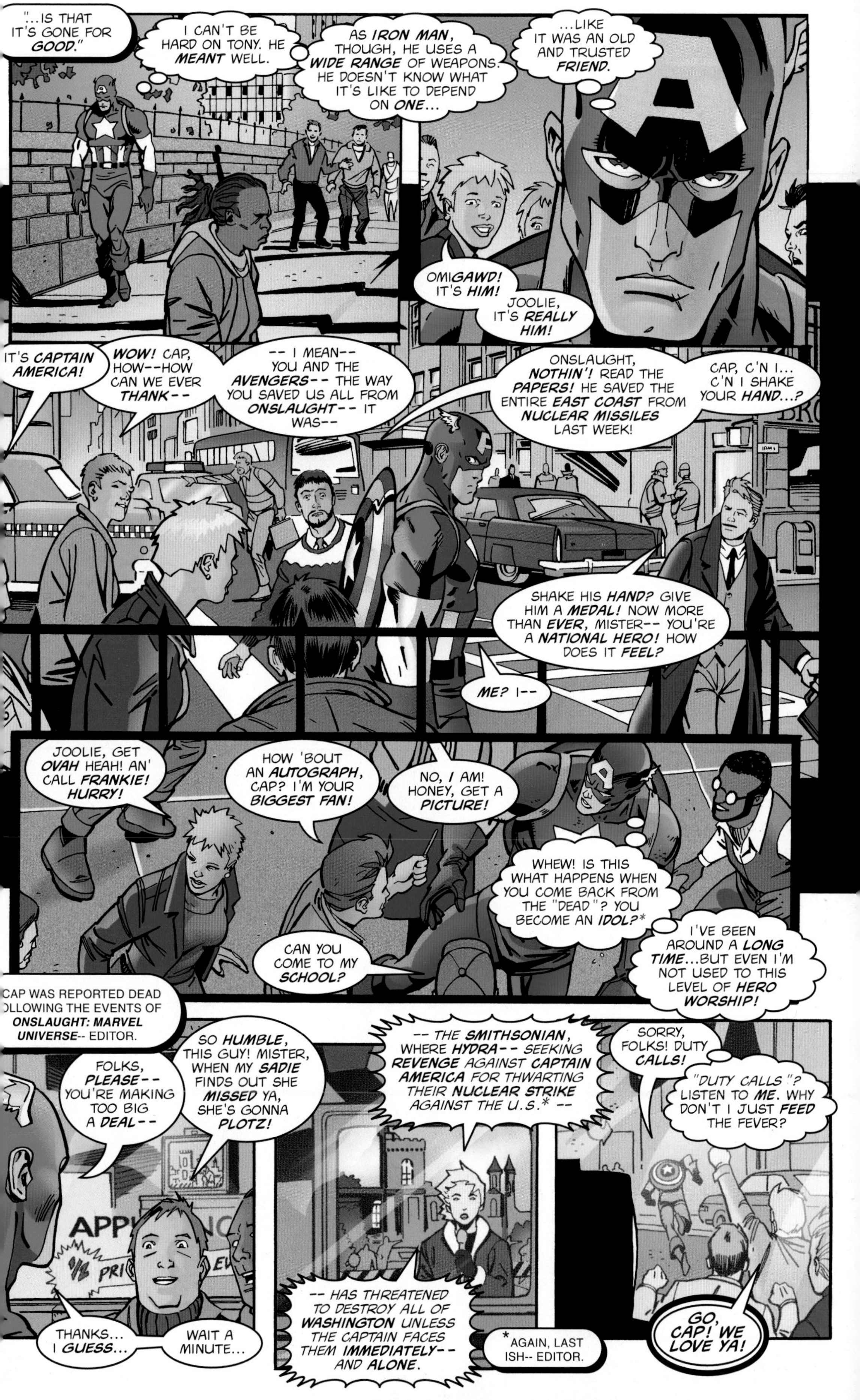

"...IS THAT IT'S GONE FOR GOOD."
I CAN'T BE HARD ON TONY. HE MEANT WELL.
AS IRON MAN, THOUGH, HE USES A WIDE RANGE OF WEAPONS. HE DOESN'T KNOW WHAT IT'S LIKE TO DEPEND ON ONE...
...LIKE IT WAS AN OLD AND TRUSTED FRIEND.
OMIGAWD! IT'S HIM!
JOOLIE, IT'S REALLY HIM!
IT'S CAPTAIN AMERICA!
WOW! CAP, HOW--HOW CAN WE EVER THANK--
-- I MEAN-- YOU AND THE AVENGERS-- THE WAY YOU SAVED US ALL FROM ONSLAUGHT-- IT WAS--
ONSLAUGHT, NOTHIN'! READ THE PAPERS! HE SAVED THE ENTIRE EAST COAST FROM NUCLEAR MISSILES LAST WEEK!
CAP, C'N I... C'N I SHAKE YOUR HAND...?
SHAKE HIS HAND? GIVE HIM A MEDAL! NOW MORE THAN EVER, MISTER-- YOU'RE A NATIONAL HERO! HOW DOES IT FEEL?
ME? I--
JOOLIE, GET OVAH HEAH! AN' CALL FRANKIE! HURRY!
HOW 'BOUT AN AUTOGRAPH, CAP? I'M YOUR BIGGEST FAN!
NO, I AM! HONEY, GET A PICTURE!
WHEW! IS THIS WHAT HAPPENS WHEN YOU COME BACK FROM THE "DEAD"? YOU BECOME AN IDOL?*
CAN YOU COME TO MY SCHOOL?
I'VE BEEN AROUND A LONG TIME...BUT EVEN I'M NOT USED TO THIS LEVEL OF HERO WORSHIP!
*CAP WAS REPORTED DEAD FOLLOWING THE EVENTS OF ONSLAUGHT: MARVEL UNIVERSE-- EDITOR.
FOLKS, PLEASE-- YOU'RE MAKING TOO BIG A DEAL--
SO HUMBLE, THIS GUY! MISTER, WHEN MY SADIE FINDS OUT SHE MISSED YA, SHE'S GONNA PLOTZ!
THANKS... I GUESS...
WAIT A MINUTE...
-- THE SMITHSONIAN, WHERE HYDRA-- SEEKING REVENGE AGAINST CAPTAIN AMERICA FOR THWARTING THEIR NUCLEAR STRIKE AGAINST THE U.S.* --
-- HAS THREATENED TO DESTROY ALL OF WASHINGTON UNLESS THE CAPTAIN FACES THEM IMMEDIATELY-- AND ALONE.
*AGAIN, LAST ISH-- EDITOR.
SORRY, FOLKS! DUTY CALLS!
"DUTY CALLS"? LISTEN TO ME. WHY DON'T I JUST FEED THE FEVER?
GO, CAP! WE LOVE YA!

HYDRA HEADQUARTERS.

I'M *TELLING* YOU, MODAM *MOVED!* I SAW HER *TWITCH!*

IMPOSSIBLE. SHE'S *DEAD.* SHE--

OH, YEAH? *LOOK!*

I AM *MODAM!*

BEWARE MY *FRIGHTFULLY LARGE HEAD!*

BEWARE MY *TEETH,* THE SIZE OF A *STOP SIGN!* BEWARE MY--

OH, NEVER MIND.

⸮GASP!⸮

SHHLRPKK

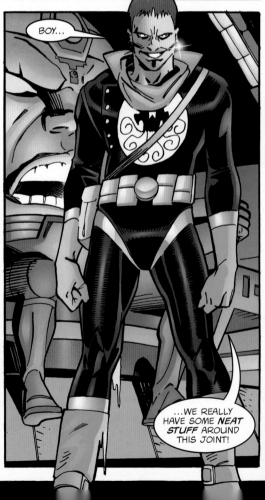

BOY...

...WE REALLY HAVE SOME *NEAT STUFF* AROUND THIS JOINT!

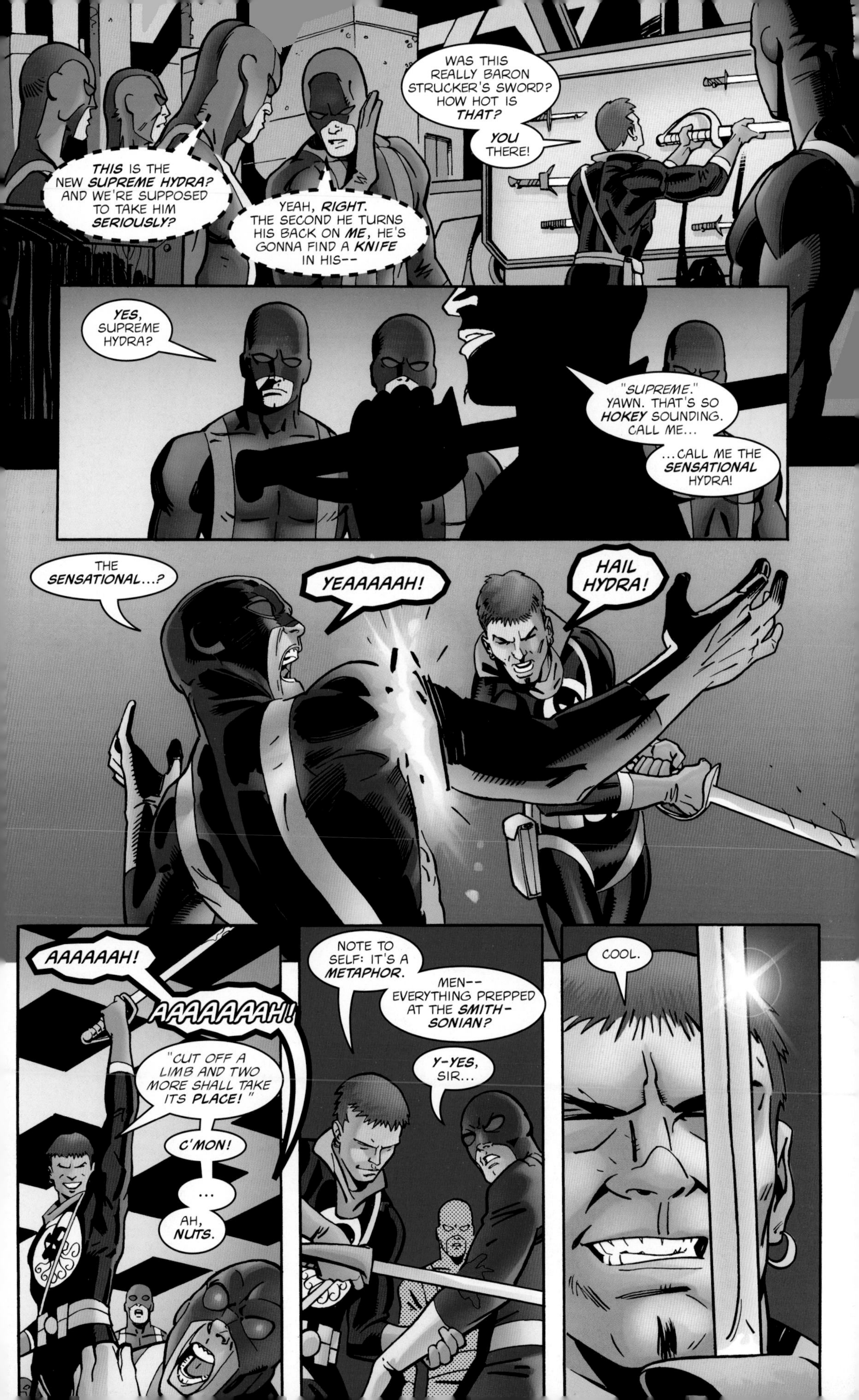

THIS IS THE NEW SUPREME HYDRA? AND WE'RE SUPPOSED TO TAKE HIM SERIOUSLY?
YEAH, RIGHT. THE SECOND HE TURNS HIS BACK ON ME, HE'S GONNA FIND A KNIFE IN HIS--
WAS THIS REALLY BARON STRUCKER'S SWORD? HOW HOT IS THAT?
YOU THERE!
YES, SUPREME HYDRA?
"SUPREME." YAWN. THAT'S SO HOKEY SOUNDING. CALL ME...
...CALL ME THE SENSATIONAL HYDRA!
THE SENSATIONAL...?
YEAAAAAH!
HAIL HYDRA!
AAAAAAH!
AAAAAAAH!
"CUT OFF A LIMB AND TWO MORE SHALL TAKE ITS PLACE!"
C'MON!
...
AH, NUTS.
NOTE TO SELF: IT'S A METAPHOR.
MEN-- EVERYTHING PREPPED AT THE SMITH-SONIAN?
Y-YES, SIR...
COOL.

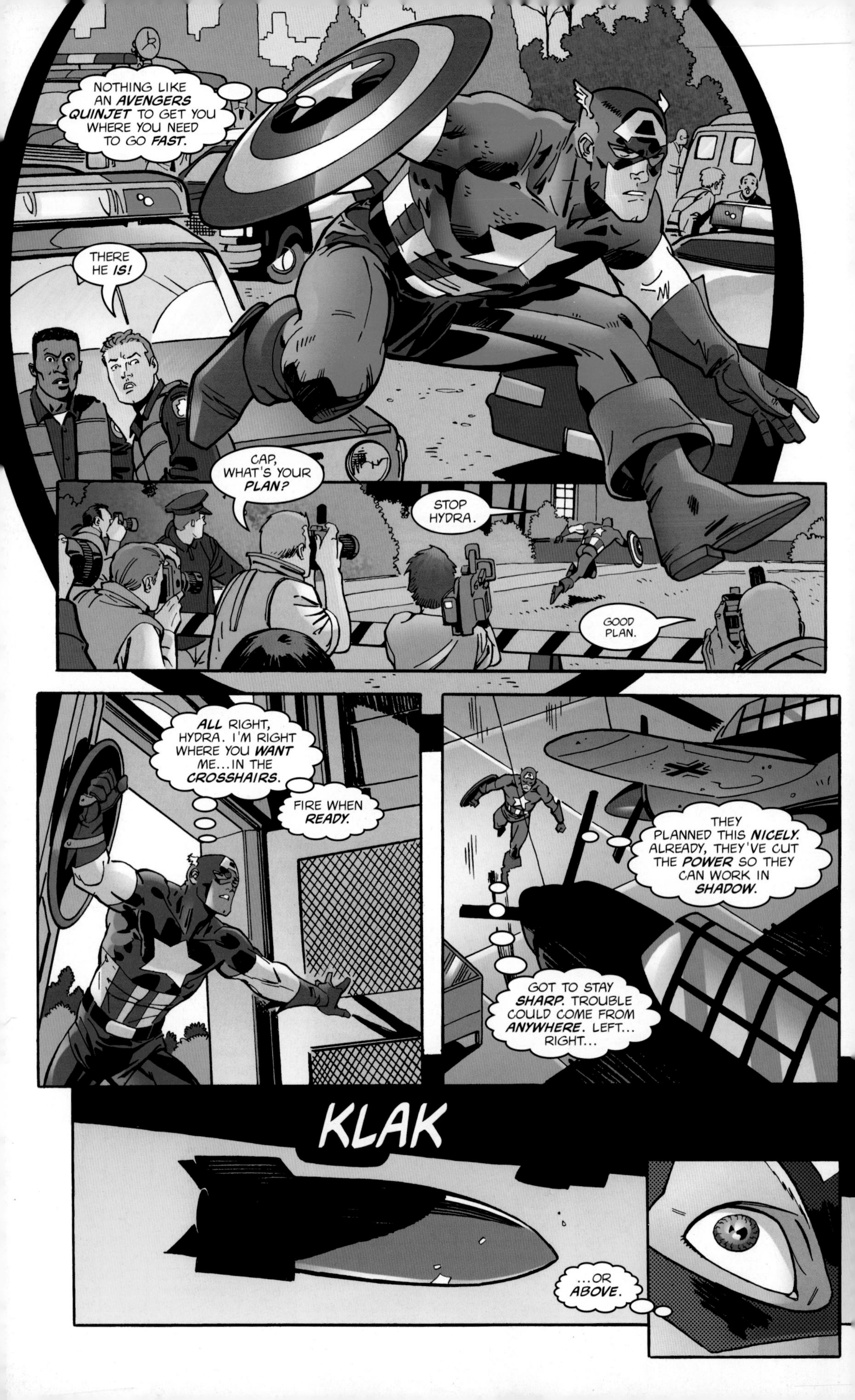

NOTHING LIKE AN AVENGERS QUINJET TO GET YOU WHERE YOU NEED TO GO FAST.
THERE HE IS!
CAP, WHAT'S YOUR PLAN?
STOP HYDRA.
GOOD PLAN.
ALL RIGHT, HYDRA. I'M RIGHT WHERE YOU WANT ME...IN THE CROSSHAIRS.
FIRE WHEN READY.
THEY PLANNED THIS NICELY. ALREADY, THEY'VE CUT THE POWER SO THEY CAN WORK IN SHADOW.
GOT TO STAY SHARP. TROUBLE COULD COME FROM ANYWHERE. LEFT... RIGHT...
KLAK
...OR ABOVE.

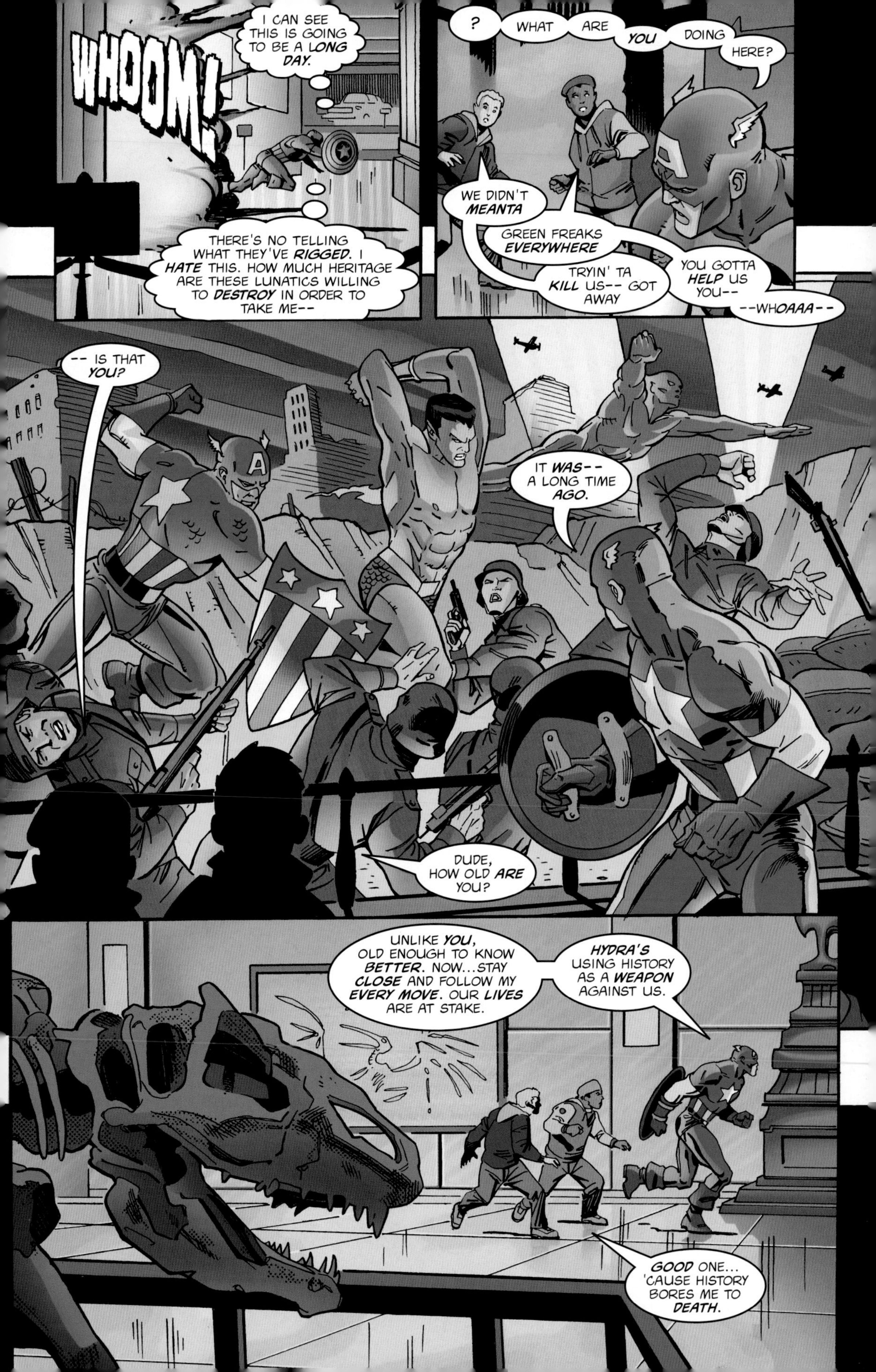
WHOOM!
I CAN SEE THIS IS GOING TO BE A LONG DAY.
THERE'S NO TELLING WHAT THEY'VE RIGGED. I HATE THIS. HOW MUCH HERITAGE ARE THESE LUNATICS WILLING TO DESTROY IN ORDER TO TAKE ME--
?
WHAT
ARE
YOU
DOING
HERE?
WE DIDN'T MEANTA
GREEN FREAKS EVERYWHERE
TRYIN' TA KILL US-- GOT AWAY
YOU GOTTA HELP US YOU--
--WHOAAA--
-- IS THAT YOU?
IT WAS-- A LONG TIME AGO.
DUDE, HOW OLD ARE YOU?
UNLIKE YOU, OLD ENOUGH TO KNOW BETTER. NOW...STAY CLOSE AND FOLLOW MY EVERY MOVE. OUR LIVES ARE AT STAKE.
HYDRA'S USING HISTORY AS A WEAPON AGAINST US.
GOOD ONE... 'CAUSE HISTORY BORES ME TO DEATH.

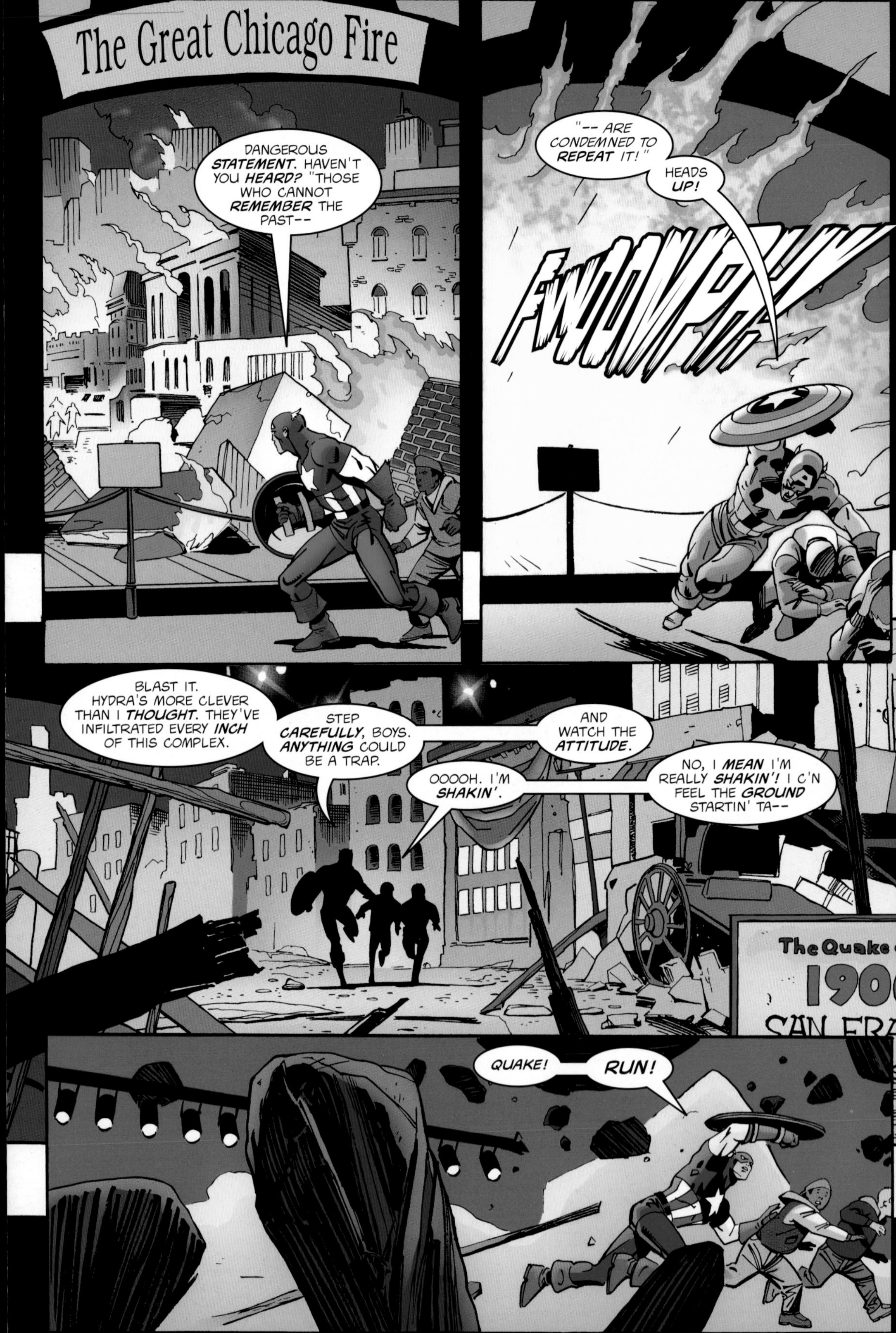
The Great Chicago Fire
DANGEROUS STATEMENT. HAVEN'T YOU HEARD? "THOSE WHO CANNOT REMEMBER THE PAST--
"-- ARE CONDEMNED TO REPEAT IT!"
HEADS UP!
FWOOMPH
BLAST IT. HYDRA'S MORE CLEVER THAN I THOUGHT. THEY'VE INFILTRATED EVERY INCH OF THIS COMPLEX.
STEP CAREFULLY, BOYS. ANYTHING COULD BE A TRAP.
AND WATCH THE ATTITUDE.
OOOOH. I'M SHAKIN'.
NO, I MEAN I'M REALLY SHAKIN'! I C'N FEEL THE GROUND STARTIN' TA--
QUAKE!
RUN!

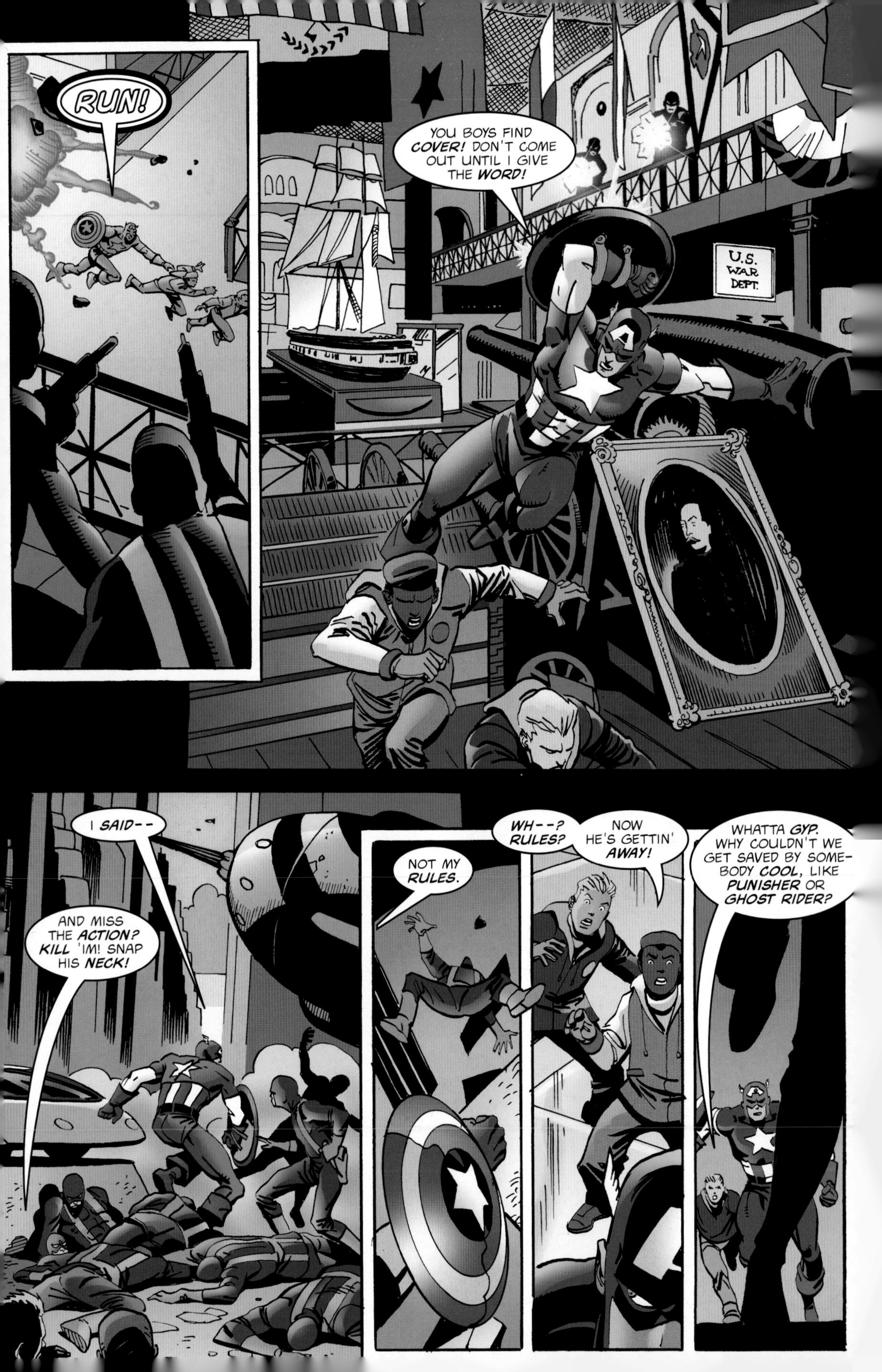
RUN!
YOU BOYS FIND COVER! DON'T COME OUT UNTIL I GIVE THE WORD!
U.S. WAR DEPT.
I SAID--
AND MISS THE ACTION? KILL 'IM! SNAP HIS NECK!
NOT MY RULES.
WH--? RULES?
NOW HE'S GETTIN' AWAY!
WHATTA GYP. WHY COULDN'T WE GET SAVED BY SOMEBODY COOL, LIKE PUNISHER OR GHOST RIDER?

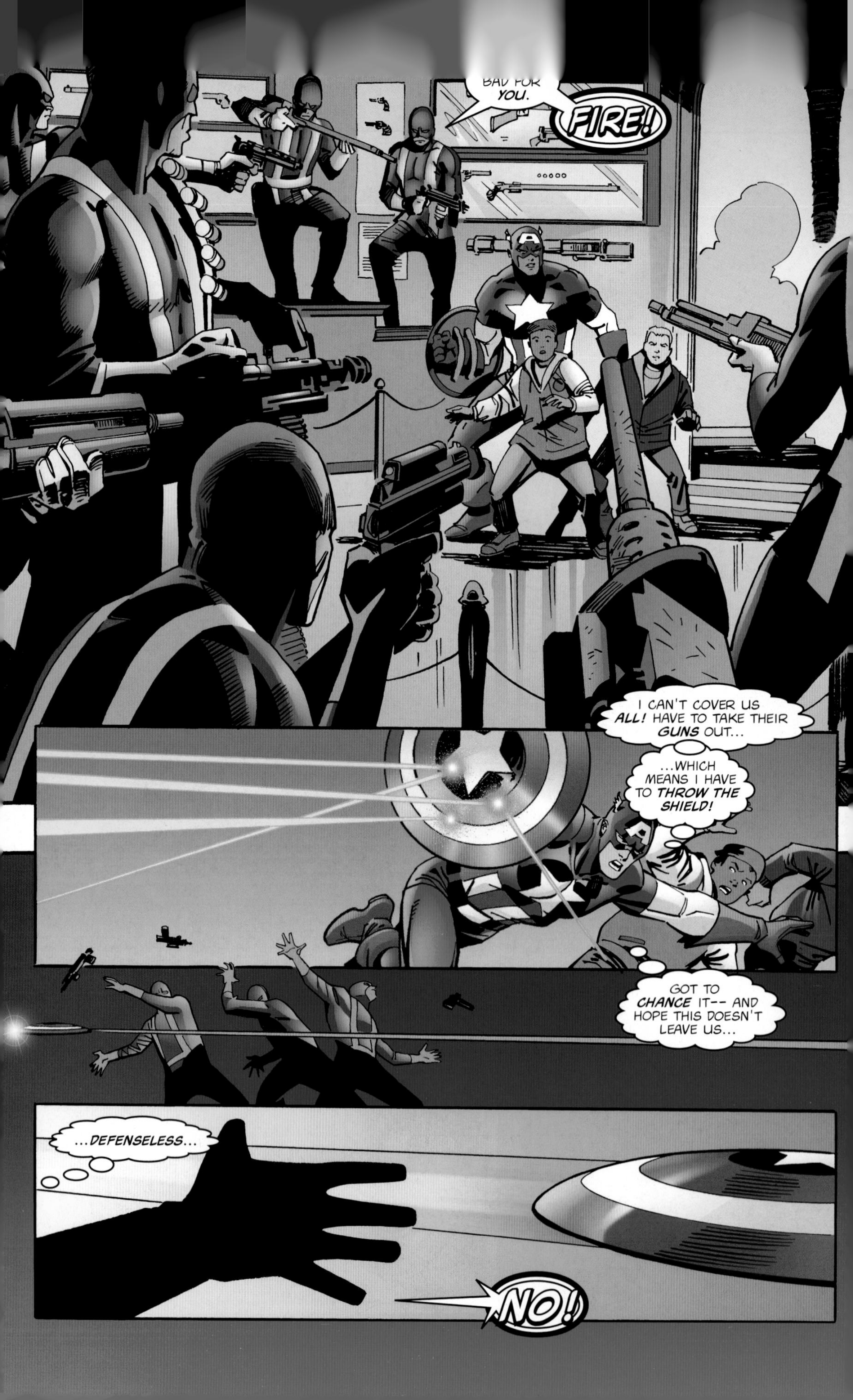
BAD FOR YOU.
FIRE!
I CAN'T COVER US ALL! HAVE TO TAKE THEIR GUNS OUT...
...WHICH MEANS I HAVE TO THROW THE SHIELD!
GOT TO CHANCE IT-- AND HOPE THIS DOESN'T LEAVE US...
...DEFENSELESS...
NO!

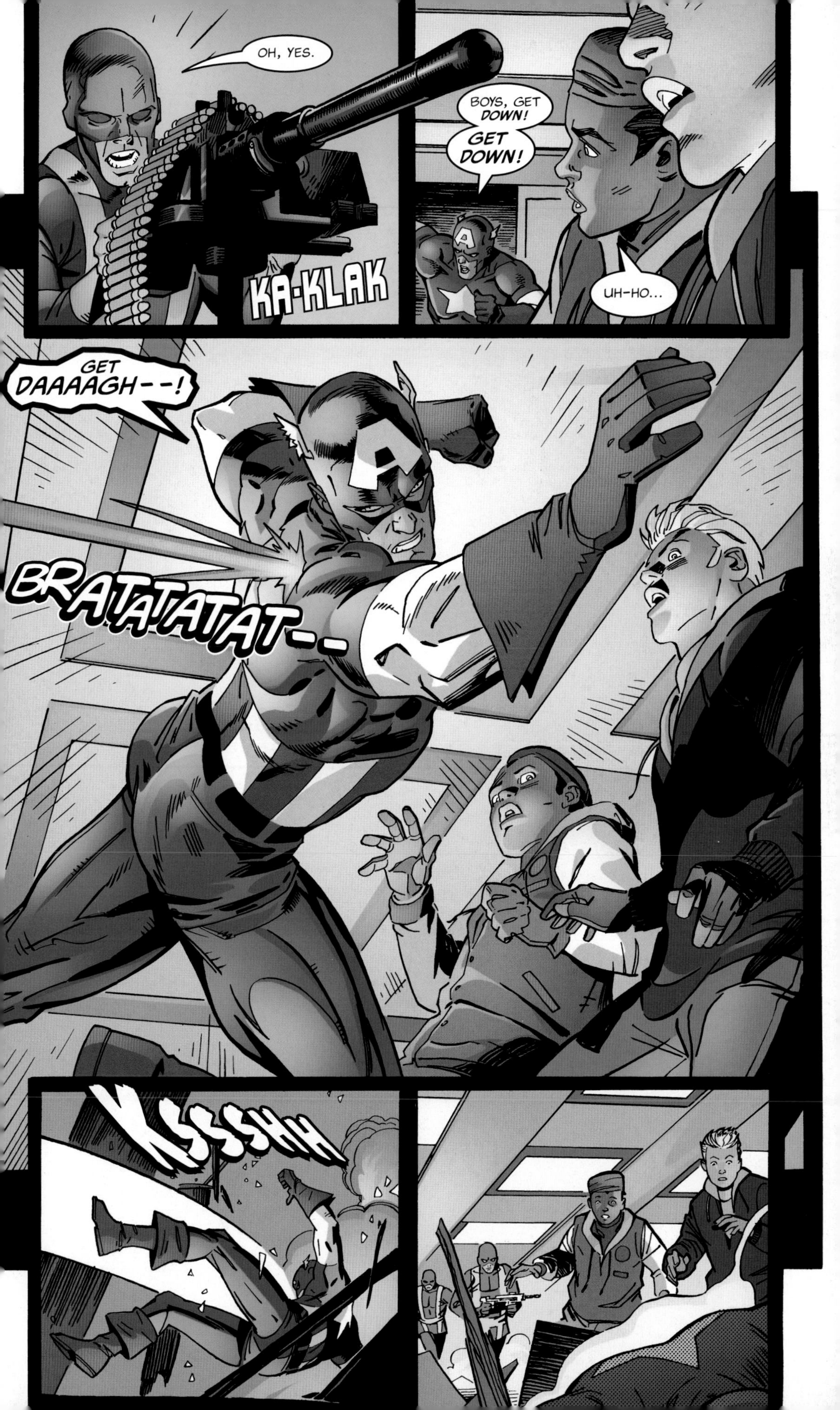
OH, YES.
KA-KLAK
BOYS, GET DOWN!
GET DOWN!
UH-HO...
GET DAAAAGH--!
BRATATATATAT--

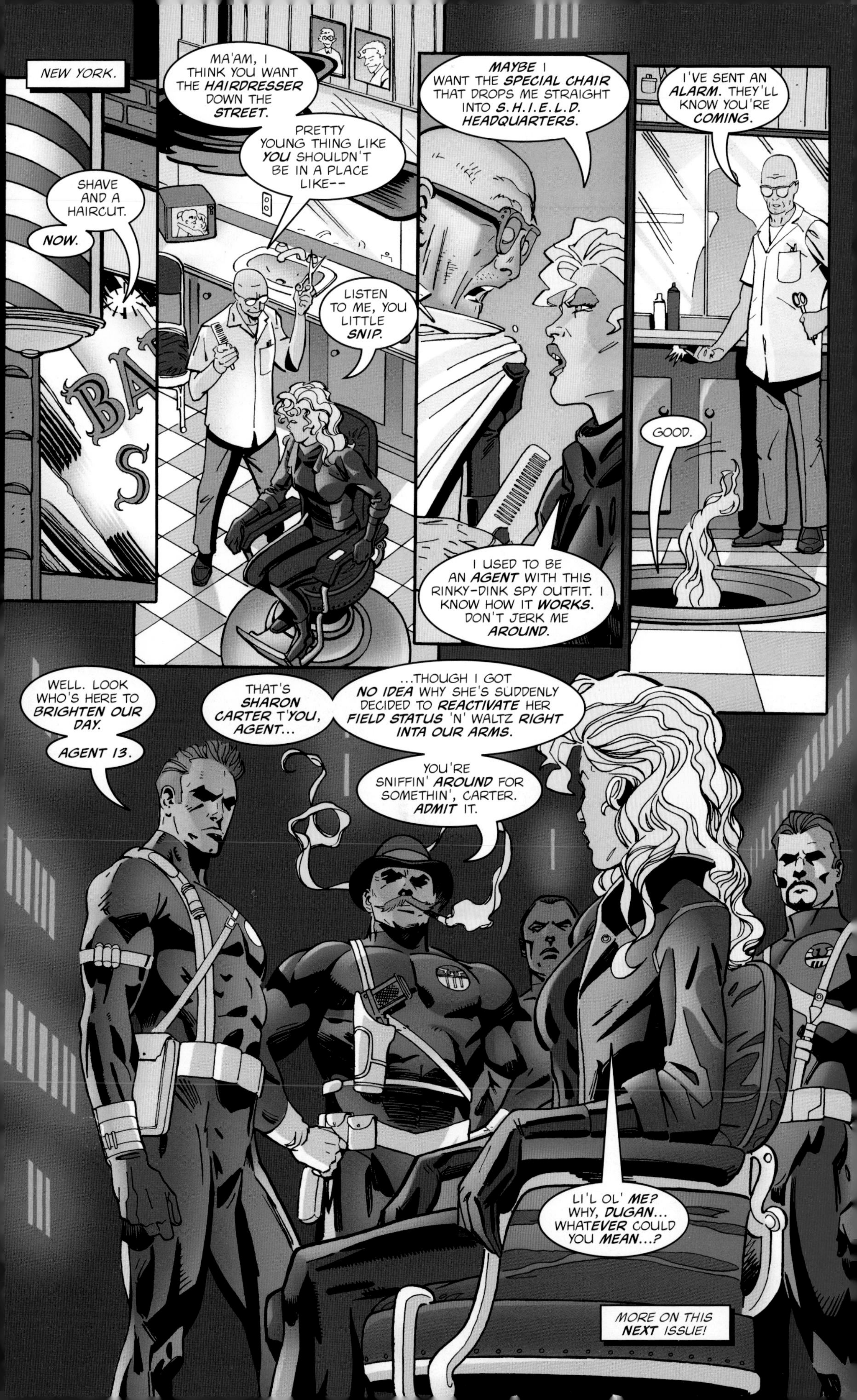
NEW YORK.
SHAVE AND A HAIRCUT.
NOW.
MA'AM, I THINK YOU WANT THE HAIRDRESSER DOWN THE STREET.
PRETTY YOUNG THING LIKE YOU SHOULDN'T BE IN A PLACE LIKE--
LISTEN TO ME, YOU LITTLE SNIP.
MAYBE I WANT THE SPECIAL CHAIR THAT DROPS ME STRAIGHT INTO S.H.I.E.L.D. HEADQUARTERS.
I USED TO BE AN AGENT WITH THIS RINKY-DINK SPY OUTFIT. I KNOW HOW IT WORKS. DON'T JERK ME AROUND.
I'VE SENT AN ALARM. THEY'LL KNOW YOU'RE COMING.
GOOD.
WELL. LOOK WHO'S HERE TO BRIGHTEN OUR DAY.
AGENT 13.
THAT'S SHARON CARTER T'YOU, AGENT...
...THOUGH I GOT NO IDEA WHY SHE'S SUDDENLY DECIDED TO REACTIVATE HER FIELD STATUS 'N' WALTZ RIGHT INTA OUR ARMS.
YOU'RE SNIFFIN' AROUND FOR SOMETHIN', CARTER. ADMIT IT.
LI'L OL' ME? WHY, DUGAN... WHATEVER COULD YOU MEAN...?
MORE ON THIS NEXT ISSUE!

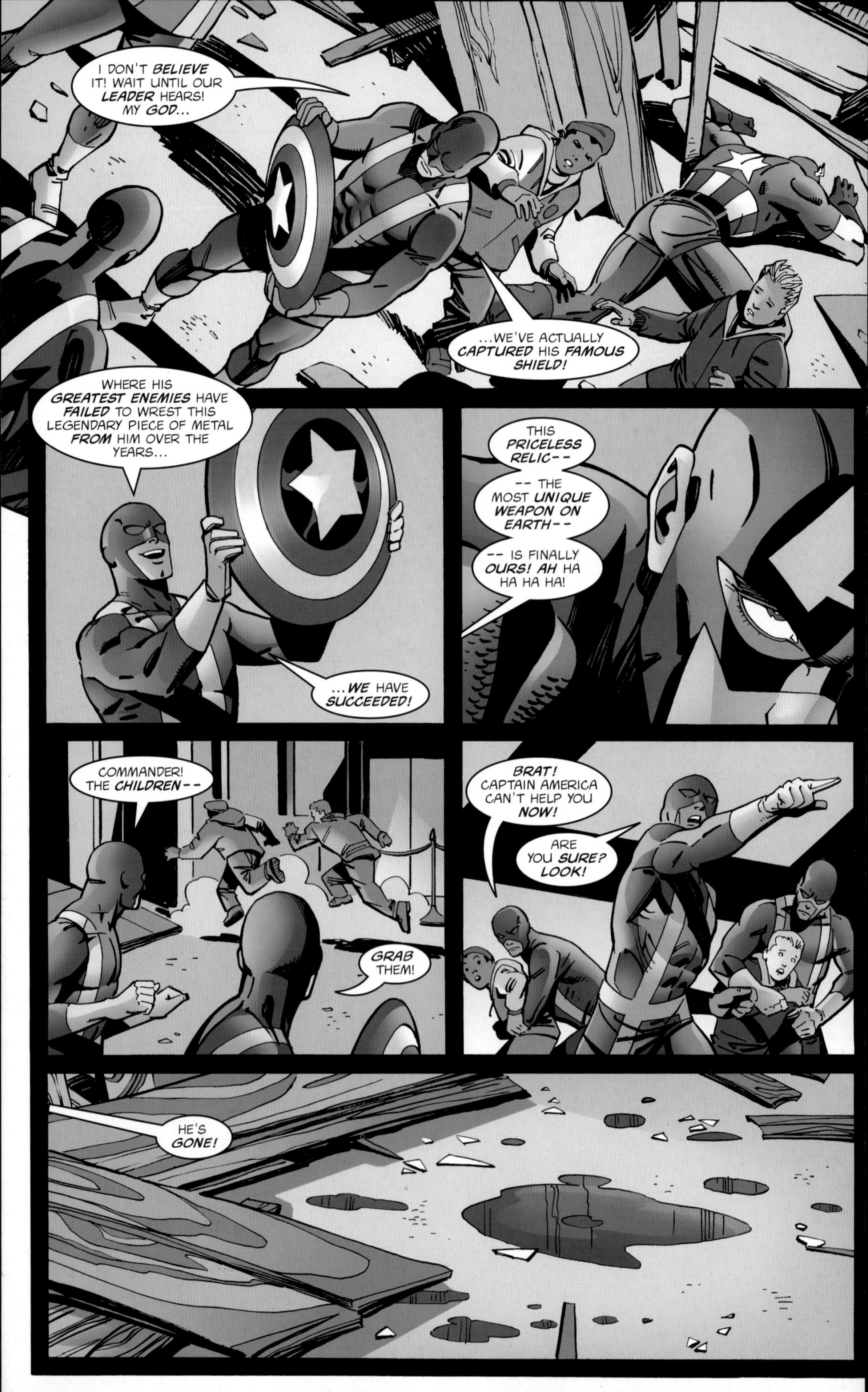
I DON'T BELIEVE IT! WAIT UNTIL OUR LEADER HEARS! MY GOD...
...WE'VE ACTUALLY CAPTURED HIS FAMOUS SHIELD!
WHERE HIS GREATEST ENEMIES HAVE FAILED TO WREST THIS LEGENDARY PIECE OF METAL FROM HIM OVER THE YEARS...
...WE HAVE SUCCEEDED!
THIS PRICELESS RELIC--
-- THE MOST UNIQUE WEAPON ON EARTH--
-- IS FINALLY OURS! AH HA HA HA HA!
COMMANDER! THE CHILDREN--
GRAB THEM!
BRAT! CAPTAIN AMERICA CAN'T HELP YOU NOW!
ARE YOU SURE? LOOK!
HE'S GONE!

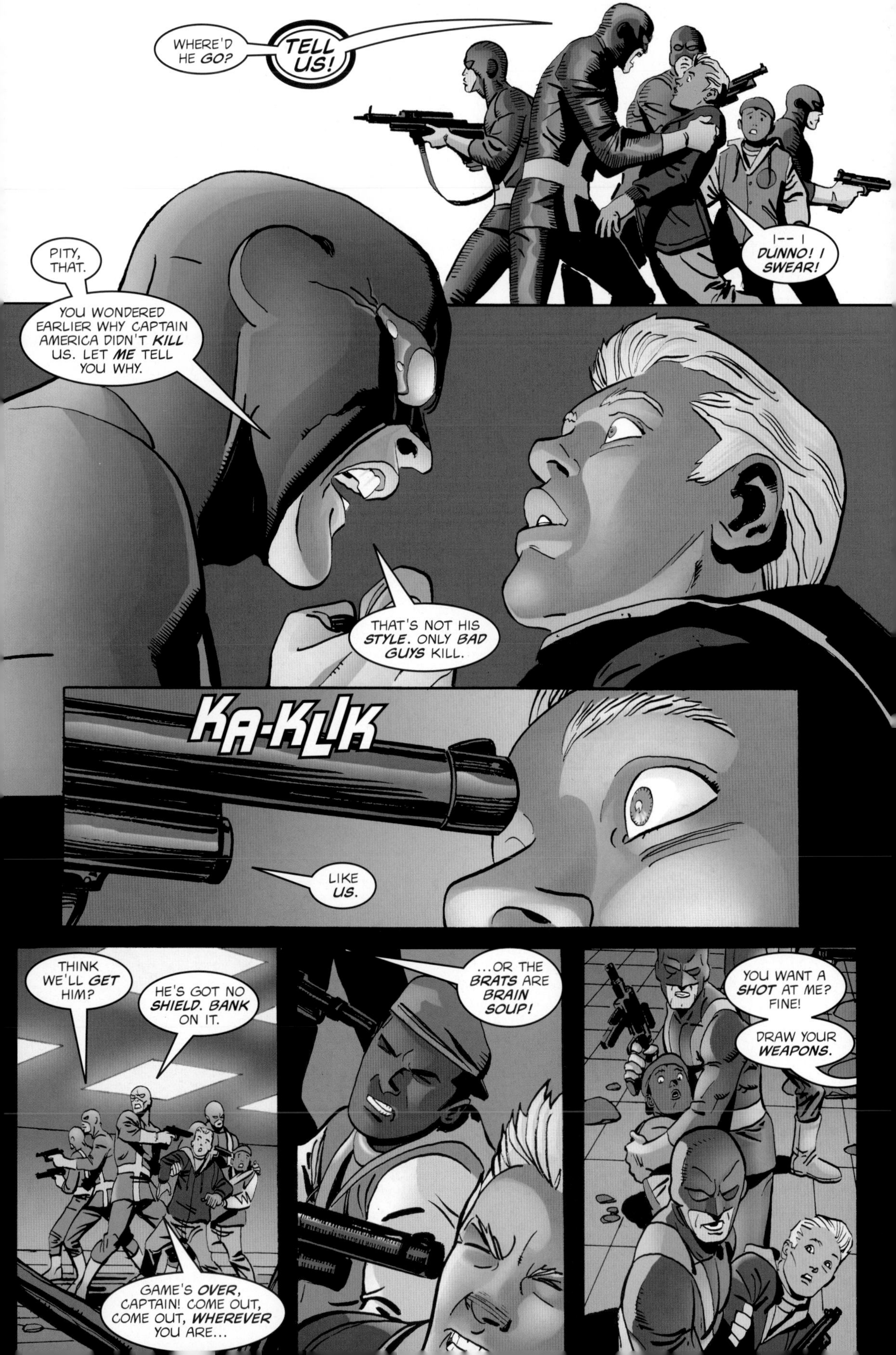
WHERE'D HE GO?
TELL US!
I-- I DUNNO! I SWEAR!
PITY, THAT.
YOU WONDERED EARLIER WHY CAPTAIN AMERICA DIDN'T KILL US. LET ME TELL YOU WHY.
THAT'S NOT HIS STYLE. ONLY BAD GUYS KILL.
KA-KLIK
LIKE US.
THINK WE'LL GET HIM?
HE'S GOT NO SHIELD. BANK ON IT.
GAME'S OVER, CAPTAIN! COME OUT, COME OUT, WHEREVER YOU ARE...
...OR THE BRATS ARE BRAIN SOUP!
YOU WANT A SHOT AT ME? FINE!
DRAW YOUR WEAPONS.

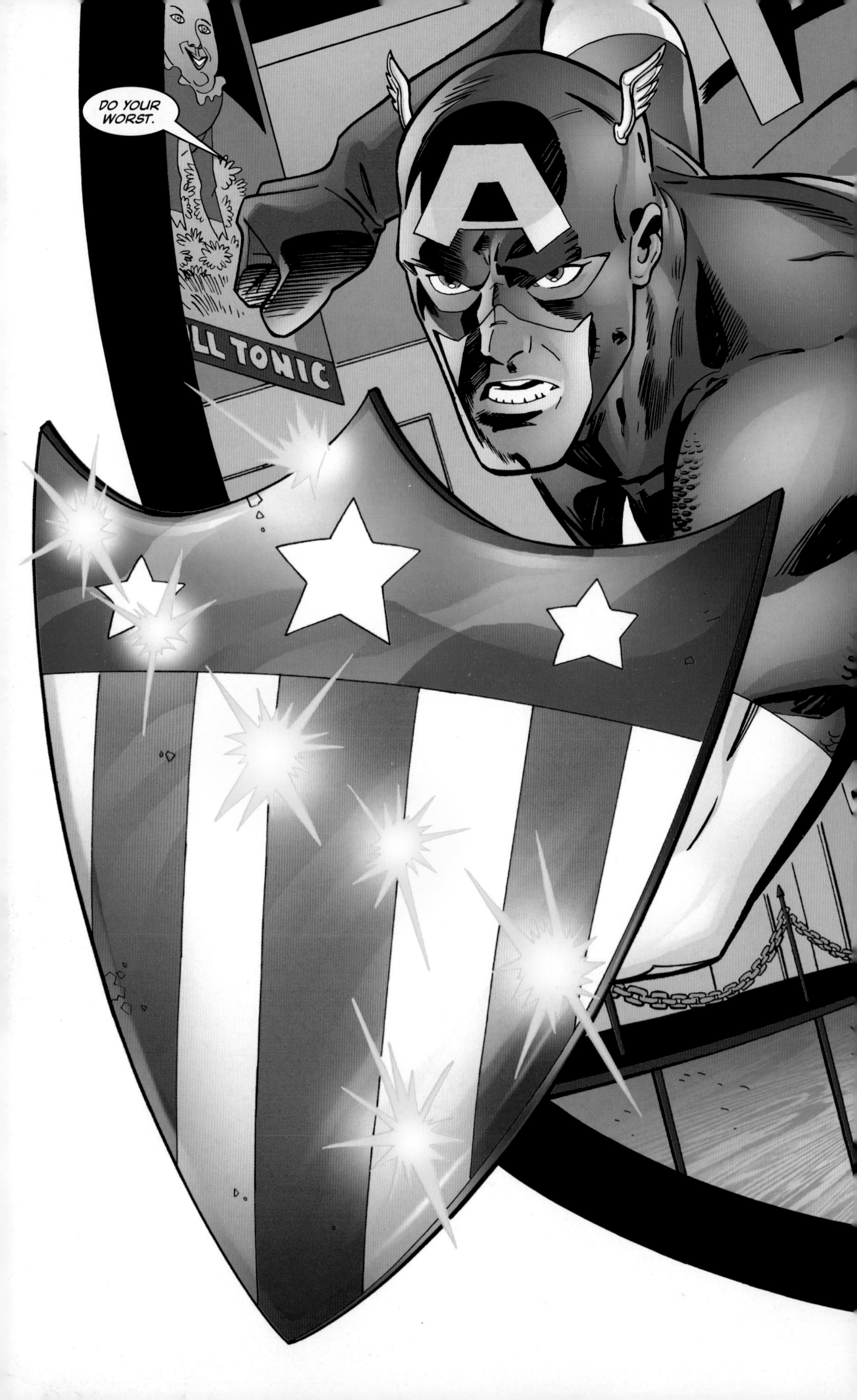
DO YOUR WORST.
LL TONIC

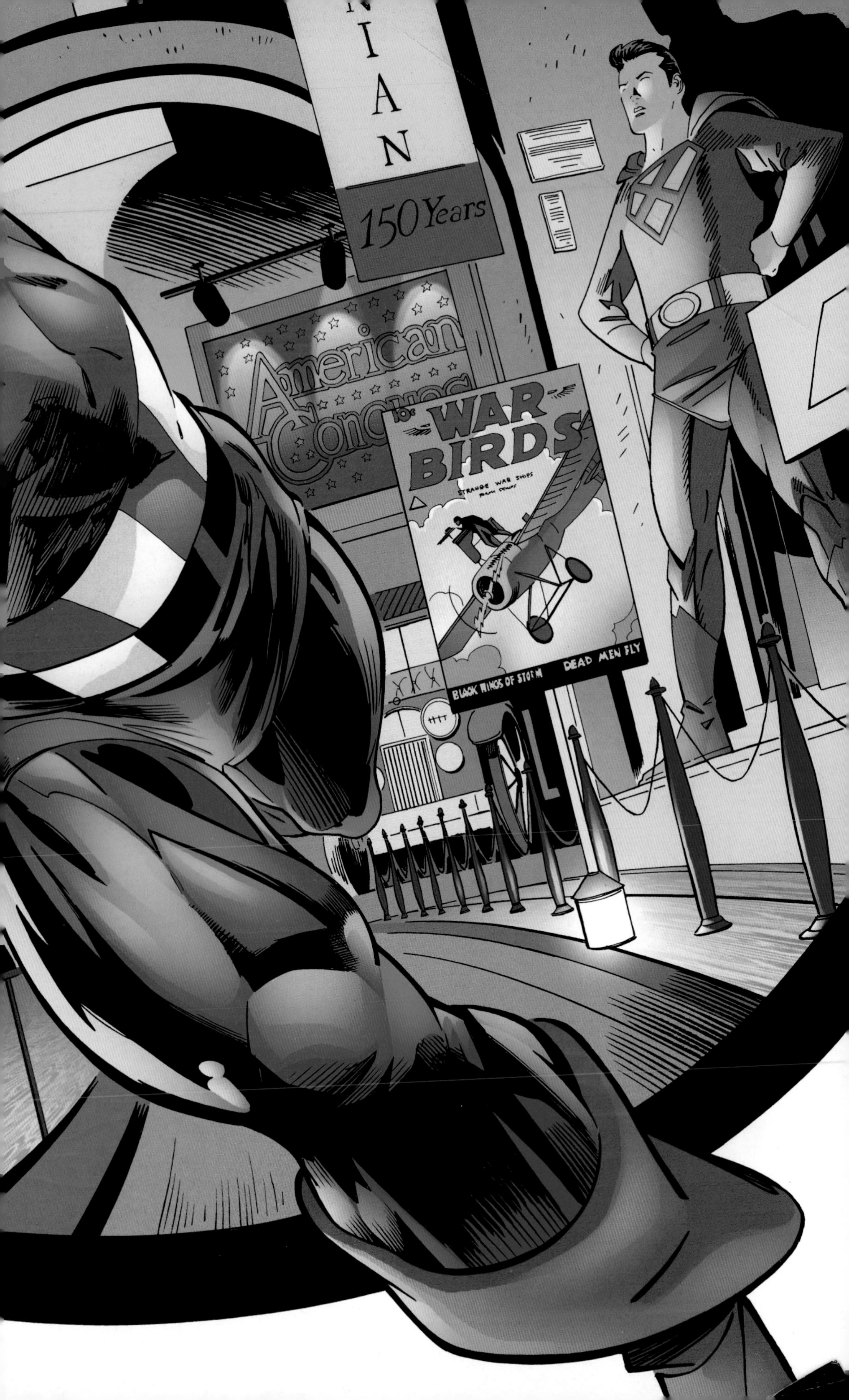
IAN
150 Years
American
10¢
WAR BIRDS
STRANGE WAR SHIPS
BLACK WINGS OF STORM
DEAD MEN FLY

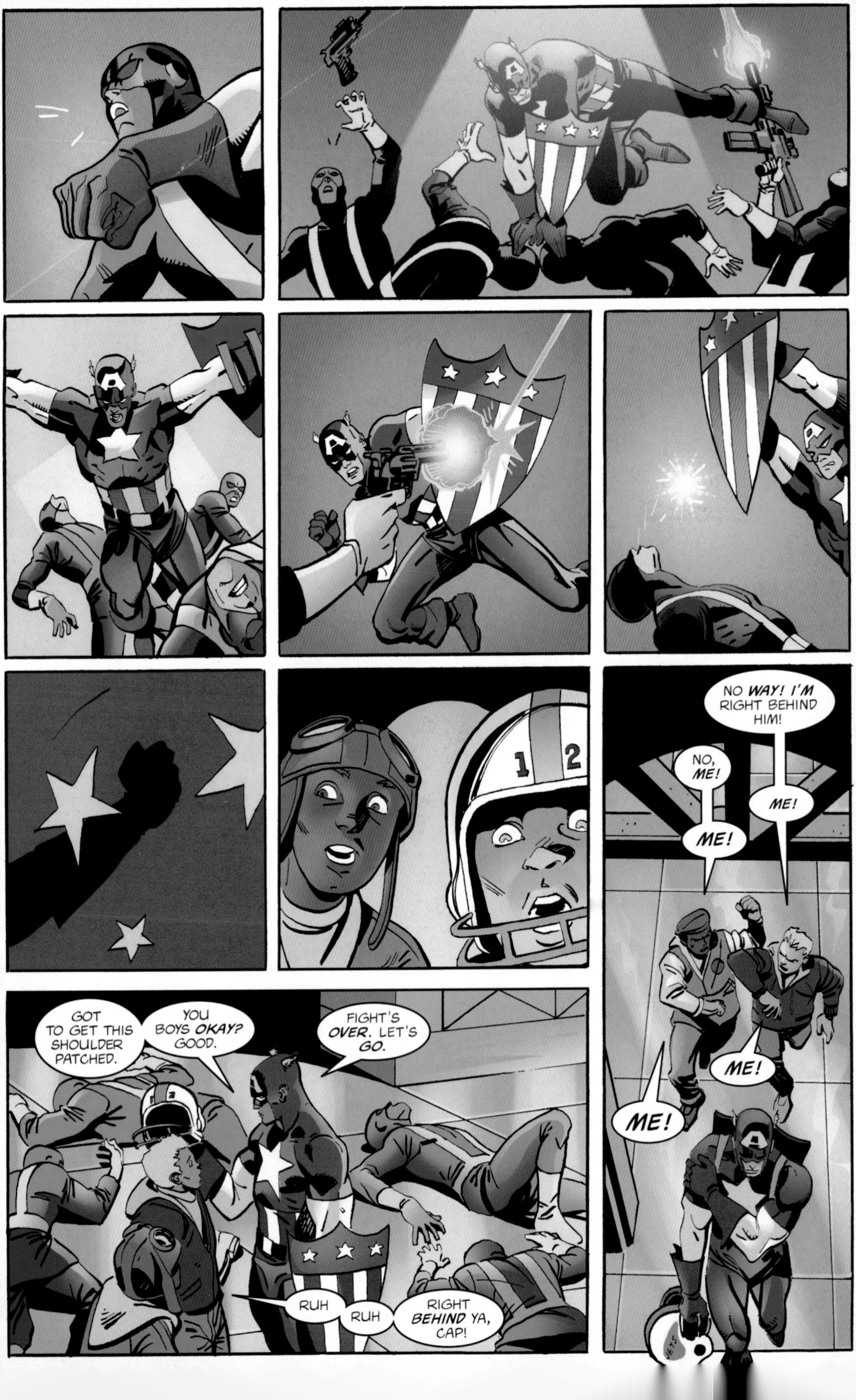
NO *WAY*! I'M RIGHT BEHIND HIM!
NO, *ME!*
ME!
ME!
ME!
ME!
GOT TO GET THIS SHOULDER PATCHED.
YOU BOYS *OKAY?* GOOD.
FIGHT'S *OVER*. LET'S *GO*.
RUH
RUH
RIGHT *BEHIND* YA, CAP!

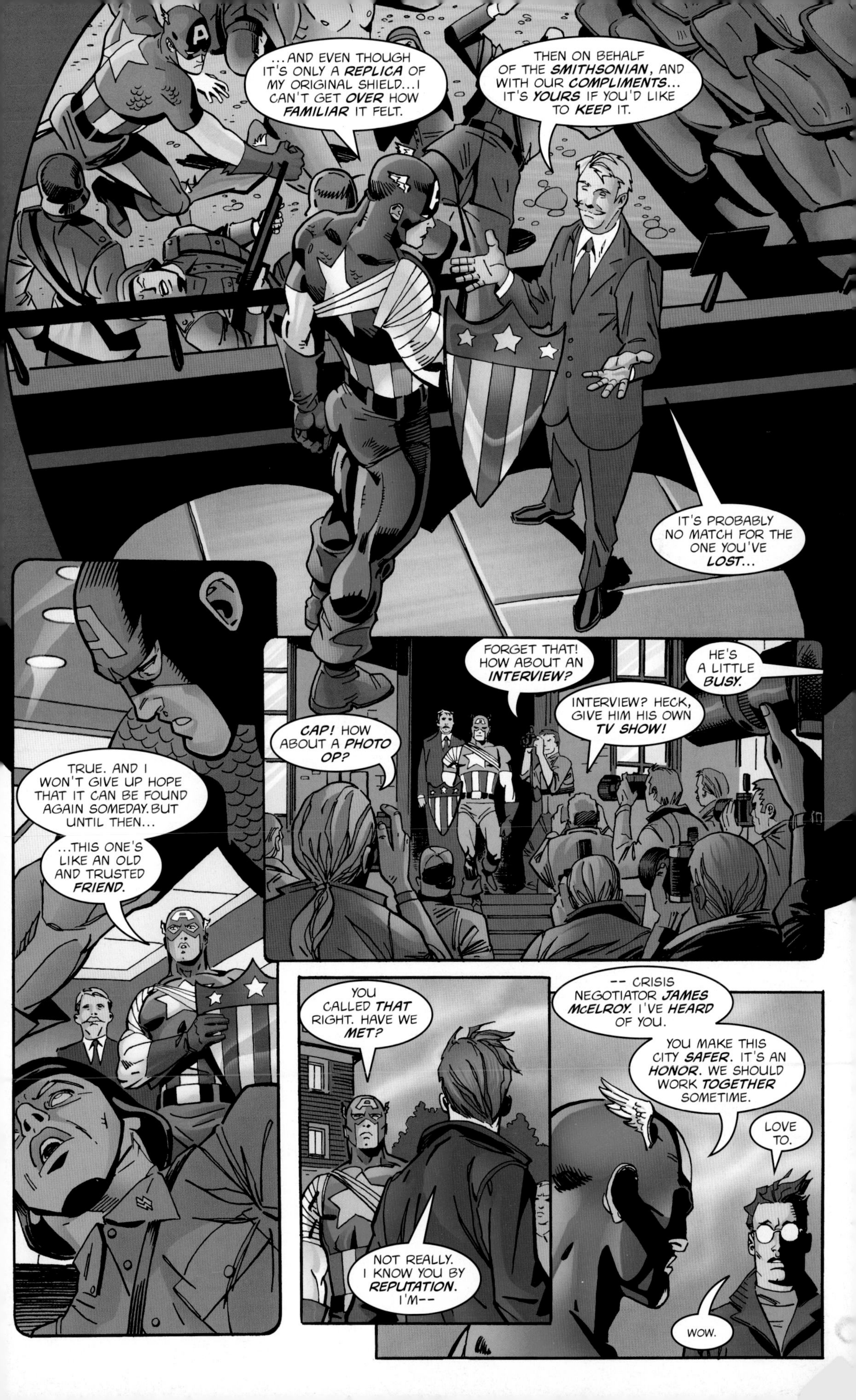
...AND EVEN THOUGH IT'S ONLY A REPLICA OF MY ORIGINAL SHIELD...I CAN'T GET OVER HOW FAMILIAR IT FELT.
THEN ON BEHALF OF THE SMITHSONIAN, AND WITH OUR COMPLIMENTS... IT'S YOURS IF YOU'D LIKE TO KEEP IT.
IT'S PROBABLY NO MATCH FOR THE ONE YOU'VE LOST...
TRUE. AND I WON'T GIVE UP HOPE THAT IT CAN BE FOUND AGAIN SOMEDAY. BUT UNTIL THEN...
...THIS ONE'S LIKE AN OLD AND TRUSTED FRIEND.
CAP! HOW ABOUT A PHOTO OP?
FORGET THAT! HOW ABOUT AN INTERVIEW?
HE'S A LITTLE BUSY.
INTERVIEW? HECK, GIVE HIM HIS OWN TV SHOW!
YOU CALLED THAT RIGHT. HAVE WE MET?
NOT REALLY. I KNOW YOU BY REPUTATION. I'M--
-- CRISIS NEGOTIATOR JAMES McELROY. I'VE HEARD OF YOU.
YOU MAKE THIS CITY SAFER. IT'S AN HONOR. WE SHOULD WORK TOGETHER SOMETIME.
LOVE TO.
WOW.

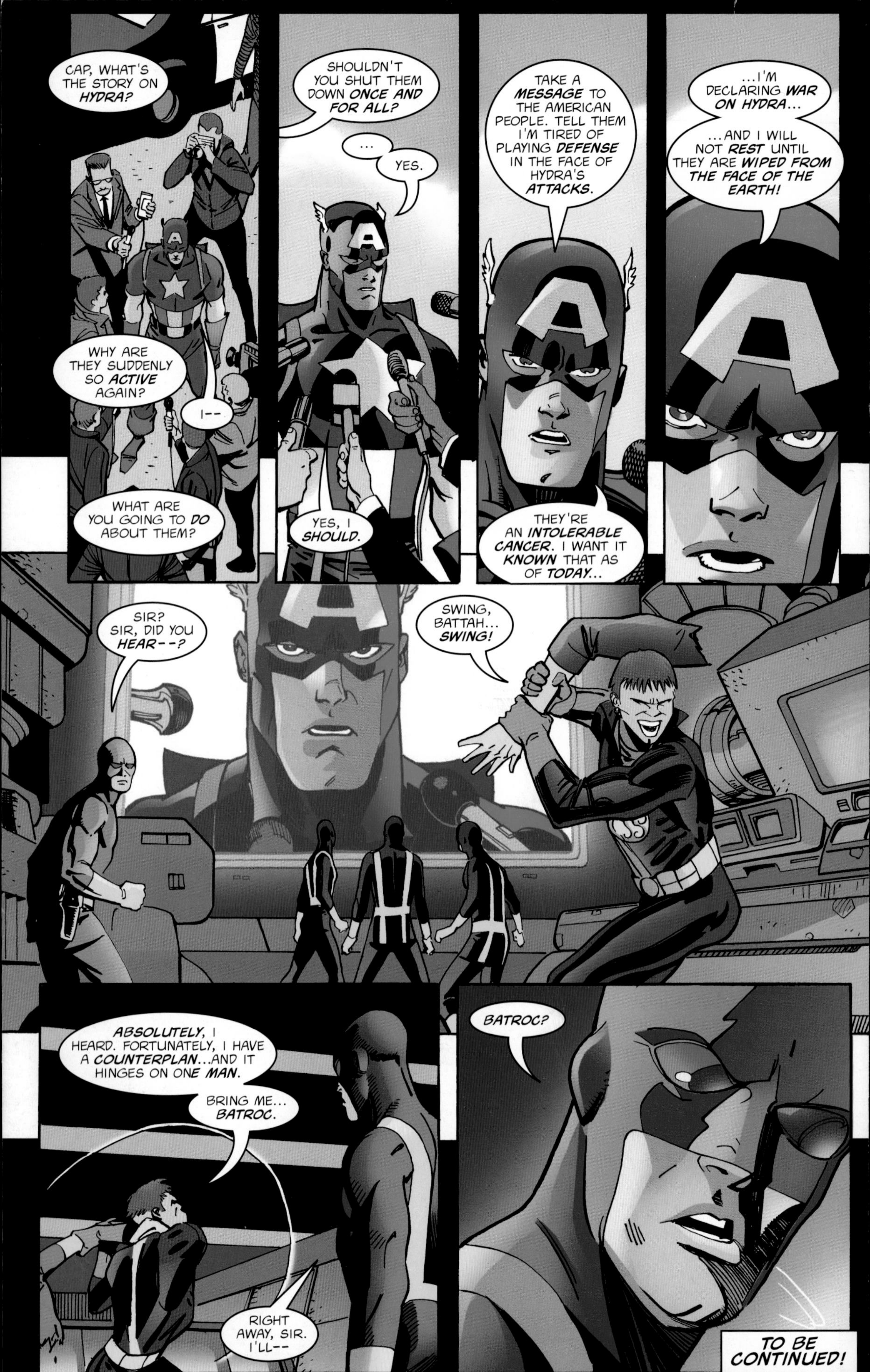
CAP, WHAT'S THE STORY ON HYDRA?
WHY ARE THEY SUDDENLY SO ACTIVE AGAIN?
I--
WHAT ARE YOU GOING TO DO ABOUT THEM?
SHOULDN'T YOU SHUT THEM DOWN ONCE AND FOR ALL?
...
YES.
YES, I SHOULD.
TAKE A MESSAGE TO THE AMERICAN PEOPLE. TELL THEM I'M TIRED OF PLAYING DEFENSE IN THE FACE OF HYDRA'S ATTACKS.
THEY'RE AN INTOLERABLE CANCER. I WANT IT KNOWN THAT AS OF TODAY...
...I'M DECLARING WAR ON HYDRA...
...AND I WILL NOT REST UNTIL THEY ARE WIPED FROM THE FACE OF THE EARTH!
SIR? SIR, DID YOU HEAR--?
SWING, BATTAH... SWING!
ABSOLUTELY, I HEARD. FORTUNATELY, I HAVE A COUNTERPLAN...AND IT HINGES ON ONE MAN.
BRING ME... BATROC.
RIGHT AWAY, SIR. I'LL--
BATROC?
TO BE CONTINUED!

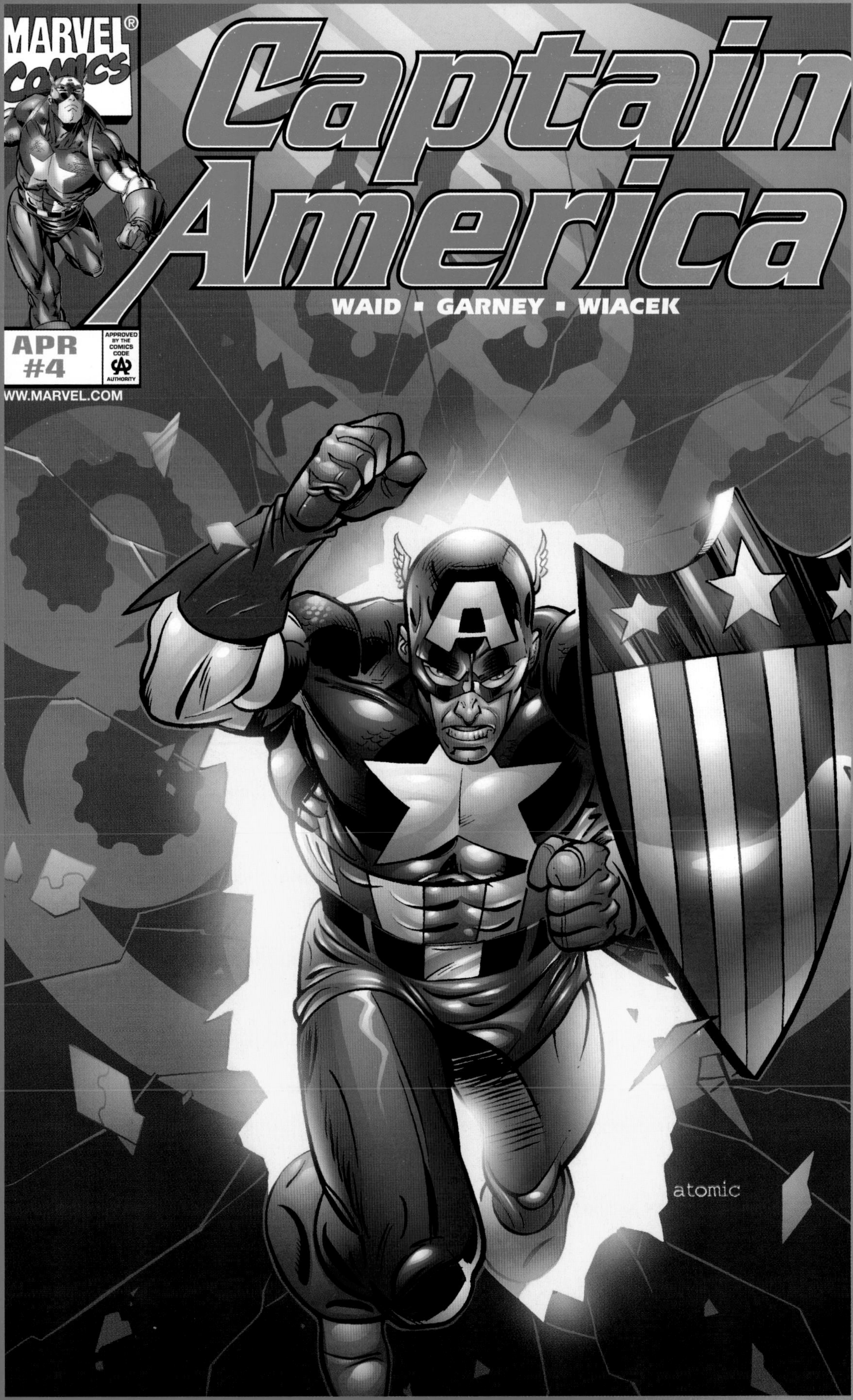
MARVEL®
COMICS
Captain America
WAID ▪ GARNEY ▪ WIACEK
APR
#4
APPROVED BY THE COMICS CODE AUTHORITY
WWW.MARVEL.COM
atomic

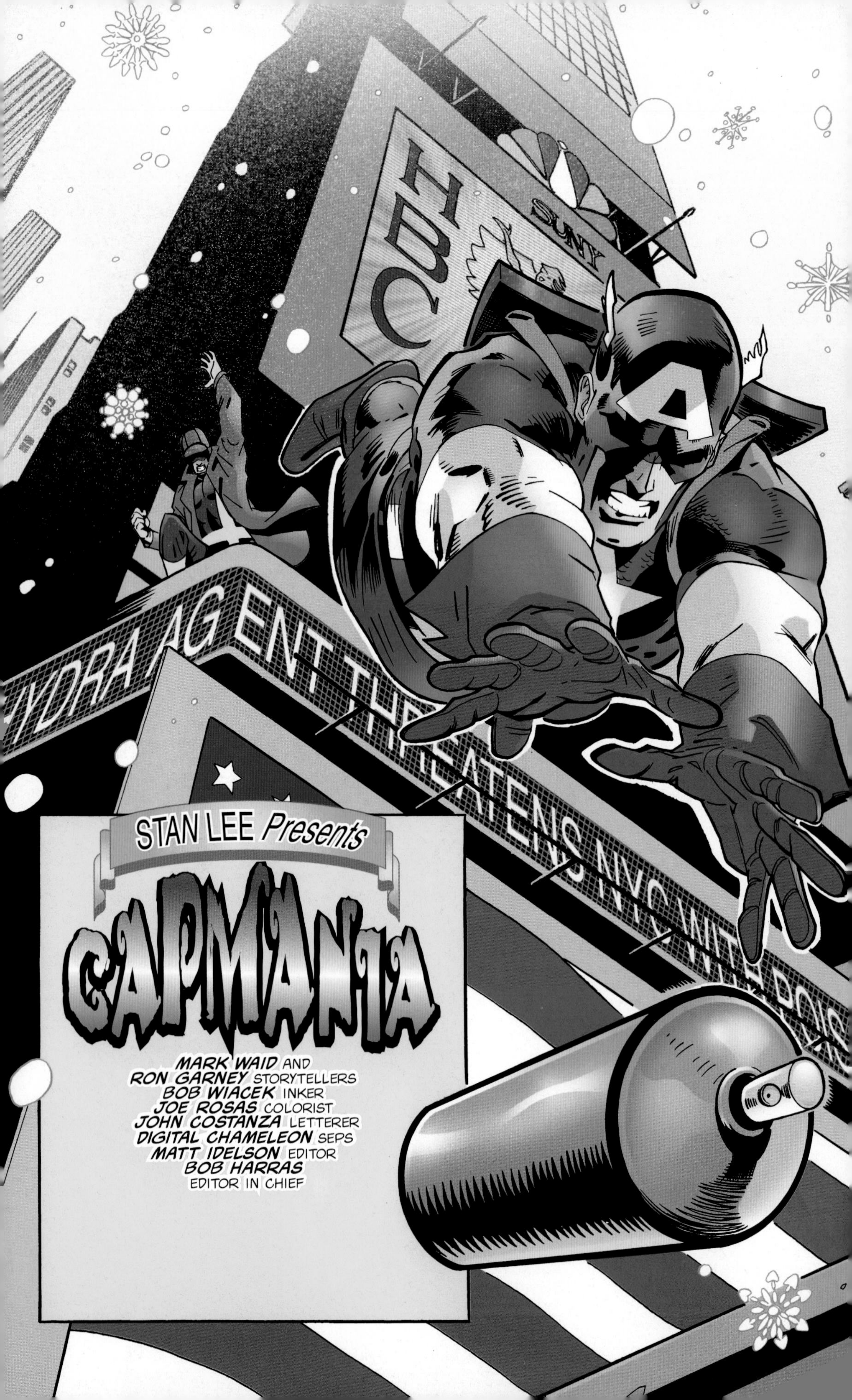

HBC
SONY
YDRA AG ENT THREATENS NYC WITH POIS
STAN LEE Presents
CAPMANIA
MARK WAID AND
RON GARNEY STORYTELLERS
BOB WIACEK INKER
JOE ROSAS COLORIST
JOHN COSTANZA LETTERER
DIGITAL CHAMELEON SEPS
MATT IDELSON EDITOR
BOB HARRAS
EDITOR IN CHIEF

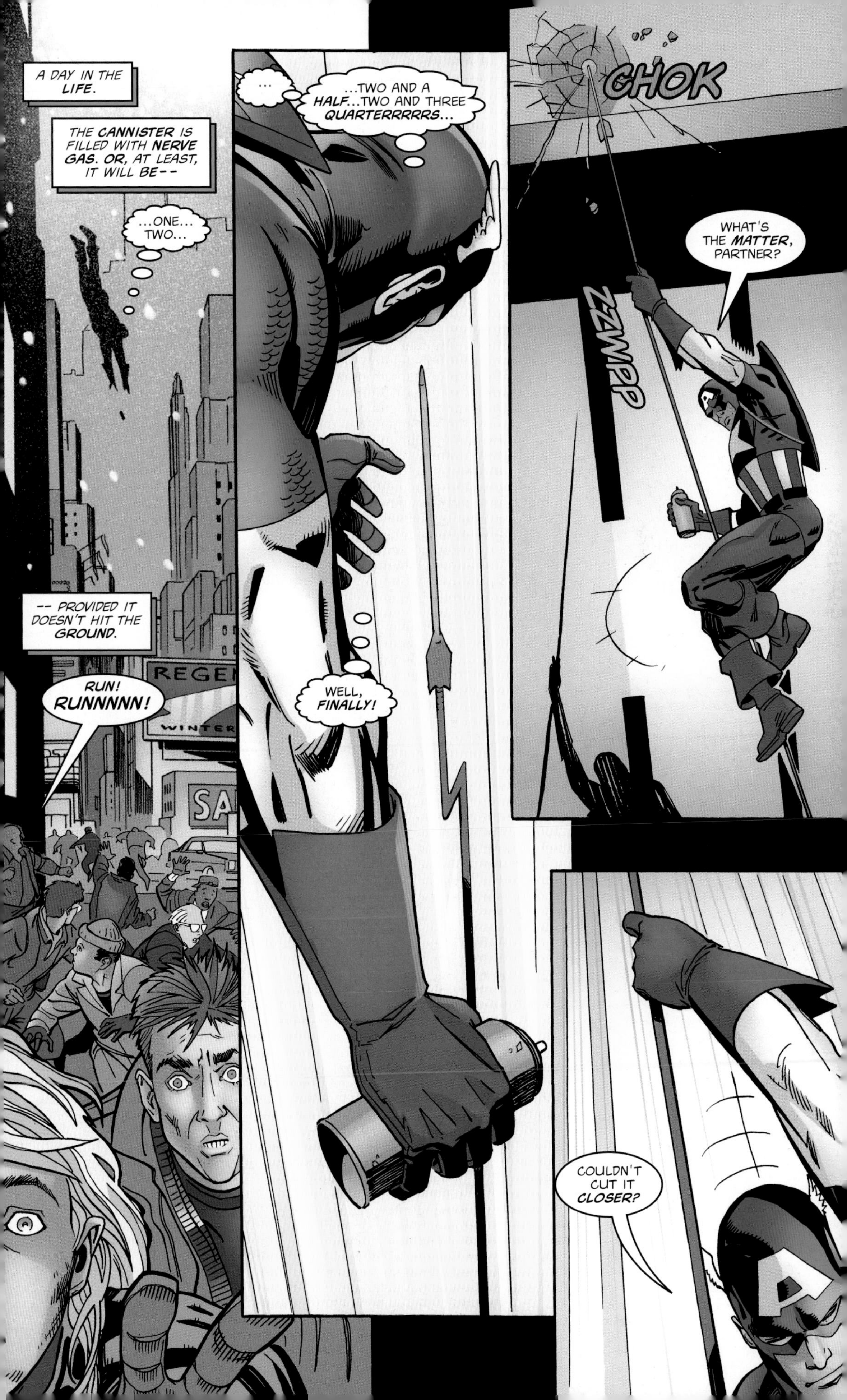

A DAY IN THE LIFE.
THE CANNISTER IS FILLED WITH NERVE GAS. OR, AT LEAST, IT WILL BE--
...ONE... TWO...
-- PROVIDED IT DOESN'T HIT THE GROUND.
REGEN
RUN! RUNNNNN!
WINTER
SA
...
...TWO AND A HALF...TWO AND THREE QUARTERRRRRS...
WELL, FINALLY!
CHOK
WHAT'S THE MATTER, PARTNER?
ZZWPP
COULDN'T CUT IT CLOSER?

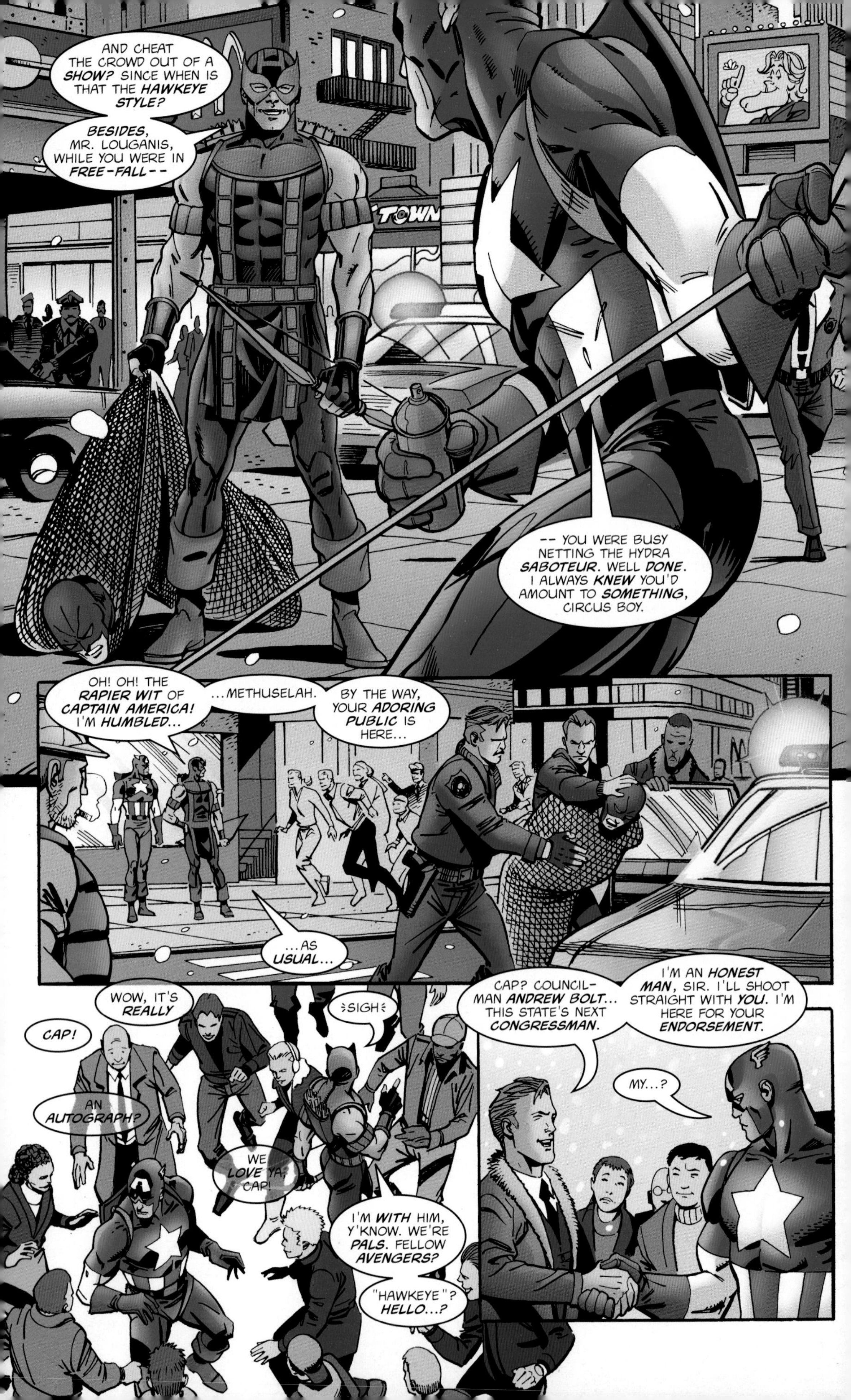

AND CHEAT THE CROWD OUT OF A SHOW? SINCE WHEN IS THAT THE HAWKEYE STYLE?
BESIDES, MR. LOUGANIS, WHILE YOU WERE IN FREE-FALL--
TOWN
-- YOU WERE BUSY NETTING THE HYDRA SABOTEUR. WELL DONE. I ALWAYS KNEW YOU'D AMOUNT TO SOMETHING, CIRCUS BOY.
OH! OH! THE RAPIER WIT OF CAPTAIN AMERICA! I'M HUMBLED...
...METHUSELAH.
BY THE WAY, YOUR ADORING PUBLIC IS HERE...
...AS USUAL...
WOW, IT'S REALLY
CAP!
AN AUTOGRAPH?
WE LOVE YA, CAP!
SIGH
I'M WITH HIM, Y'KNOW. WE'RE PALS. FELLOW AVENGERS?
"HAWKEYE"? HELLO...?
CAP? COUNCIL-MAN ANDREW BOLT... THIS STATE'S NEXT CONGRESSMAN.
I'M AN HONEST MAN, SIR. I'LL SHOOT STRAIGHT WITH YOU. I'M HERE FOR YOUR ENDORSEMENT.
MY...?

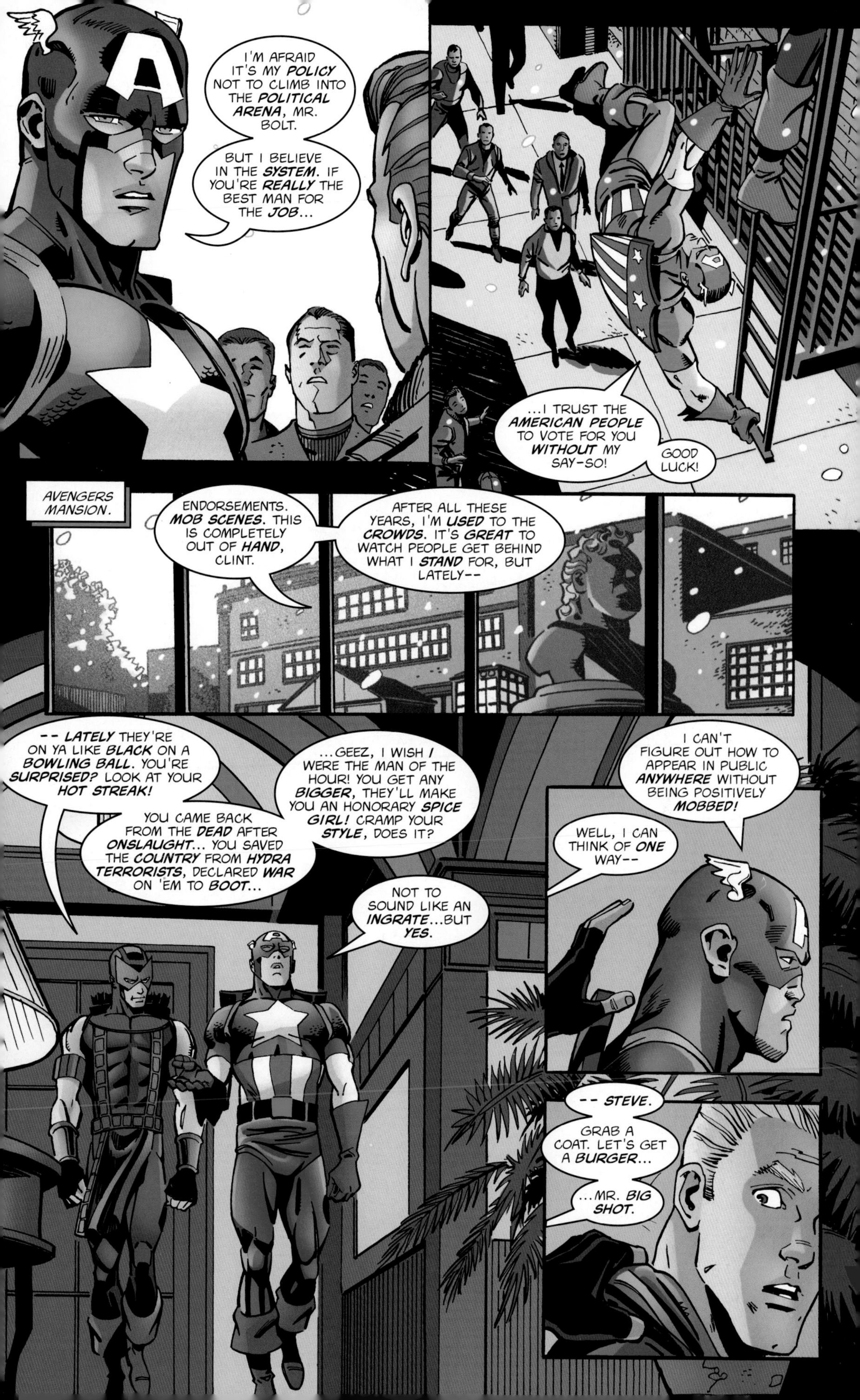
I'M AFRAID IT'S MY POLICY NOT TO CLIMB INTO THE POLITICAL ARENA, MR. BOLT.
BUT I BELIEVE IN THE SYSTEM. IF YOU'RE REALLY THE BEST MAN FOR THE JOB...
...I TRUST THE AMERICAN PEOPLE TO VOTE FOR YOU WITHOUT MY SAY-SO!
GOOD LUCK!
AVENGERS MANSION.
ENDORSEMENTS. MOB SCENES. THIS IS COMPLETELY OUT OF HAND, CLINT.
AFTER ALL THESE YEARS, I'M USED TO THE CROWDS. IT'S GREAT TO WATCH PEOPLE GET BEHIND WHAT I STAND FOR, BUT LATELY--
-- LATELY THEY'RE ON YA LIKE BLACK ON A BOWLING BALL. YOU'RE SURPRISED? LOOK AT YOUR HOT STREAK!
YOU CAME BACK FROM THE DEAD AFTER ONSLAUGHT... YOU SAVED THE COUNTRY FROM HYDRA TERRORISTS, DECLARED WAR ON 'EM TO BOOT...
...GEEZ, I WISH I WERE THE MAN OF THE HOUR! YOU GET ANY BIGGER, THEY'LL MAKE YOU AN HONORARY SPICE GIRL! CRAMP YOUR STYLE, DOES IT?
NOT TO SOUND LIKE AN INGRATE...BUT YES.
I CAN'T FIGURE OUT HOW TO APPEAR IN PUBLIC ANYWHERE WITHOUT BEING POSITIVELY MOBBED!
WELL, I CAN THINK OF ONE WAY--
-- STEVE.
GRAB A COAT. LET'S GET A BURGER...
...MR. BIG SHOT.

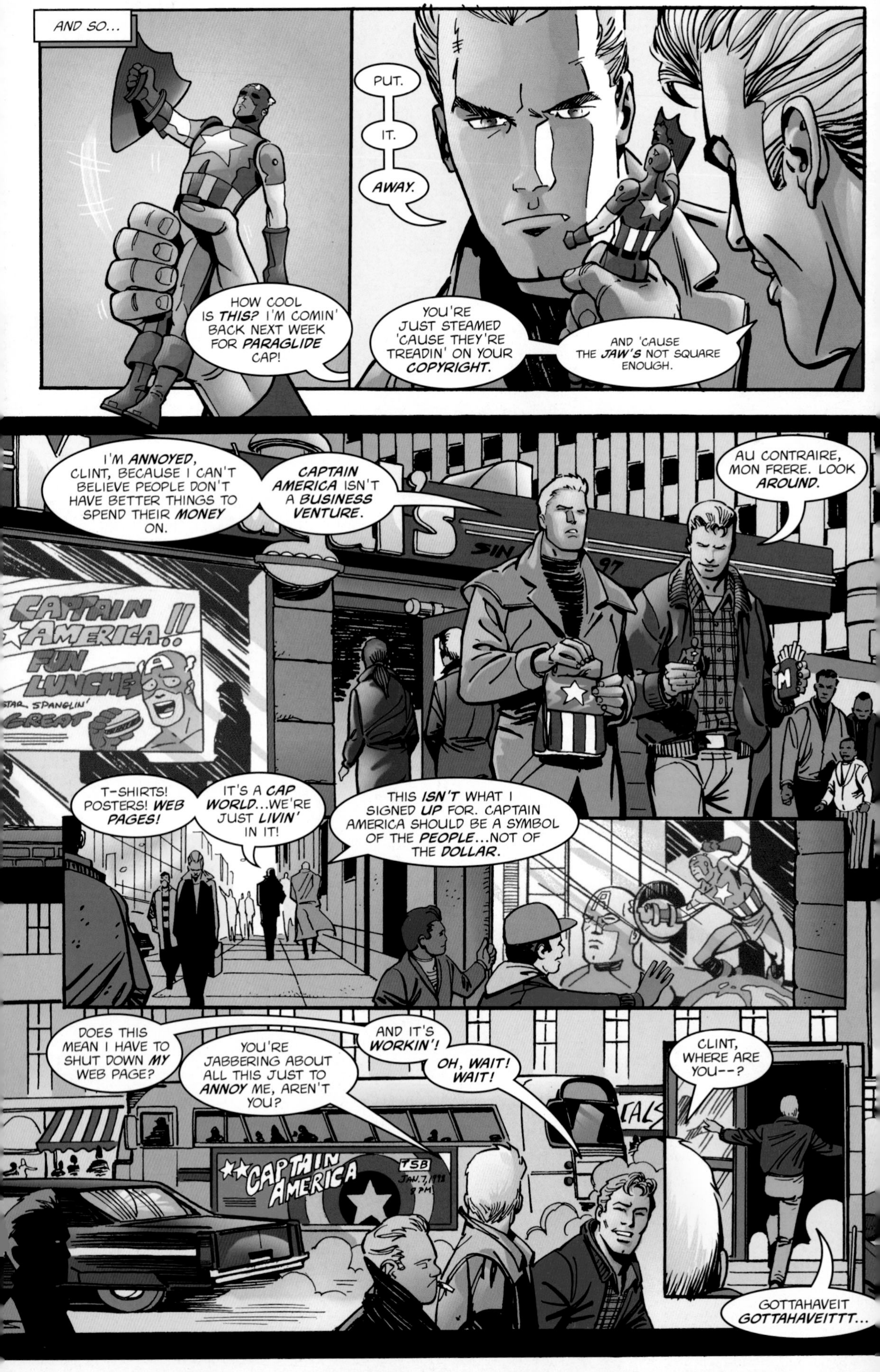
AND SO...
PUT.
IT.
AWAY.
HOW COOL IS THIS? I'M COMIN' BACK NEXT WEEK FOR PARAGLIDE CAP!
YOU'RE JUST STEAMED 'CAUSE THEY'RE TREADIN' ON YOUR COPYRIGHT.
AND 'CAUSE THE JAW'S NOT SQUARE ENOUGH.
I'M ANNOYED, CLINT, BECAUSE I CAN'T BELIEVE PEOPLE DON'T HAVE BETTER THINGS TO SPEND THEIR MONEY ON.
CAPTAIN AMERICA ISN'T A BUSINESS VENTURE.
AU CONTRAIRE, MON FRERE. LOOK AROUND.
CAPTAIN AMERICA!!
FUN LUNCHES
STAR SPANGLIN' GREAT
T-SHIRTS! POSTERS! WEB PAGES!
IT'S A CAP WORLD...WE'RE JUST LIVIN' IN IT!
THIS ISN'T WHAT I SIGNED UP FOR. CAPTAIN AMERICA SHOULD BE A SYMBOL OF THE PEOPLE...NOT OF THE DOLLAR.
DOES THIS MEAN I HAVE TO SHUT DOWN MY WEB PAGE?
AND IT'S WORKIN'!
YOU'RE JABBERING ABOUT ALL THIS JUST TO ANNOY ME, AREN'T YOU?
OH, WAIT! WAIT!
CLINT, WHERE ARE YOU--?
CAPTAIN AMERICA
TSB
JAN. 7, 1998
8 PM
GOTTAHAVEIT GOTTAHAVEITTT...

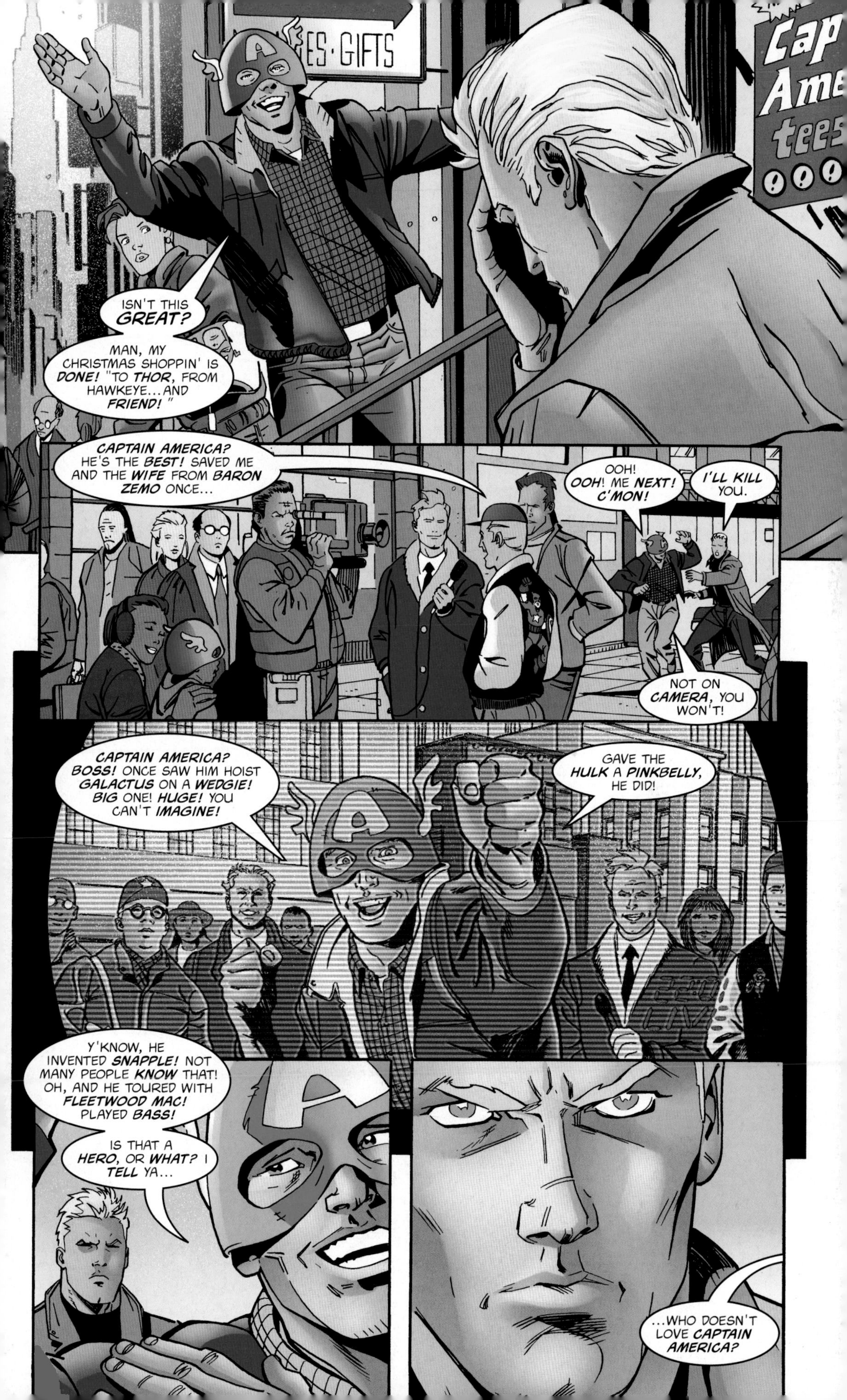

ES·GIFTS
Cap Ame tees
ISN'T THIS GREAT?
MAN, MY CHRISTMAS SHOPPIN' IS DONE! "TO THOR, FROM HAWKEYE...AND FRIEND!"
CAPTAIN AMERICA? HE'S THE BEST! SAVED ME AND THE WIFE FROM BARON ZEMO ONCE...
OOH! OOH! ME NEXT! C'MON!
I'LL KILL YOU.
NOT ON CAMERA, YOU WON'T!
CAPTAIN AMERICA? BOSS! ONCE SAW HIM HOIST GALACTUS ON A WEDGIE! BIG ONE! HUGE! YOU CAN'T IMAGINE!
GAVE THE HULK A PINKBELLY, HE DID!
Y'KNOW, HE INVENTED SNAPPLE! NOT MANY PEOPLE KNOW THAT! OH, AND HE TOURED WITH FLEETWOOD MAC! PLAYED BASS!
IS THAT A HERO, OR WHAT? I TELL YA...
...WHO DOESN'T LOVE CAPTAIN AMERICA?

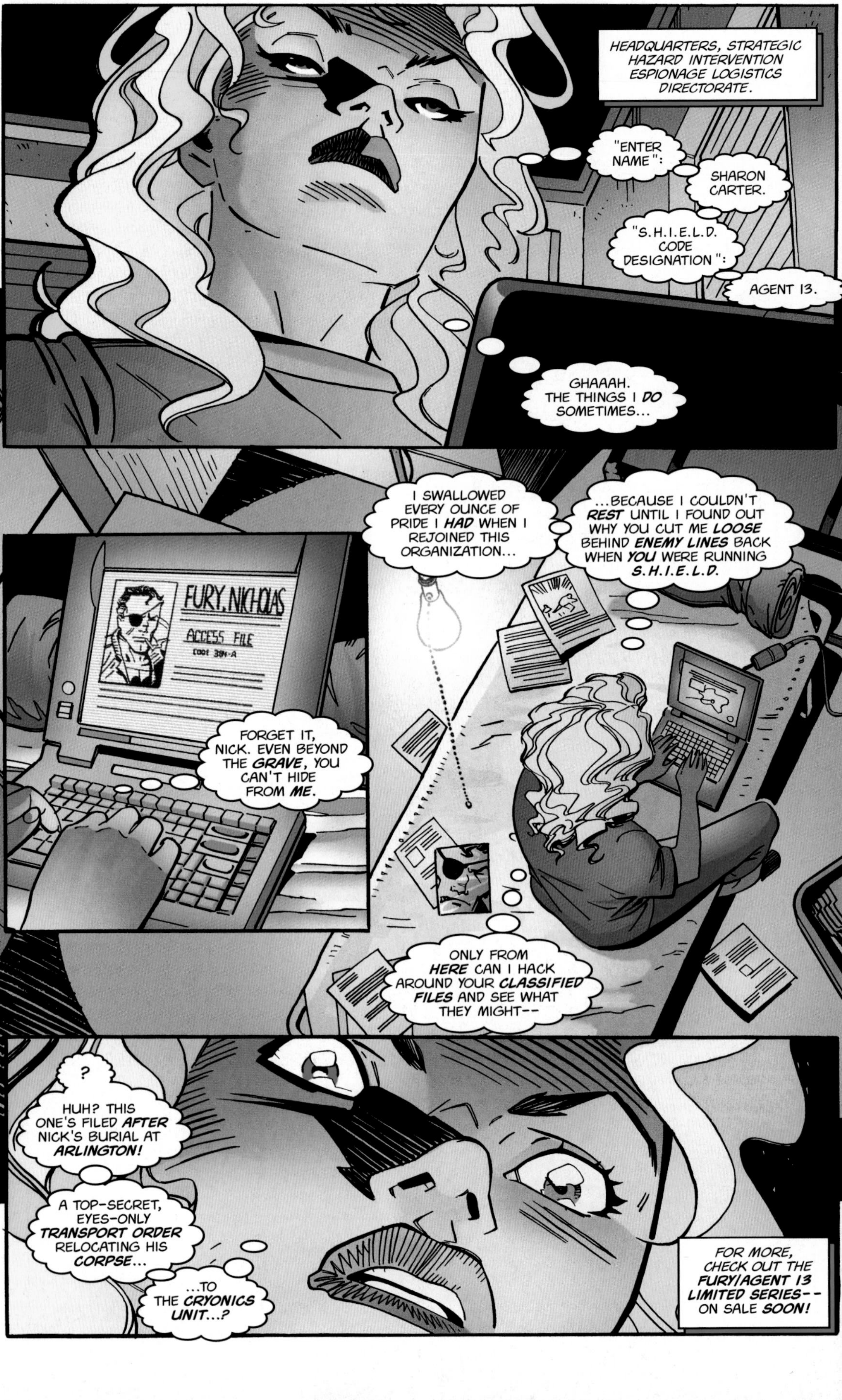
HEADQUARTERS, STRATEGIC HAZARD INTERVENTION ESPIONAGE LOGISTICS DIRECTORATE.
"ENTER NAME":
SHARON CARTER.
"S.H.I.E.L.D. CODE DESIGNATION":
AGENT 13.
GHAAAH. THE THINGS I DO SOMETIMES...
I SWALLOWED EVERY OUNCE OF PRIDE I HAD WHEN I REJOINED THIS ORGANIZATION...
...BECAUSE I COULDN'T REST UNTIL I FOUND OUT WHY YOU CUT ME LOOSE BEHIND ENEMY LINES BACK WHEN YOU WERE RUNNING S.H.I.E.L.D.
FURY, NICHOLAS
ACCESS FILE
FORGET IT, NICK. EVEN BEYOND THE GRAVE, YOU CAN'T HIDE FROM ME.
ONLY FROM HERE CAN I HACK AROUND YOUR CLASSIFIED FILES AND SEE WHAT THEY MIGHT--
?
HUH? THIS ONE'S FILED AFTER NICK'S BURIAL AT ARLINGTON!
A TOP-SECRET, EYES-ONLY TRANSPORT ORDER RELOCATING HIS CORPSE...
...TO THE CRYONICS UNIT...?
FOR MORE, CHECK OUT THE FURY/AGENT 13 LIMITED SERIES--ON SALE SOON!

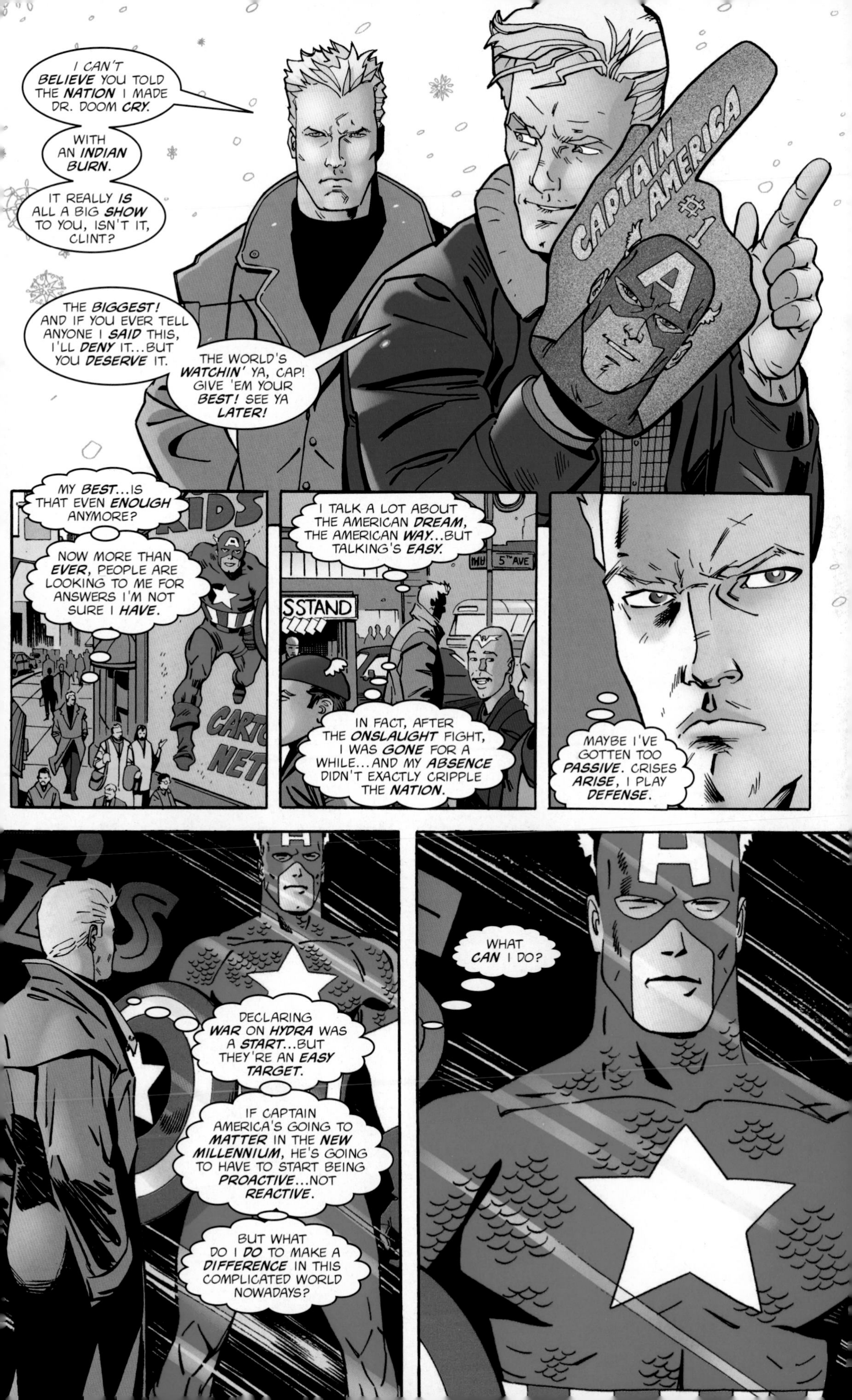
I CAN'T BELIEVE YOU TOLD THE NATION I MADE DR. DOOM CRY.
WITH AN INDIAN BURN.
IT REALLY IS ALL A BIG SHOW TO YOU, ISN'T IT, CLINT?
CAPTAIN AMERICA #1
THE BIGGEST! AND IF YOU EVER TELL ANYONE I SAID THIS, I'LL DENY IT...BUT YOU DESERVE IT.
THE WORLD'S WATCHIN' YA, CAP! GIVE 'EM YOUR BEST! SEE YA LATER!
MY BEST...IS THAT EVEN ENOUGH ANYMORE?
NOW MORE THAN EVER, PEOPLE ARE LOOKING TO ME FOR ANSWERS I'M NOT SURE I HAVE.
I TALK A LOT ABOUT THE AMERICAN DREAM, THE AMERICAN WAY...BUT TALKING'S EASY.
5TH AVE
SSTAND
IN FACT, AFTER THE ONSLAUGHT FIGHT, I WAS GONE FOR A WHILE...AND MY ABSENCE DIDN'T EXACTLY CRIPPLE THE NATION.
MAYBE I'VE GOTTEN TOO PASSIVE. CRISES ARISE, I PLAY DEFENSE.
DECLARING WAR ON HYDRA WAS A START...BUT THEY'RE AN EASY TARGET.
IF CAPTAIN AMERICA'S GOING TO MATTER IN THE NEW MILLENNIUM, HE'S GOING TO HAVE TO START BEING PROACTIVE...NOT REACTIVE.
BUT WHAT DO I DO TO MAKE A DIFFERENCE IN THIS COMPLICATED WORLD NOWADAYS?
WHAT CAN I DO?

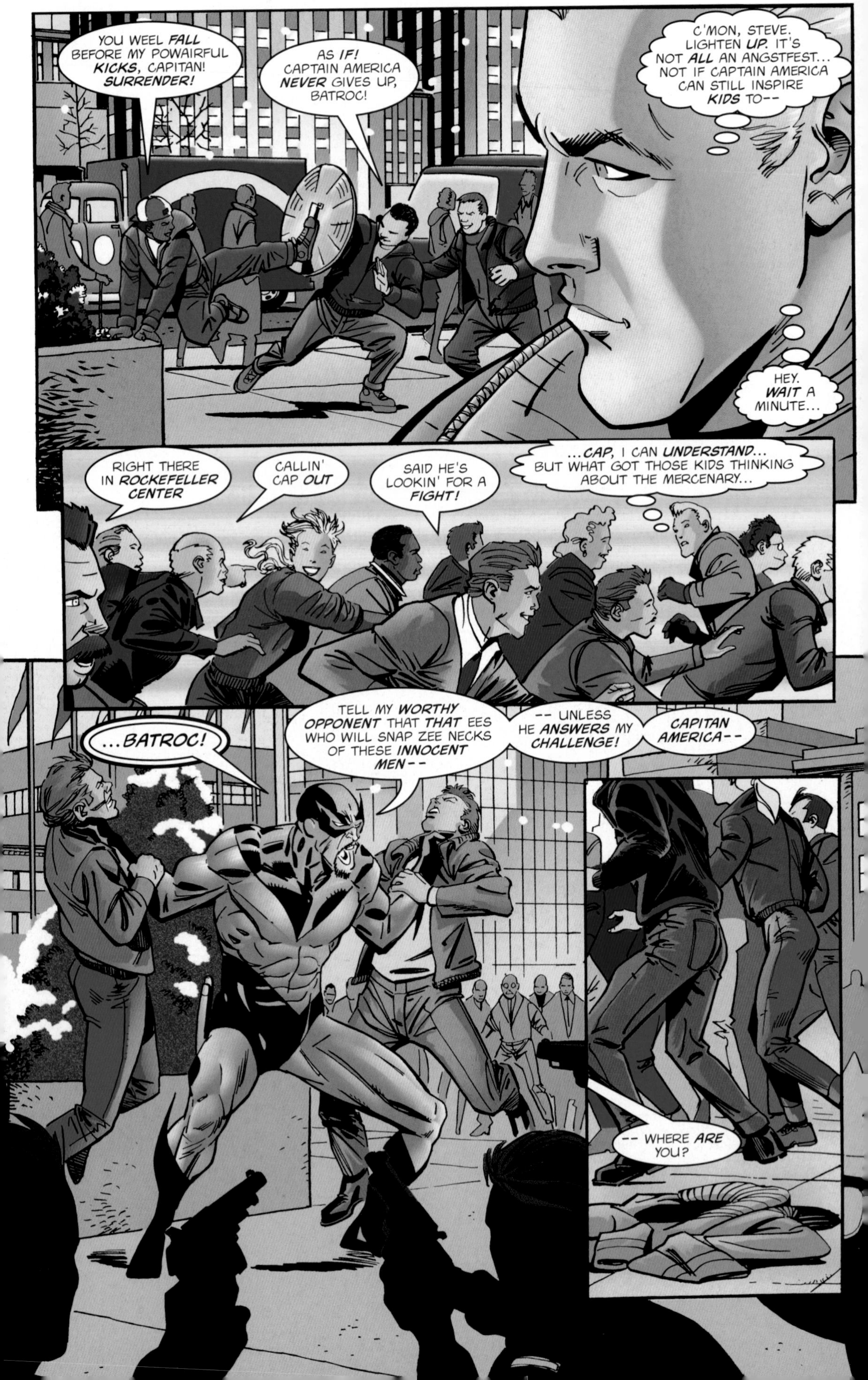
YOU WEEL FALL BEFORE MY POWAIRFUL KICKS, CAPITAN! SURRENDER!
AS IF! CAPTAIN AMERICA NEVER GIVES UP, BATROC!
C'MON, STEVE. LIGHTEN UP. IT'S NOT ALL AN ANGSTFEST... NOT IF CAPTAIN AMERICA CAN STILL INSPIRE KIDS TO--
HEY. WAIT A MINUTE...
RIGHT THERE IN ROCKEFELLER CENTER
CALLIN' CAP OUT
SAID HE'S LOOKIN' FOR A FIGHT!
...CAP, I CAN UNDERSTAND... BUT WHAT GOT THOSE KIDS THINKING ABOUT THE MERCENARY...
...BATROC!
TELL MY WORTHY OPPONENT THAT THAT EES WHO WILL SNAP ZEE NECKS OF THESE INNOCENT MEN--
-- UNLESS HE ANSWERS MY CHALLENGE!
CAPITAN AMERICA--
-- WHERE ARE YOU?

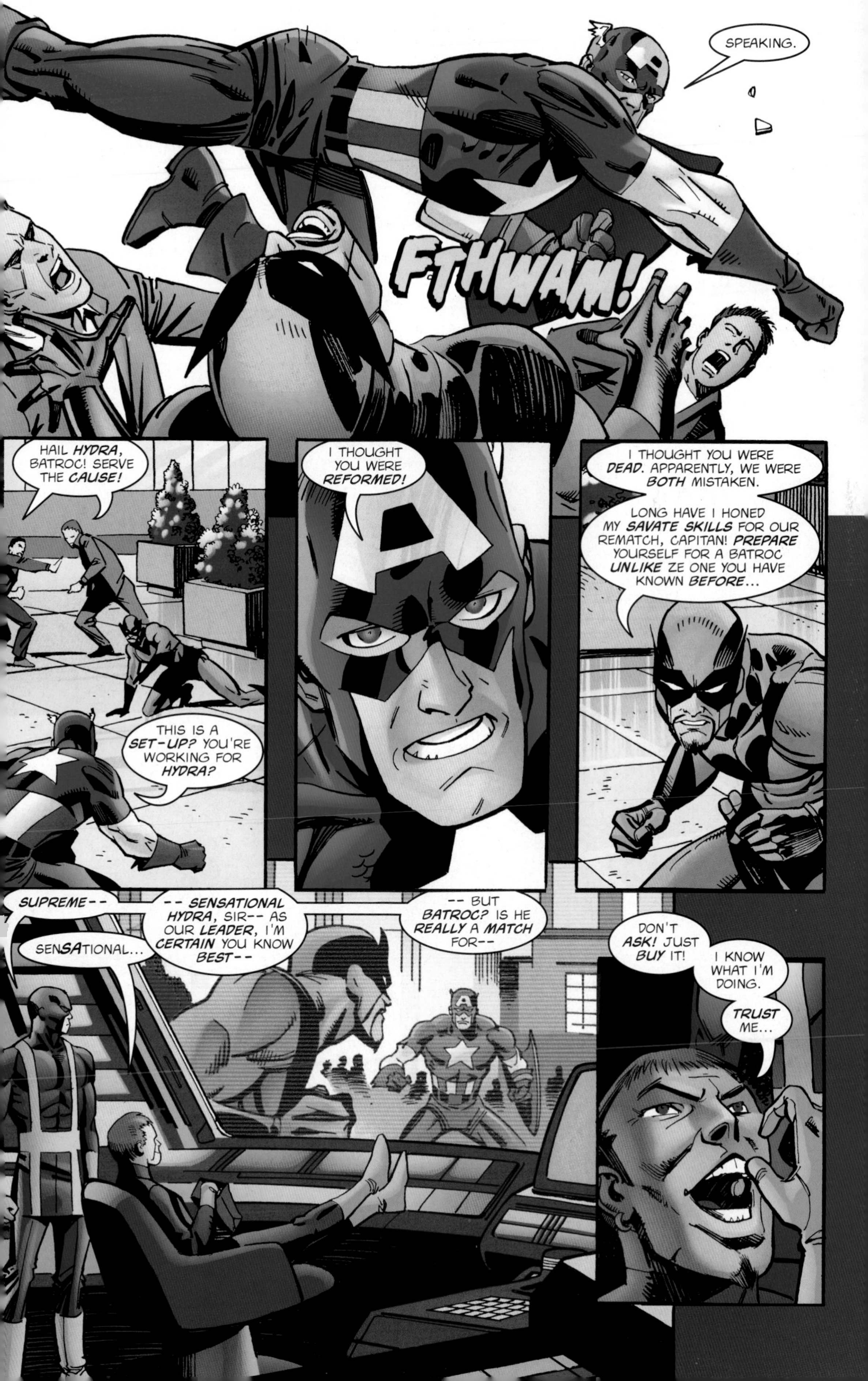
SPEAKING.
FTHWAM!
HAIL HYDRA, BATROC! SERVE THE CAUSE!
THIS IS A SET-UP? YOU'RE WORKING FOR HYDRA?
I THOUGHT YOU WERE REFORMED!
I THOUGHT YOU WERE DEAD. APPARENTLY, WE WERE BOTH MISTAKEN.
LONG HAVE I HONED MY SAVATE SKILLS FOR OUR REMATCH, CAPITAN! PREPARE YOURSELF FOR A BATROC UNLIKE ZE ONE YOU HAVE KNOWN BEFORE...
SUPREME--
SENSATIONAL...
-- SENSATIONAL HYDRA, SIR-- AS OUR LEADER, I'M CERTAIN YOU KNOW BEST--
-- BUT BATROC? IS HE REALLY A MATCH FOR--
DON'T ASK! JUST BUY IT!
I KNOW WHAT I'M DOING.
TRUST ME...

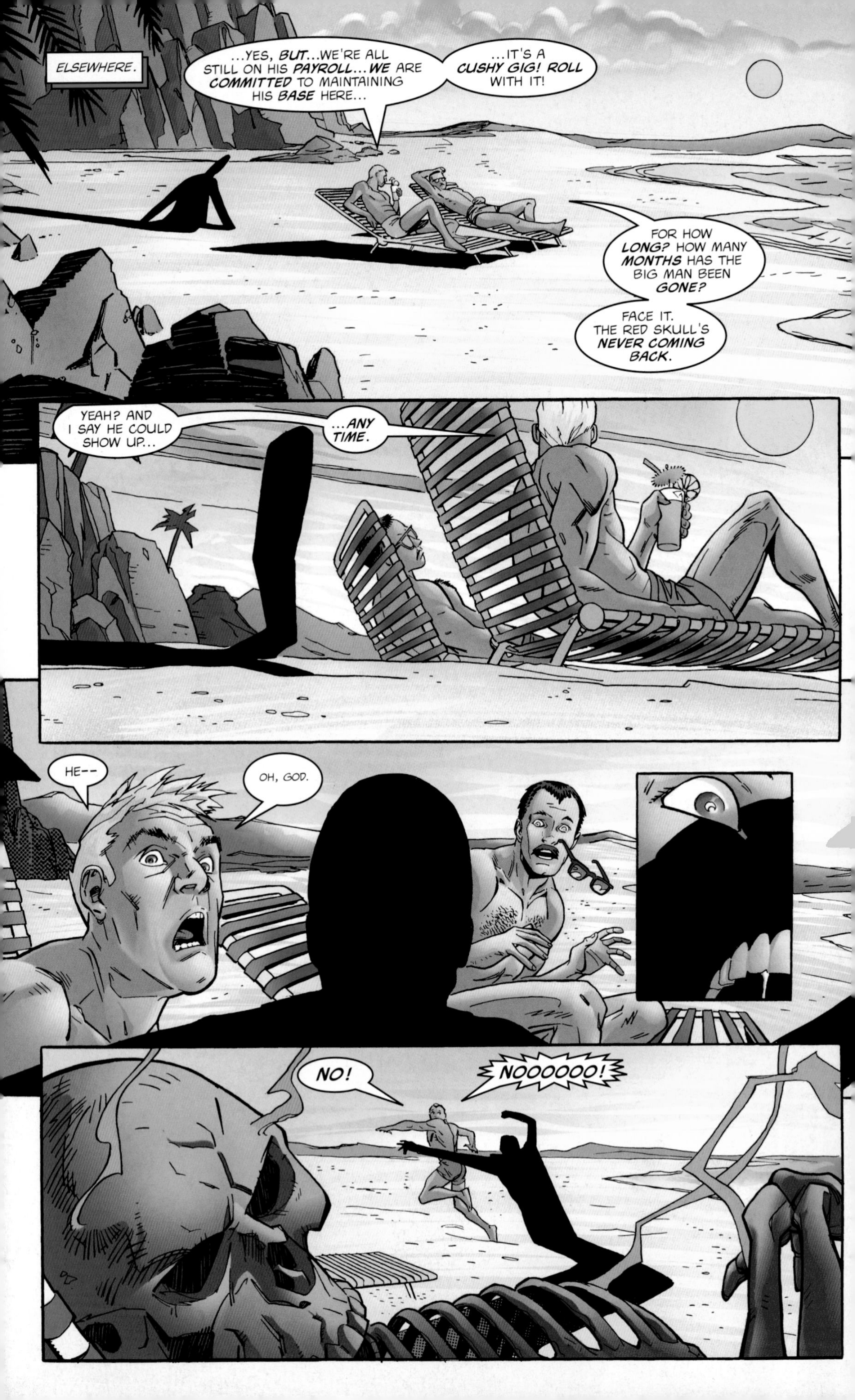
ELSEWHERE.
...YES, BUT...WE'RE ALL STILL ON HIS PAYROLL...WE ARE COMMITTED TO MAINTAINING HIS BASE HERE...
...IT'S A CUSHY GIG! ROLL WITH IT!
FOR HOW LONG? HOW MANY MONTHS HAS THE BIG MAN BEEN GONE?
FACE IT. THE RED SKULL'S NEVER COMING BACK.
YEAH? AND I SAY HE COULD SHOW UP...
...ANY TIME.
HE--
OH, GOD.
NO!
NOOOOOO!

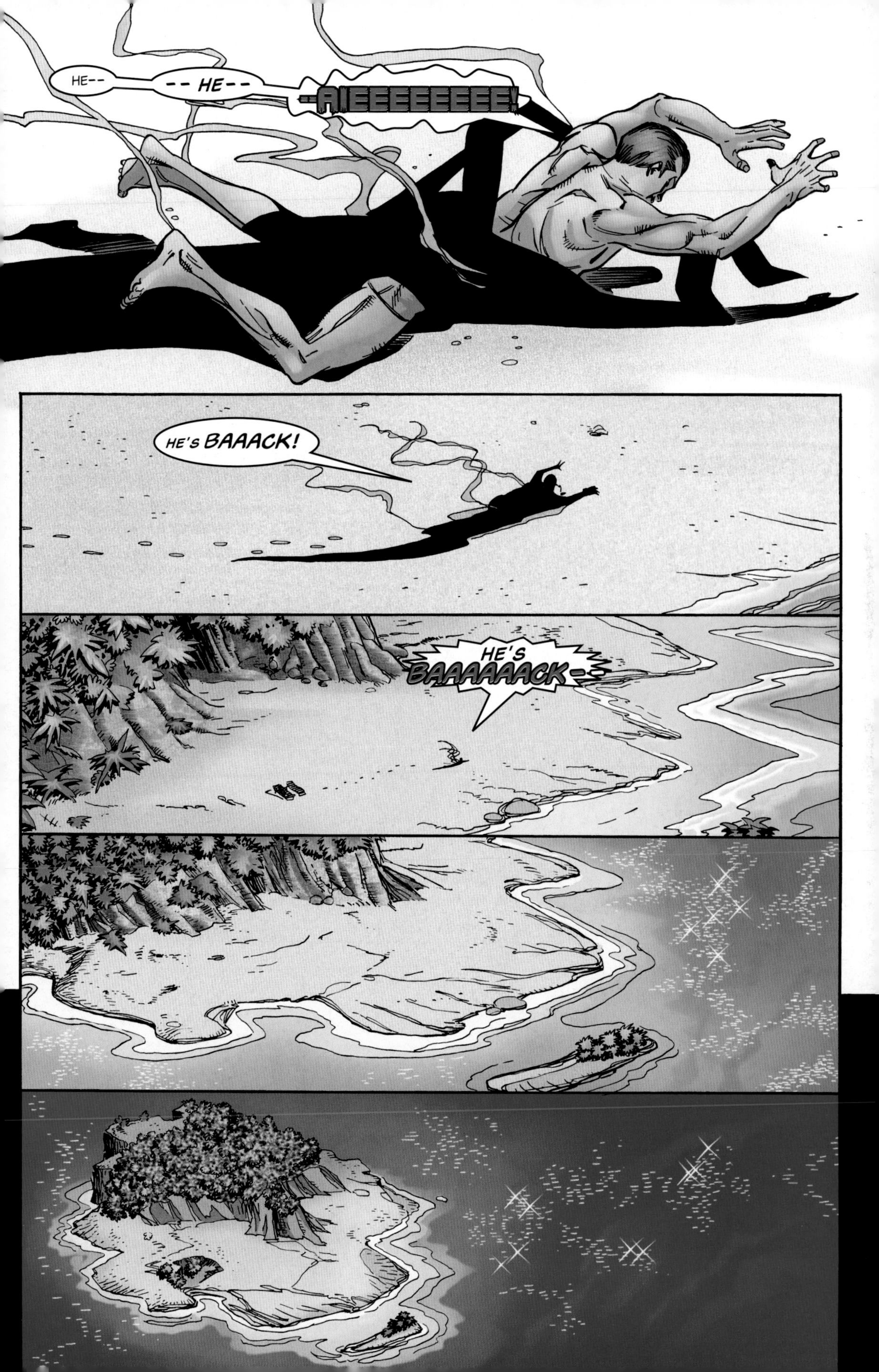
HE--
-- HE--
--AIEEEEEEEEE!
HE'S BAAACK!
HE'S BAAAAAACK--

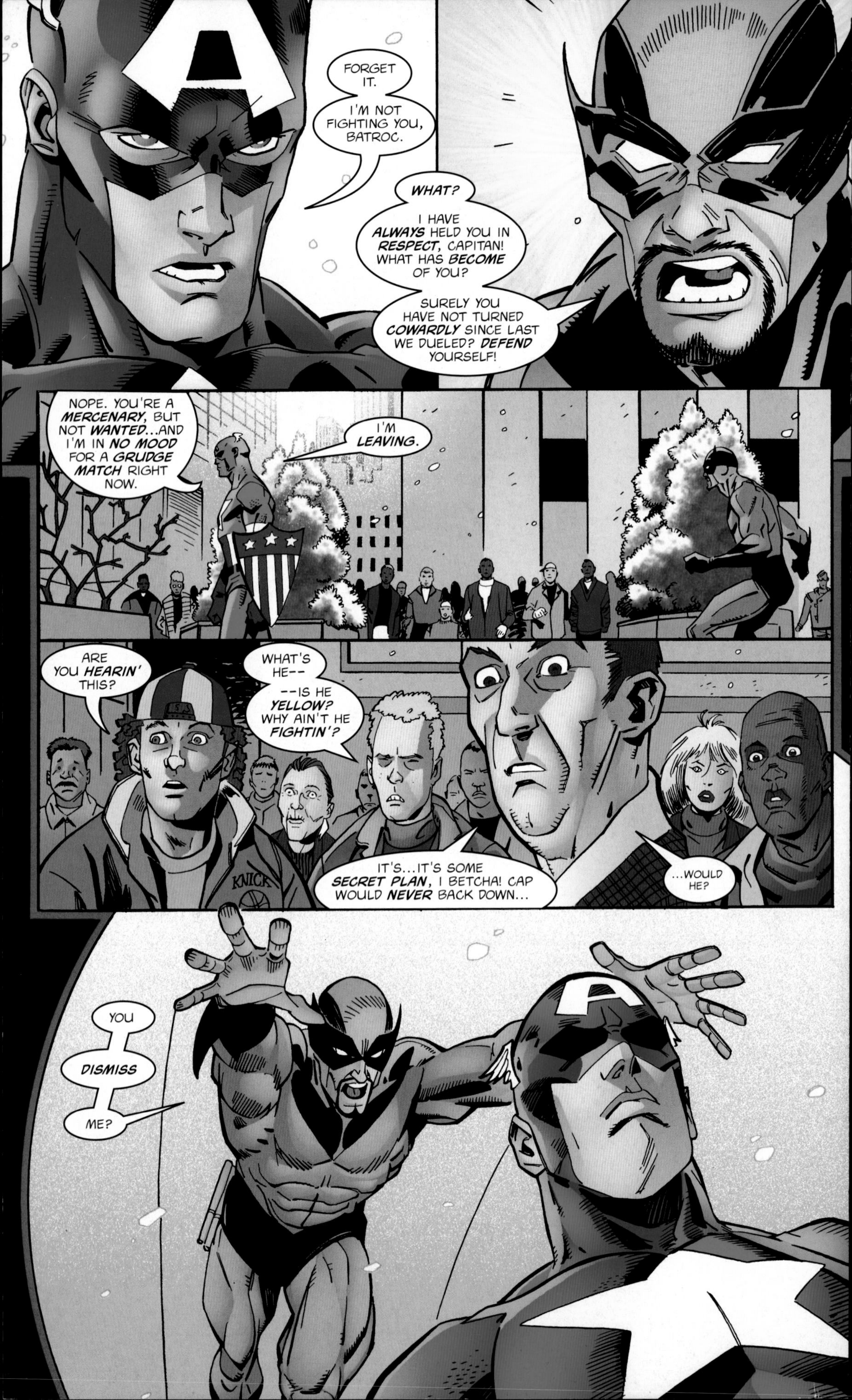
FORGET IT.
I'M NOT FIGHTING YOU, BATROC.
WHAT?
I HAVE ALWAYS HELD YOU IN RESPECT, CAPITAN! WHAT HAS BECOME OF YOU?
SURELY YOU HAVE NOT TURNED COWARDLY SINCE LAST WE DUELED? DEFEND YOURSELF!
NOPE. YOU'RE A MERCENARY, BUT NOT WANTED...AND I'M IN NO MOOD FOR A GRUDGE MATCH RIGHT NOW.
I'M LEAVING.
ARE YOU HEARIN' THIS?
WHAT'S HE--
--IS HE YELLOW? WHY AIN'T HE FIGHTIN'?
IT'S...IT'S SOME SECRET PLAN, I BETCHA! CAP WOULD NEVER BACK DOWN...
...WOULD HE?
KNICK
YOU
DISMISS
ME?

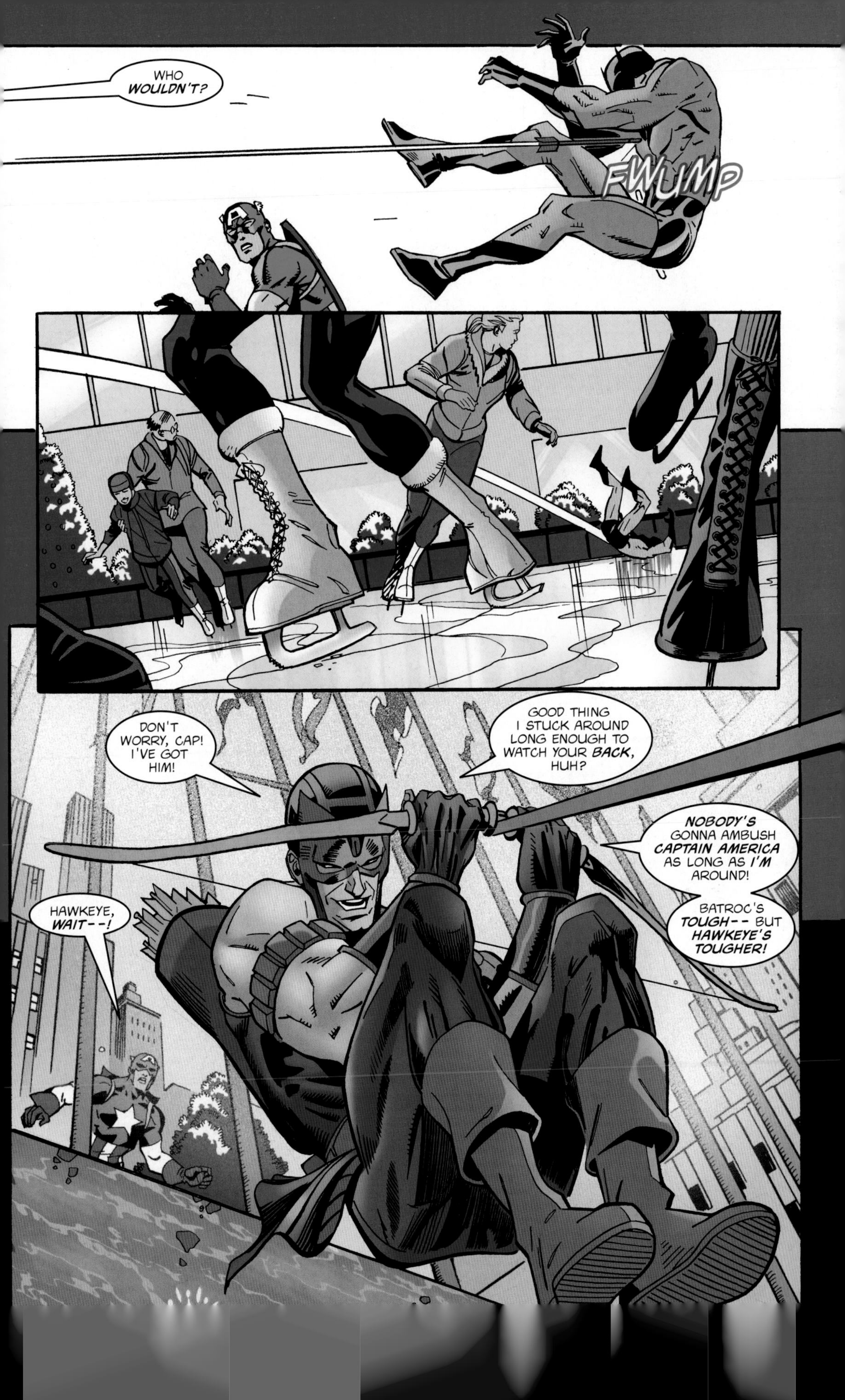
WHO WOULDN'T?
FWUMP
DON'T WORRY, CAP! I'VE GOT HIM!
GOOD THING I STUCK AROUND LONG ENOUGH TO WATCH YOUR BACK, HUH?
HAWKEYE, WAIT--!
NOBODY'S GONNA AMBUSH CAPTAIN AMERICA AS LONG AS I'M AROUND!
BATROC'S TOUGH-- BUT HAWKEYE'S TOUGHER!

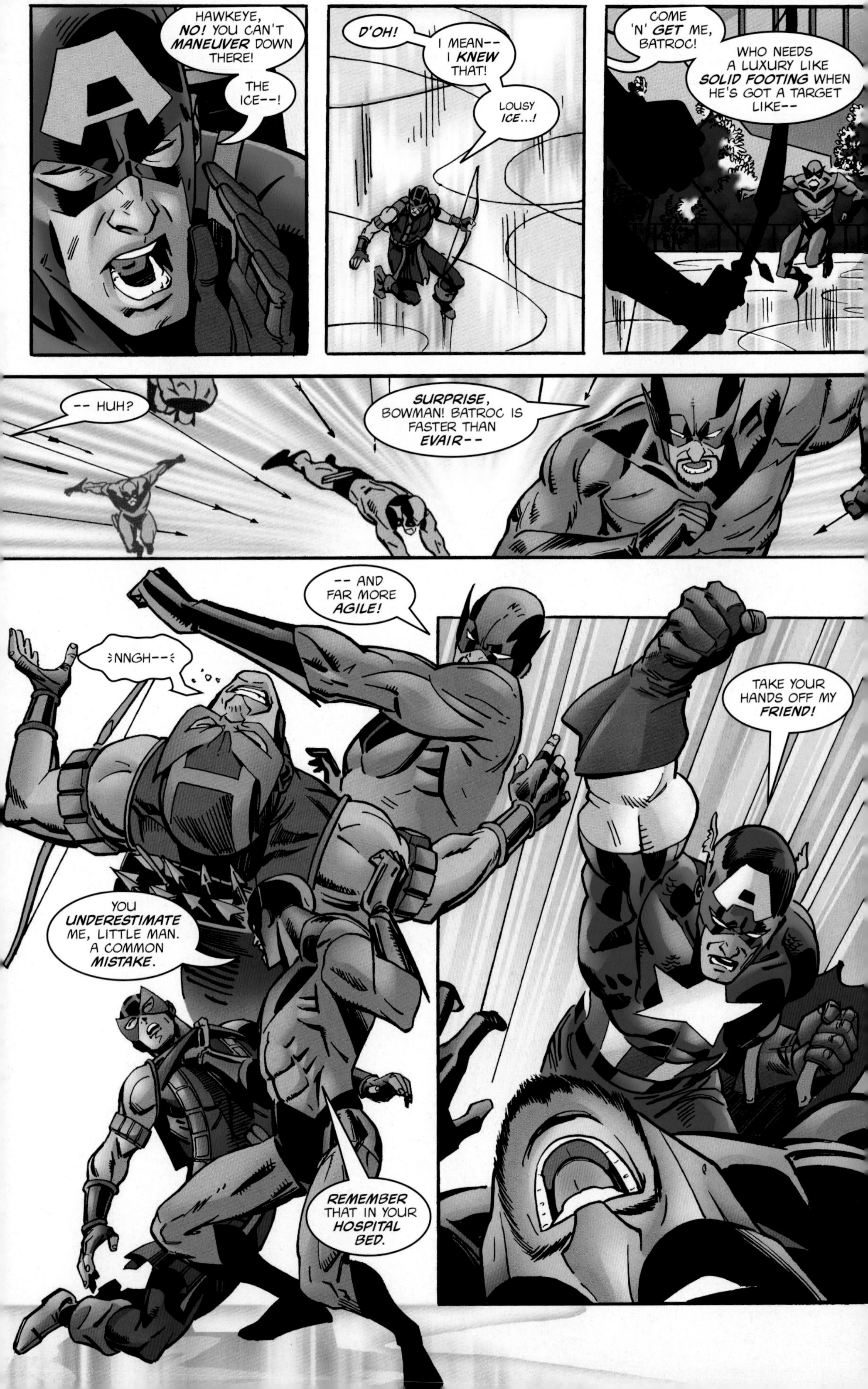
HAWKEYE, NO! YOU CAN'T MANEUVER DOWN THERE!
THE ICE--!
D'OH!
I MEAN-- I KNEW THAT!
LOUSY ICE...!
COME 'N' GET ME, BATROC!
WHO NEEDS A LUXURY LIKE SOLID FOOTING WHEN HE'S GOT A TARGET LIKE--
-- HUH?
SURPRISE, BOWMAN! BATROC IS FASTER THAN EVAIR--
-- AND FAR MORE AGILE!
NNGH--
YOU UNDERESTIMATE ME, LITTLE MAN. A COMMON MISTAKE.
REMEMBER THAT IN YOUR HOSPITAL BED.
TAKE YOUR HANDS OFF MY FRIEND!

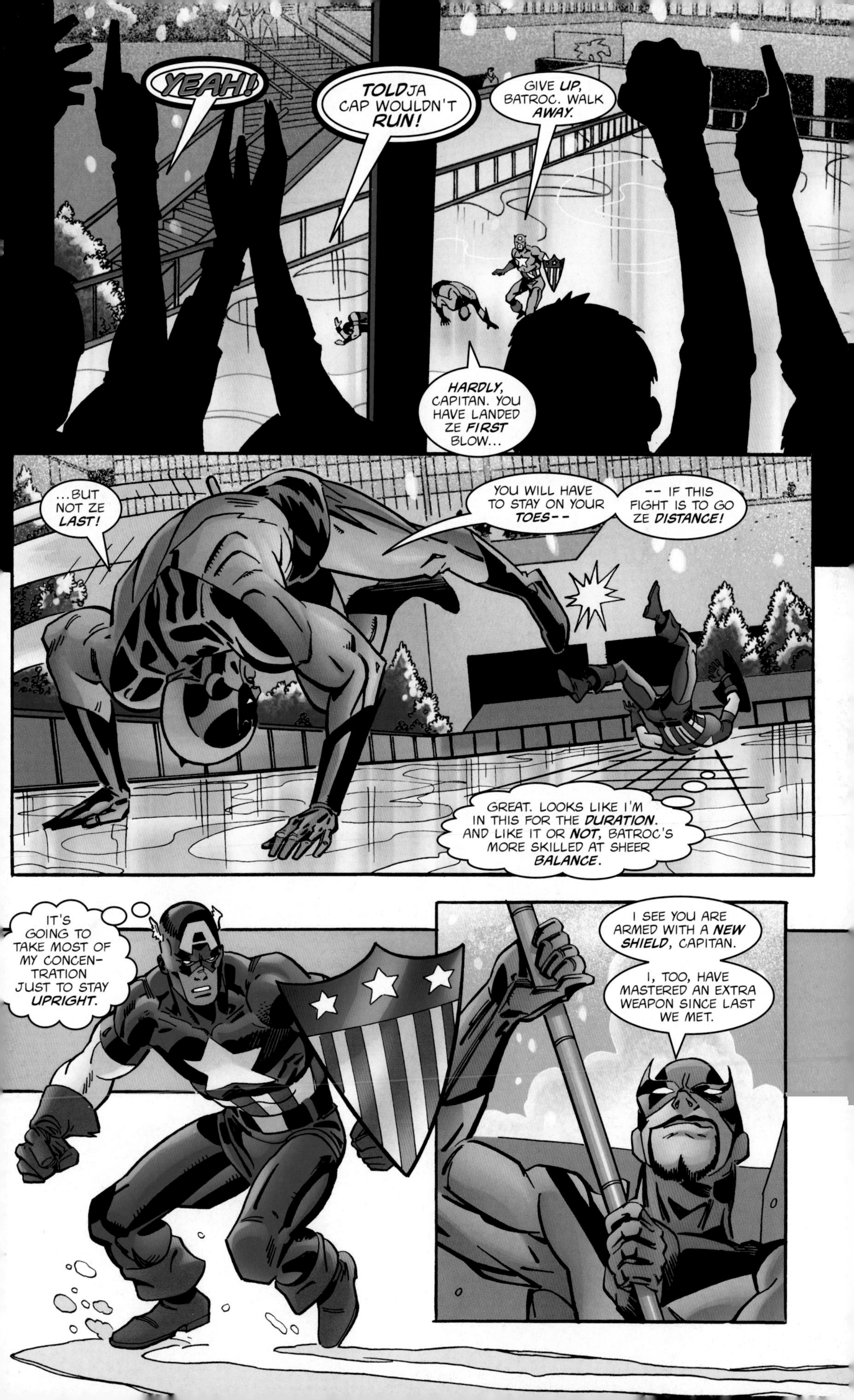
YEAH!
TOLDJA CAP WOULDN'T RUN!
GIVE UP, BATROC. WALK AWAY.
HARDLY, CAPITAN. YOU HAVE LANDED ZE FIRST BLOW...
...BUT NOT ZE LAST!
YOU WILL HAVE TO STAY ON YOUR TOES--
-- IF THIS FIGHT IS TO GO ZE DISTANCE!
GREAT. LOOKS LIKE I'M IN THIS FOR THE DURATION. AND LIKE IT OR NOT, BATROC'S MORE SKILLED AT SHEER BALANCE.
IT'S GOING TO TAKE MOST OF MY CONCENTRATION JUST TO STAY UPRIGHT.
I SEE YOU ARE ARMED WITH A NEW SHIELD, CAPITAN.
I, TOO, HAVE MASTERED AN EXTRA WEAPON SINCE LAST WE MET.

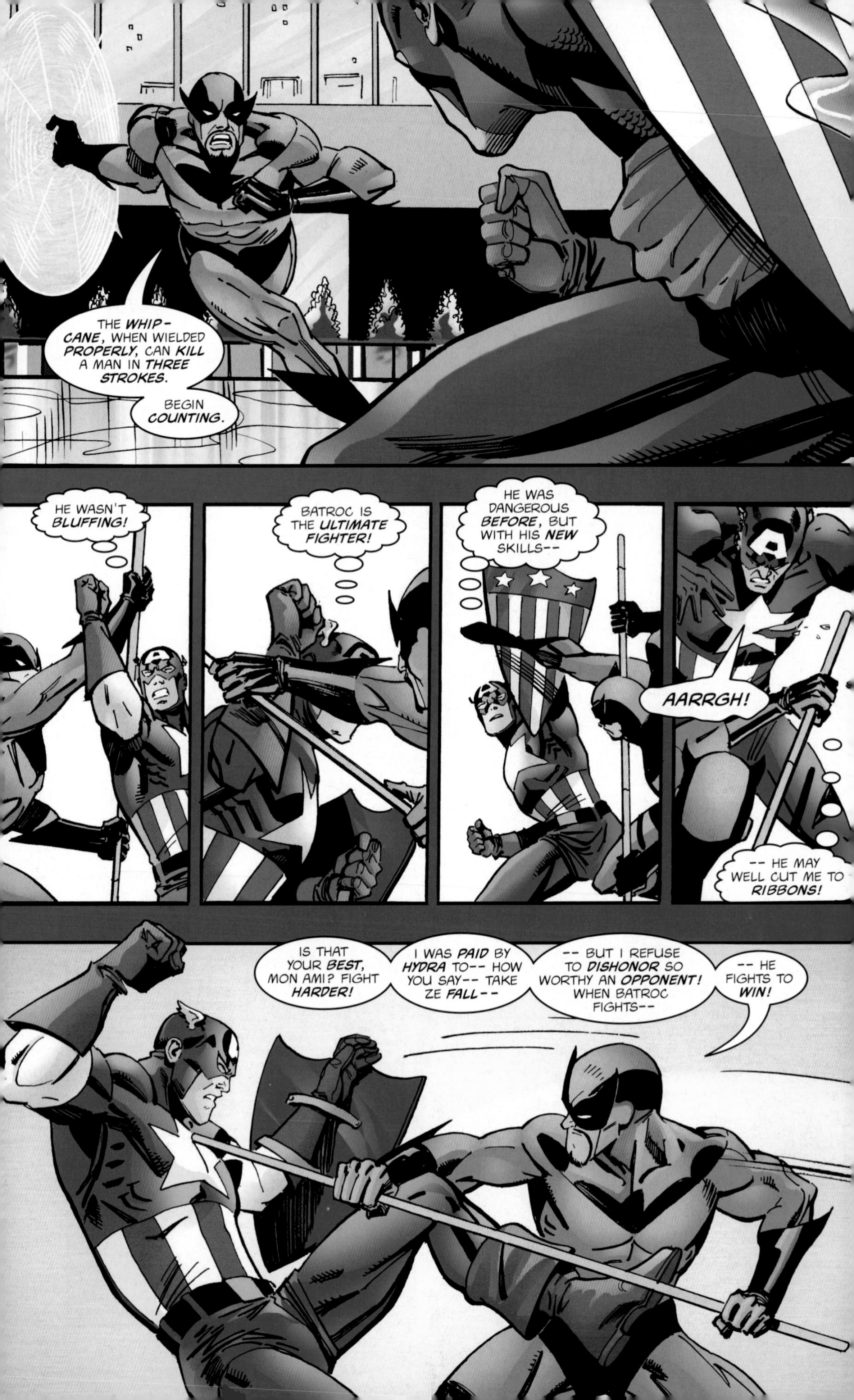
THE WHIP-CANE, WHEN WIELDED PROPERLY, CAN KILL A MAN IN THREE STROKES.
BEGIN COUNTING.
HE WASN'T BLUFFING!
BATROC IS THE ULTIMATE FIGHTER!
HE WAS DANGEROUS BEFORE, BUT WITH HIS NEW SKILLS--
AARRGH!
-- HE MAY WELL CUT ME TO RIBBONS!
IS THAT YOUR BEST, MON AMI? FIGHT HARDER!
I WAS PAID BY HYDRA TO-- HOW YOU SAY-- TAKE ZE FALL--
-- BUT I REFUSE TO DISHONOR SO WORTHY AN OPPONENT! WHEN BATROC FIGHTS--
-- HE FIGHTS TO WIN!

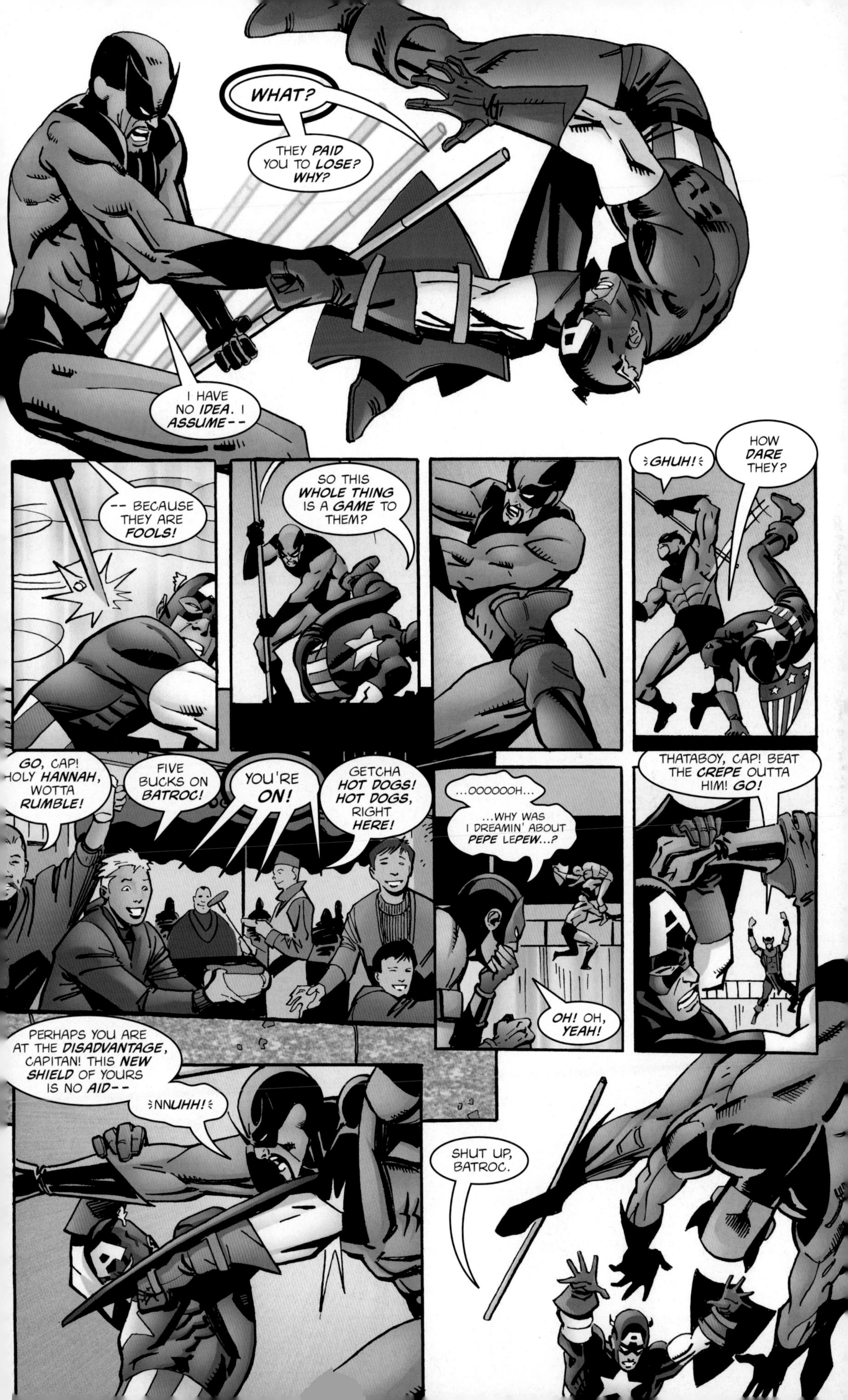
WHAT?
THEY PAID YOU TO LOSE? WHY?
I HAVE NO IDEA. I ASSUME--
-- BECAUSE THEY ARE FOOLS!
SO THIS WHOLE THING IS A GAME TO THEM?
GHUH!
HOW DARE THEY?
GO, CAP! HOLY HANNAH, WOTTA RUMBLE!
FIVE BUCKS ON BATROC!
YOU'RE ON!
GETCHA HOT DOGS! HOT DOGS, RIGHT HERE!
...OOOOOOH...
...WHY WAS I DREAMIN' ABOUT PEPE LEPEW...?
OH! OH, YEAH!
THATABOY, CAP! BEAT THE CREPE OUTTA HIM! GO!
PERHAPS YOU ARE AT THE DISADVANTAGE, CAPITAN! THIS NEW SHIELD OF YOURS IS NO AID--
NNUHH!
SHUT UP, BATROC.

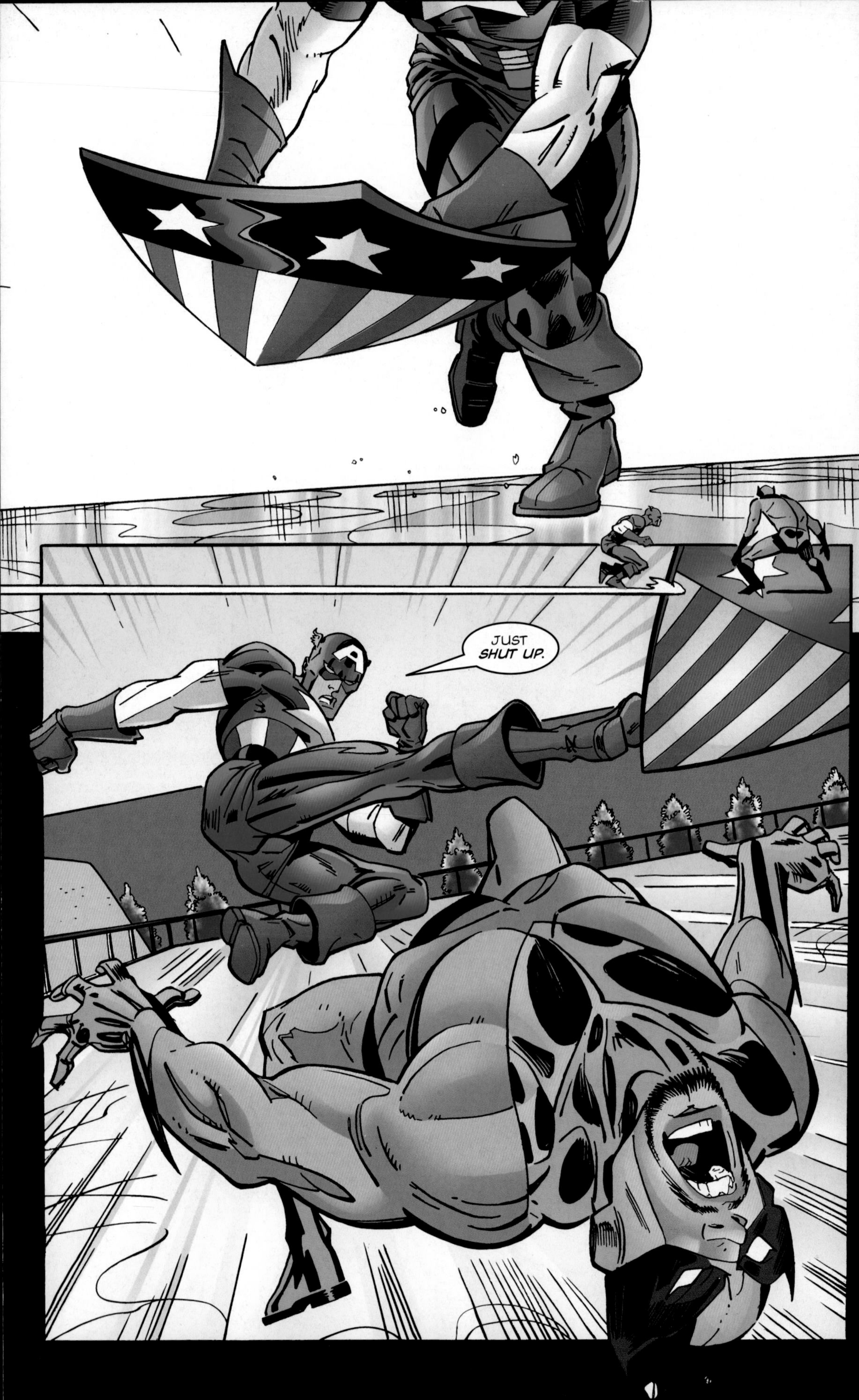
JUST SHUT UP.

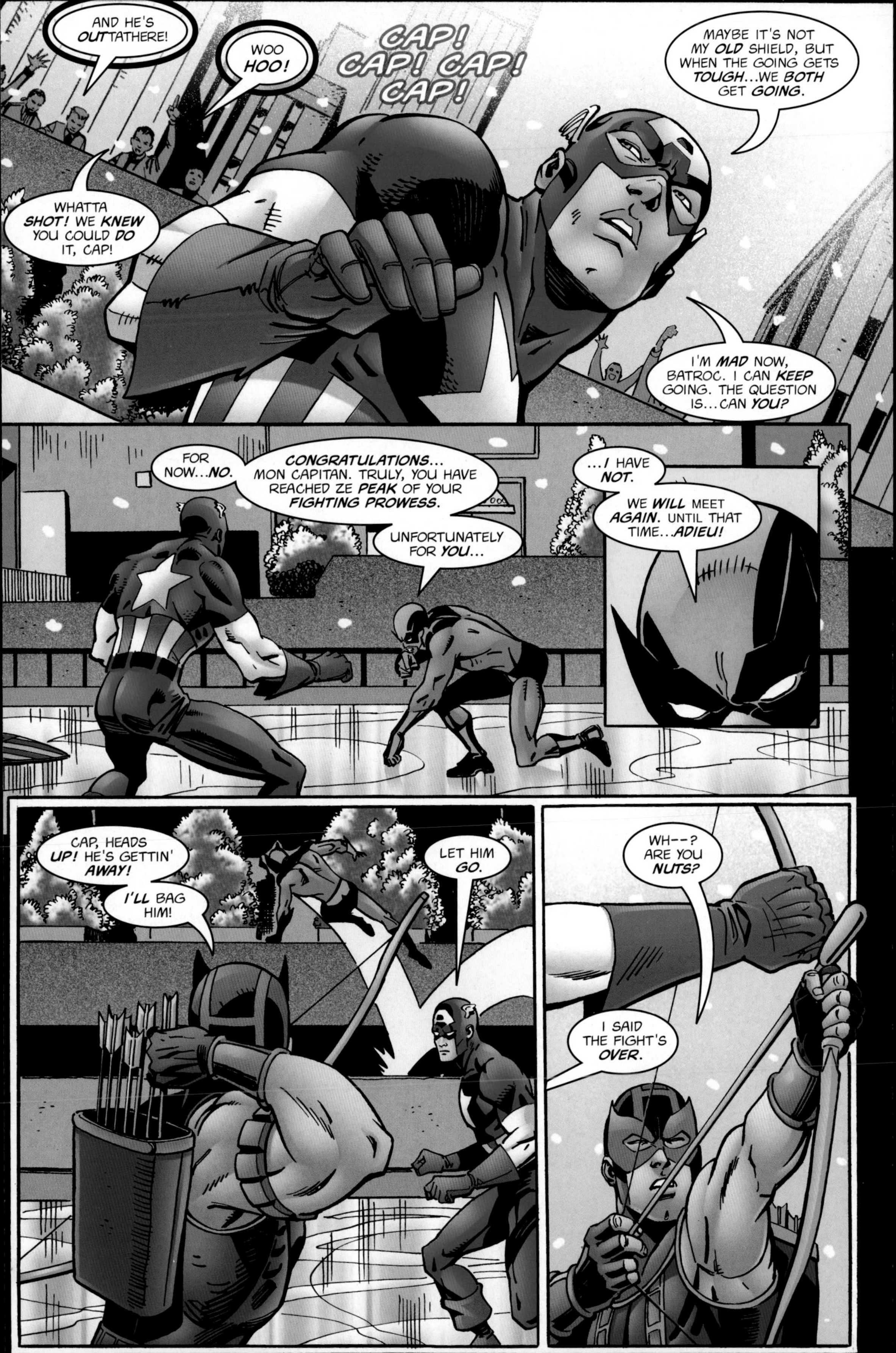

AND HE'S OUTTATHERE!
WOO HOO!
CAP! CAP! CAP! CAP!
MAYBE IT'S NOT MY OLD SHIELD, BUT WHEN THE GOING GETS TOUGH...WE BOTH GET GOING.
WHATTA SHOT! WE KNEW YOU COULD DO IT, CAP!
I'M MAD NOW, BATROC. I CAN KEEP GOING. THE QUESTION IS...CAN YOU?
CONGRATULATIONS... MON CAPITAN. TRULY, YOU HAVE REACHED ZE PEAK OF YOUR FIGHTING PROWESS.
FOR NOW...NO.
UNFORTUNATELY FOR YOU...
...I HAVE NOT.
WE WILL MEET AGAIN. UNTIL THAT TIME...ADIEU!
CAP, HEADS UP! HE'S GETTIN' AWAY!
I'LL BAG HIM!
LET HIM GO.
WH--? ARE YOU NUTS?
I SAID THE FIGHT'S OVER.

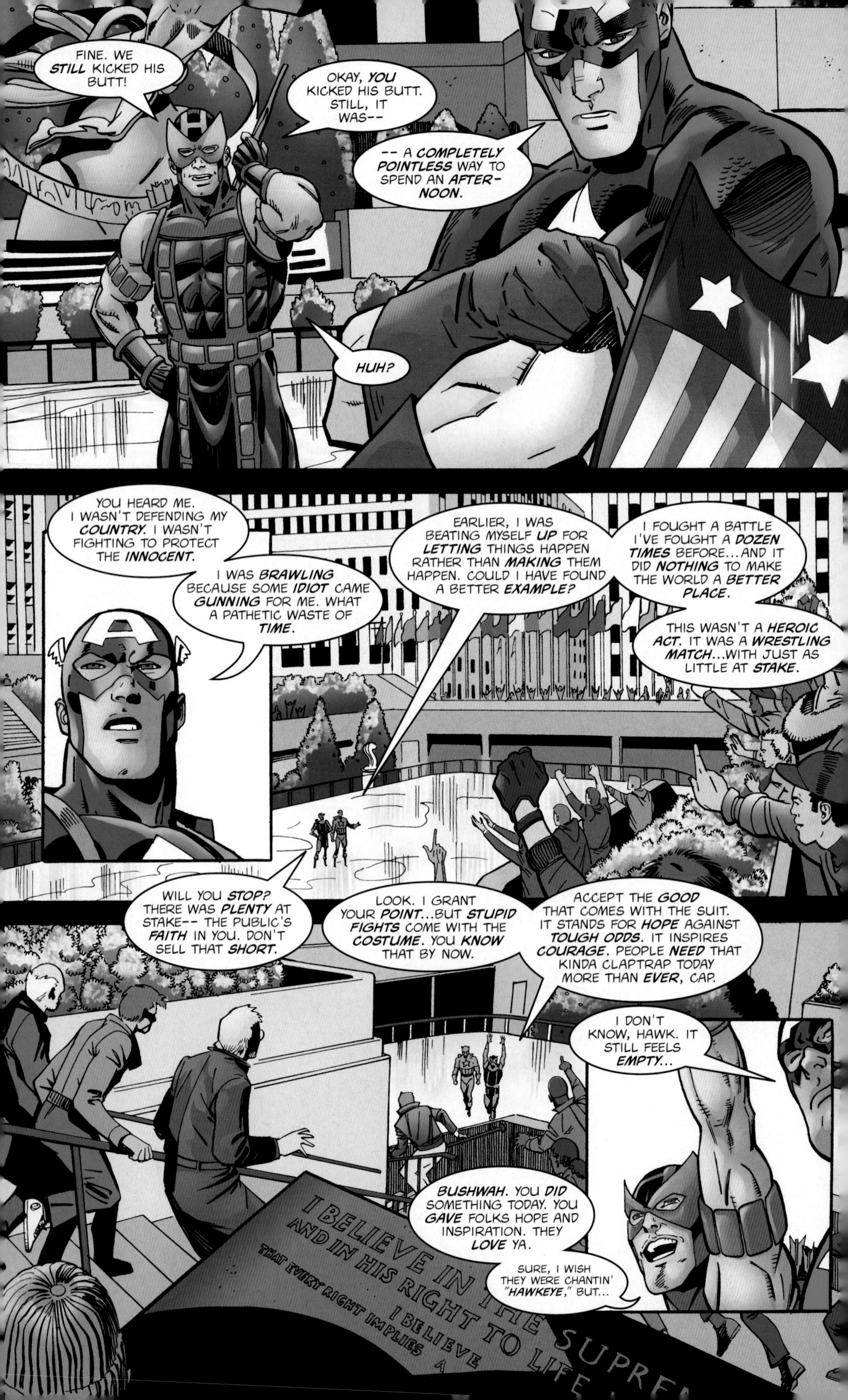

FINE. WE STILL KICKED HIS BUTT!
OKAY, YOU KICKED HIS BUTT. STILL, IT WAS--
-- A COMPLETELY POINTLESS WAY TO SPEND AN AFTER-NOON.
HUH?
YOU HEARD ME. I WASN'T DEFENDING MY COUNTRY. I WASN'T FIGHTING TO PROTECT THE INNOCENT.
I WAS BRAWLING BECAUSE SOME IDIOT CAME GUNNING FOR ME. WHAT A PATHETIC WASTE OF TIME.
EARLIER, I WAS BEATING MYSELF UP FOR LETTING THINGS HAPPEN RATHER THAN MAKING THEM HAPPEN. COULD I HAVE FOUND A BETTER EXAMPLE?
I FOUGHT A BATTLE I'VE FOUGHT A DOZEN TIMES BEFORE...AND IT DID NOTHING TO MAKE THE WORLD A BETTER PLACE.
THIS WASN'T A HEROIC ACT. IT WAS A WRESTLING MATCH...WITH JUST AS LITTLE AT STAKE.
WILL YOU STOP? THERE WAS PLENTY AT STAKE-- THE PUBLIC'S FAITH IN YOU. DON'T SELL THAT SHORT.
LOOK. I GRANT YOUR POINT...BUT STUPID FIGHTS COME WITH THE COSTUME. YOU KNOW THAT BY NOW.
ACCEPT THE GOOD THAT COMES WITH THE SUIT. IT STANDS FOR HOPE AGAINST TOUGH ODDS. IT INSPIRES COURAGE. PEOPLE NEED THAT KINDA CLAPTRAP TODAY MORE THAN EVER, CAP.
I DON'T KNOW, HAWK. IT STILL FEELS EMPTY...
BUSHWAH. YOU DID SOMETHING TODAY. YOU GAVE FOLKS HOPE AND INSPIRATION. THEY LOVE YA.
SURE, I WISH THEY WERE CHANTIN' "HAWKEYE," BUT...
I BELIEVE IN THE
AND IN HIS RIGHT TO LIFE
THAT EVERY RIGHT IMPLIES A
I BELIEVE

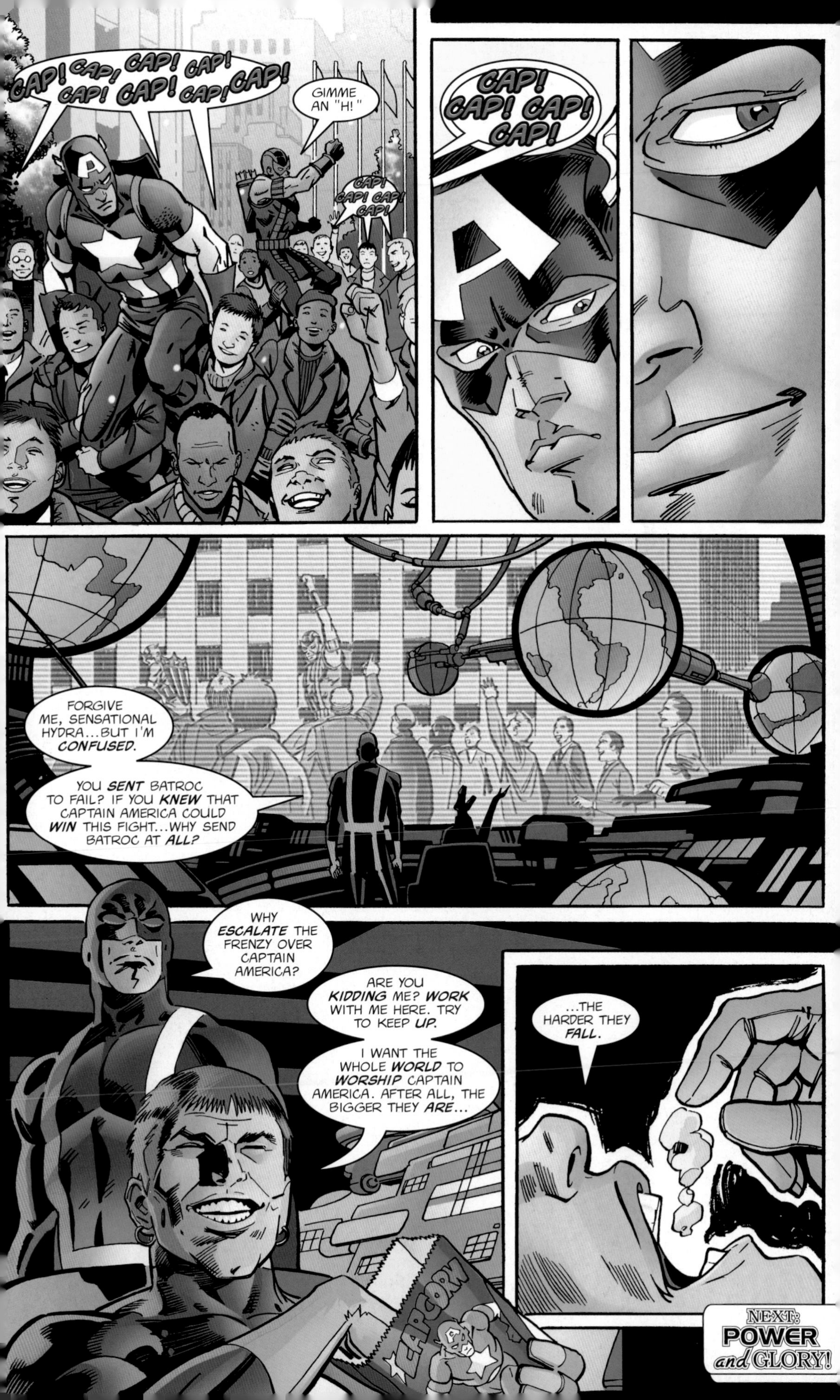
CAP! CAP! CAP! CAP! CAP! CAP! CAP! CAP!
GIMME AN "H!"
CAP! CAP! CAP! CAP!
CAP! CAP! CAP! CAP!
FORGIVE ME, SENSATIONAL HYDRA...BUT I'M CONFUSED.
YOU SENT BATROC TO FAIL? IF YOU KNEW THAT CAPTAIN AMERICA COULD WIN THIS FIGHT...WHY SEND BATROC AT ALL?
WHY ESCALATE THE FRENZY OVER CAPTAIN AMERICA?
ARE YOU KIDDING ME? WORK WITH ME HERE. TRY TO KEEP UP.
I WANT THE WHOLE WORLD TO WORSHIP CAPTAIN AMERICA. AFTER ALL, THE BIGGER THEY ARE...
...THE HARDER THEY FALL.
CAPCORN
NEXT: POWER and GLORY!

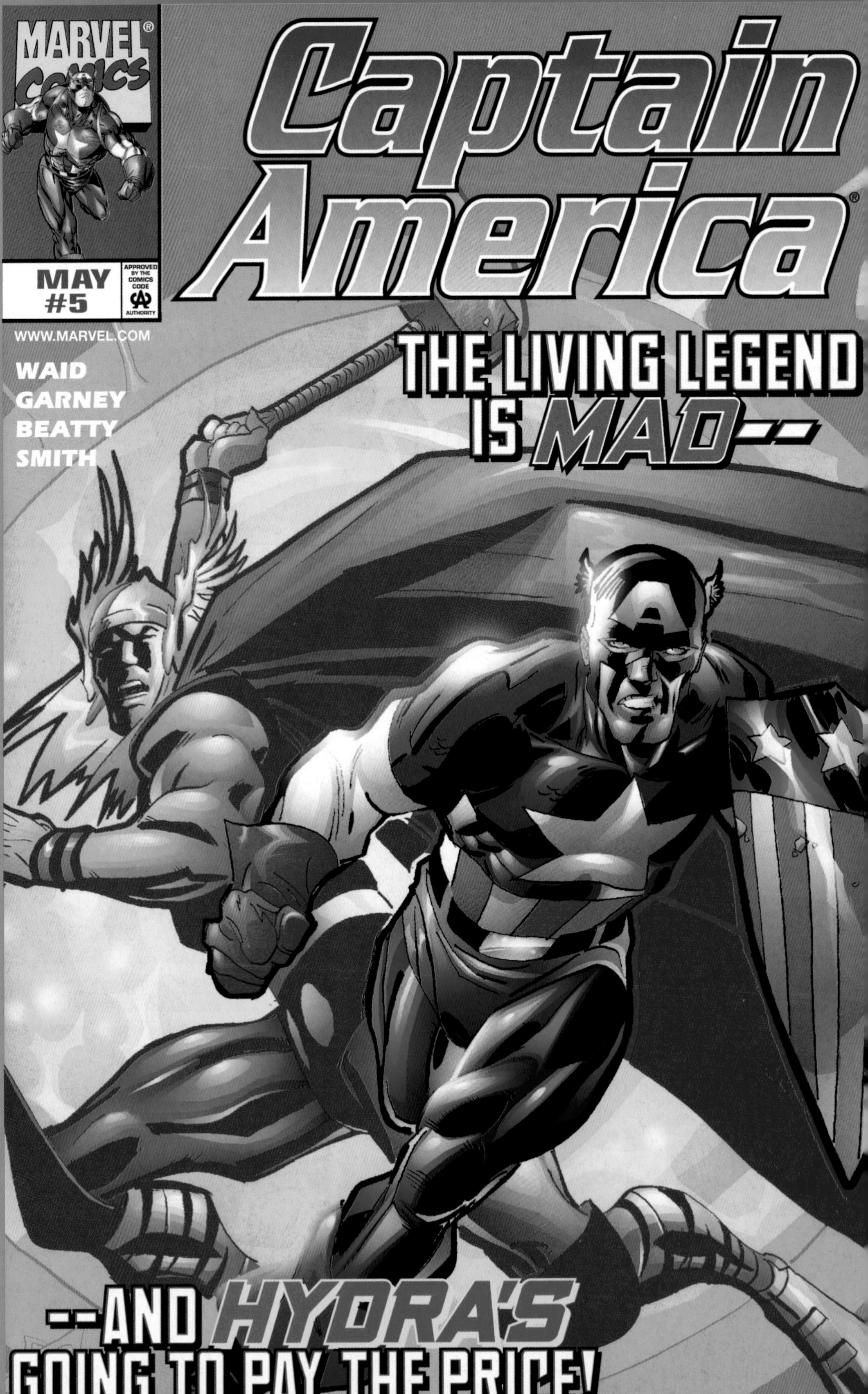
MARVEL® COMICS
Captain America®
MAY #5
APPROVED BY THE COMICS CODE AUTHORITY
WWW.MARVEL.COM
WAID
GARNEY
BEATTY
SMITH
THE LIVING LEGEND IS MAD--
--AND HYDRA'S GOING TO PAY THE PRICE!

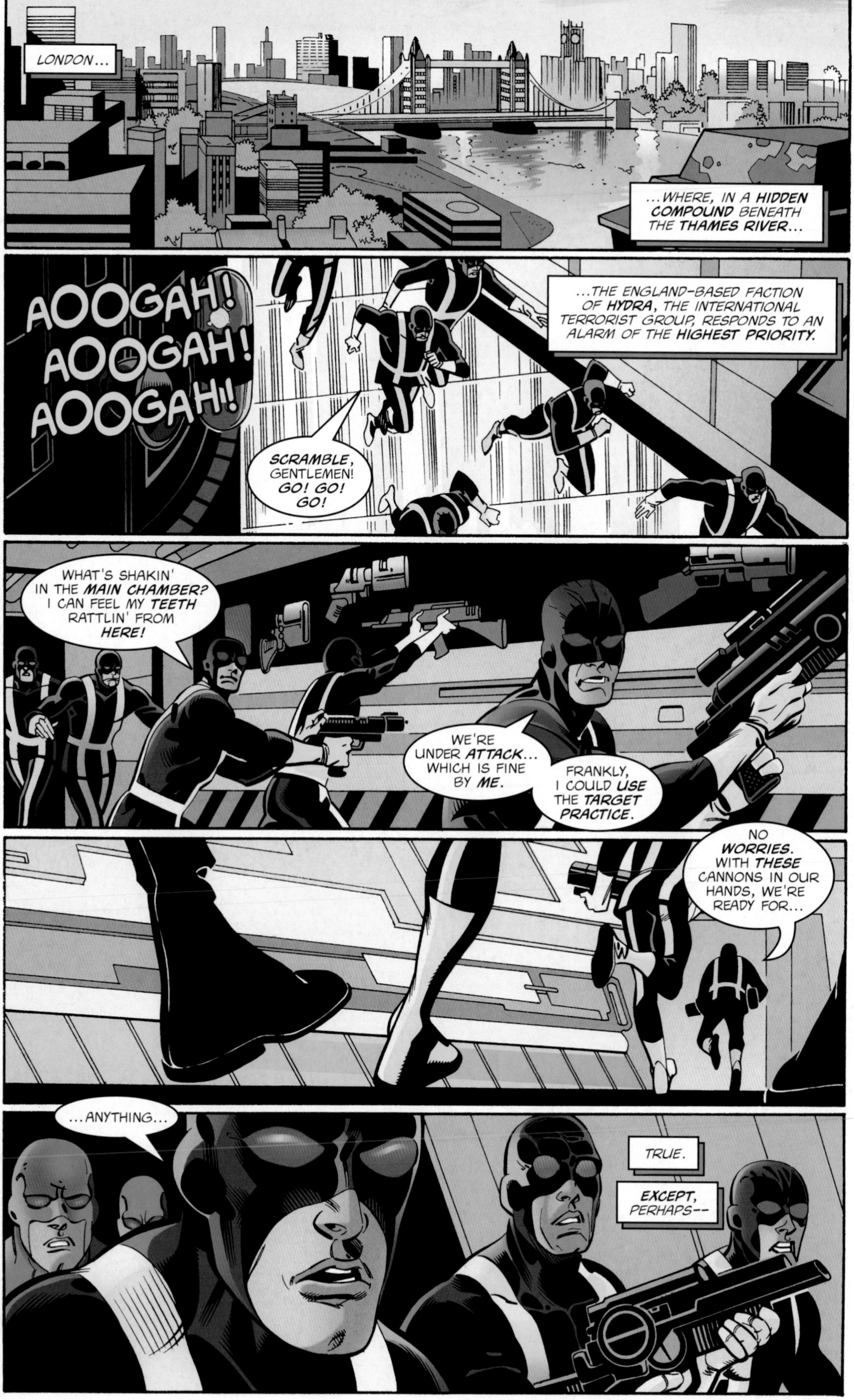
LONDON...
...WHERE, IN A HIDDEN COMPOUND BENEATH THE THAMES RIVER...
AOOGAH! AOOGAH! AOOGAH!
...THE ENGLAND-BASED FACTION OF HYDRA, THE INTERNATIONAL TERRORIST GROUP, RESPONDS TO AN ALARM OF THE HIGHEST PRIORITY.
SCRAMBLE, GENTLEMEN! GO! GO! GO!
WHAT'S SHAKIN' IN THE MAIN CHAMBER? I CAN FEEL MY TEETH RATTLIN' FROM HERE!
WE'RE UNDER ATTACK... WHICH IS FINE BY ME.
FRANKLY, I COULD USE THE TARGET PRACTICE.
NO WORRIES. WITH THESE CANNONS IN OUR HANDS, WE'RE READY FOR...
...ANYTHING...
TRUE.
EXCEPT, PERHAPS--

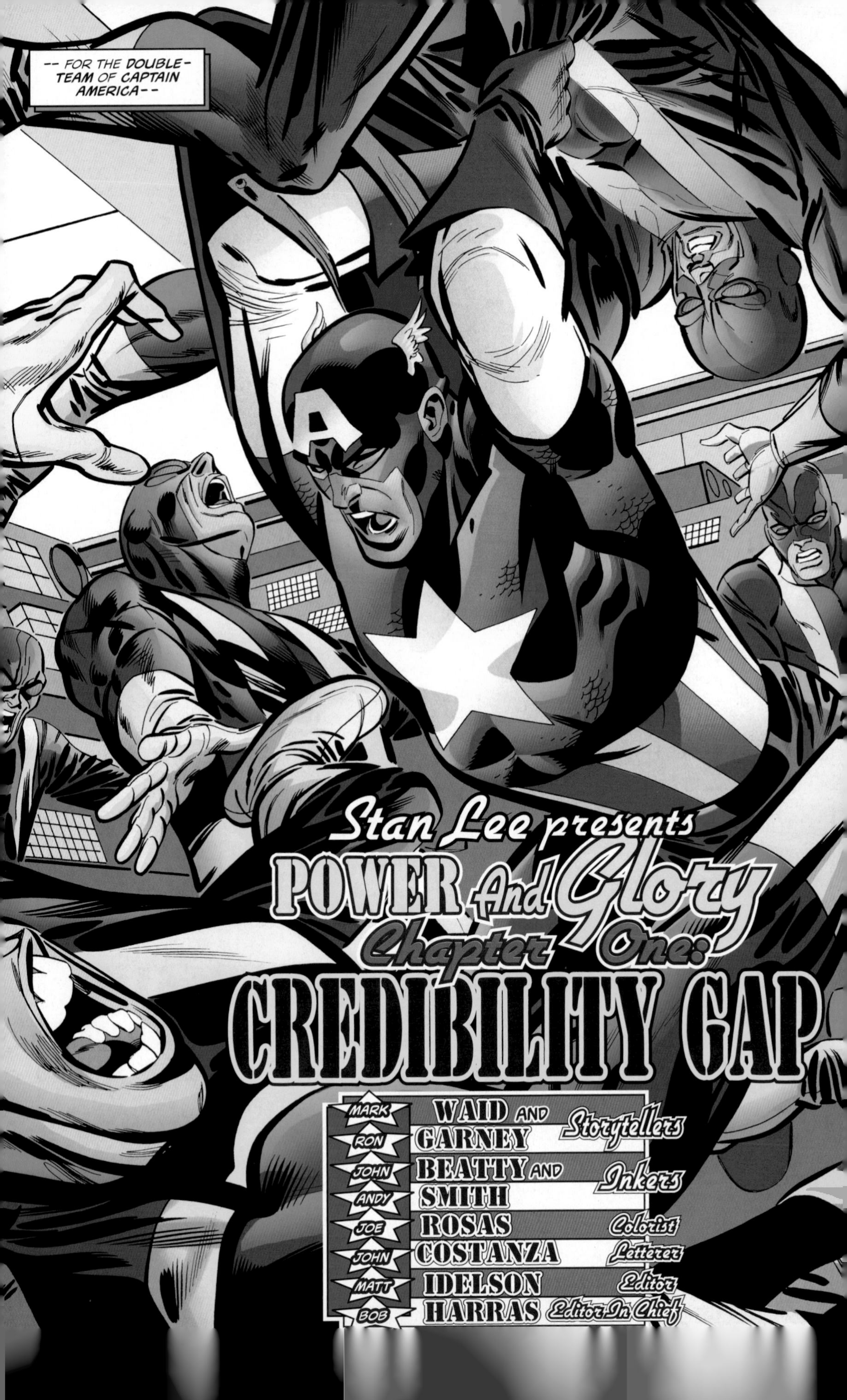
-- FOR THE DOUBLE-TEAM OF CAPTAIN AMERICA--
Stan Lee presents
POWER And Glory
Chapter One:
CREDIBILITY GAP
MARK WAID AND RON GARNEY Storytellers
JOHN BEATTY AND ANDY SMITH Inkers
JOE ROSAS Colorist
JOHN COSTANZA Letterer
MATT IDELSON Editor
BOB HARRAS Editor In Chief

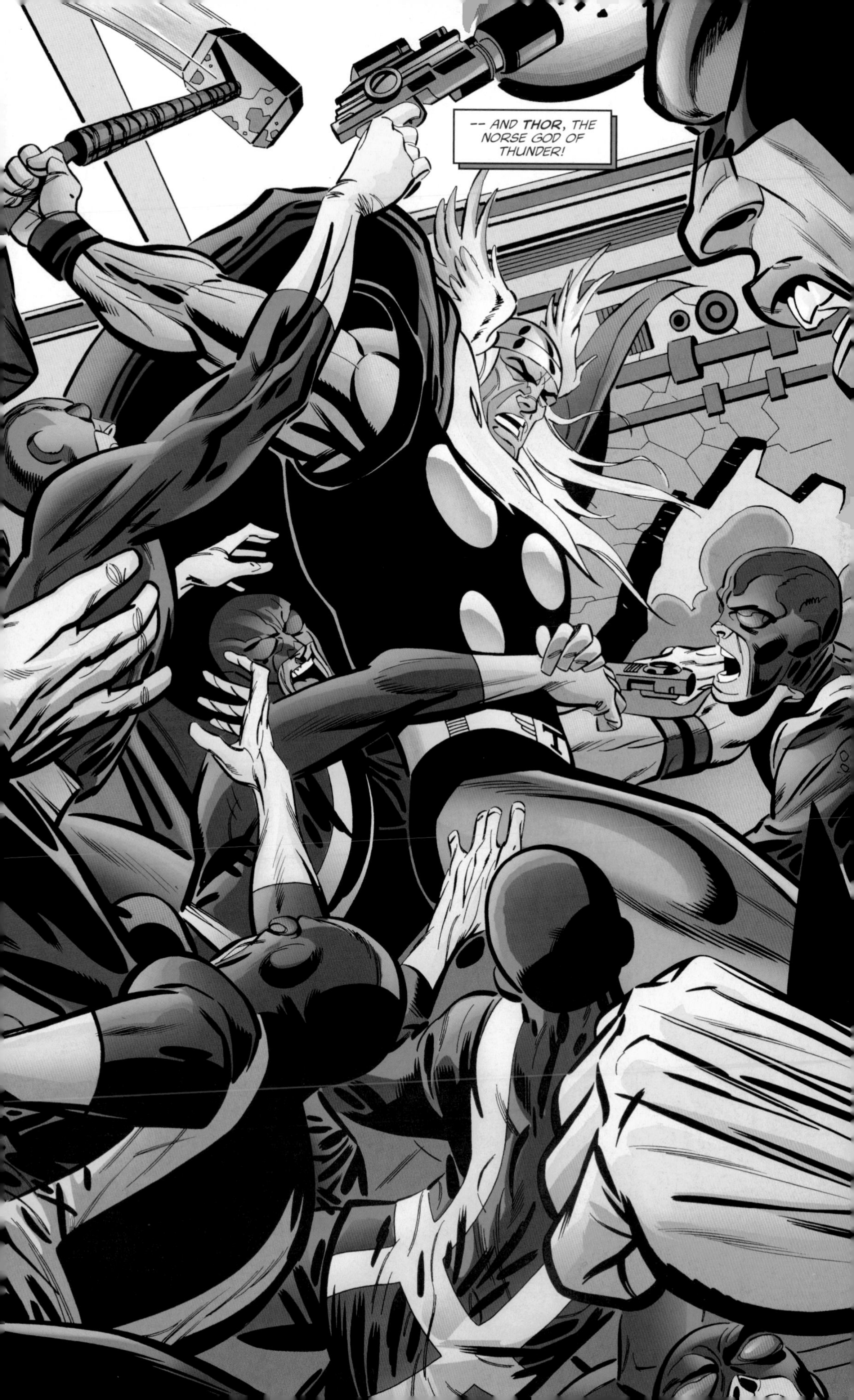
-- AND THOR, THE NORSE GOD OF THUNDER!

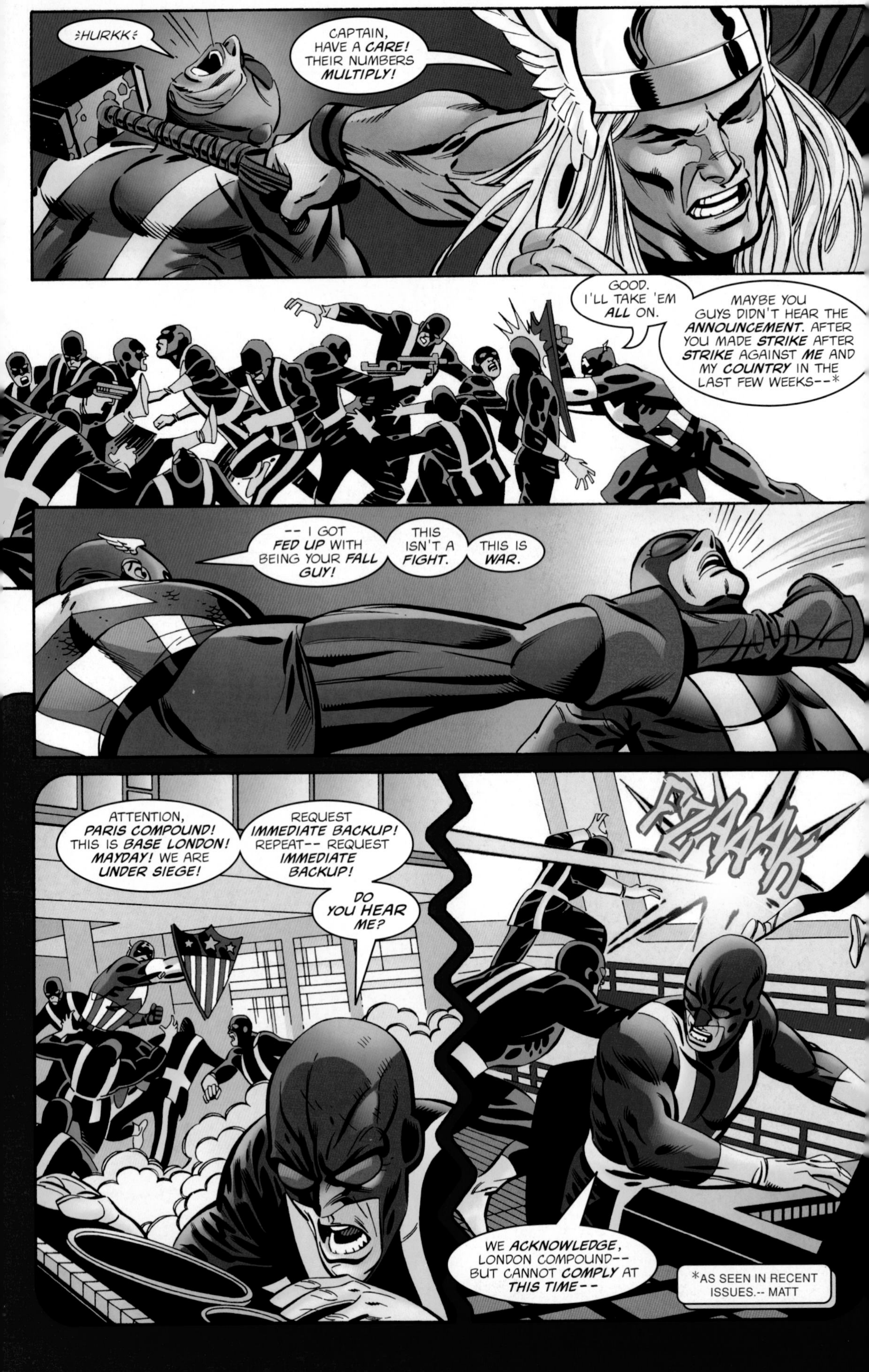

HURKK
CAPTAIN, HAVE A CARE! THEIR NUMBERS MULTIPLY!
GOOD. I'LL TAKE 'EM ALL ON.
MAYBE YOU GUYS DIDN'T HEAR THE ANNOUNCEMENT. AFTER YOU MADE STRIKE AFTER STRIKE AGAINST ME AND MY COUNTRY IN THE LAST FEW WEEKS--*
-- I GOT FED UP WITH BEING YOUR FALL GUY!
THIS ISN'T A FIGHT.
THIS IS WAR.
ATTENTION, PARIS COMPOUND! THIS IS BASE LONDON! MAYDAY! WE ARE UNDER SIEGE!
REQUEST IMMEDIATE BACKUP! REPEAT-- REQUEST IMMEDIATE BACKUP!
DO YOU HEAR ME?
FZAAAK
WE ACKNOWLEDGE, LONDON COMPOUND-- BUT CANNOT COMPLY AT THIS TIME--
*AS SEEN IN RECENT ISSUES.-- MATT

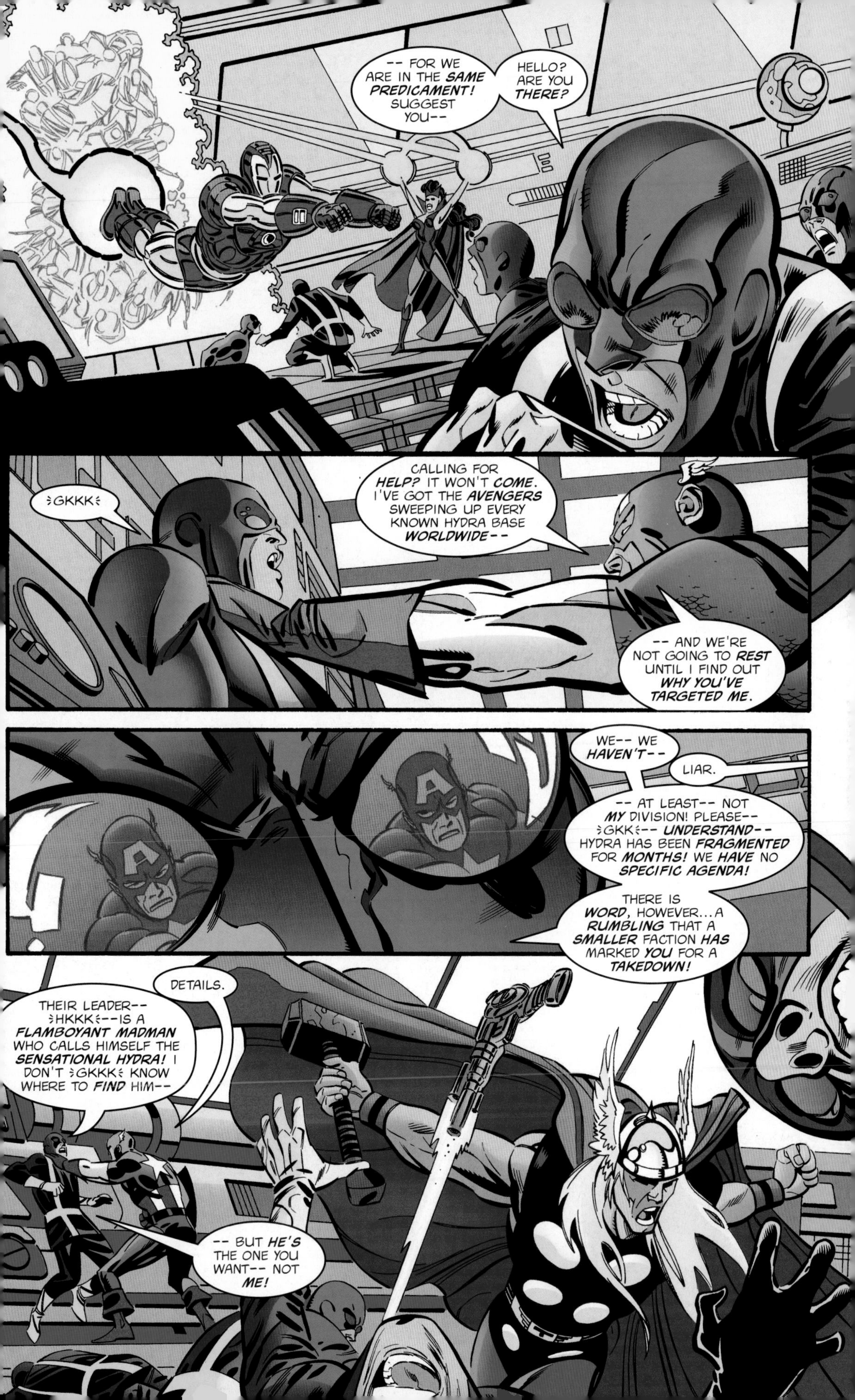
-- FOR WE ARE IN THE SAME PREDICAMENT! SUGGEST YOU--
HELLO? ARE YOU THERE?
≶GKKK≶
CALLING FOR HELP? IT WON'T COME. I'VE GOT THE AVENGERS SWEEPING UP EVERY KNOWN HYDRA BASE WORLDWIDE--
-- AND WE'RE NOT GOING TO REST UNTIL I FIND OUT WHY YOU'VE TARGETED ME.
WE-- WE HAVEN'T--
LIAR.
-- AT LEAST-- NOT MY DIVISION! PLEASE-- ≶GKK≶-- UNDERSTAND-- HYDRA HAS BEEN FRAGMENTED FOR MONTHS! WE HAVE NO SPECIFIC AGENDA!
THERE IS WORD, HOWEVER... A RUMBLING THAT A SMALLER FACTION HAS MARKED YOU FOR A TAKEDOWN!
DETAILS.
THEIR LEADER-- ≶HKKK≶--IS A FLAMBOYANT MADMAN WHO CALLS HIMSELF THE SENSATIONAL HYDRA! I DON'T ≶GKKK≶ KNOW WHERE TO FIND HIM--
-- BUT HE'S THE ONE YOU WANT-- NOT ME!

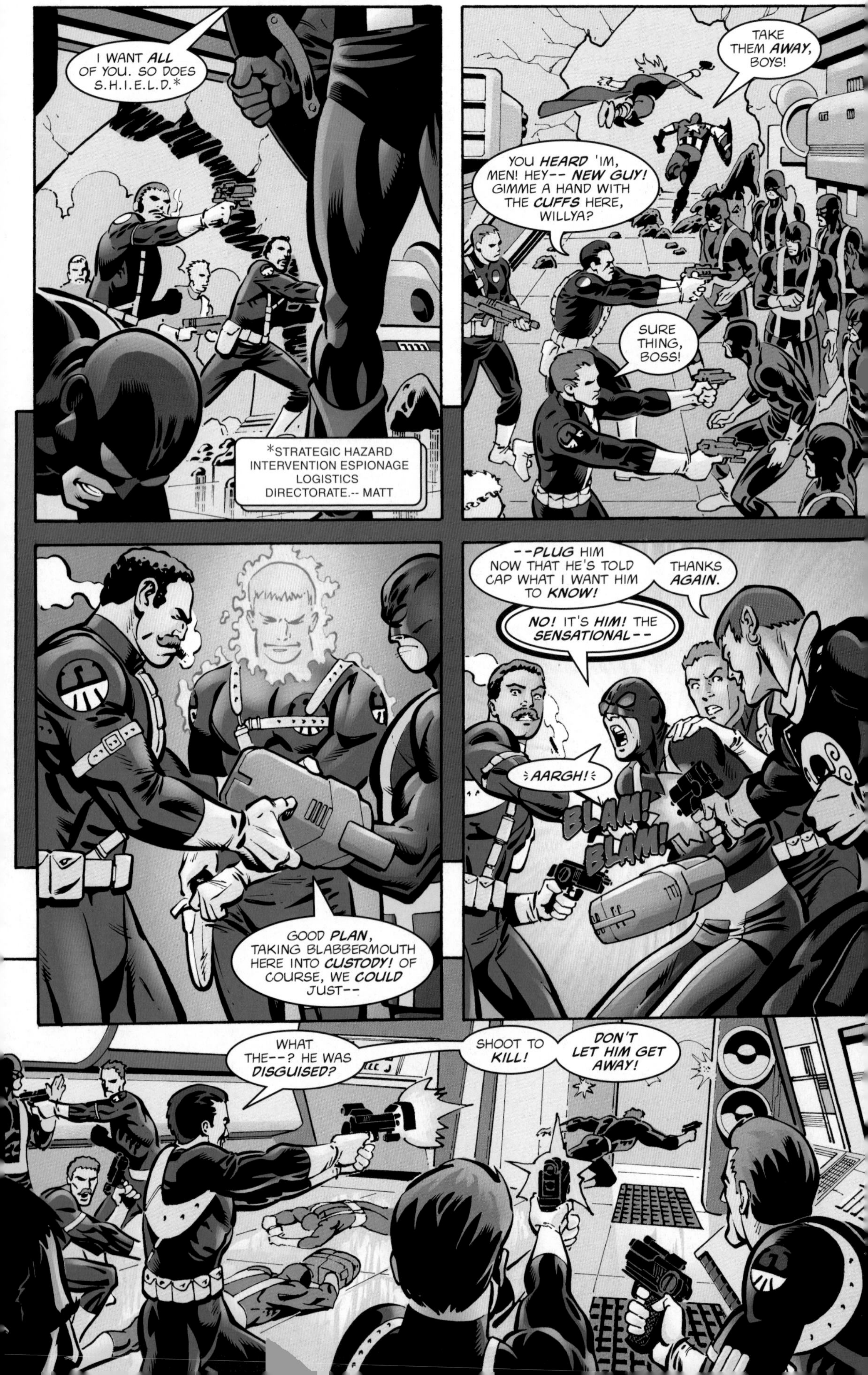
I WANT ALL OF YOU. SO DOES S.H.I.E.L.D.*
*STRATEGIC HAZARD INTERVENTION ESPIONAGE LOGISTICS DIRECTORATE.-- MATT
TAKE THEM AWAY, BOYS!
YOU HEARD 'IM, MEN! HEY-- NEW GUY! GIMME A HAND WITH THE CUFFS HERE, WILLYA?
SURE THING, BOSS!
GOOD PLAN, TAKING BLABBERMOUTH HERE INTO CUSTODY! OF COURSE, WE COULD JUST--
--PLUG HIM NOW THAT HE'S TOLD CAP WHAT I WANT HIM TO KNOW!
THANKS AGAIN.
NO! IT'S HIM! THE SENSATIONAL--
AARGH!
BLAM!
BLAM!
WHAT THE--? HE WAS DISGUISED?
SHOOT TO KILL!
DON'T LET HIM GET AWAY!

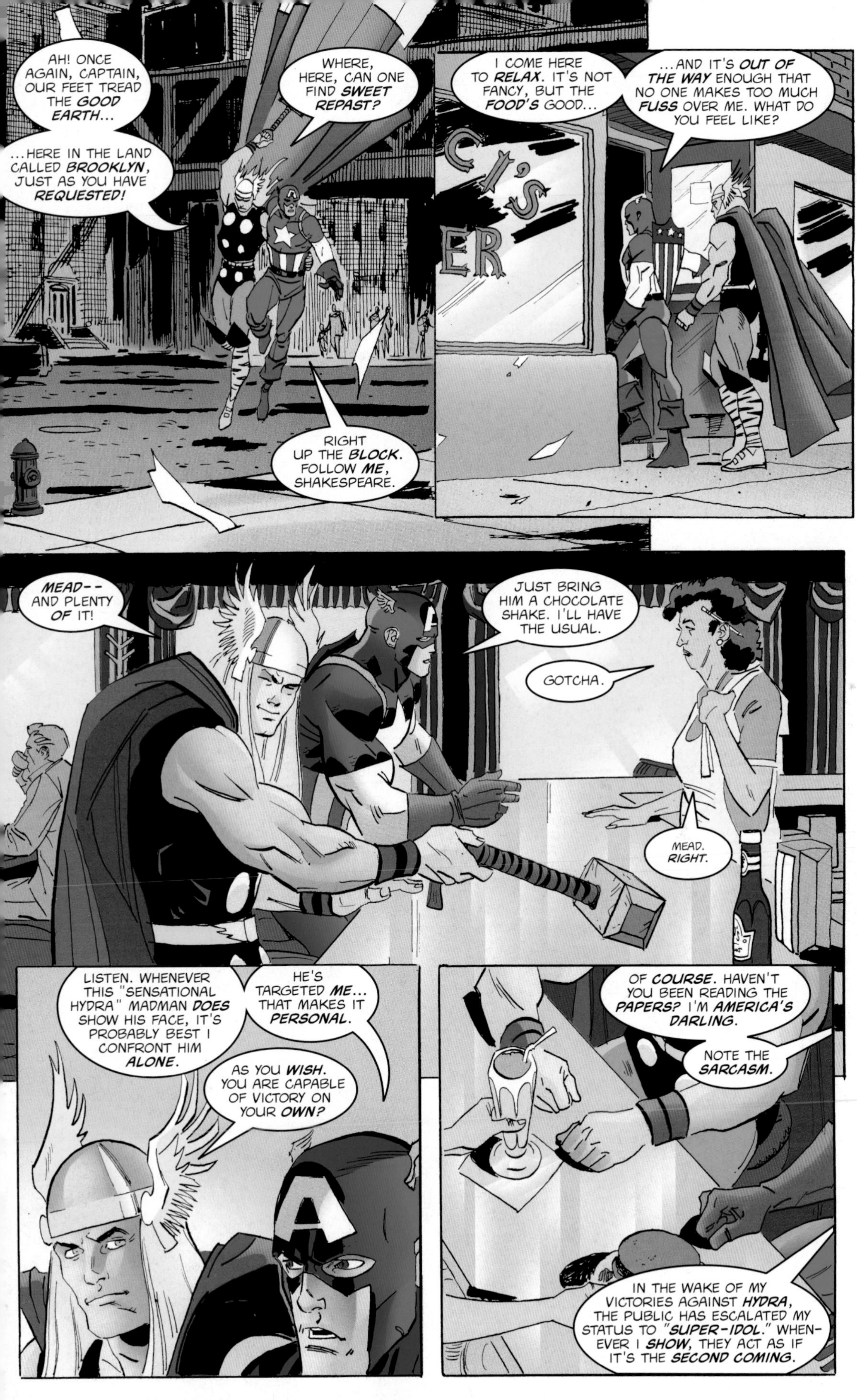

AH! ONCE AGAIN, CAPTAIN, OUR FEET TREAD THE GOOD EARTH...
...HERE IN THE LAND CALLED BROOKLYN, JUST AS YOU HAVE REQUESTED!
WHERE, HERE, CAN ONE FIND SWEET REPAST?
RIGHT UP THE BLOCK. FOLLOW ME, SHAKESPEARE.
I COME HERE TO RELAX. IT'S NOT FANCY, BUT THE FOOD'S GOOD...
...AND IT'S OUT OF THE WAY ENOUGH THAT NO ONE MAKES TOO MUCH FUSS OVER ME. WHAT DO YOU FEEL LIKE?
MEAD-- AND PLENTY OF IT!
JUST BRING HIM A CHOCOLATE SHAKE. I'LL HAVE THE USUAL.
GOTCHA.
MEAD. RIGHT.
LISTEN. WHENEVER THIS "SENSATIONAL HYDRA" MADMAN DOES SHOW HIS FACE, IT'S PROBABLY BEST I CONFRONT HIM ALONE.
HE'S TARGETED ME... THAT MAKES IT PERSONAL.
AS YOU WISH. YOU ARE CAPABLE OF VICTORY ON YOUR OWN?
OF COURSE. HAVEN'T YOU BEEN READING THE PAPERS? I'M AMERICA'S DARLING.
NOTE THE SARCASM.
IN THE WAKE OF MY VICTORIES AGAINST HYDRA, THE PUBLIC HAS ESCALATED MY STATUS TO "SUPER-IDOL." WHENEVER I SHOW, THEY ACT AS IF IT'S THE SECOND COMING.

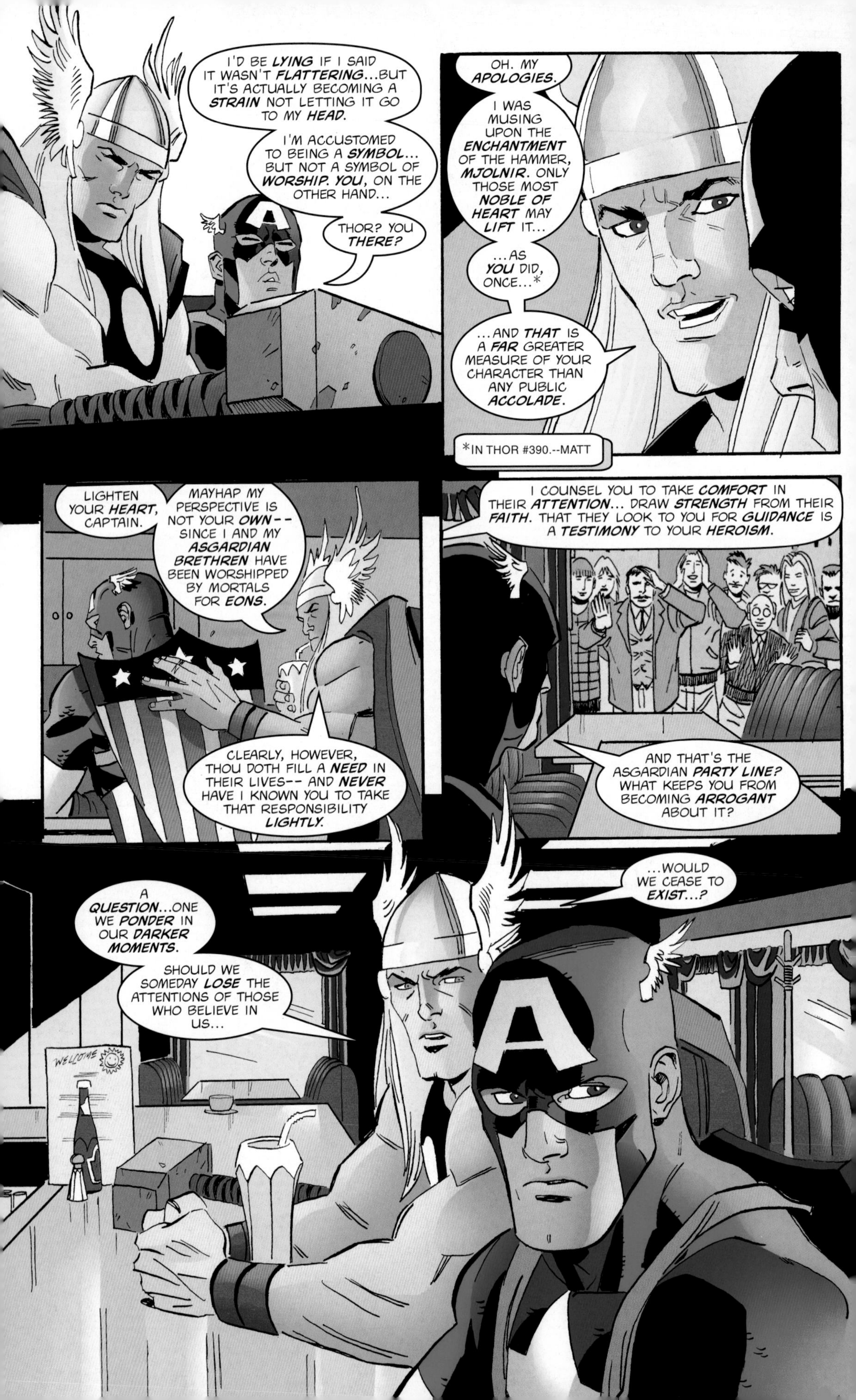

I'D BE LYING IF I SAID IT WASN'T FLATTERING...BUT IT'S ACTUALLY BECOMING A STRAIN NOT LETTING IT GO TO MY HEAD.
I'M ACCUSTOMED TO BEING A SYMBOL... BUT NOT A SYMBOL OF WORSHIP. YOU, ON THE OTHER HAND...
THOR? YOU THERE?
OH. MY APOLOGIES.
I WAS MUSING UPON THE ENCHANTMENT OF THE HAMMER, MJOLNIR. ONLY THOSE MOST NOBLE OF HEART MAY LIFT IT...
...AS YOU DID, ONCE...*
...AND THAT IS A FAR GREATER MEASURE OF YOUR CHARACTER THAN ANY PUBLIC ACCOLADE.
*IN THOR #390.--MATT
LIGHTEN YOUR HEART, CAPTAIN.
MAYHAP MY PERSPECTIVE IS NOT YOUR OWN-- SINCE I AND MY ASGARDIAN BRETHREN HAVE BEEN WORSHIPPED BY MORTALS FOR EONS.
CLEARLY, HOWEVER, THOU DOTH FILL A NEED IN THEIR LIVES-- AND NEVER HAVE I KNOWN YOU TO TAKE THAT RESPONSIBILITY LIGHTLY.
I COUNSEL YOU TO TAKE COMFORT IN THEIR ATTENTION... DRAW STRENGTH FROM THEIR FAITH. THAT THEY LOOK TO YOU FOR GUIDANCE IS A TESTIMONY TO YOUR HEROISM.
AND THAT'S THE ASGARDIAN PARTY LINE? WHAT KEEPS YOU FROM BECOMING ARROGANT ABOUT IT?
A QUESTION...ONE WE PONDER IN OUR DARKER MOMENTS.
SHOULD WE SOMEDAY LOSE THE ATTENTIONS OF THOSE WHO BELIEVE IN US...
...WOULD WE CEASE TO EXIST...?
WELCOME

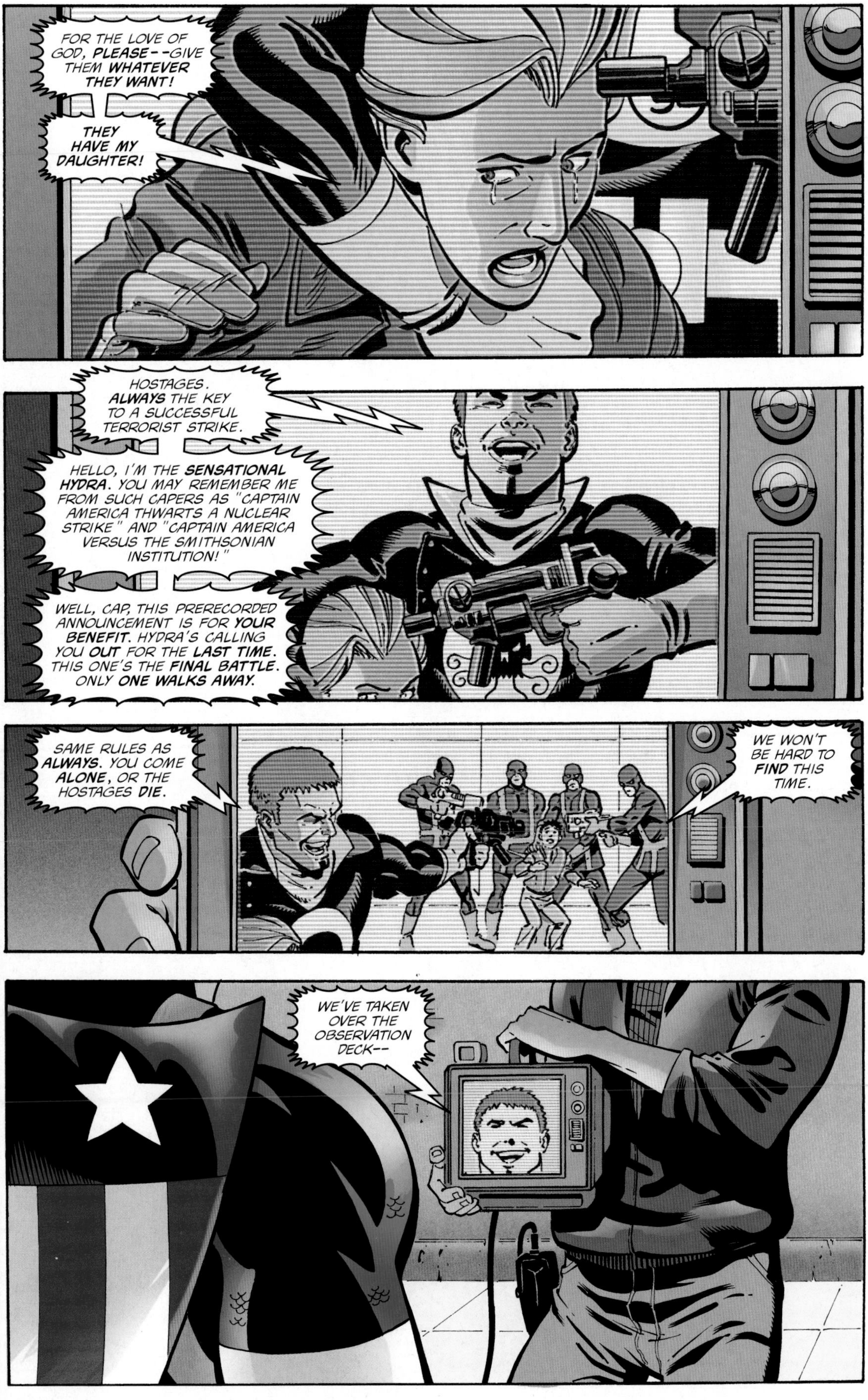
FOR THE LOVE OF GOD, PLEASE--GIVE THEM WHATEVER THEY WANT!
THEY HAVE MY DAUGHTER!
HOSTAGES. ALWAYS THE KEY TO A SUCCESSFUL TERRORIST STRIKE.
HELLO, I'M THE SENSATIONAL HYDRA. YOU MAY REMEMBER ME FROM SUCH CAPERS AS "CAPTAIN AMERICA THWARTS A NUCLEAR STRIKE" AND "CAPTAIN AMERICA VERSUS THE SMITHSONIAN INSTITUTION!"
WELL, CAP, THIS PRERECORDED ANNOUNCEMENT IS FOR YOUR BENEFIT. HYDRA'S CALLING YOU OUT FOR THE LAST TIME. THIS ONE'S THE FINAL BATTLE. ONLY ONE WALKS AWAY.
SAME RULES AS ALWAYS. YOU COME ALONE, OR THE HOSTAGES DIE.
WE WON'T BE HARD TO FIND THIS TIME.
WE'VE TAKEN OVER THE OBSERVATION DECK--

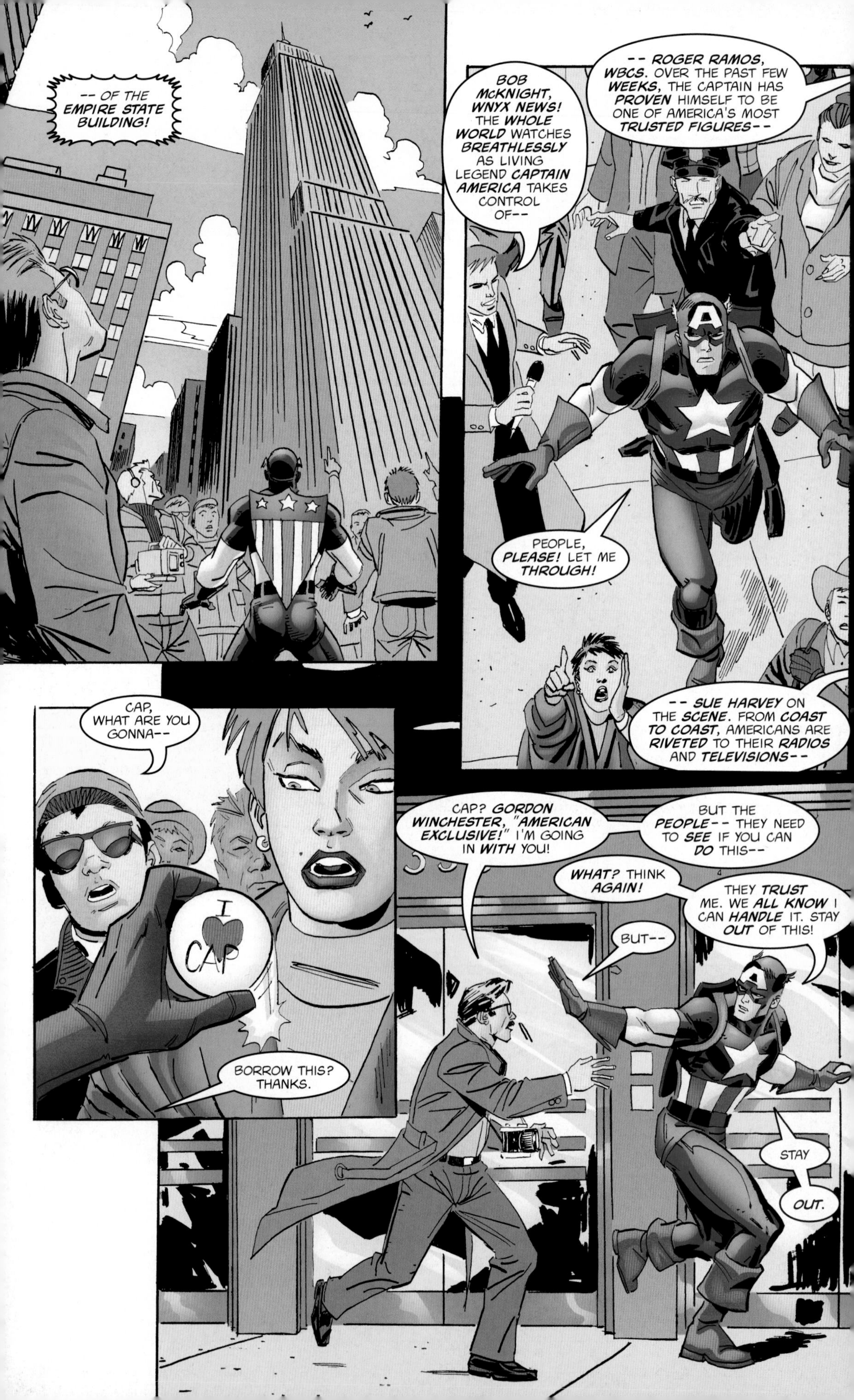
-- OF THE EMPIRE STATE BUILDING!
BOB McKNIGHT, WNYX NEWS! THE WHOLE WORLD WATCHES BREATHLESSLY AS LIVING LEGEND CAPTAIN AMERICA TAKES CONTROL OF--
-- ROGER RAMOS, WBCS. OVER THE PAST FEW WEEKS, THE CAPTAIN HAS PROVEN HIMSELF TO BE ONE OF AMERICA'S MOST TRUSTED FIGURES--
PEOPLE, PLEASE! LET ME THROUGH!
-- SUE HARVEY ON THE SCENE. FROM COAST TO COAST, AMERICANS ARE RIVETED TO THEIR RADIOS AND TELEVISIONS--
CAP, WHAT ARE YOU GONNA--
I ♥ CAP
BORROW THIS? THANKS.
CAP? GORDON WINCHESTER, "AMERICAN EXCLUSIVE!" I'M GOING IN WITH YOU!
BUT THE PEOPLE-- THEY NEED TO SEE IF YOU CAN DO THIS--
WHAT? THINK AGAIN!
THEY TRUST ME. WE ALL KNOW I CAN HANDLE IT. STAY OUT OF THIS!
BUT--
STAY
OUT.

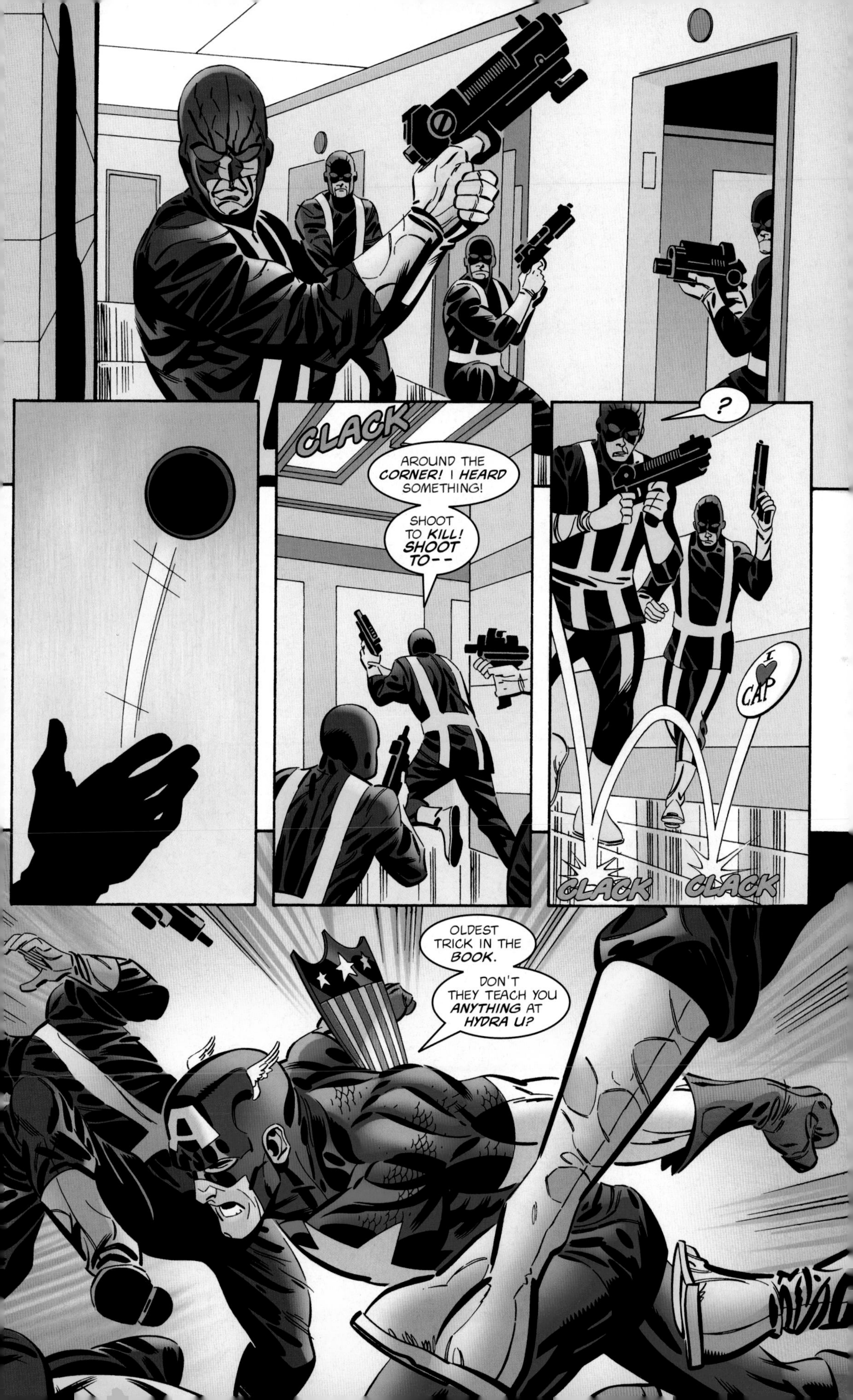
CLACK
AROUND THE CORNER! I HEARD SOMETHING!
SHOOT TO KILL! SHOOT TO--
?
I ♥ CAP
CLACK
CLACK
OLDEST TRICK IN THE BOOK.
DON'T THEY TEACH YOU ANYTHING AT HYDRA U?

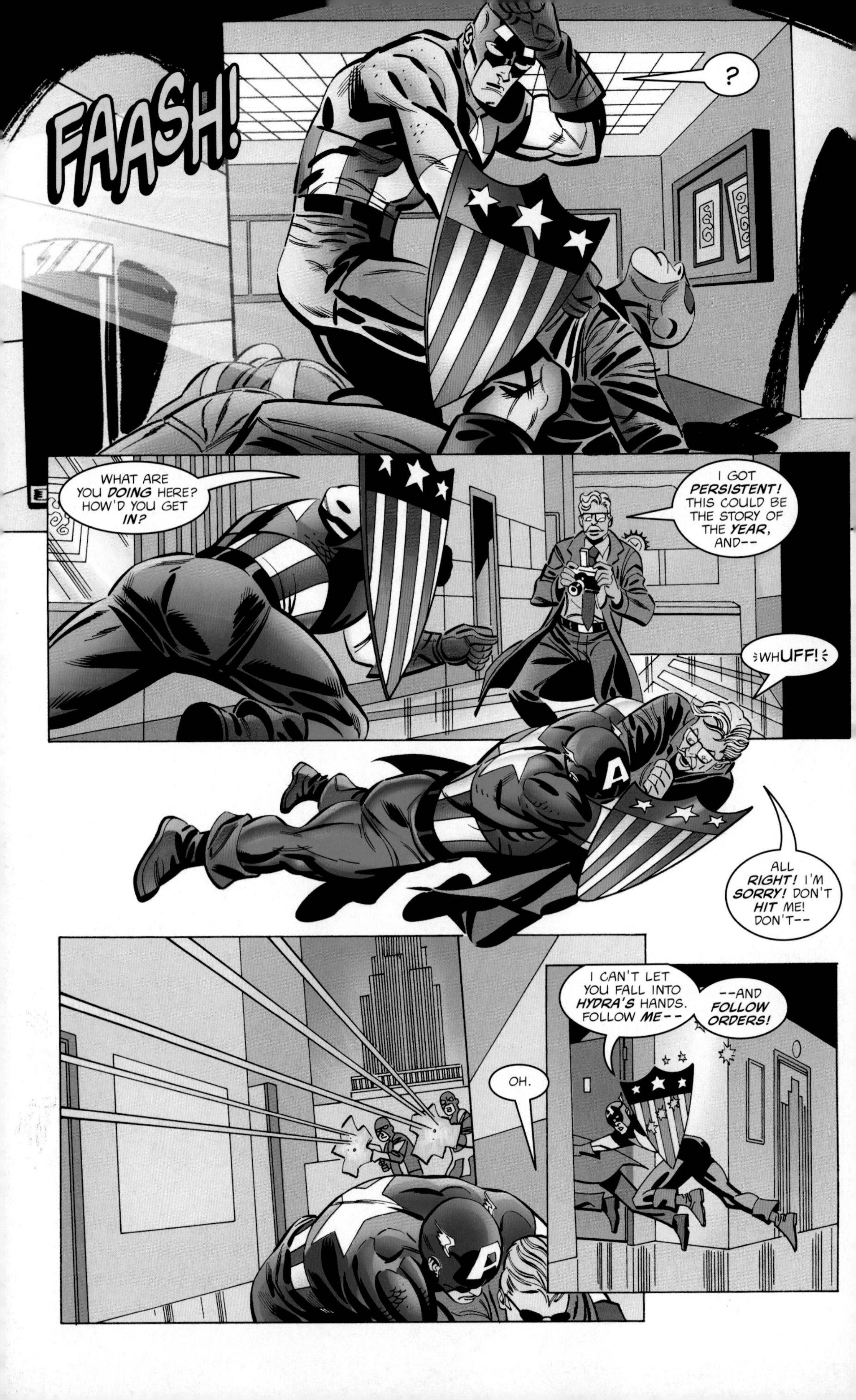
FAASH!
?
WHAT ARE YOU DOING HERE? HOW'D YOU GET IN?
I GOT PERSISTENT! THIS COULD BE THE STORY OF THE YEAR, AND--
WHUFF!
ALL RIGHT! I'M SORRY! DON'T HIT ME! DON'T--
OH.
I CAN'T LET YOU FALL INTO HYDRA'S HANDS. FOLLOW ME--
--AND FOLLOW ORDERS!

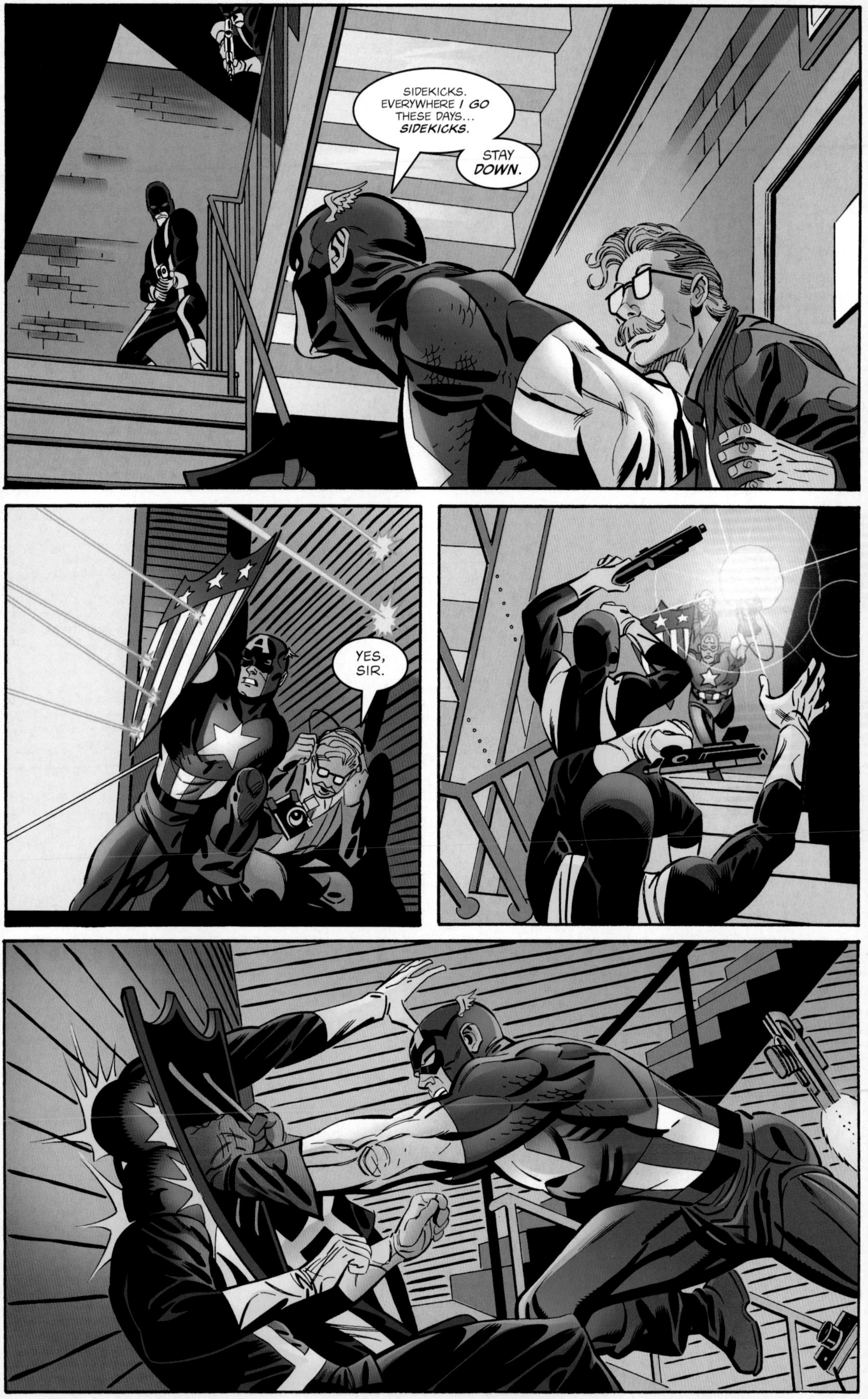
SIDEKICKS. EVERYWHERE I GO THESE DAYS... SIDEKICKS.
STAY DOWN.
YES, SIR.

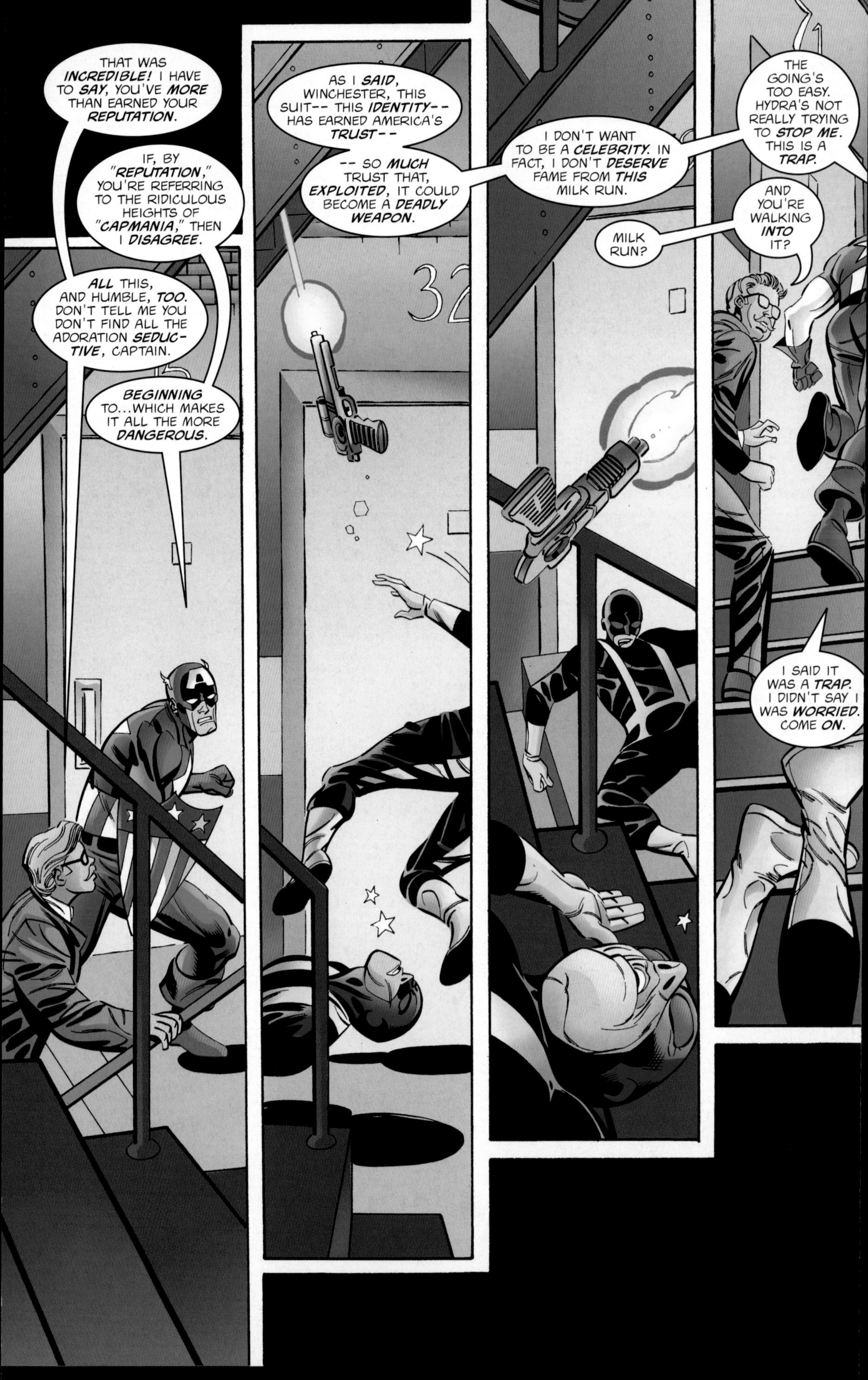
THAT WAS INCREDIBLE! I HAVE TO SAY, YOU'VE MORE THAN EARNED YOUR REPUTATION.
IF, BY "REPUTATION," YOU'RE REFERRING TO THE RIDICULOUS HEIGHTS OF "CAPMANIA," THEN I DISAGREE.
ALL THIS, AND HUMBLE, TOO. DON'T TELL ME YOU DON'T FIND ALL THE ADORATION SEDUCTIVE, CAPTAIN.
BEGINNING TO...WHICH MAKES IT ALL THE MORE DANGEROUS.
AS I SAID, WINCHESTER, THIS SUIT-- THIS IDENTITY-- HAS EARNED AMERICA'S TRUST--
-- SO MUCH TRUST THAT, EXPLOITED, IT COULD BECOME A DEADLY WEAPON.
32
I DON'T WANT TO BE A CELEBRITY. IN FACT, I DON'T DESERVE FAME FROM THIS MILK RUN.
MILK RUN?
THE GOING'S TOO EASY. HYDRA'S NOT REALLY TRYING TO STOP ME. THIS IS A TRAP.
AND YOU'RE WALKING INTO IT?
I SAID IT WAS A TRAP. I DIDN'T SAY I WAS WORRIED. COME ON.

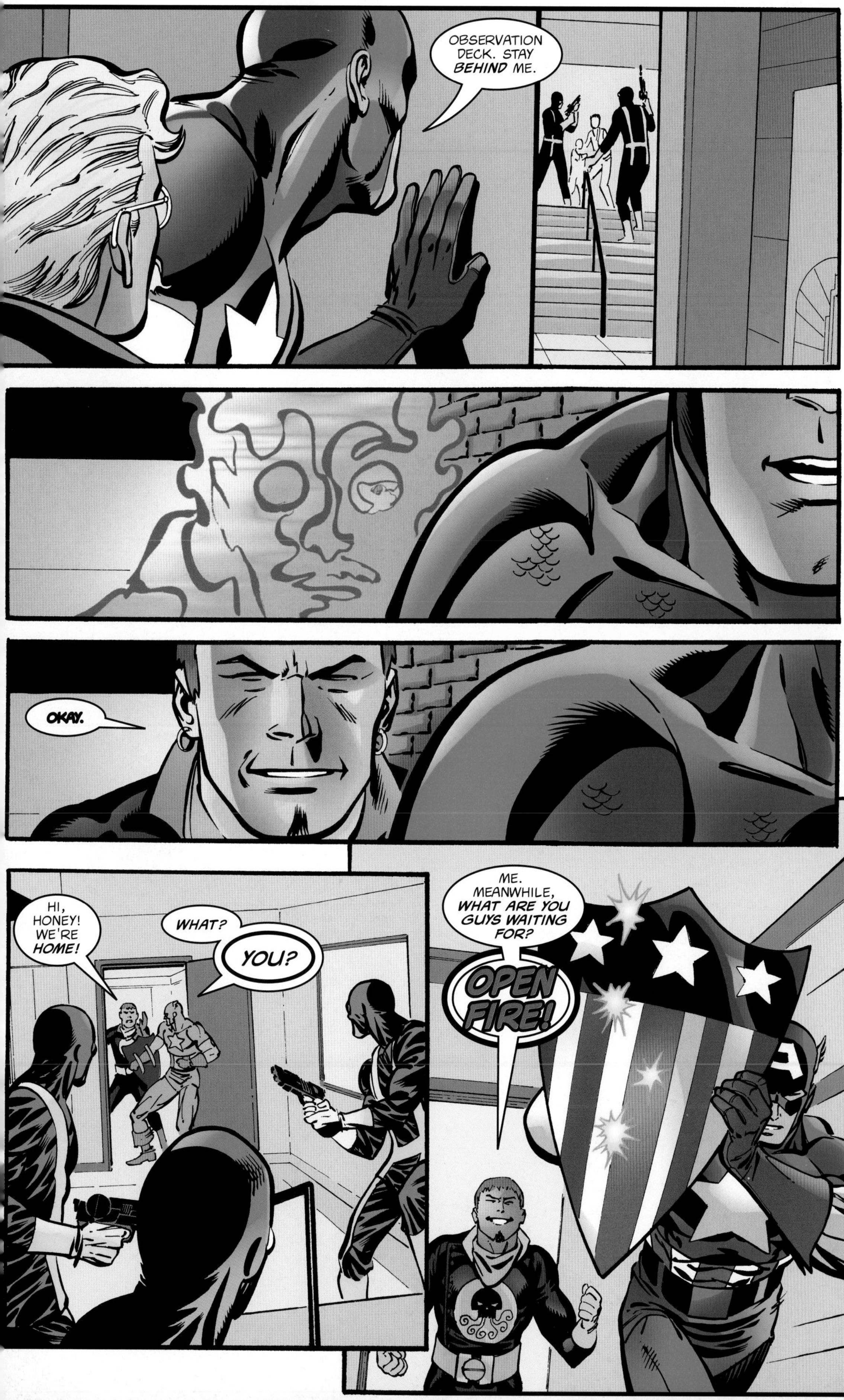
OBSERVATION DECK. STAY BEHIND ME.
OKAY.
HI, HONEY! WE'RE HOME!
WHAT?
YOU?
ME. MEANWHILE, WHAT ARE YOU GUYS WAITING FOR?
OPEN FIRE!

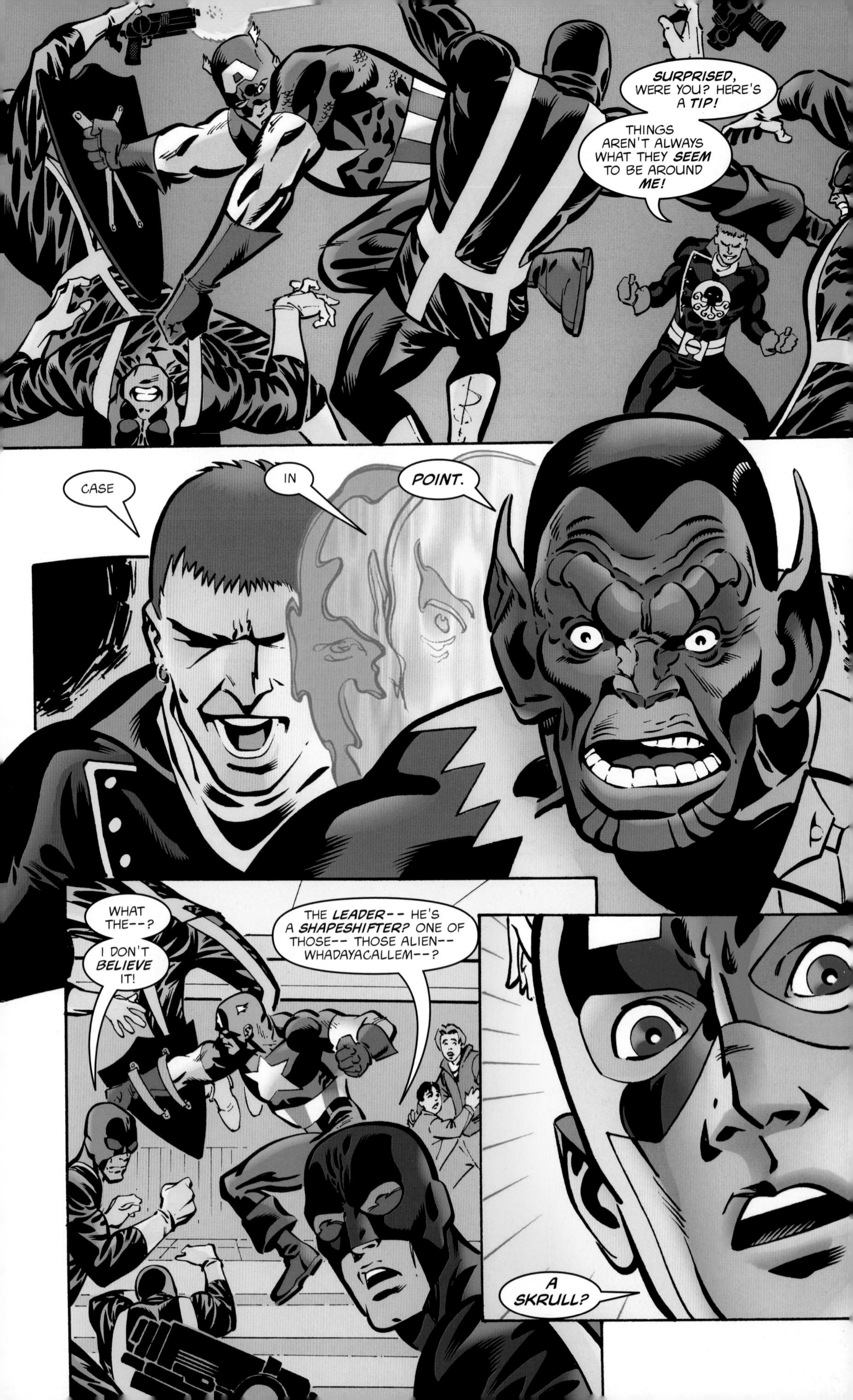
SURPRISED, WERE YOU? HERE'S A TIP!
THINGS AREN'T ALWAYS WHAT THEY SEEM TO BE AROUND ME!
CASE
IN
POINT.
WHAT THE--?
I DON'T BELIEVE IT!
THE LEADER-- HE'S A SHAPESHIFTER? ONE OF THOSE-- THOSE ALIEN-- WHADAYACALLEM--?
A SKRULL?

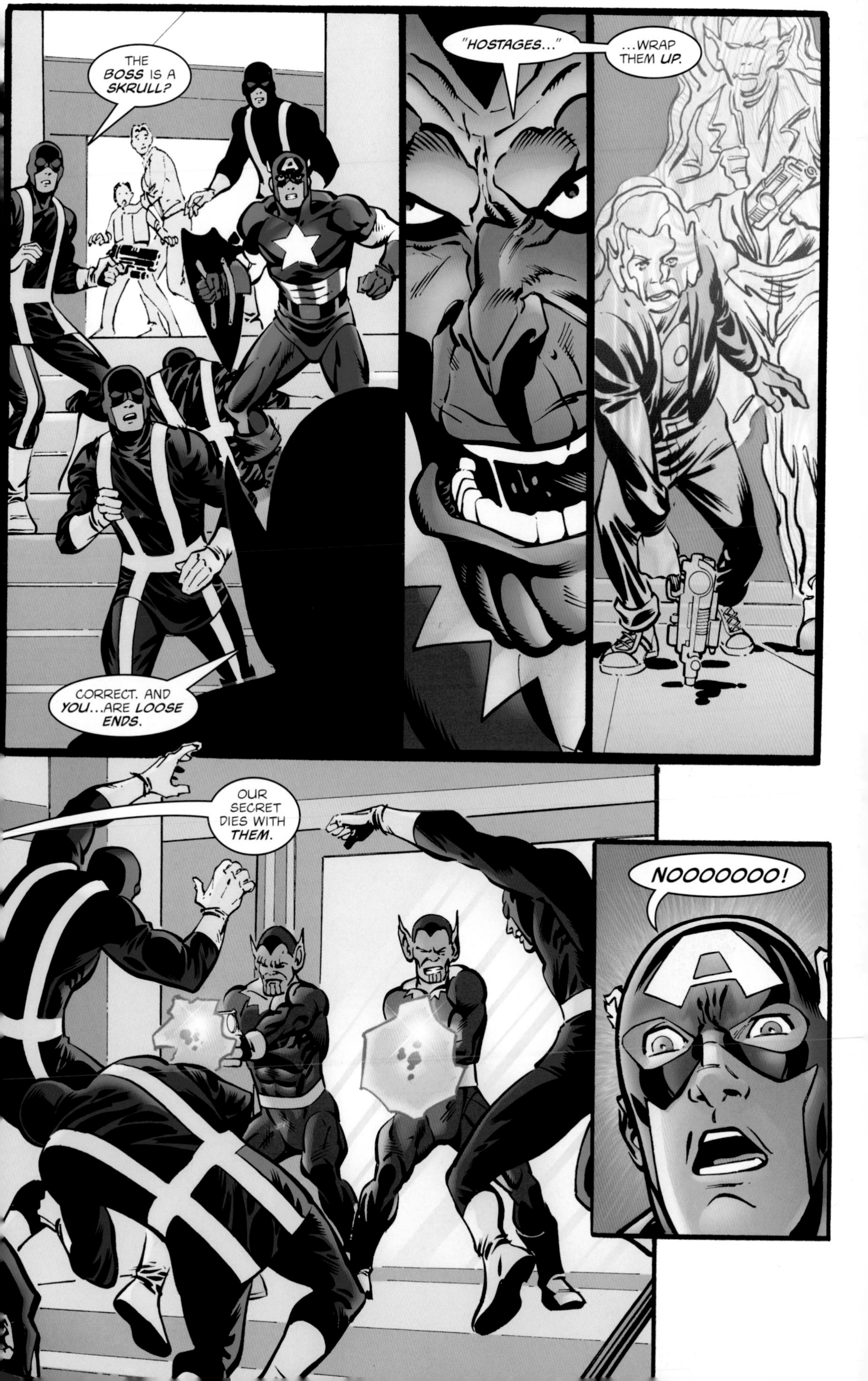
THE BOSS IS A SKRULL?
CORRECT. AND YOU...ARE LOOSE ENDS.
"HOSTAGES..."
...WRAP THEM UP.
OUR SECRET DIES WITH THEM.
NOOOOOOO!

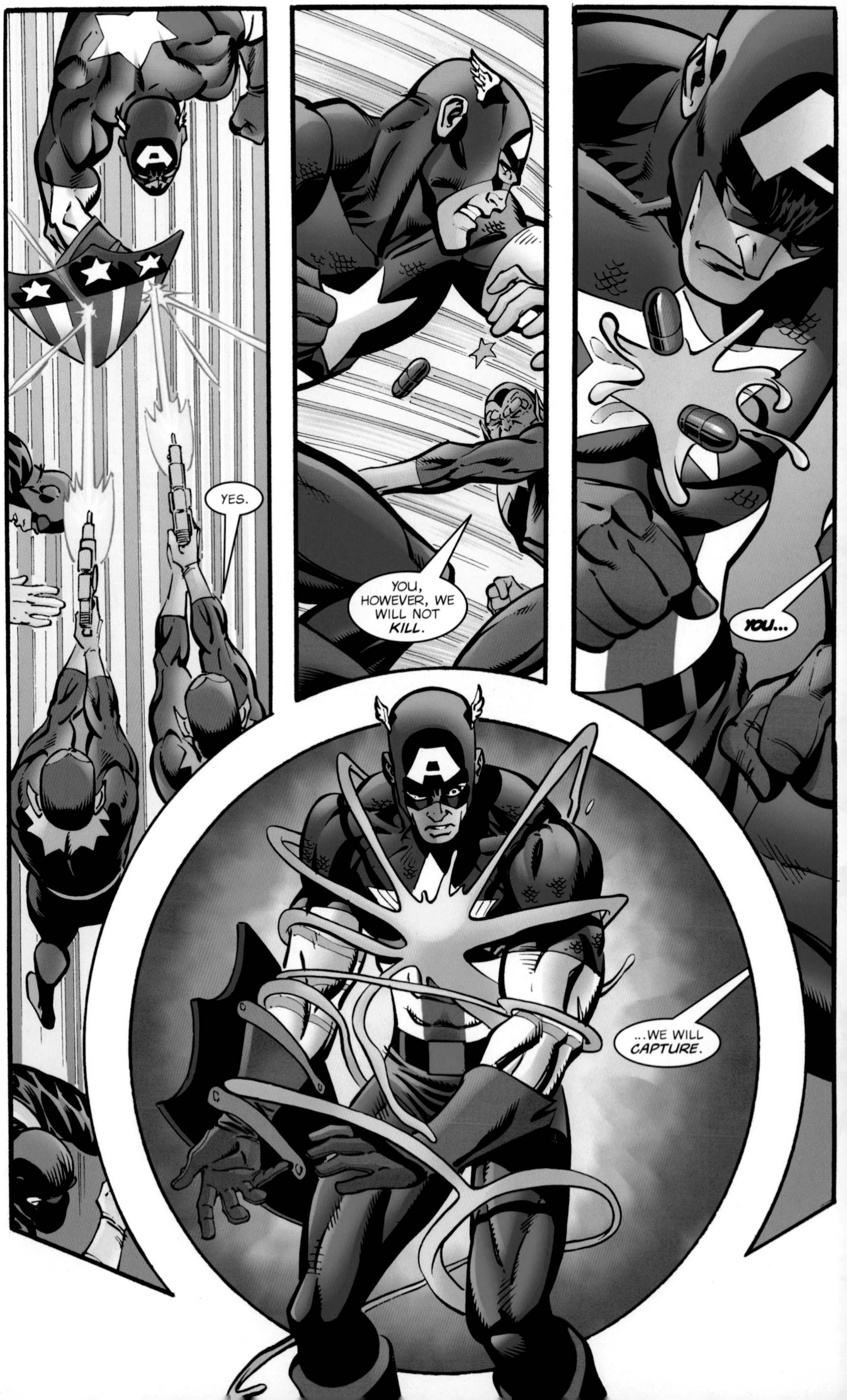
YES.
YOU, HOWEVER, WE WILL NOT KILL.
YOU...
...WE WILL CAPTURE.

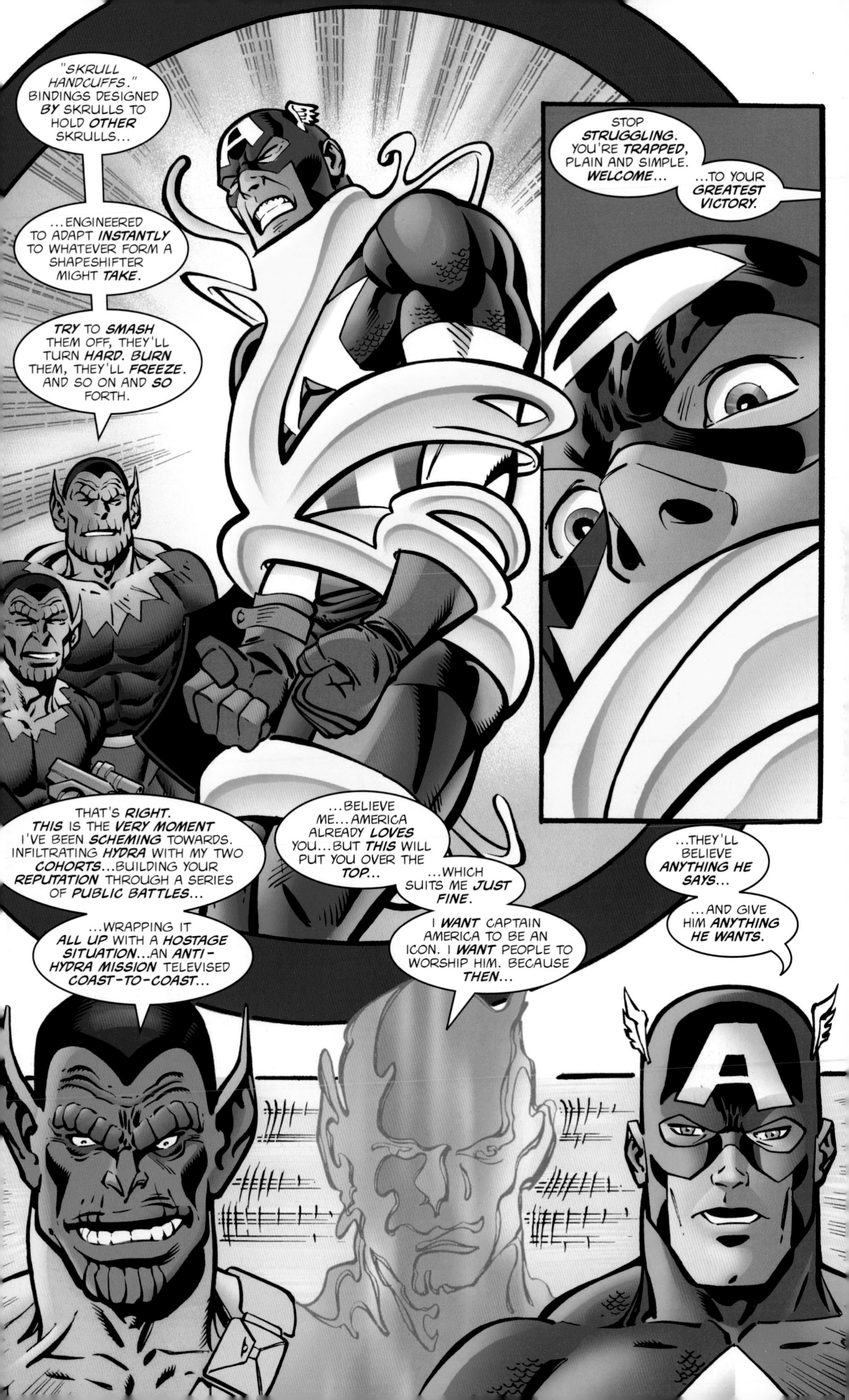
"SKRULL HANDCUFFS." BINDINGS DESIGNED BY SKRULLS TO HOLD OTHER SKRULLS...
...ENGINEERED TO ADAPT INSTANTLY TO WHATEVER FORM A SHAPESHIFTER MIGHT TAKE.
TRY TO SMASH THEM OFF, THEY'LL TURN HARD. BURN THEM, THEY'LL FREEZE. AND SO ON AND SO FORTH.
STOP STRUGGLING. YOU'RE TRAPPED, PLAIN AND SIMPLE. WELCOME...
...TO YOUR GREATEST VICTORY.
THAT'S RIGHT. THIS IS THE VERY MOMENT I'VE BEEN SCHEMING TOWARDS. INFILTRATING HYDRA WITH MY TWO COHORTS...BUILDING YOUR REPUTATION THROUGH A SERIES OF PUBLIC BATTLES...
...WRAPPING IT ALL UP WITH A HOSTAGE SITUATION...AN ANTI-HYDRA MISSION TELEVISED COAST-TO-COAST...
...BELIEVE ME...AMERICA ALREADY LOVES YOU...BUT THIS WILL PUT YOU OVER THE TOP...
...WHICH SUITS ME JUST FINE.
I WANT CAPTAIN AMERICA TO BE AN ICON. I WANT PEOPLE TO WORSHIP HIM. BECAUSE THEN...
...THEY'LL BELIEVE ANYTHING HE SAYS...
...AND GIVE HIM ANYTHING HE WANTS.

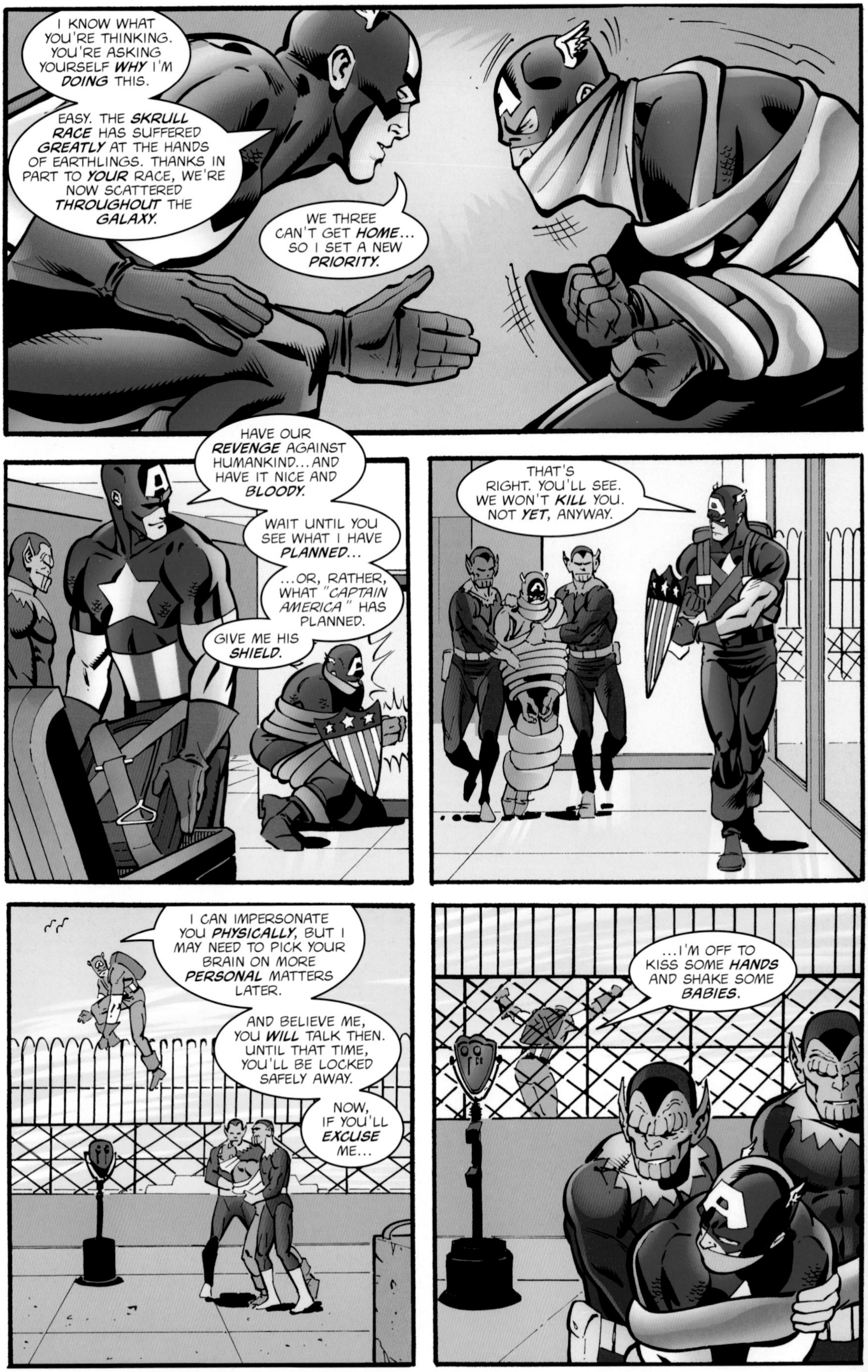
I KNOW WHAT YOU'RE THINKING. YOU'RE ASKING YOURSELF WHY I'M DOING THIS.
EASY. THE SKRULL RACE HAS SUFFERED GREATLY AT THE HANDS OF EARTHLINGS. THANKS IN PART TO YOUR RACE, WE'RE NOW SCATTERED THROUGHOUT THE GALAXY.
WE THREE CAN'T GET HOME... SO I SET A NEW PRIORITY.
HAVE OUR REVENGE AGAINST HUMANKIND... AND HAVE IT NICE AND BLOODY.
WAIT UNTIL YOU SEE WHAT I HAVE PLANNED...
...OR, RATHER, WHAT "CAPTAIN AMERICA" HAS PLANNED.
GIVE ME HIS SHIELD.
THAT'S RIGHT. YOU'LL SEE. WE WON'T KILL YOU. NOT YET, ANYWAY.
I CAN IMPERSONATE YOU PHYSICALLY, BUT I MAY NEED TO PICK YOUR BRAIN ON MORE PERSONAL MATTERS LATER.
AND BELIEVE ME, YOU WILL TALK THEN. UNTIL THAT TIME, YOU'LL BE LOCKED SAFELY AWAY.
NOW, IF YOU'LL EXCUSE ME...
...I'M OFF TO KISS SOME HANDS AND SHAKE SOME BABIES.

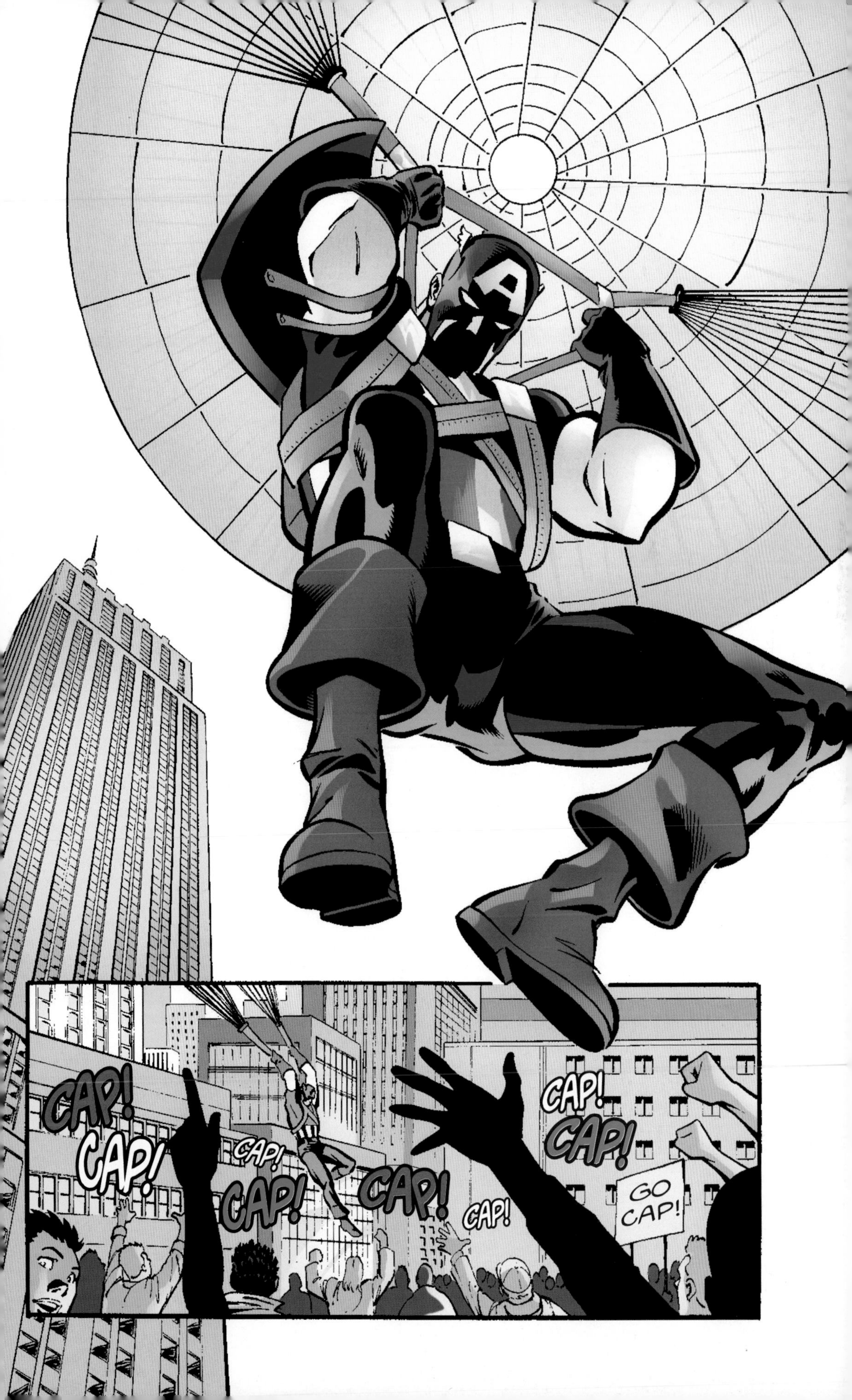
CAP!
CAP!
CAP!
CAP!
CAP!
CAP!
CAP!
CAP!
GO CAP!

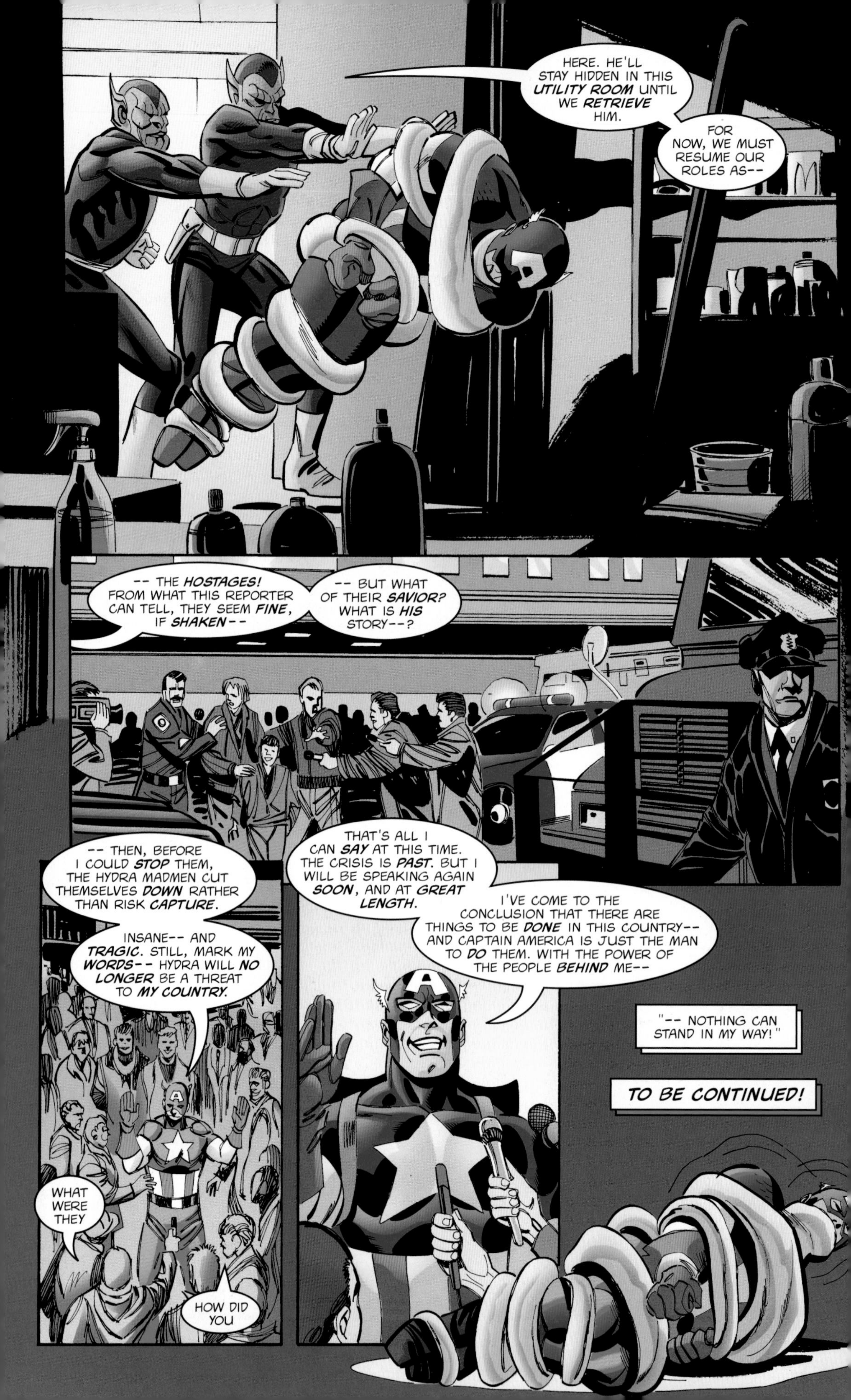
HERE. HE'LL STAY HIDDEN IN THIS UTILITY ROOM UNTIL WE RETRIEVE HIM.
FOR NOW, WE MUST RESUME OUR ROLES AS--
-- THE HOSTAGES! FROM WHAT THIS REPORTER CAN TELL, THEY SEEM FINE, IF SHAKEN--
-- BUT WHAT OF THEIR SAVIOR? WHAT IS HIS STORY--?
-- THEN, BEFORE I COULD STOP THEM, THE HYDRA MADMEN CUT THEMSELVES DOWN RATHER THAN RISK CAPTURE.
INSANE-- AND TRAGIC. STILL, MARK MY WORDS-- HYDRA WILL NO LONGER BE A THREAT TO MY COUNTRY.
WHAT WERE THEY
HOW DID YOU
THAT'S ALL I CAN SAY AT THIS TIME. THE CRISIS IS PAST. BUT I WILL BE SPEAKING AGAIN SOON, AND AT GREAT LENGTH.
I'VE COME TO THE CONCLUSION THAT THERE ARE THINGS TO BE DONE IN THIS COUNTRY-- AND CAPTAIN AMERICA IS JUST THE MAN TO DO THEM. WITH THE POWER OF THE PEOPLE BEHIND ME--
"-- NOTHING CAN STAND IN MY WAY!"
TO BE CONTINUED!

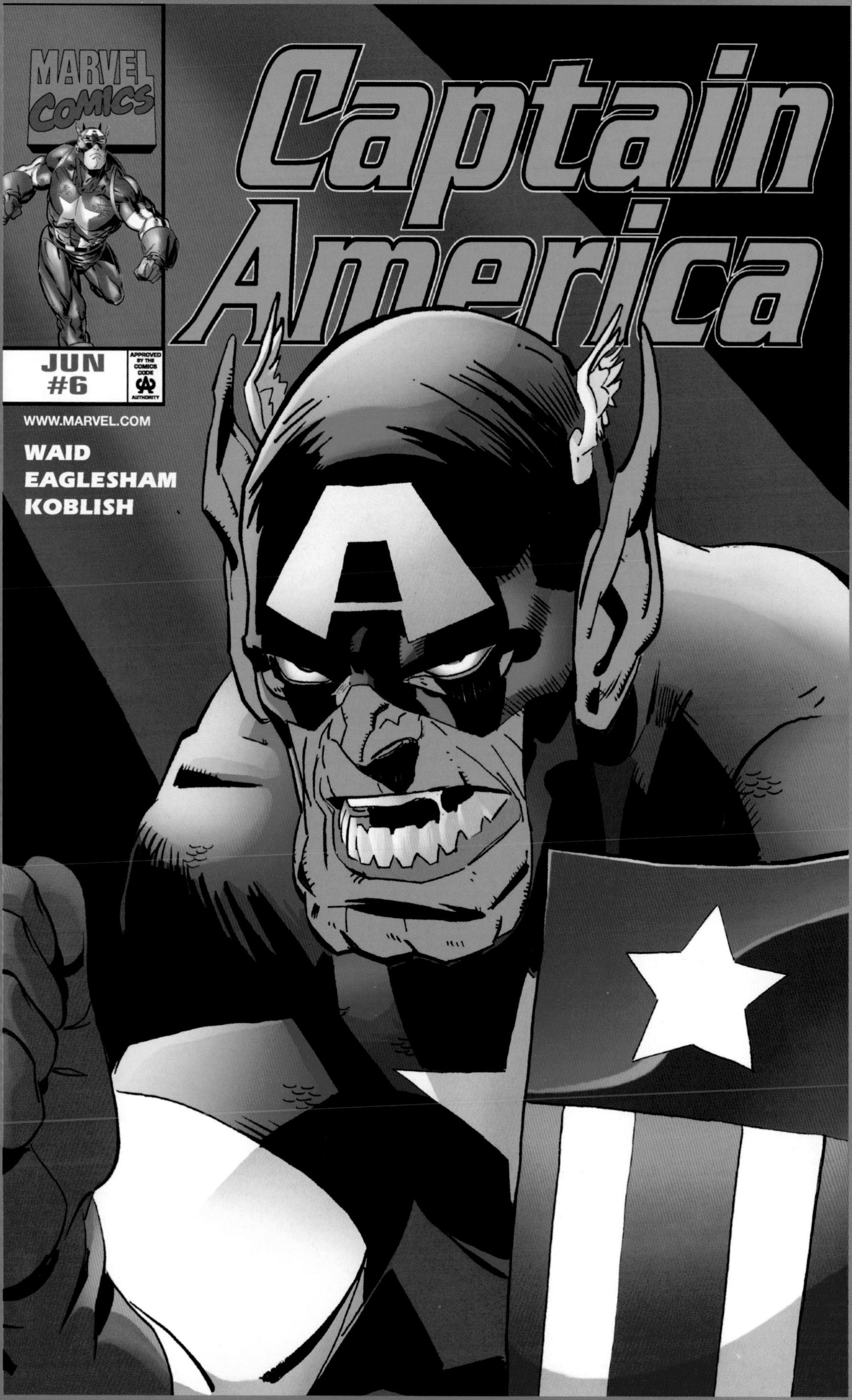
MARVEL COMICS
Captain America
JUN #6
APPROVED BY THE COMICS CODE AUTHORITY
WWW.MARVEL.COM
WAID
EAGLESHAM
KOBLISH

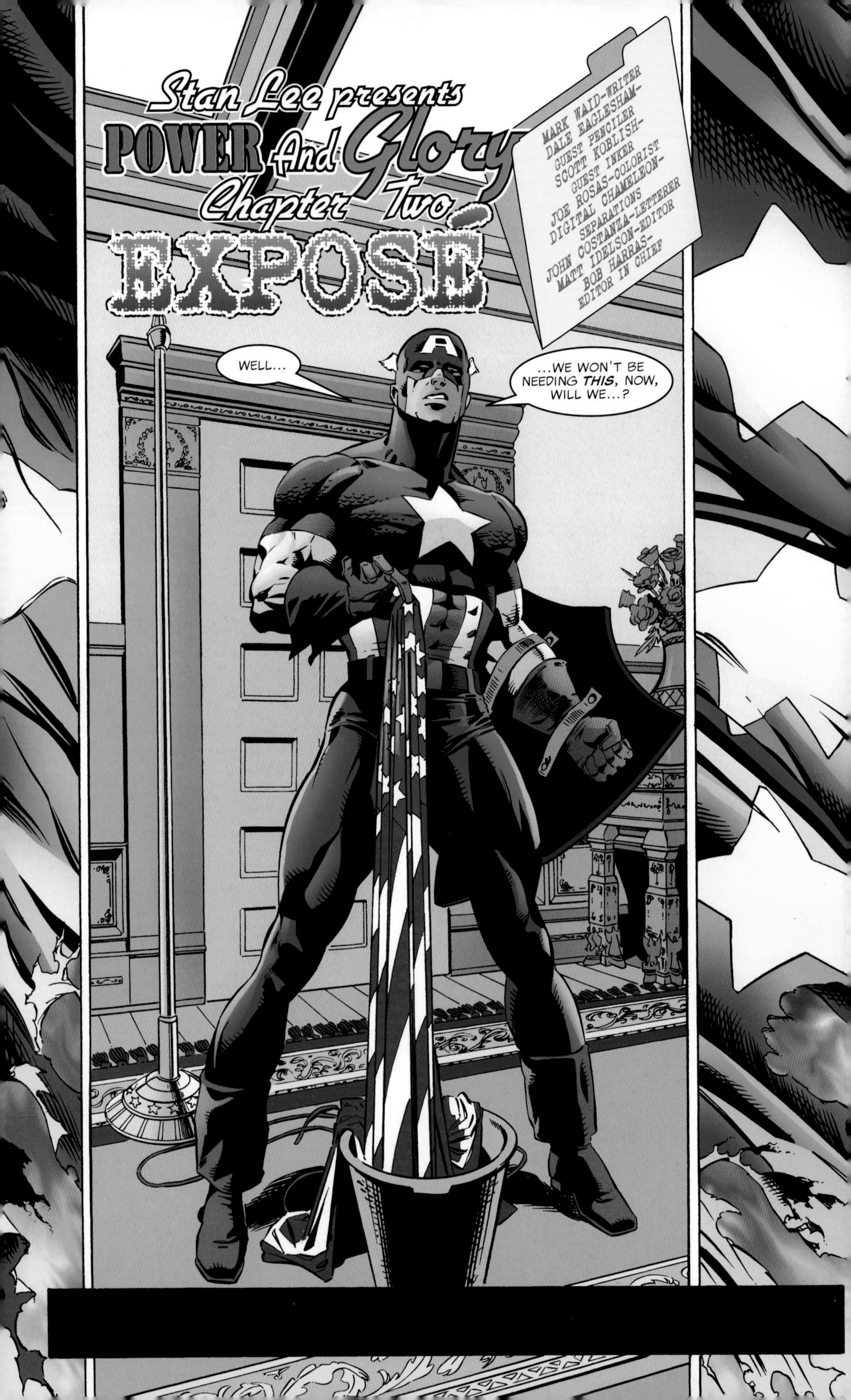
Stan Lee presents
POWER And Glory
Chapter Two!
EXPOSÉ
MARK WAID-WRITER
DALE EAGLESHAM-GUEST PENCILER
SCOTT KOBLISH-GUEST INKER
JOE ROSAS-COLORIST
DIGITAL CHAMELEON-SEPARATIONS
JOHN COSTANZA-LETTERER
MATT IDELSON-EDITOR
BOB HARRAS-EDITOR IN CHIEF
WELL...
...WE WON'T BE NEEDING *THIS*, NOW, WILL WE...?
[redacted]

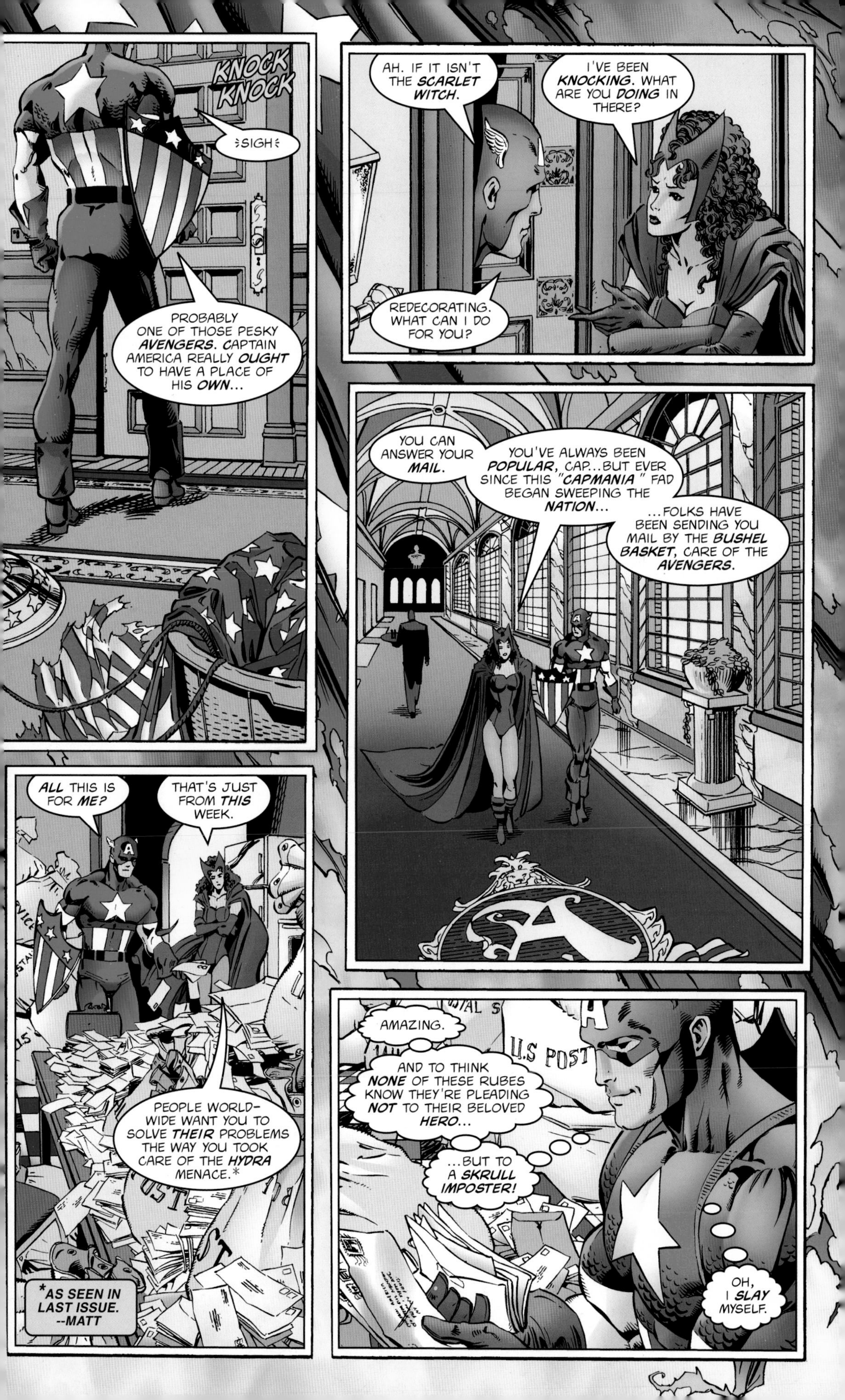
KNOCK KNOCK
SIGH
PROBABLY ONE OF THOSE PESKY AVENGERS. CAPTAIN AMERICA REALLY OUGHT TO HAVE A PLACE OF HIS OWN...
AH. IF IT ISN'T THE SCARLET WITCH.
I'VE BEEN KNOCKING. WHAT ARE YOU DOING IN THERE?
REDECORATING. WHAT CAN I DO FOR YOU?
YOU CAN ANSWER YOUR MAIL.
YOU'VE ALWAYS BEEN POPULAR, CAP...BUT EVER SINCE THIS "CAPMANIA" FAD BEGAN SWEEPING THE NATION...
...FOLKS HAVE BEEN SENDING YOU MAIL BY THE BUSHEL BASKET, CARE OF THE AVENGERS.
ALL THIS IS FOR ME?
THAT'S JUST FROM THIS WEEK.
PEOPLE WORLD-WIDE WANT YOU TO SOLVE THEIR PROBLEMS THE WAY YOU TOOK CARE OF THE HYDRA MENACE.*
*AS SEEN IN LAST ISSUE. --MATT
AMAZING.
U.S POST
AND TO THINK NONE OF THESE RUBES KNOW THEY'RE PLEADING NOT TO THEIR BELOVED HERO...
...BUT TO A SKRULL IMPOSTER!
OH, I SLAY MYSELF.

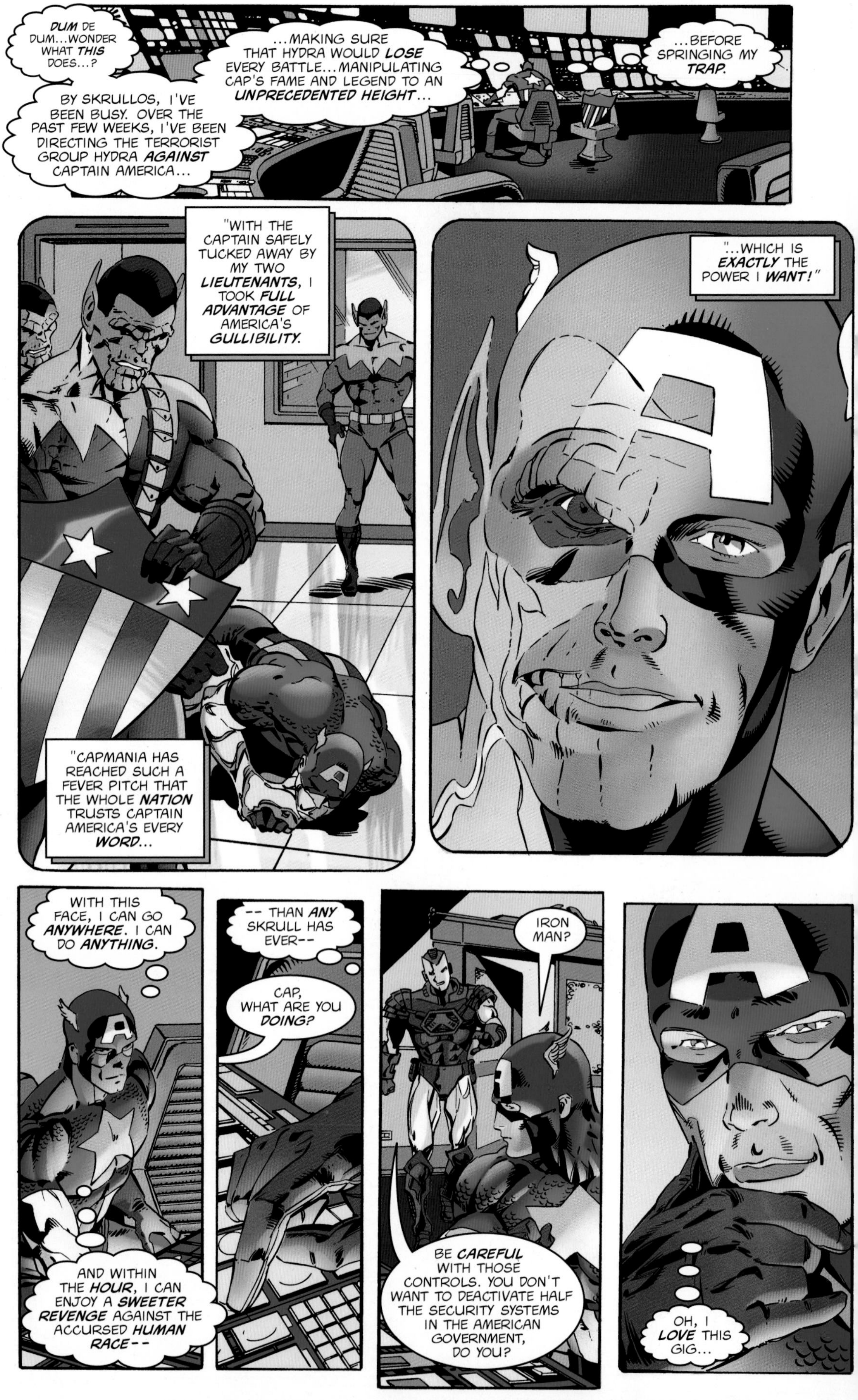
DUM DE DUM...WONDER WHAT THIS DOES...?
BY SKRULLOS, I'VE BEEN BUSY. OVER THE PAST FEW WEEKS, I'VE BEEN DIRECTING THE TERRORIST GROUP HYDRA AGAINST CAPTAIN AMERICA...
...MAKING SURE THAT HYDRA WOULD LOSE EVERY BATTLE...MANIPULATING CAP'S FAME AND LEGEND TO AN UNPRECEDENTED HEIGHT...
...BEFORE SPRINGING MY TRAP.
"WITH THE CAPTAIN SAFELY TUCKED AWAY BY MY TWO LIEUTENANTS, I TOOK FULL ADVANTAGE OF AMERICA'S GULLIBILITY.
"CAPMANIA HAS REACHED SUCH A FEVER PITCH THAT THE WHOLE NATION TRUSTS CAPTAIN AMERICA'S EVERY WORD...
"...WHICH IS EXACTLY THE POWER I WANT!"
WITH THIS FACE, I CAN GO ANYWHERE. I CAN DO ANYTHING.
AND WITHIN THE HOUR, I CAN ENJOY A SWEETER REVENGE AGAINST THE ACCURSED HUMAN RACE--
-- THAN ANY SKRULL HAS EVER--
CAP, WHAT ARE YOU DOING?
IRON MAN?
BE CAREFUL WITH THOSE CONTROLS. YOU DON'T WANT TO DEACTIVATE HALF THE SECURITY SYSTEMS IN THE AMERICAN GOVERNMENT, DO YOU?
OH, I LOVE THIS GIG...

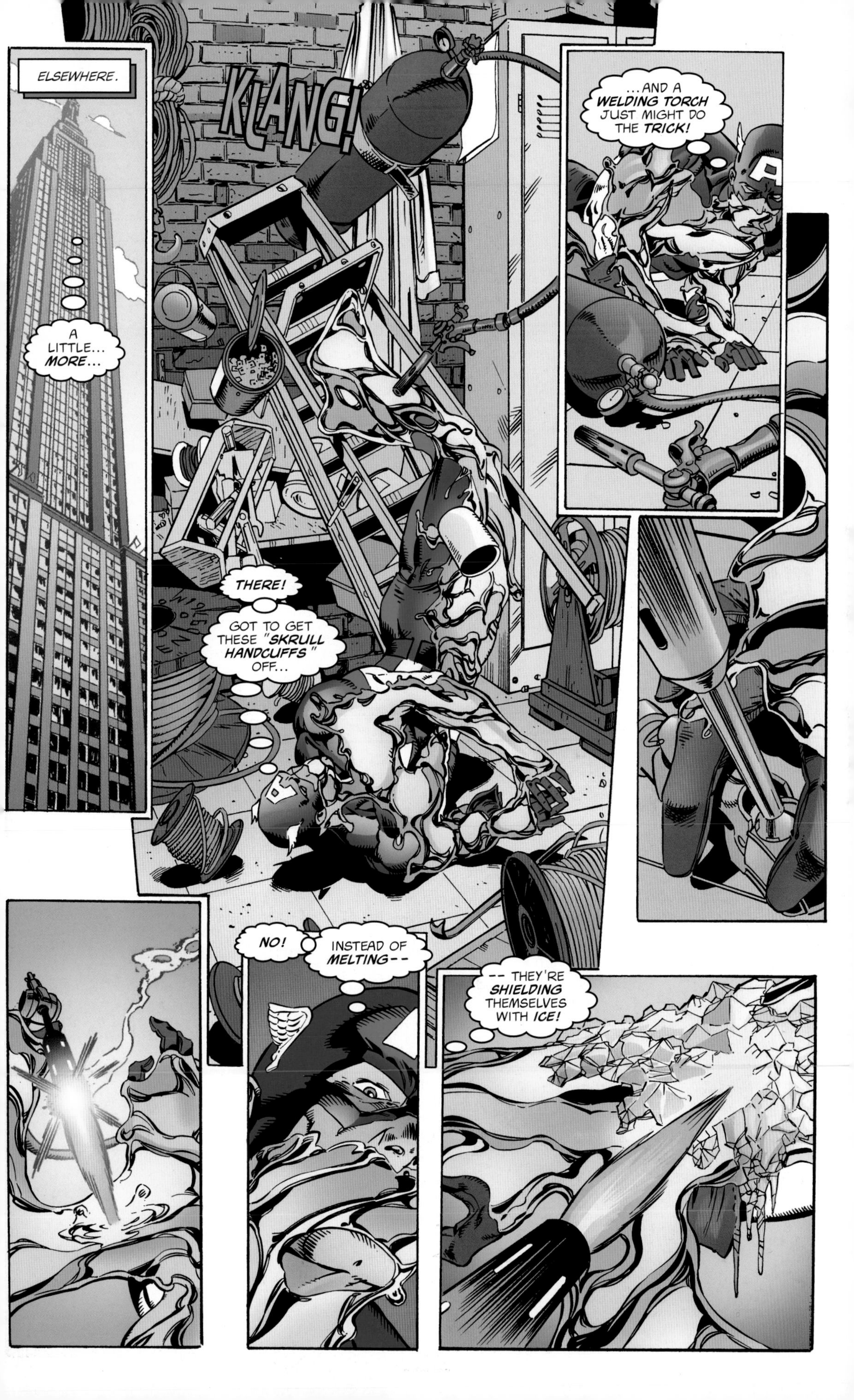
ELSEWHERE.
A LITTLE... MORE...
KLANG!
...AND A WELDING TORCH JUST MIGHT DO THE TRICK!
THERE!
GOT TO GET THESE "SKRULL HANDCUFFS" OFF...
NO!
INSTEAD OF MELTING--
-- THEY'RE SHIELDING THEMSELVES WITH ICE!

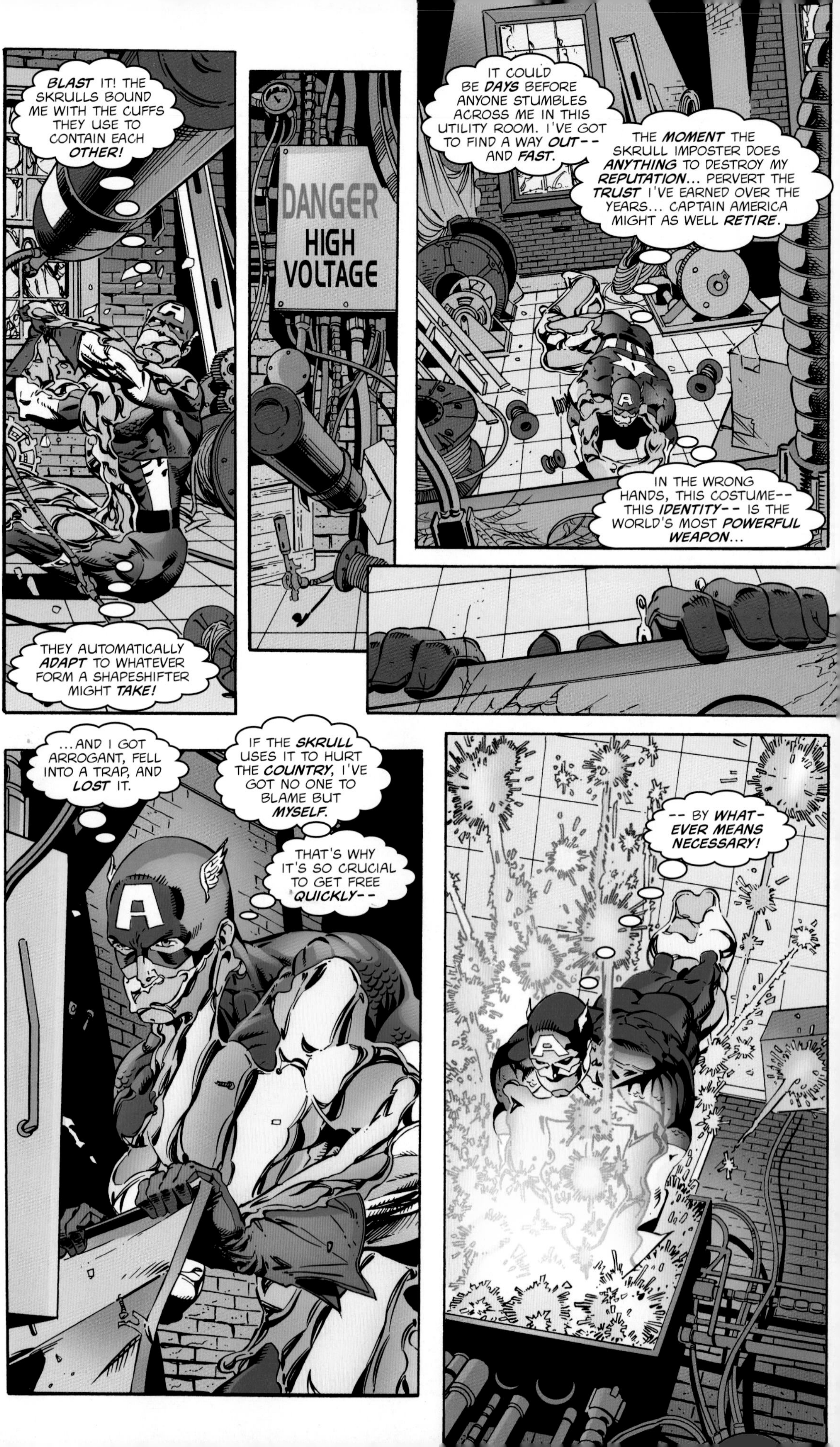
BLAST IT! THE SKRULLS BOUND ME WITH THE CUFFS THEY USE TO CONTAIN EACH OTHER!
THEY AUTOMATICALLY ADAPT TO WHATEVER FORM A SHAPESHIFTER MIGHT TAKE!
DANGER
HIGH VOLTAGE
IT COULD BE DAYS BEFORE ANYONE STUMBLES ACROSS ME IN THIS UTILITY ROOM. I'VE GOT TO FIND A WAY OUT-- AND FAST.
THE MOMENT THE SKRULL IMPOSTER DOES ANYTHING TO DESTROY MY REPUTATION... PERVERT THE TRUST I'VE EARNED OVER THE YEARS... CAPTAIN AMERICA MIGHT AS WELL RETIRE.
IN THE WRONG HANDS, THIS COSTUME-- THIS IDENTITY-- IS THE WORLD'S MOST POWERFUL WEAPON...
...AND I GOT ARROGANT, FELL INTO A TRAP, AND LOST IT.
IF THE SKRULL USES IT TO HURT THE COUNTRY, I'VE GOT NO ONE TO BLAME BUT MYSELF.
THAT'S WHY IT'S SO CRUCIAL TO GET FREE QUICKLY--
-- BY WHAT-EVER MEANS NECESSARY!

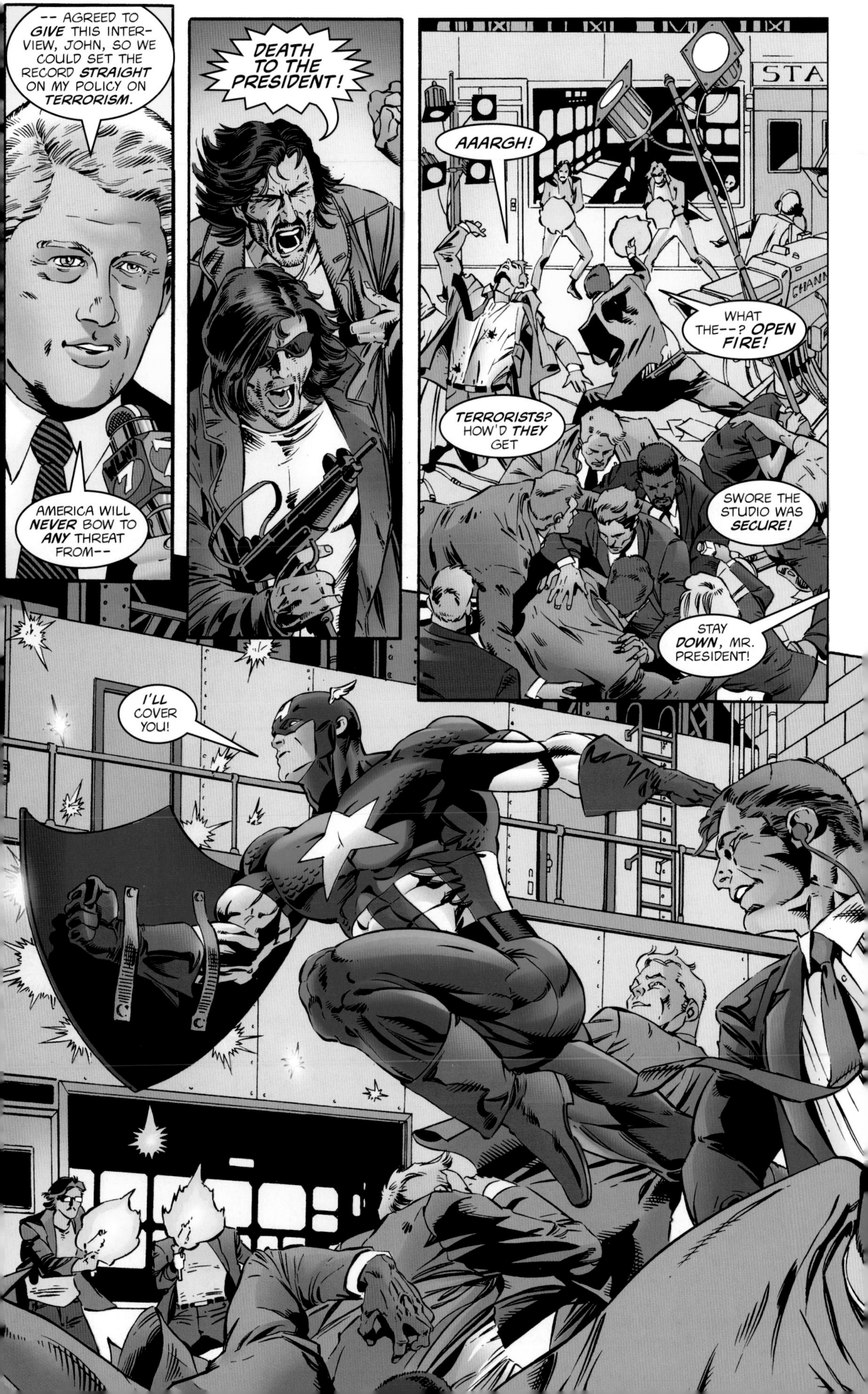
-- AGREED TO GIVE THIS INTERVIEW, JOHN, SO WE COULD SET THE RECORD STRAIGHT ON MY POLICY ON TERRORISM.
AMERICA WILL NEVER BOW TO ANY THREAT FROM--
DEATH TO THE PRESIDENT!
AAARGH!
WHAT THE--? OPEN FIRE!
TERRORISTS? HOW'D THEY GET
SWORE THE STUDIO WAS SECURE!
STAY DOWN, MR. PRESIDENT!
I'LL COVER YOU!

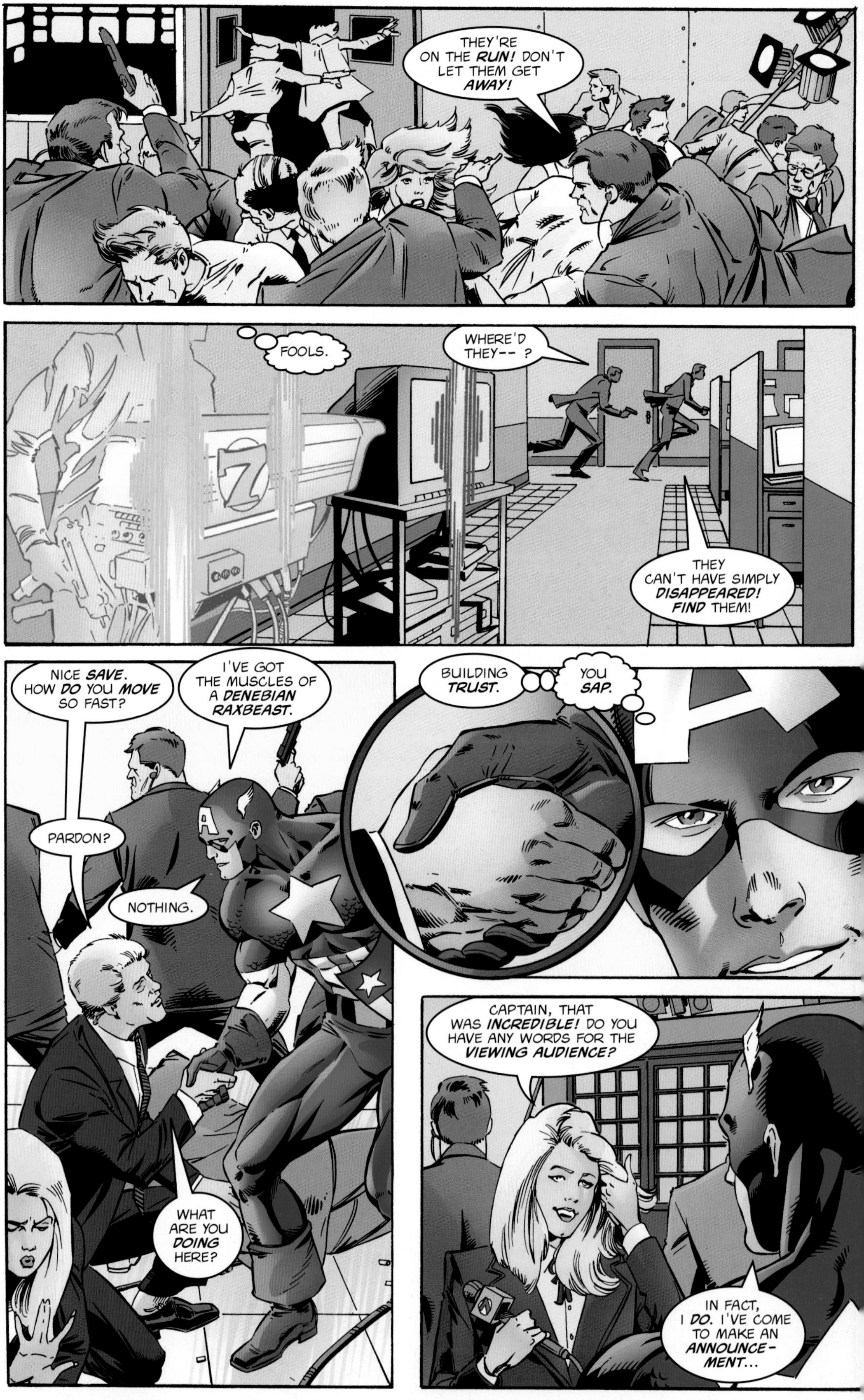
THEY'RE ON THE RUN! DON'T LET THEM GET AWAY!
FOOLS.
WHERE'D THEY-- ?
THEY CAN'T HAVE SIMPLY DISAPPEARED! FIND THEM!
NICE SAVE. HOW DO YOU MOVE SO FAST?
I'VE GOT THE MUSCLES OF A DENEBIAN RAXBEAST.
PARDON?
NOTHING.
WHAT ARE YOU DOING HERE?
BUILDING TRUST.
YOU SAP.
CAPTAIN, THAT WAS INCREDIBLE! DO YOU HAVE ANY WORDS FOR THE VIEWING AUDIENCE?
IN FACT, I DO. I'VE COME TO MAKE AN ANNOUNCE-MENT...

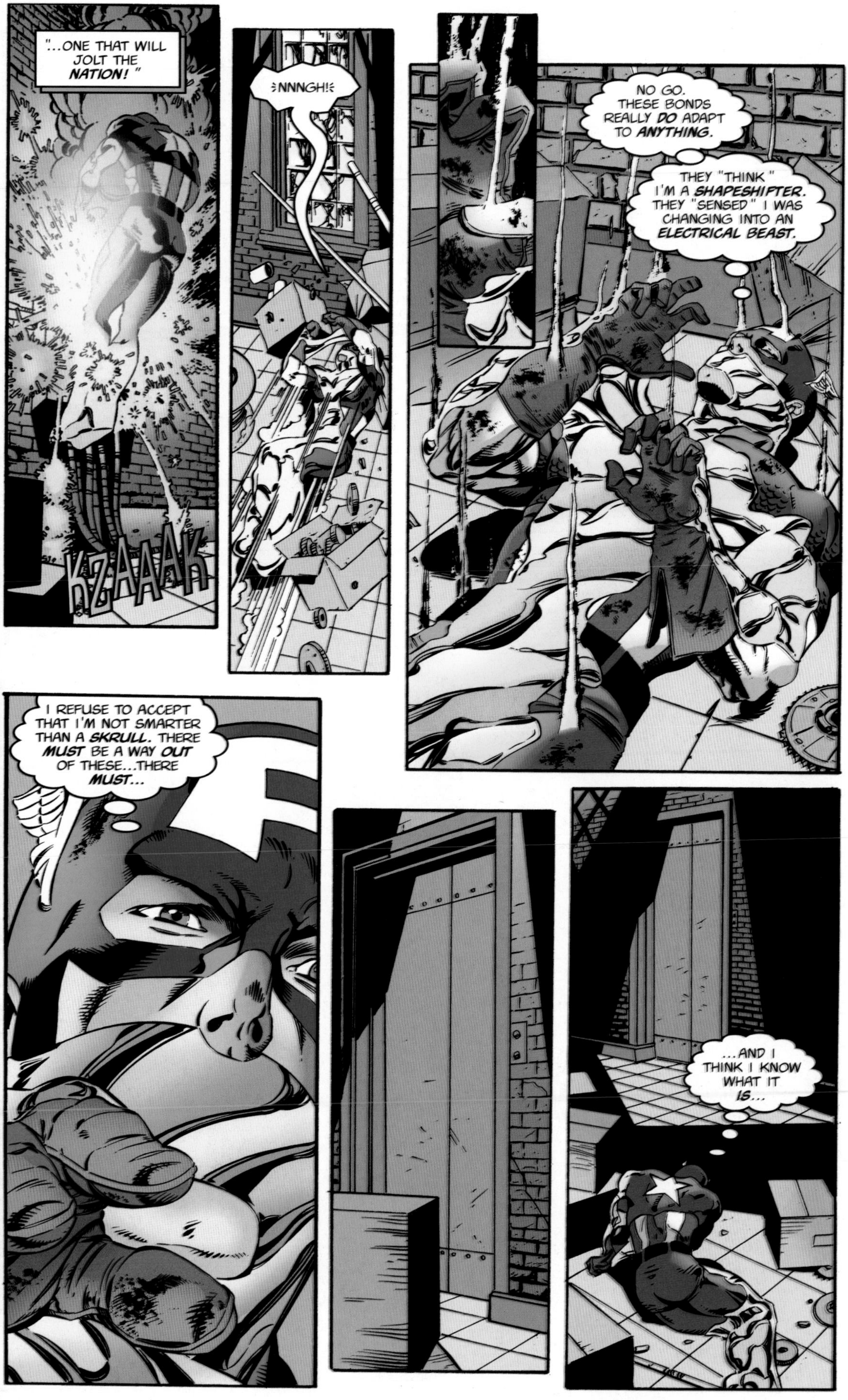
"...ONE THAT WILL JOLT THE NATION!"
KZAAAK
NNNGH!
NO GO. THESE BONDS REALLY DO ADAPT TO ANYTHING.
THEY "THINK" I'M A SHAPESHIFTER. THEY "SENSED" I WAS CHANGING INTO AN ELECTRICAL BEAST.
I REFUSE TO ACCEPT THAT I'M NOT SMARTER THAN A SKRULL. THERE MUST BE A WAY OUT OF THESE...THERE MUST...
...AND I THINK I KNOW WHAT IT IS...

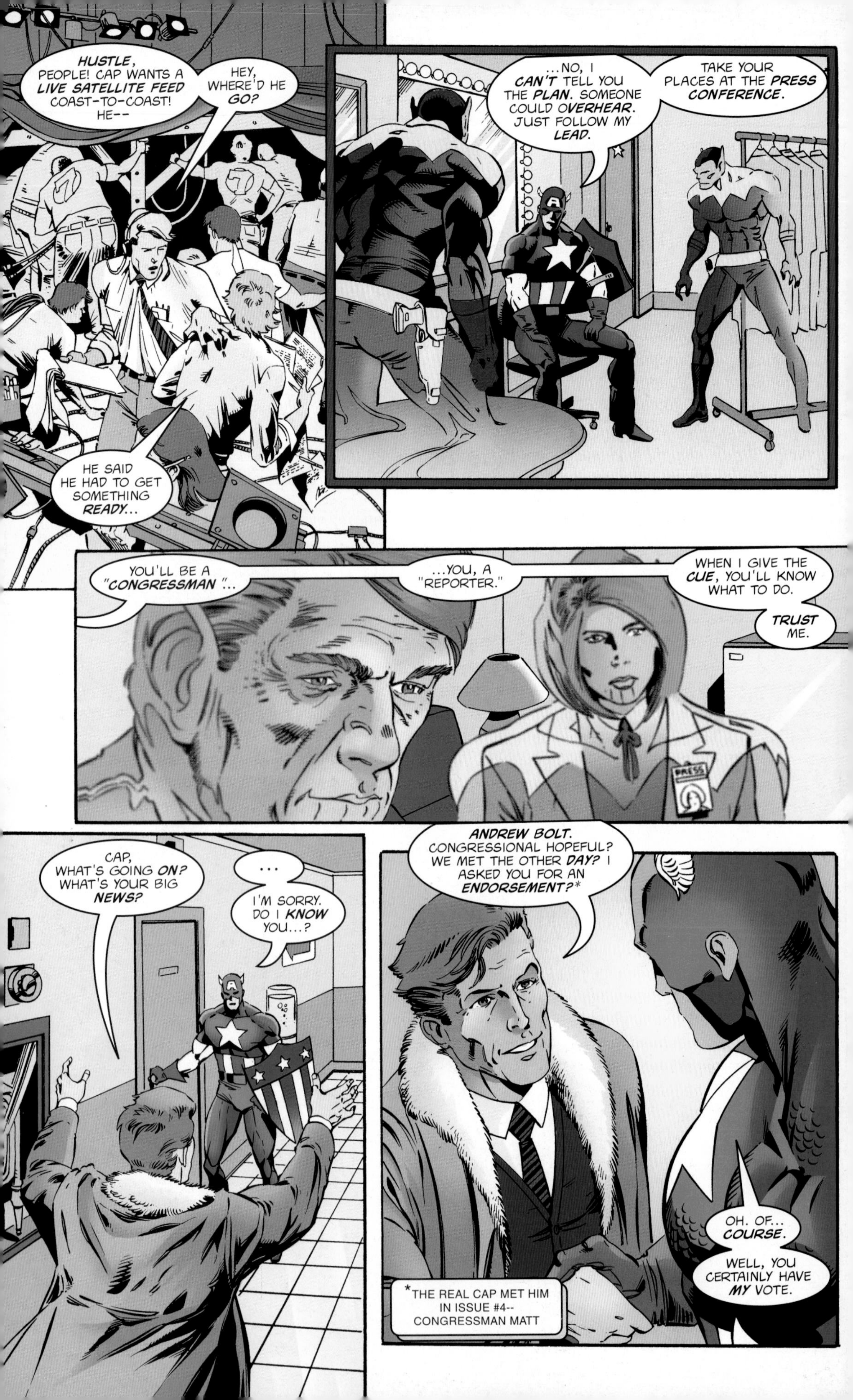
HUSTLE, PEOPLE! CAP WANTS A LIVE SATELLITE FEED COAST-TO-COAST! HE--
HEY, WHERE'D HE GO?
HE SAID HE HAD TO GET SOMETHING READY...
...NO, I CAN'T TELL YOU THE PLAN. SOMEONE COULD OVERHEAR. JUST FOLLOW MY LEAD.
TAKE YOUR PLACES AT THE PRESS CONFERENCE.
YOU'LL BE A "CONGRESSMAN"...
...YOU, A "REPORTER."
WHEN I GIVE THE CUE, YOU'LL KNOW WHAT TO DO.
TRUST ME.
PRESS
CAP, WHAT'S GOING ON? WHAT'S YOUR BIG NEWS?
...
I'M SORRY. DO I KNOW YOU...?
ANDREW BOLT. CONGRESSIONAL HOPEFUL? WE MET THE OTHER DAY? I ASKED YOU FOR AN ENDORSEMENT?*
OH. OF... COURSE.
WELL, YOU CERTAINLY HAVE MY VOTE.
*THE REAL CAP MET HIM IN ISSUE #4-- CONGRESSMAN MATT

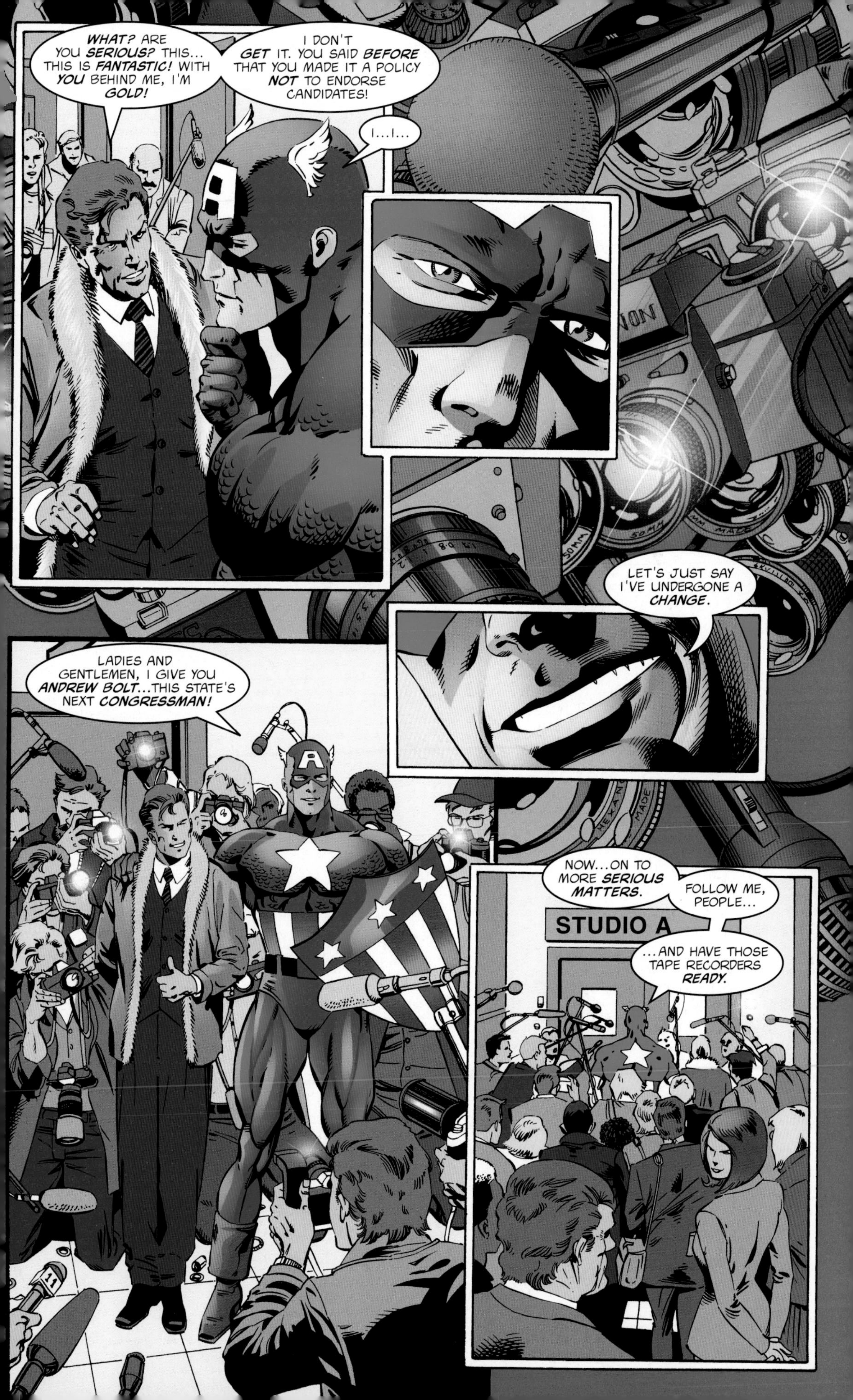
WHAT? ARE YOU SERIOUS? THIS... THIS IS FANTASTIC! WITH YOU BEHIND ME, I'M GOLD!
I DON'T GET IT. YOU SAID BEFORE THAT YOU MADE IT A POLICY NOT TO ENDORSE CANDIDATES!
I...I...
LET'S JUST SAY I'VE UNDERGONE A CHANGE.
LADIES AND GENTLEMEN, I GIVE YOU ANDREW BOLT...THIS STATE'S NEXT CONGRESSMAN!
NOW...ON TO MORE SERIOUS MATTERS.
FOLLOW ME, PEOPLE...
...AND HAVE THOSE TAPE RECORDERS READY.
STUDIO A

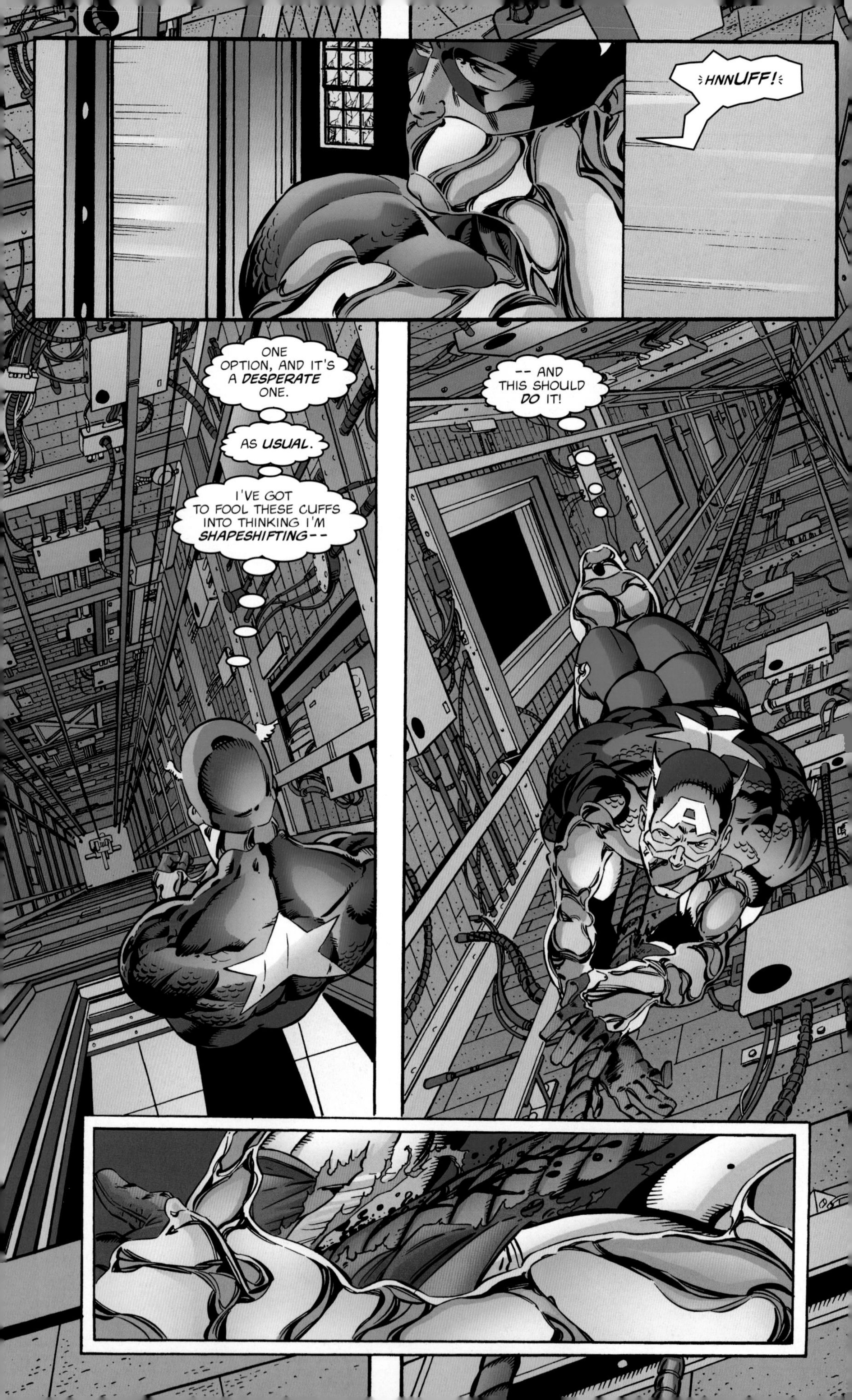
HNNUFF!
ONE OPTION, AND IT'S A DESPERATE ONE.
AS USUAL.
I'VE GOT TO FOOL THESE CUFFS INTO THINKING I'M SHAPESHIFTING--
-- AND THIS SHOULD DO IT!

MMMRRGHH!
COME ON...
...COME ON...
...YES!

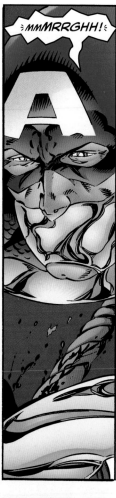

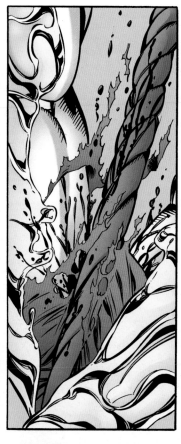

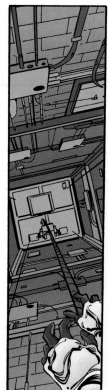

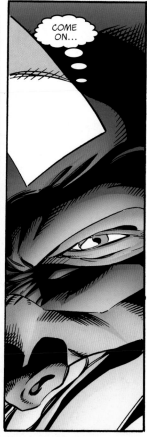

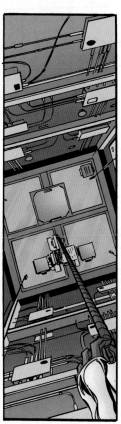

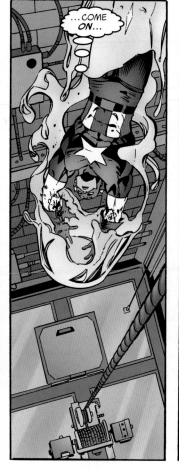

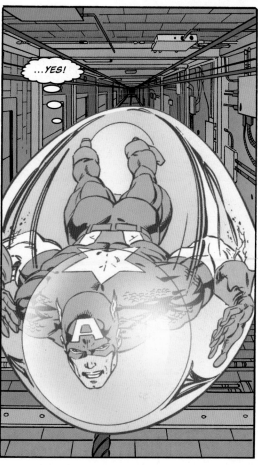

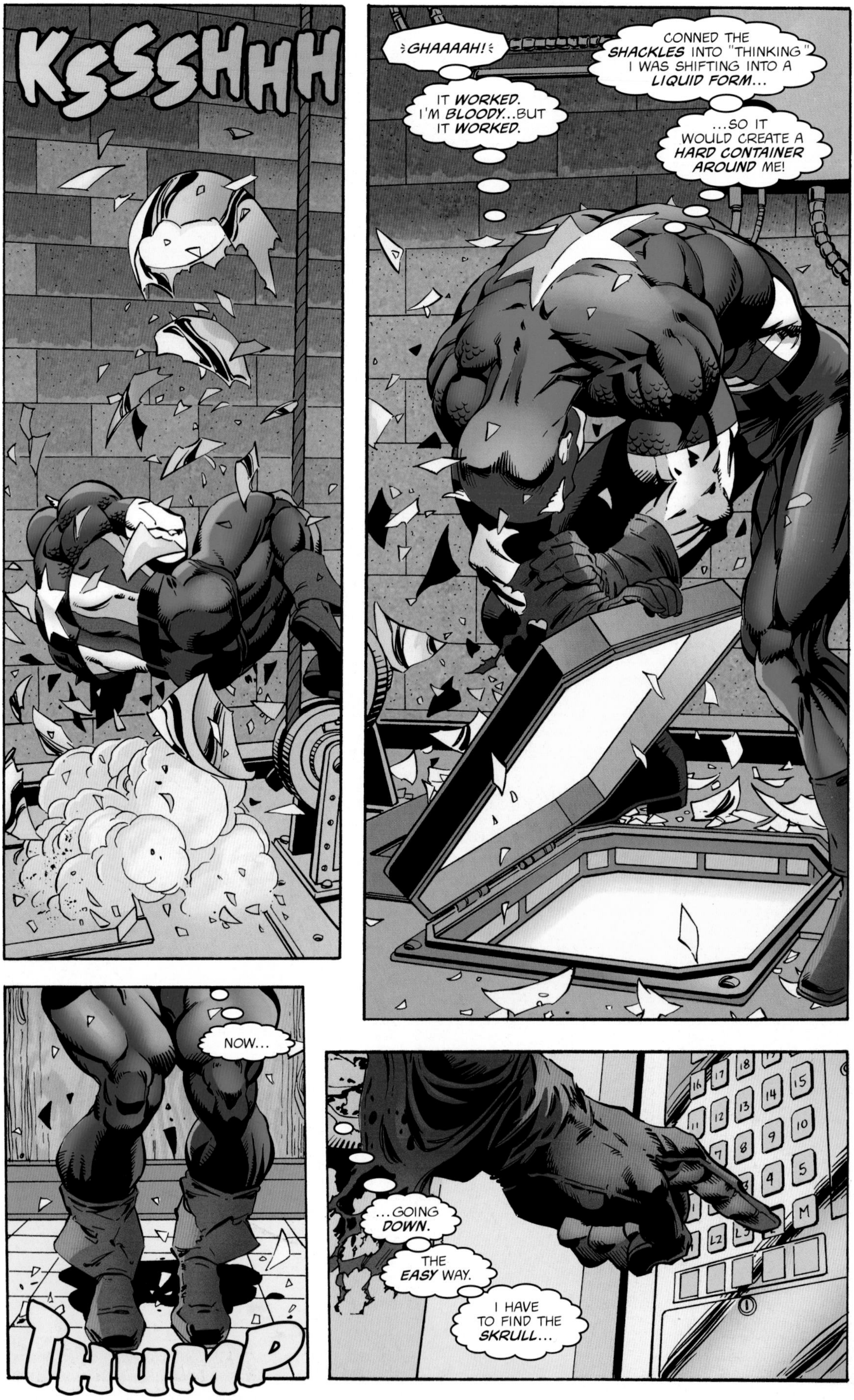
KSSSHHH
GHAAAAH!
IT WORKED. I'M BLOODY...BUT IT WORKED.
CONNED THE SHACKLES INTO "THINKING" I WAS SHIFTING INTO A LIQUID FORM...
...SO IT WOULD CREATE A HARD CONTAINER AROUND ME!
NOW...
THUMP
...GOING DOWN.
THE EASY WAY.
I HAVE TO FIND THE SKRULL...

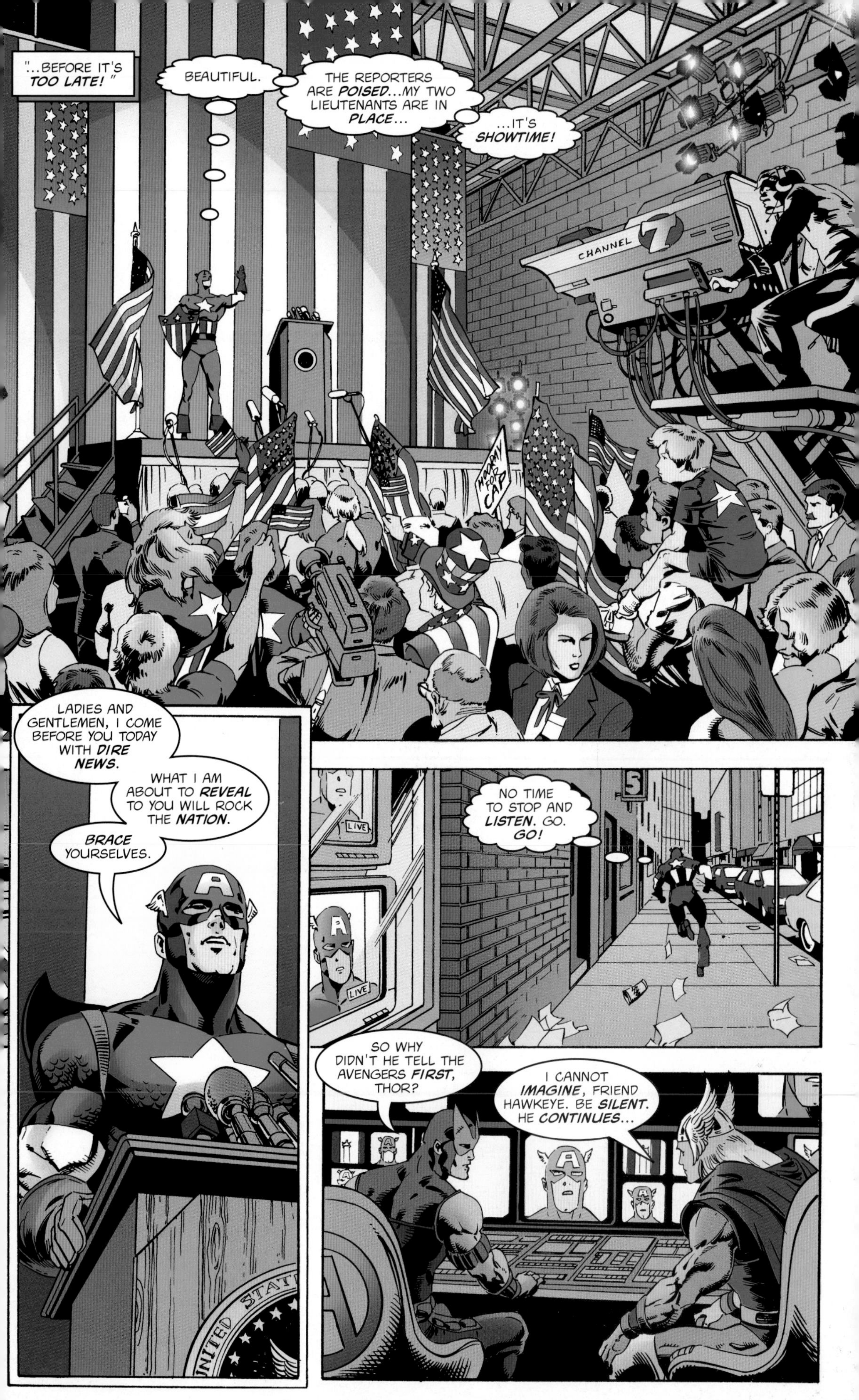

"...BEFORE IT'S *TOO LATE!*"
BEAUTIFUL.
THE REPORTERS ARE *POISED*...MY TWO LIEUTENANTS ARE IN *PLACE*...
...IT'S *SHOWTIME!*
CHANNEL 7
HOORAY FOR CAP
LADIES AND GENTLEMEN, I COME BEFORE YOU TODAY WITH *DIRE NEWS*.
WHAT I AM ABOUT TO *REVEAL* TO YOU WILL ROCK THE *NATION*.
BRACE YOURSELVES.
LIVE
LIVE
NO TIME TO STOP AND *LISTEN*. GO. *GO!*
5
SO WHY DIDN'T HE TELL THE AVENGERS *FIRST*, THOR?
I CANNOT *IMAGINE*, FRIEND HAWKEYE. BE *SILENT*. HE *CONTINUES*...

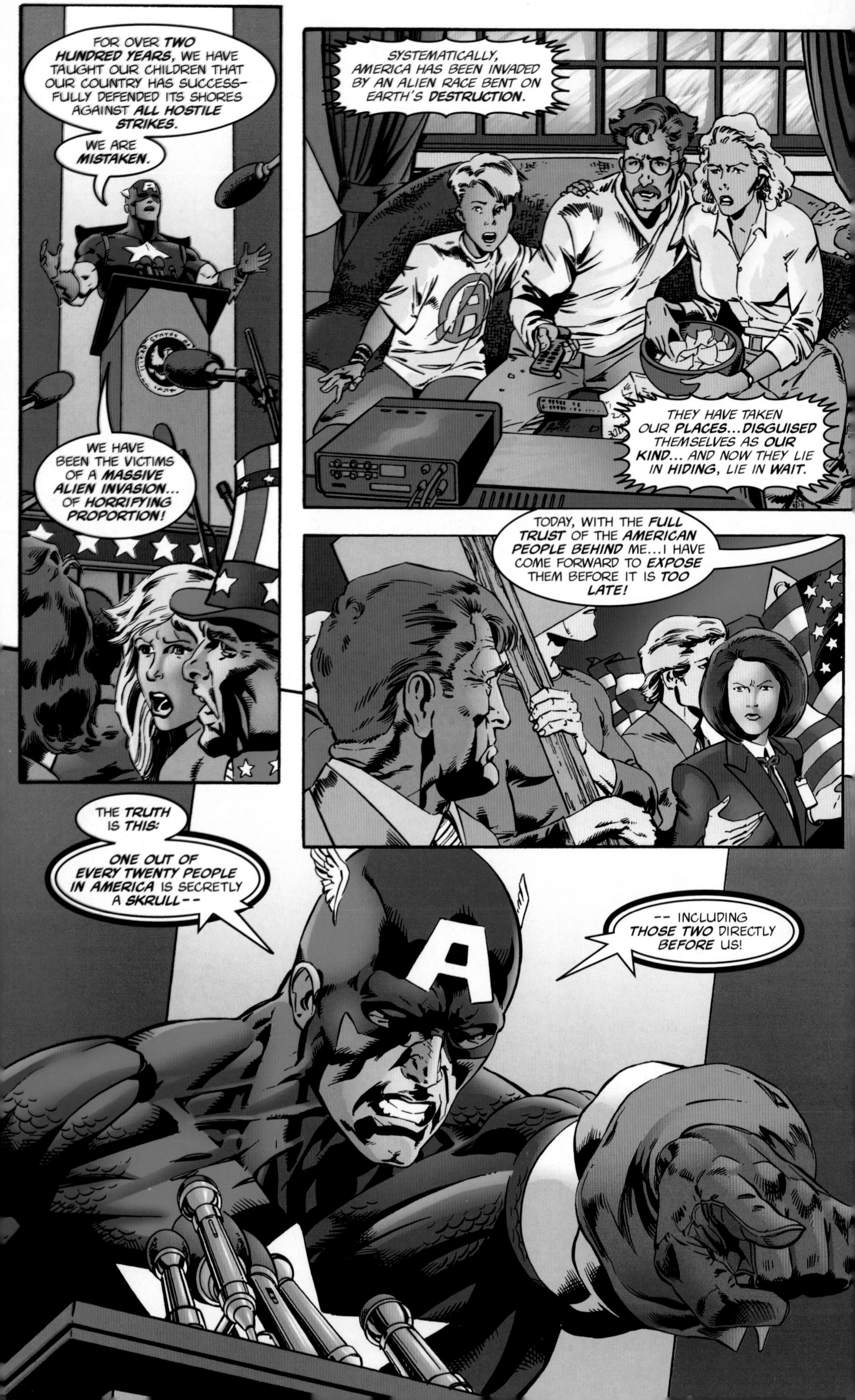
FOR OVER TWO HUNDRED YEARS, WE HAVE TAUGHT OUR CHILDREN THAT OUR COUNTRY HAS SUCCESSFULLY DEFENDED ITS SHORES AGAINST ALL HOSTILE STRIKES.
WE ARE MISTAKEN.
SYSTEMATICALLY, AMERICA HAS BEEN INVADED BY AN ALIEN RACE BENT ON EARTH'S DESTRUCTION.
THEY HAVE TAKEN OUR PLACES...DISGUISED THEMSELVES AS OUR KIND... AND NOW THEY LIE IN HIDING, LIE IN WAIT.
WE HAVE BEEN THE VICTIMS OF A MASSIVE ALIEN INVASION... OF HORRIFYING PROPORTION!
TODAY, WITH THE FULL TRUST OF THE AMERICAN PEOPLE BEHIND ME...I HAVE COME FORWARD TO EXPOSE THEM BEFORE IT IS TOO LATE!
THE TRUTH IS THIS:
ONE OUT OF EVERY TWENTY PEOPLE IN AMERICA IS SECRETLY A SKRULL--
-- INCLUDING THOSE TWO DIRECTLY BEFORE US!

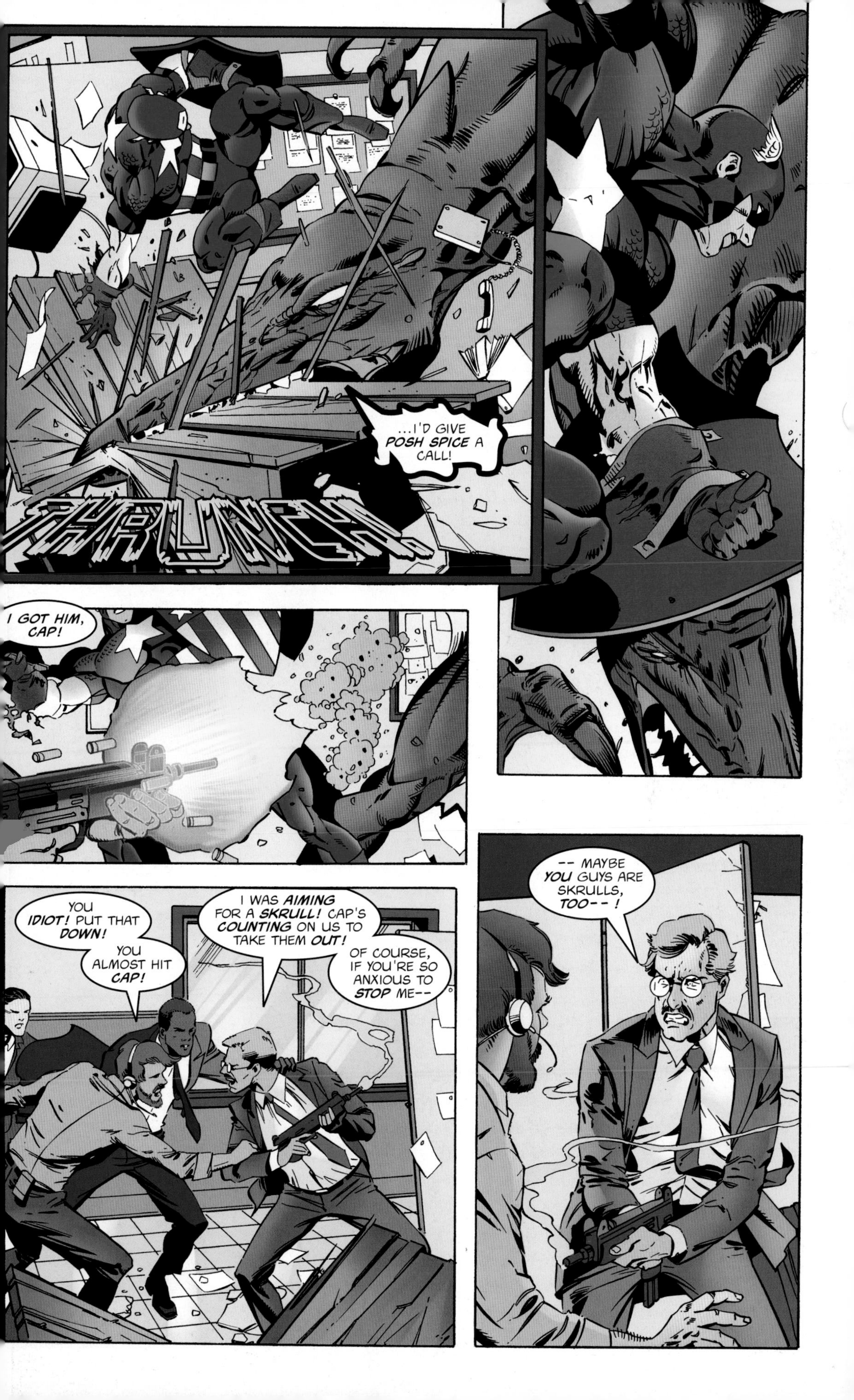
...I'D GIVE POSH SPICE A CALL!
THRUNCH!
I GOT HIM, CAP!
YOU IDIOT! PUT THAT DOWN!
YOU ALMOST HIT CAP!
I WAS AIMING FOR A SKRULL! CAP'S COUNTING ON US TO TAKE THEM OUT!
OF COURSE, IF YOU'RE SO ANXIOUS TO STOP ME--
-- MAYBE YOU GUYS ARE SKRULLS, TOO-- !

CH-CHAK

STOP!

WHAT DO YOU *MEAN* I'M "*COUNTING*" ON YOU?

TELL *ME!*

Y-YOU *SAID*-- SKRULLS WERE *EVERYWHERE*--

-- INVADING-- HUH*HIDING*--

-- T-TOLD US TO FUH*FIND* THEM--!

I DID *WHAT?*

YOU!

ME.

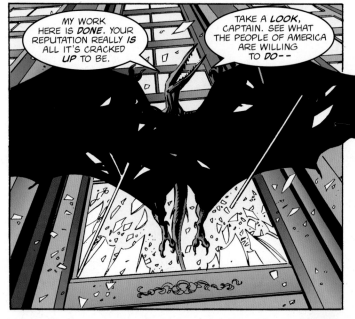

MY WORK HERE IS *DONE.* YOUR REPUTATION REALLY *IS* ALL IT'S CRACKED *UP* TO BE.

TAKE A *LOOK,* CAPTAIN. SEE WHAT THE PEOPLE OF AMERICA ARE WILLING TO *DO*--

-- IN *YOUR NAME.*

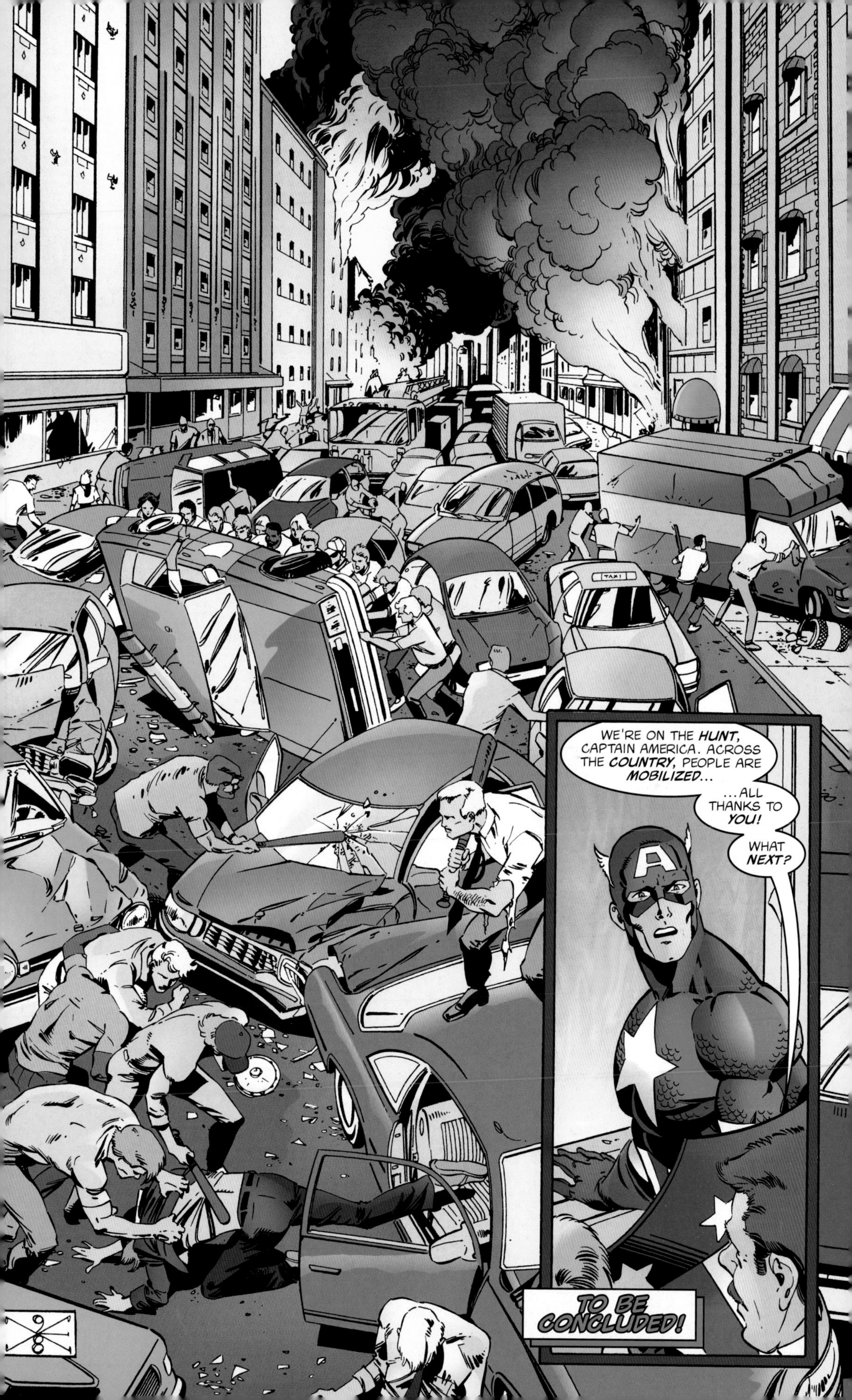
TAXI
WE'RE ON THE HUNT, CAPTAIN AMERICA. ACROSS THE COUNTRY, PEOPLE ARE MOBILIZED...
...ALL THANKS TO YOU!
WHAT NEXT?
TO BE CONCLUDED!

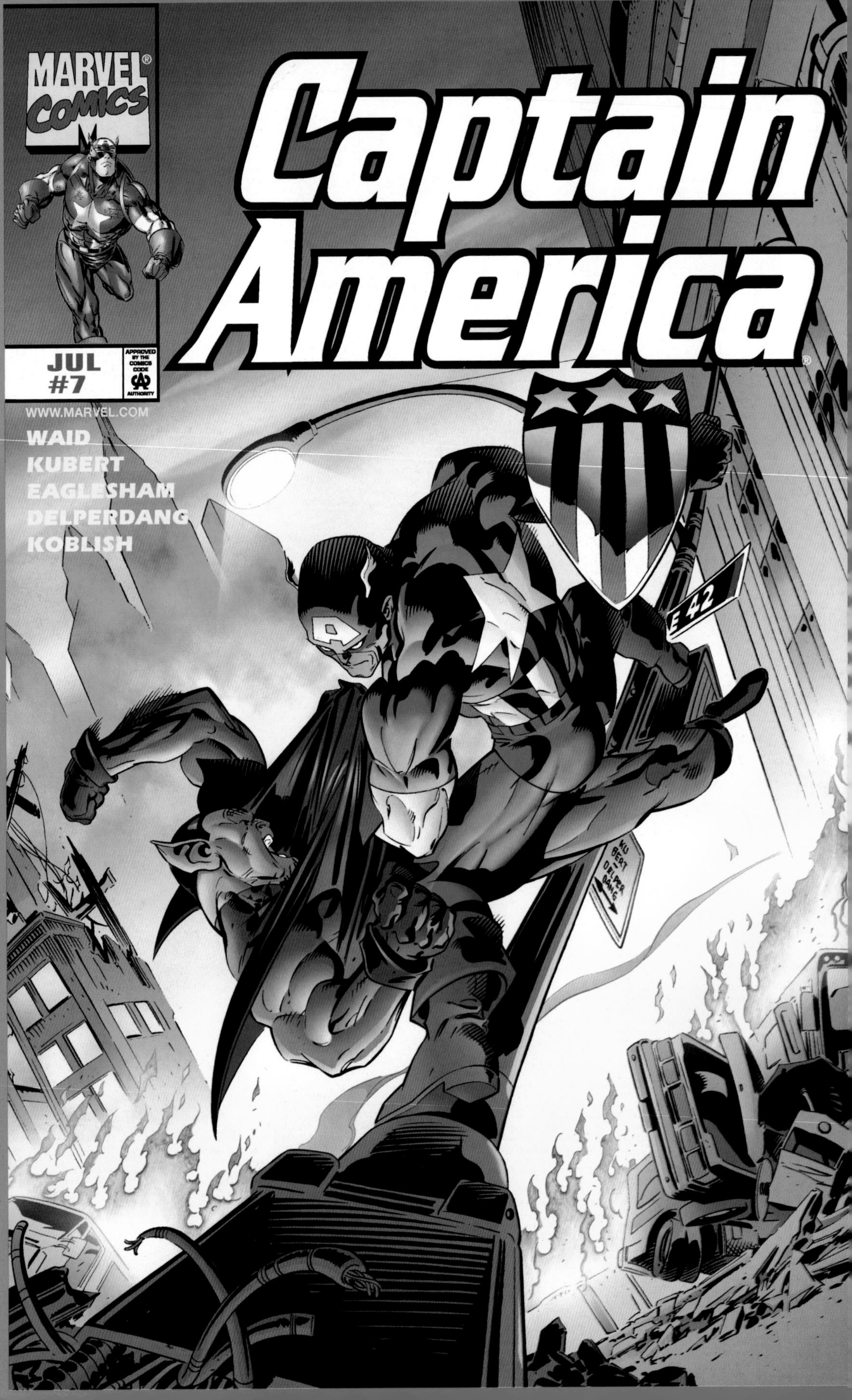
MARVEL® COMICS
Captain America®
JUL
#7
APPROVED BY THE COMICS CODE AUTHORITY
WWW.MARVEL.COM
WAID
KUBERT
EAGLESHAM
DELPERDANG
KOBLISH
E 42

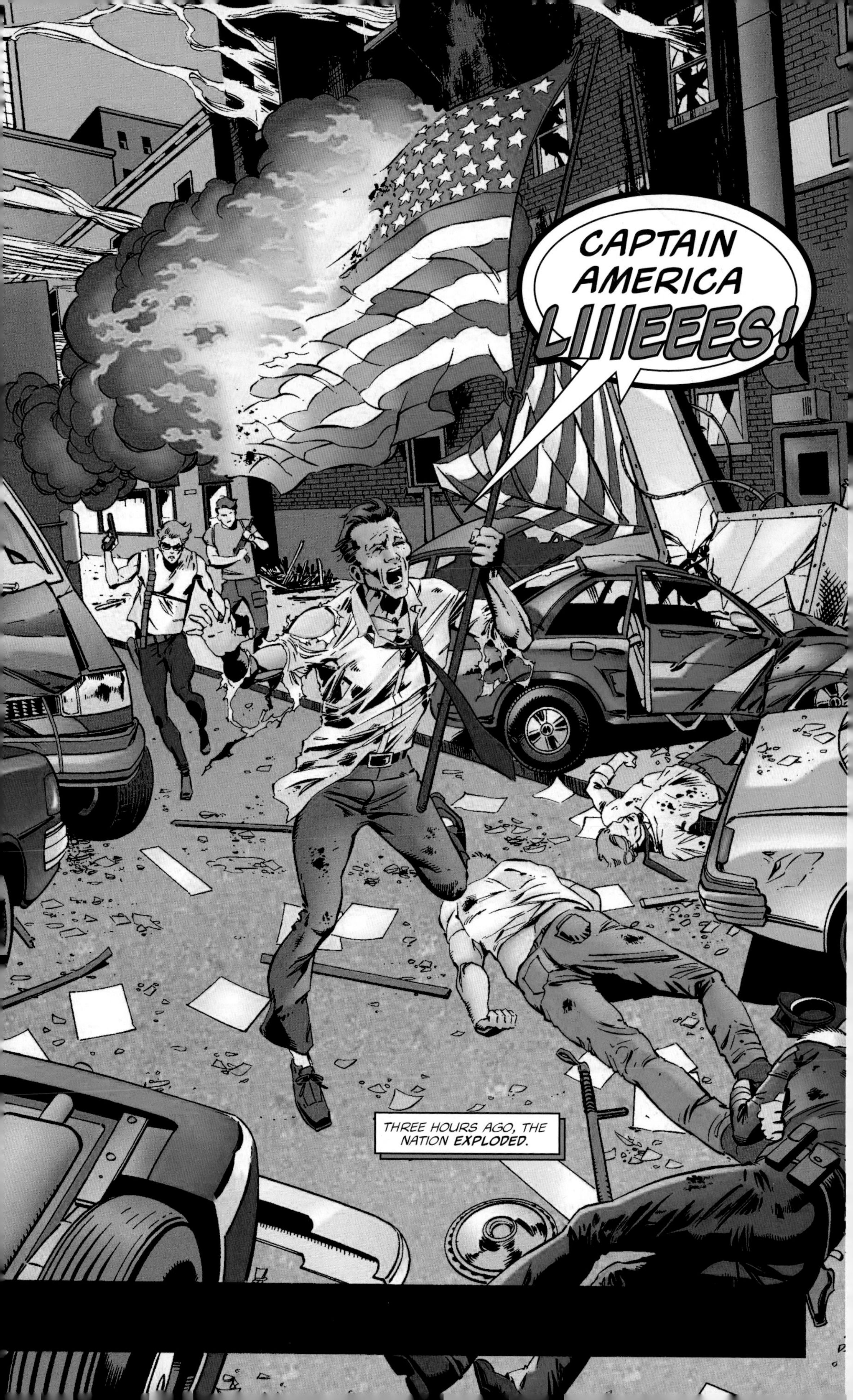
CAPTAIN AMERICA LIIIEEES!
THREE HOURS AGO, THE NATION EXPLODED.

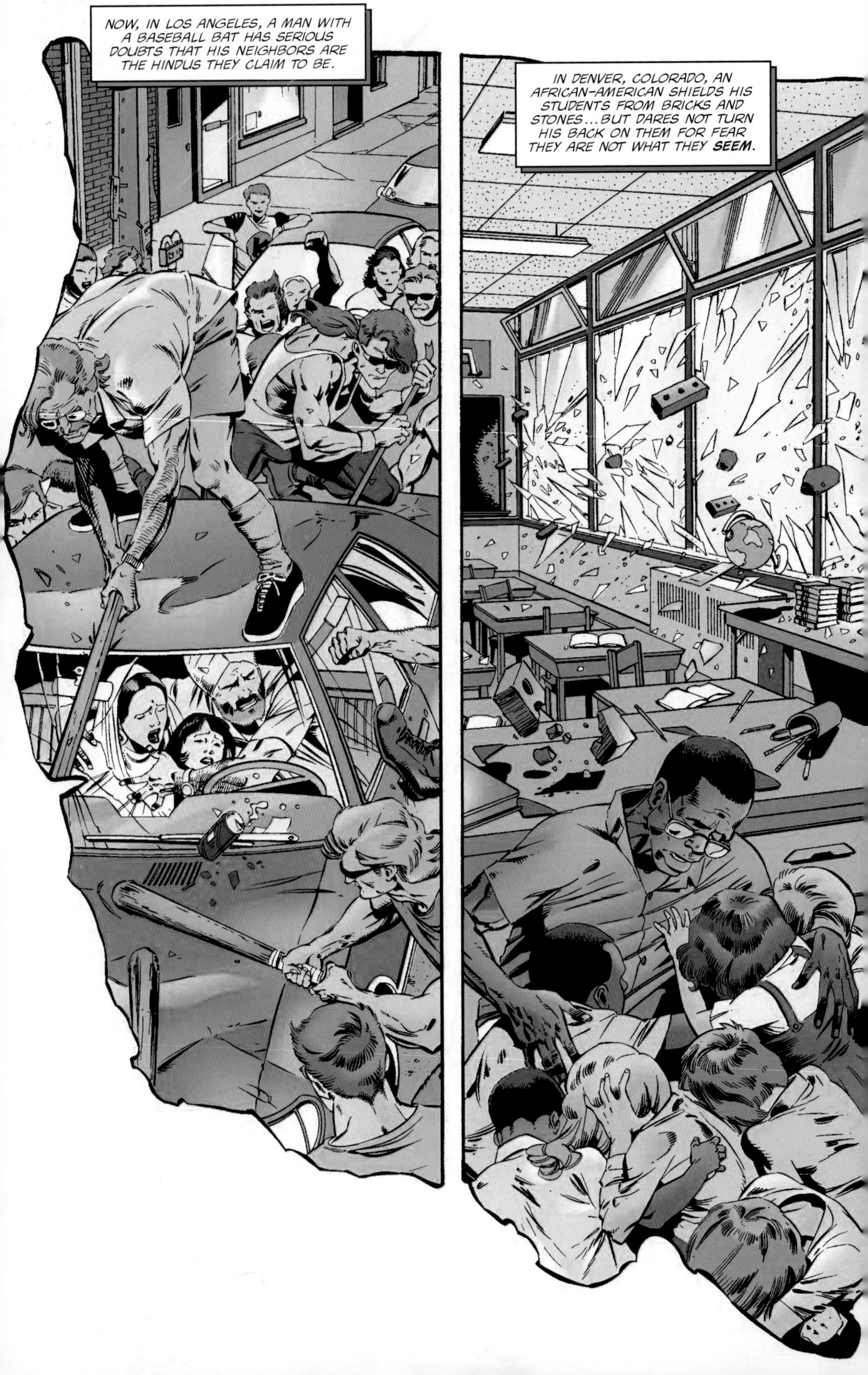
NOW, IN LOS ANGELES, A MAN WITH A BASEBALL BAT HAS SERIOUS DOUBTS THAT HIS NEIGHBORS ARE THE HINDUS THEY CLAIM TO BE.
IN DENVER, COLORADO, AN AFRICAN-AMERICAN SHIELDS HIS STUDENTS FROM BRICKS AND STONES...BUT DARES NOT TURN HIS BACK ON THEM FOR FEAR THEY ARE NOT WHAT THEY SEEM.

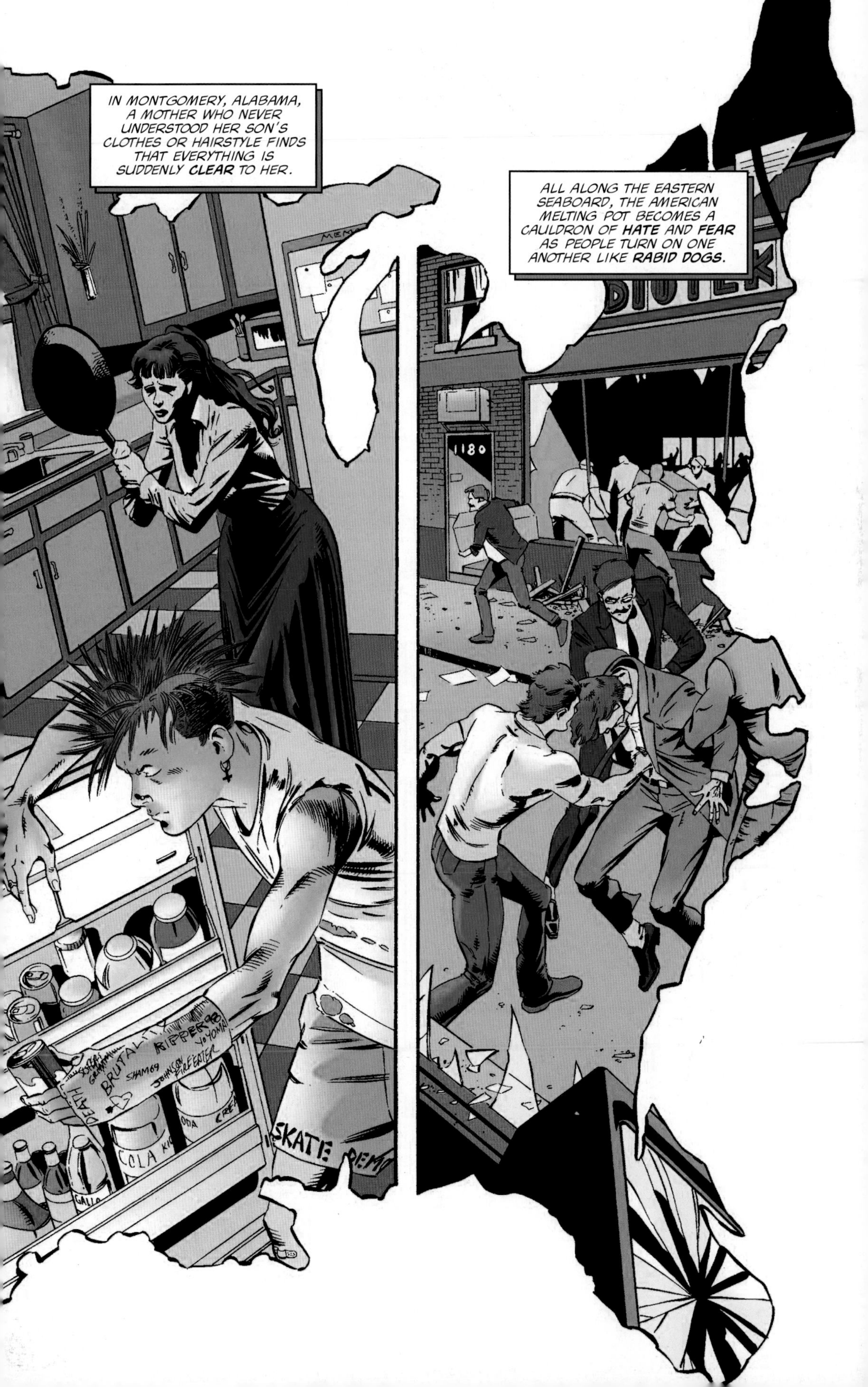
IN MONTGOMERY, ALABAMA, A MOTHER WHO NEVER UNDERSTOOD HER SON'S CLOTHES OR HAIRSTYLE FINDS THAT EVERYTHING IS SUDDENLY **CLEAR** TO HER.
ALL ALONG THE EASTERN SEABOARD, THE AMERICAN MELTING POT BECOMES A CAULDRON OF **HATE** AND **FEAR** AS PEOPLE TURN ON ONE ANOTHER LIKE **RABID DOGS**.
1180
COLA
SKATE

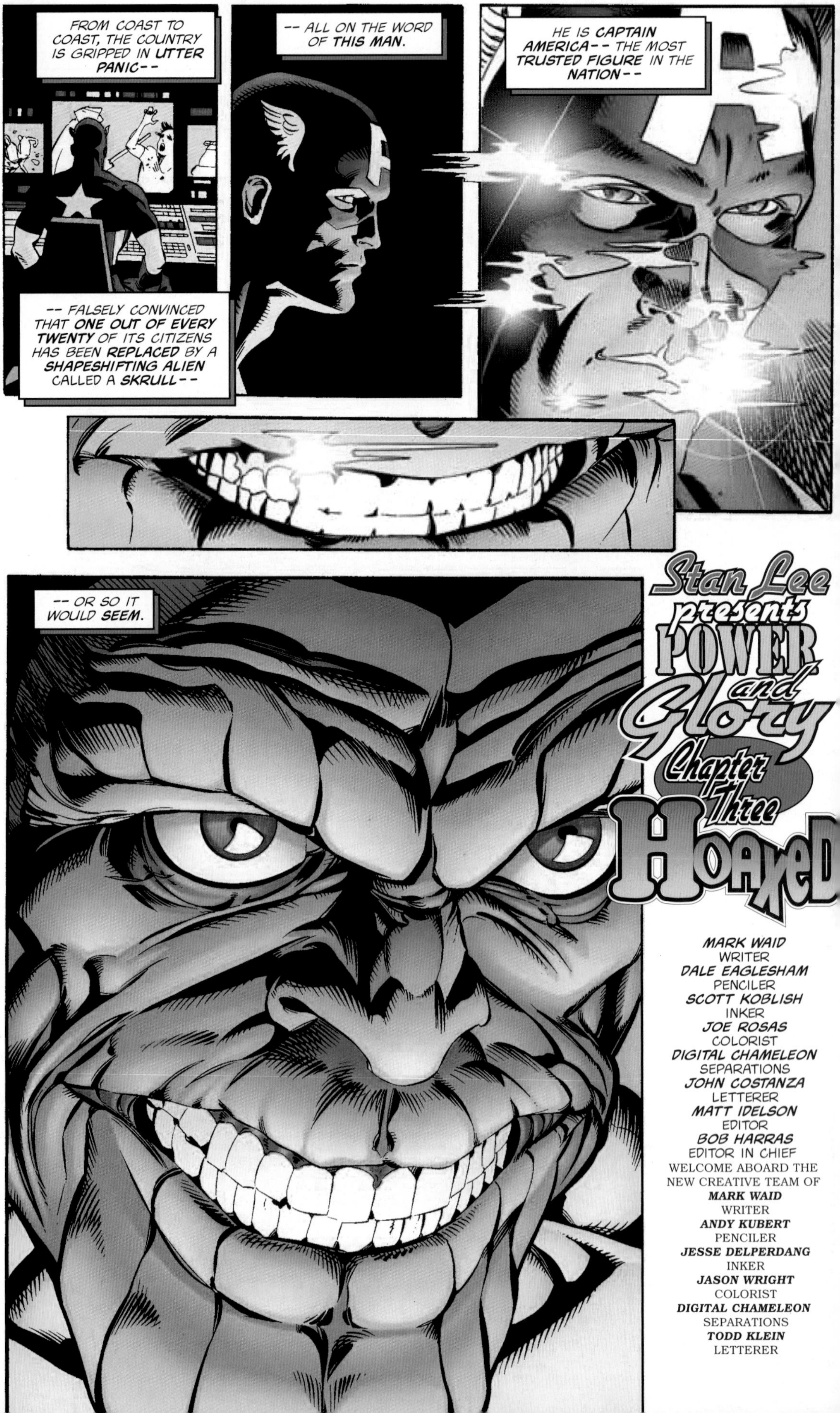
FROM COAST TO COAST, THE COUNTRY IS GRIPPED IN UTTER PANIC--
-- ALL ON THE WORD OF THIS MAN.
HE IS CAPTAIN AMERICA-- THE MOST TRUSTED FIGURE IN THE NATION--
-- FALSELY CONVINCED THAT ONE OUT OF EVERY TWENTY OF ITS CITIZENS HAS BEEN REPLACED BY A SHAPESHIFTING ALIEN CALLED A SKRULL--
-- OR SO IT WOULD SEEM.
Stan Lee presents POWER and Glory
Chapter Three
HOAXED
MARK WAID
WRITER
DALE EAGLESHAM
PENCILER
SCOTT KOBLISH
INKER
JOE ROSAS
COLORIST
DIGITAL CHAMELEON
SEPARATIONS
JOHN COSTANZA
LETTERER
MATT IDELSON
EDITOR
BOB HARRAS
EDITOR IN CHIEF
WELCOME ABOARD THE NEW CREATIVE TEAM OF
MARK WAID
WRITER
ANDY KUBERT
PENCILER
JESSE DELPERDANG
INKER
JASON WRIGHT
COLORIST
DIGITAL CHAMELEON
SEPARATIONS
TODD KLEIN
LETTERER

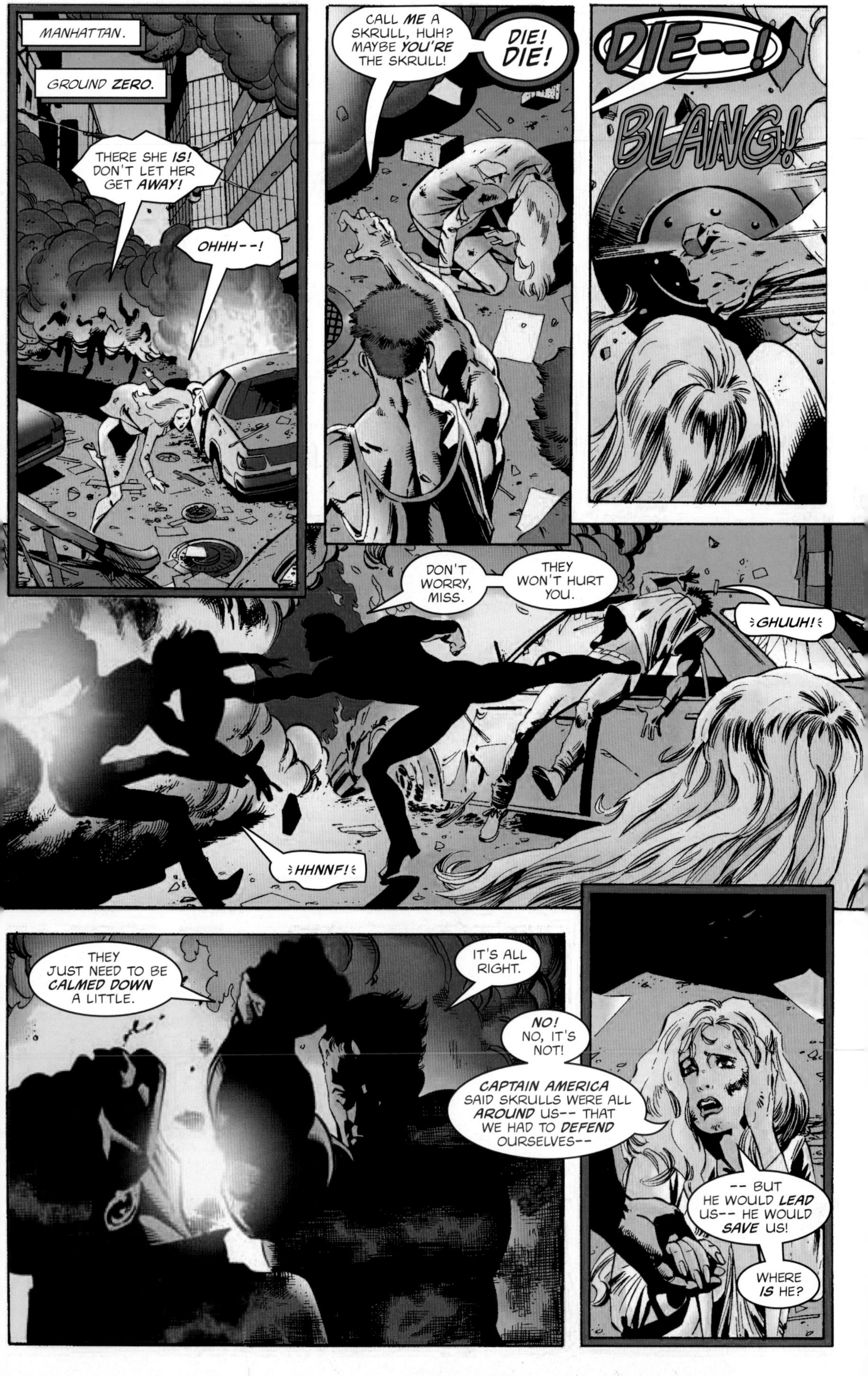

MANHATTAN.
GROUND ZERO.
THERE SHE IS! DON'T LET HER GET AWAY!
OHHH--!
CALL ME A SKRULL, HUH? MAYBE YOU'RE THE SKRULL!
DIE! DIE!
DIE--!
BLANG!
DON'T WORRY, MISS.
THEY WON'T HURT YOU.
GHUUH!
HHNNF!
THEY JUST NEED TO BE CALMED DOWN A LITTLE.
IT'S ALL RIGHT.
NO! NO, IT'S NOT!
CAPTAIN AMERICA SAID SKRULLS WERE ALL AROUND US-- THAT WE HAD TO DEFEND OURSELVES--
-- BUT HE WOULD LEAD US-- HE WOULD SAVE US!
WHERE IS HE?

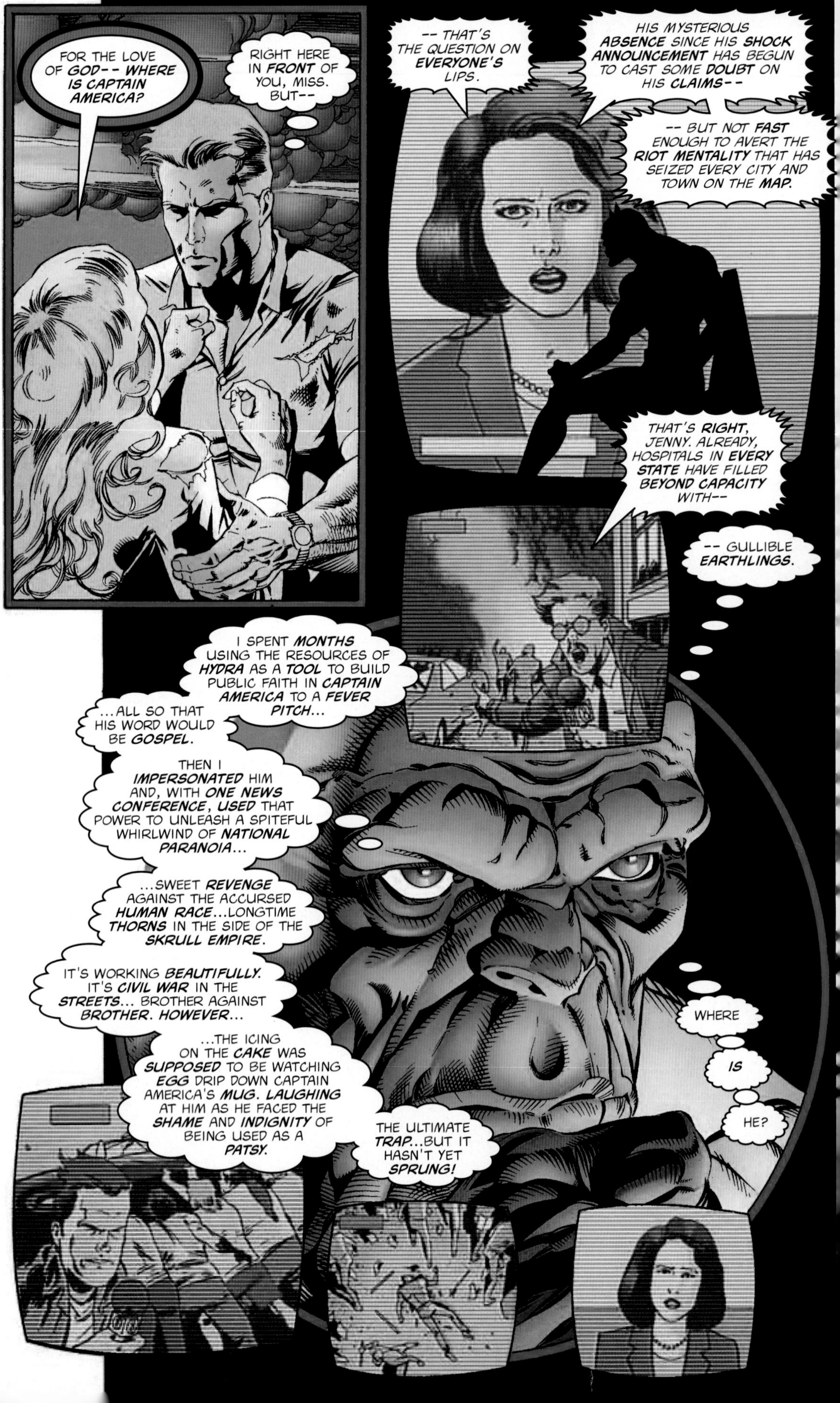
FOR THE LOVE OF GOD-- WHERE IS CAPTAIN AMERICA?
RIGHT HERE IN FRONT OF YOU, MISS. BUT--
-- THAT'S THE QUESTION ON EVERYONE'S LIPS.
HIS MYSTERIOUS ABSENCE SINCE HIS SHOCK ANNOUNCEMENT HAS BEGUN TO CAST SOME DOUBT ON HIS CLAIMS--
-- BUT NOT FAST ENOUGH TO AVERT THE RIOT MENTALITY THAT HAS SEIZED EVERY CITY AND TOWN ON THE MAP.
THAT'S RIGHT, JENNY. ALREADY, HOSPITALS IN EVERY STATE HAVE FILLED BEYOND CAPACITY WITH--
-- GULLIBLE EARTHLINGS.
I SPENT MONTHS USING THE RESOURCES OF HYDRA AS A TOOL TO BUILD PUBLIC FAITH IN CAPTAIN AMERICA TO A FEVER PITCH...
...ALL SO THAT HIS WORD WOULD BE GOSPEL.
THEN I IMPERSONATED HIM AND, WITH ONE NEWS CONFERENCE, USED THAT POWER TO UNLEASH A SPITEFUL WHIRLWIND OF NATIONAL PARANOIA...
...SWEET REVENGE AGAINST THE ACCURSED HUMAN RACE...LONGTIME THORNS IN THE SIDE OF THE SKRULL EMPIRE.
IT'S WORKING BEAUTIFULLY. IT'S CIVIL WAR IN THE STREETS... BROTHER AGAINST BROTHER. HOWEVER...
...THE ICING ON THE CAKE WAS SUPPOSED TO BE WATCHING EGG DRIP DOWN CAPTAIN AMERICA'S MUG. LAUGHING AT HIM AS HE FACED THE SHAME AND INDIGNITY OF BEING USED AS A PATSY.
THE ULTIMATE TRAP...BUT IT HASN'T YET SPRUNG!
WHERE
IS
HE?

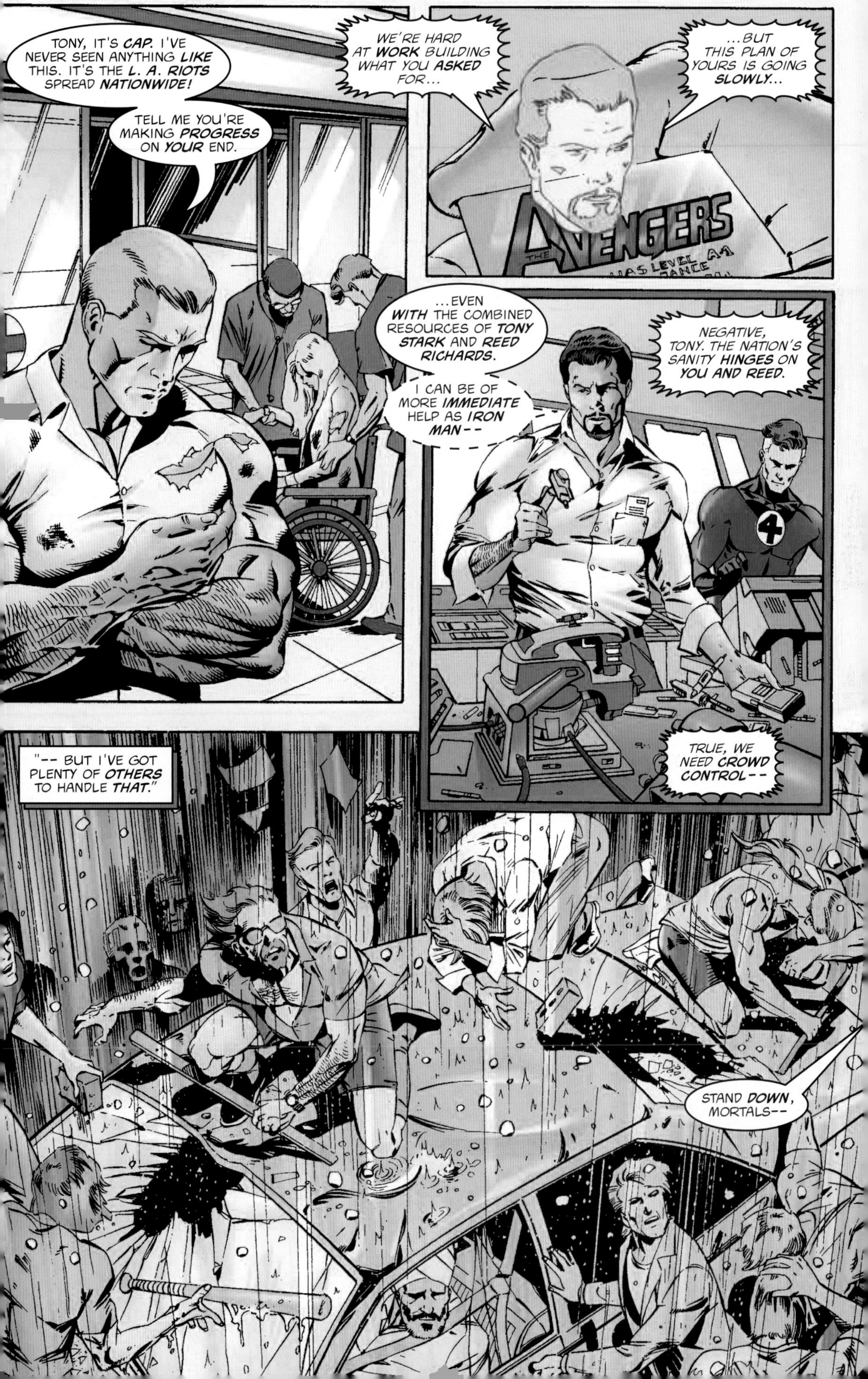

TONY, IT'S CAP. I'VE NEVER SEEN ANYTHING LIKE THIS. IT'S THE L. A. RIOTS SPREAD NATIONWIDE!
TELL ME YOU'RE MAKING PROGRESS ON YOUR END.
WE'RE HARD AT WORK BUILDING WHAT YOU ASKED FOR...
...BUT THIS PLAN OF YOURS IS GOING SLOWLY...
THE AVENGERS
...EVEN WITH THE COMBINED RESOURCES OF TONY STARK AND REED RICHARDS.
I CAN BE OF MORE IMMEDIATE HELP AS IRON MAN--
NEGATIVE, TONY. THE NATION'S SANITY HINGES ON YOU AND REED.
TRUE, WE NEED CROWD CONTROL--
"-- BUT I'VE GOT PLENTY OF OTHERS TO HANDLE THAT."
STAND DOWN, MORTALS--

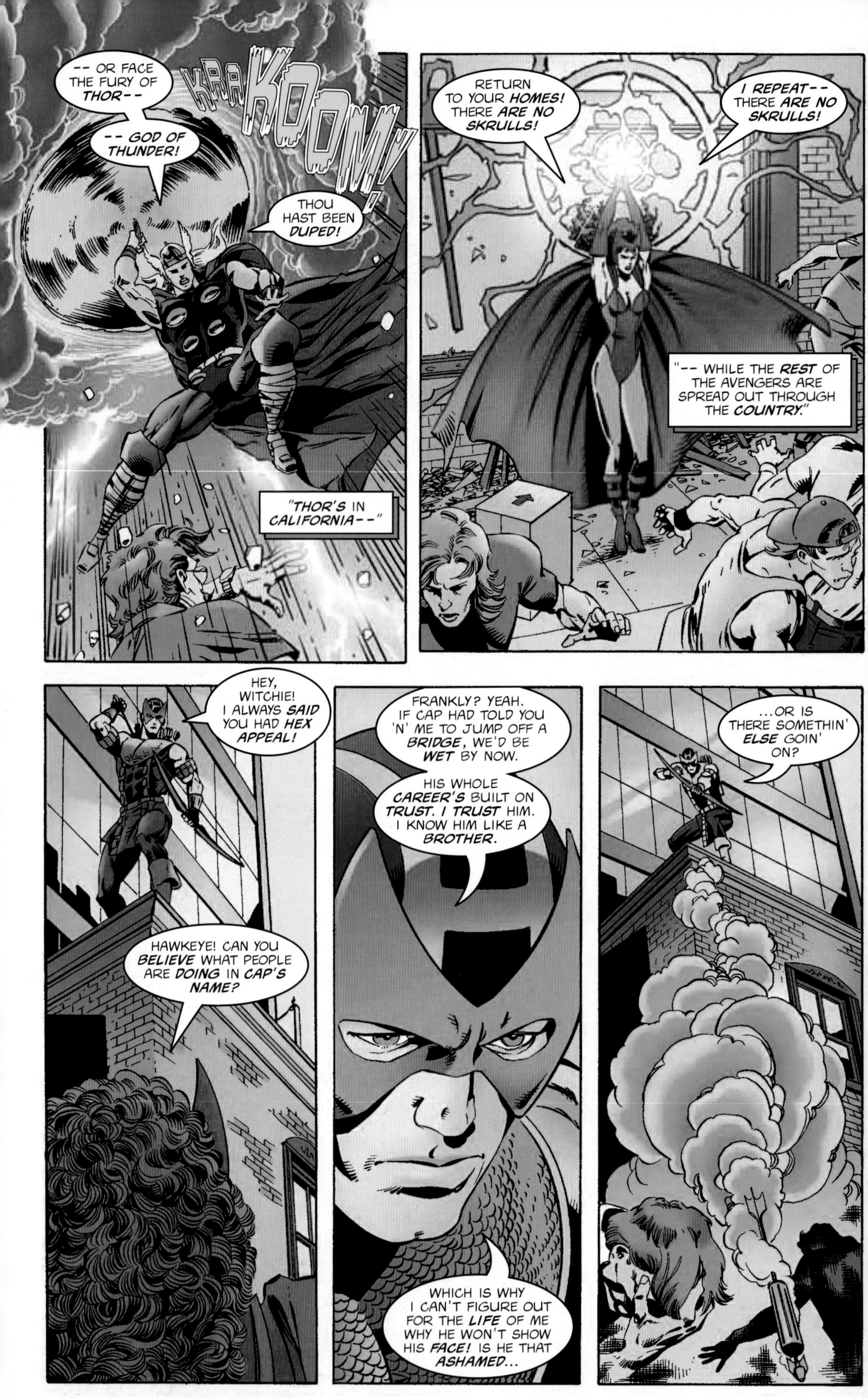
-- OR FACE THE FURY OF THOR--
KRAKOOM!
-- GOD OF THUNDER!
THOU HAST BEEN DUPED!
"THOR'S IN CALIFORNIA--"
RETURN TO YOUR HOMES! THERE ARE NO SKRULLS!
I REPEAT-- THERE ARE NO SKRULLS!
"-- WHILE THE REST OF THE AVENGERS ARE SPREAD OUT THROUGH THE COUNTRY."
HEY, WITCHIE! I ALWAYS SAID YOU HAD HEX APPEAL!
HAWKEYE! CAN YOU BELIEVE WHAT PEOPLE ARE DOING IN CAP'S NAME?
FRANKLY? YEAH. IF CAP HAD TOLD YOU 'N' ME TO JUMP OFF A BRIDGE, WE'D BE WET BY NOW.
HIS WHOLE CAREER'S BUILT ON TRUST. I TRUST HIM. I KNOW HIM LIKE A BROTHER.
WHICH IS WHY I CAN'T FIGURE OUT FOR THE LIFE OF ME WHY HE WON'T SHOW HIS FACE! IS HE THAT ASHAMED...
...OR IS THERE SOMETHIN' ELSE GOIN' ON?

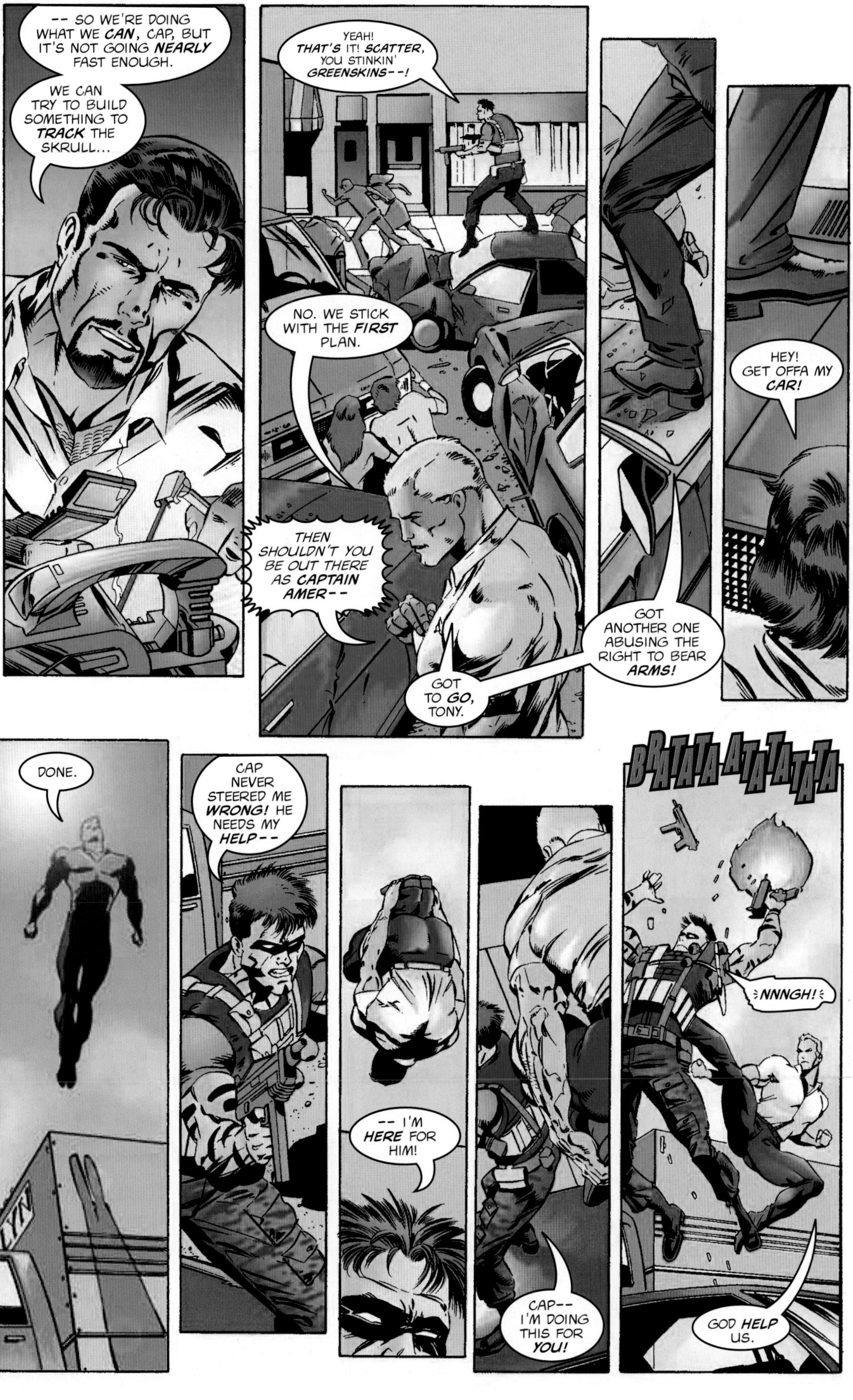

-- SO WE'RE DOING WHAT WE CAN, CAP, BUT IT'S NOT GOING NEARLY FAST ENOUGH.
WE CAN TRY TO BUILD SOMETHING TO TRACK THE SKRULL...
YEAH! THAT'S IT! SCATTER, YOU STINKIN' GREENSKINS--!
NO. WE STICK WITH THE FIRST PLAN.
THEN SHOULDN'T YOU BE OUT THERE AS CAPTAIN AMER--
GOT TO GO, TONY.
GOT ANOTHER ONE ABUSING THE RIGHT TO BEAR ARMS!
HEY! GET OFFA MY CAR!
DONE.
LYN
CAP NEVER STEERED ME WRONG! HE NEEDS MY HELP--
-- I'M HERE FOR HIM!
CAP-- I'M DOING THIS FOR YOU!
BRATATA ATATATATA
NNNGH!
GOD HELP US.

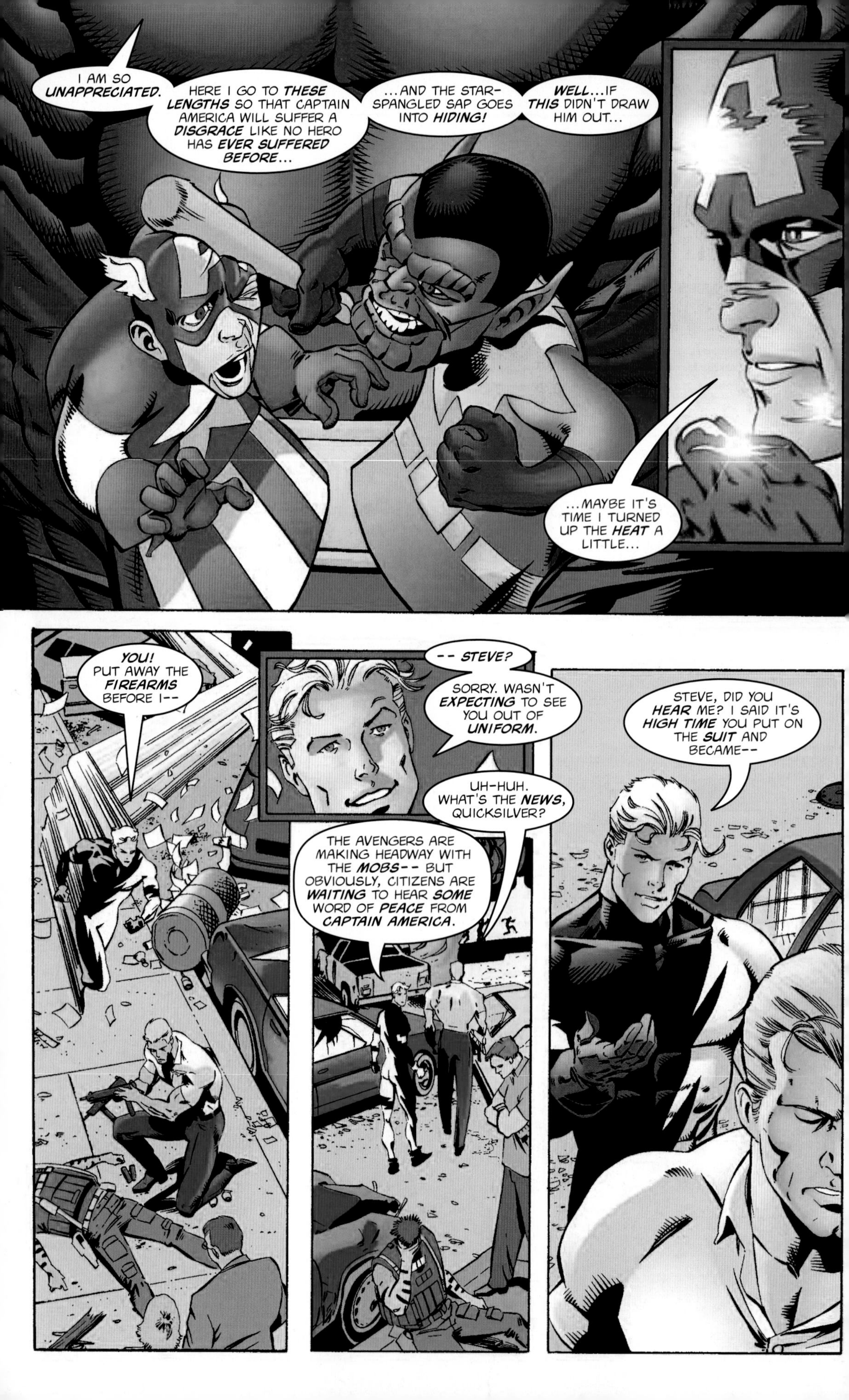
I AM SO UNAPPRECIATED.
HERE I GO TO THESE LENGTHS SO THAT CAPTAIN AMERICA WILL SUFFER A DISGRACE LIKE NO HERO HAS EVER SUFFERED BEFORE...
...AND THE STAR-SPANGLED SAP GOES INTO HIDING!
WELL...IF THIS DIDN'T DRAW HIM OUT...
...MAYBE IT'S TIME I TURNED UP THE HEAT A LITTLE...
YOU! PUT AWAY THE FIREARMS BEFORE I--
-- STEVE?
SORRY. WASN'T EXPECTING TO SEE YOU OUT OF UNIFORM.
UH-HUH. WHAT'S THE NEWS, QUICKSILVER?
THE AVENGERS ARE MAKING HEADWAY WITH THE MOBS-- BUT OBVIOUSLY, CITIZENS ARE WAITING TO HEAR SOME WORD OF PEACE FROM CAPTAIN AMERICA.
STEVE, DID YOU HEAR ME? I SAID IT'S HIGH TIME YOU PUT ON THE SUIT AND BECAME--

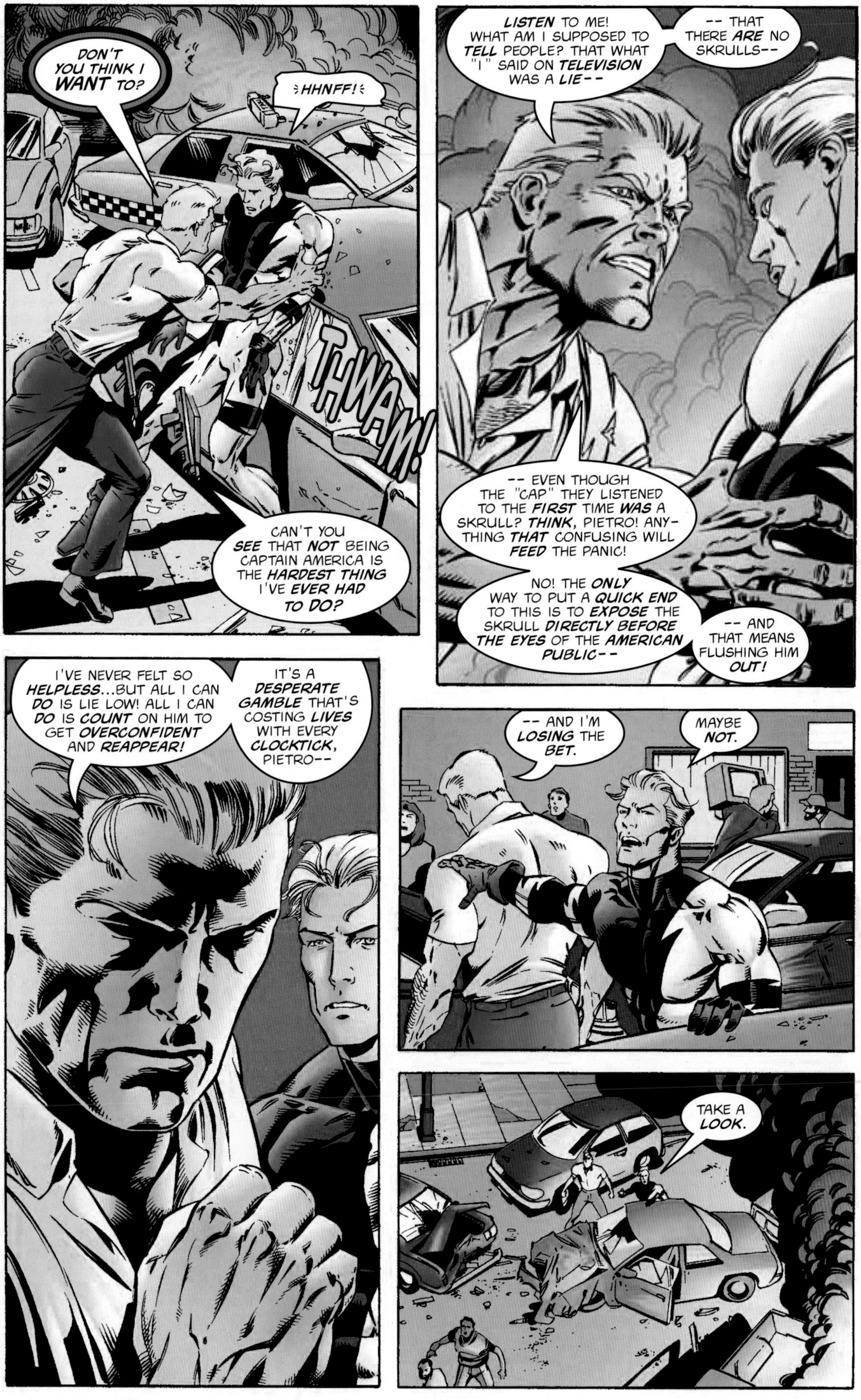
DON'T YOU THINK I WANT TO?
HHNFF!
THWAM!
CAN'T YOU SEE THAT NOT BEING CAPTAIN AMERICA IS THE HARDEST THING I'VE EVER HAD TO DO?
LISTEN TO ME! WHAT AM I SUPPOSED TO TELL PEOPLE? THAT WHAT "I" SAID ON TELEVISION WAS A LIE--
-- THAT THERE ARE NO SKRULLS--
-- EVEN THOUGH THE "CAP" THEY LISTENED TO THE FIRST TIME WAS A SKRULL? THINK, PIETRO! ANYTHING THAT CONFUSING WILL FEED THE PANIC!
NO! THE ONLY WAY TO PUT A QUICK END TO THIS IS TO EXPOSE THE SKRULL DIRECTLY BEFORE THE EYES OF THE AMERICAN PUBLIC--
-- AND THAT MEANS FLUSHING HIM OUT!
I'VE NEVER FELT SO HELPLESS...BUT ALL I CAN DO IS LIE LOW! ALL I CAN DO IS COUNT ON HIM TO GET OVERCONFIDENT AND REAPPEAR!
IT'S A DESPERATE GAMBLE THAT'S COSTING LIVES WITH EVERY CLOCKTICK, PIETRO--
-- AND I'M LOSING THE BET.
MAYBE NOT.
TAKE A LOOK.

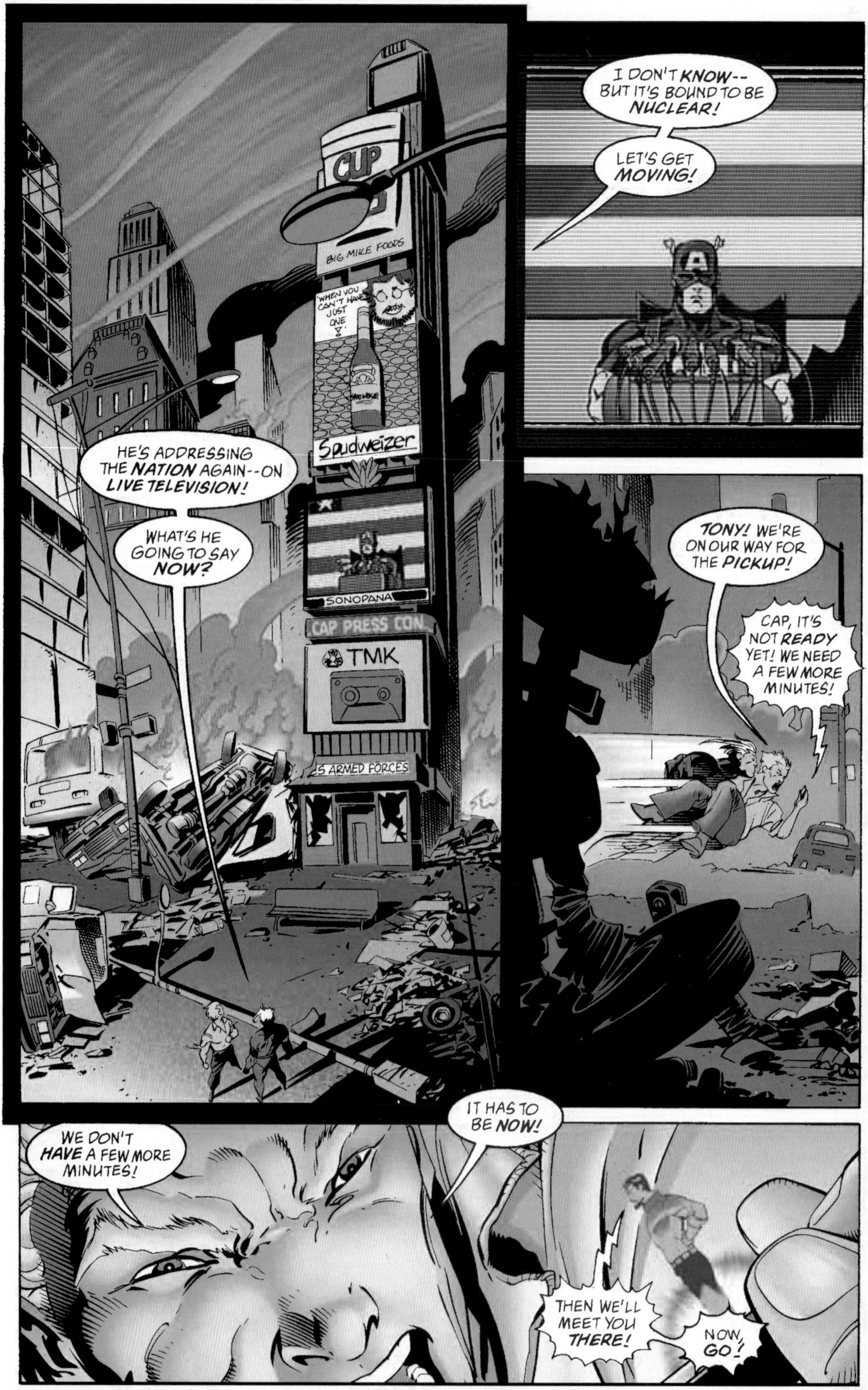
CUP
BIG MIKE FOODS
'WHEN YOU CAN'T HAVE JUST ONE'
Spudweizer
SONOPANA
CAP PRESS CON.
TMK
S ARMED FORCES
HE'S ADDRESSING THE NATION AGAIN--ON LIVE TELEVISION!
WHAT'S HE GOING TO SAY NOW?
I DON'T KNOW-- BUT IT'S BOUND TO BE NUCLEAR!
LET'S GET MOVING!
TONY! WE'RE ON OUR WAY FOR THE PICKUP!
CAP, IT'S NOT READY YET! WE NEED A FEW MORE MINUTES!
WE DON'T HAVE A FEW MORE MINUTES!
IT HAS TO BE NOW!
THEN WE'LL MEET YOU THERE!
NOW, GO!

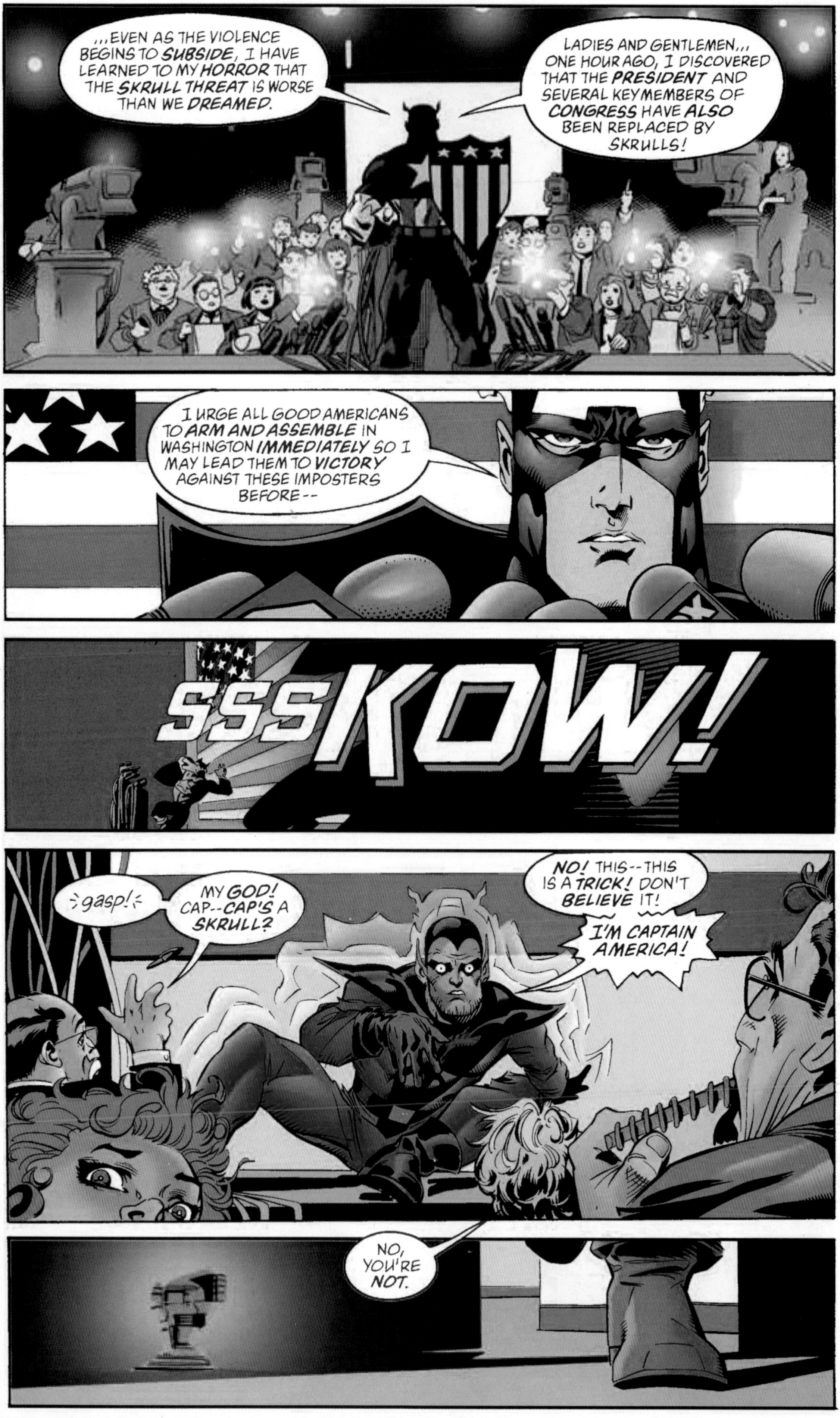
...EVEN AS THE VIOLENCE BEGINS TO SUBSIDE, I HAVE LEARNED TO MY HORROR THAT THE SKRULL THREAT IS WORSE THAN WE DREAMED.
LADIES AND GENTLEMEN... ONE HOUR AGO, I DISCOVERED THAT THE PRESIDENT AND SEVERAL KEY MEMBERS OF CONGRESS HAVE ALSO BEEN REPLACED BY SKRULLS!
I URGE ALL GOOD AMERICANS TO ARM AND ASSEMBLE IN WASHINGTON IMMEDIATELY SO I MAY LEAD THEM TO VICTORY AGAINST THESE IMPOSTERS BEFORE--
SSSKOW!
gasp!
MY GOD! CAP--CAP'S A SKRULL?
NO! THIS--THIS IS A TRICK! DON'T BELIEVE IT!
I'M CAPTAIN AMERICA!
NO, YOU'RE NOT.

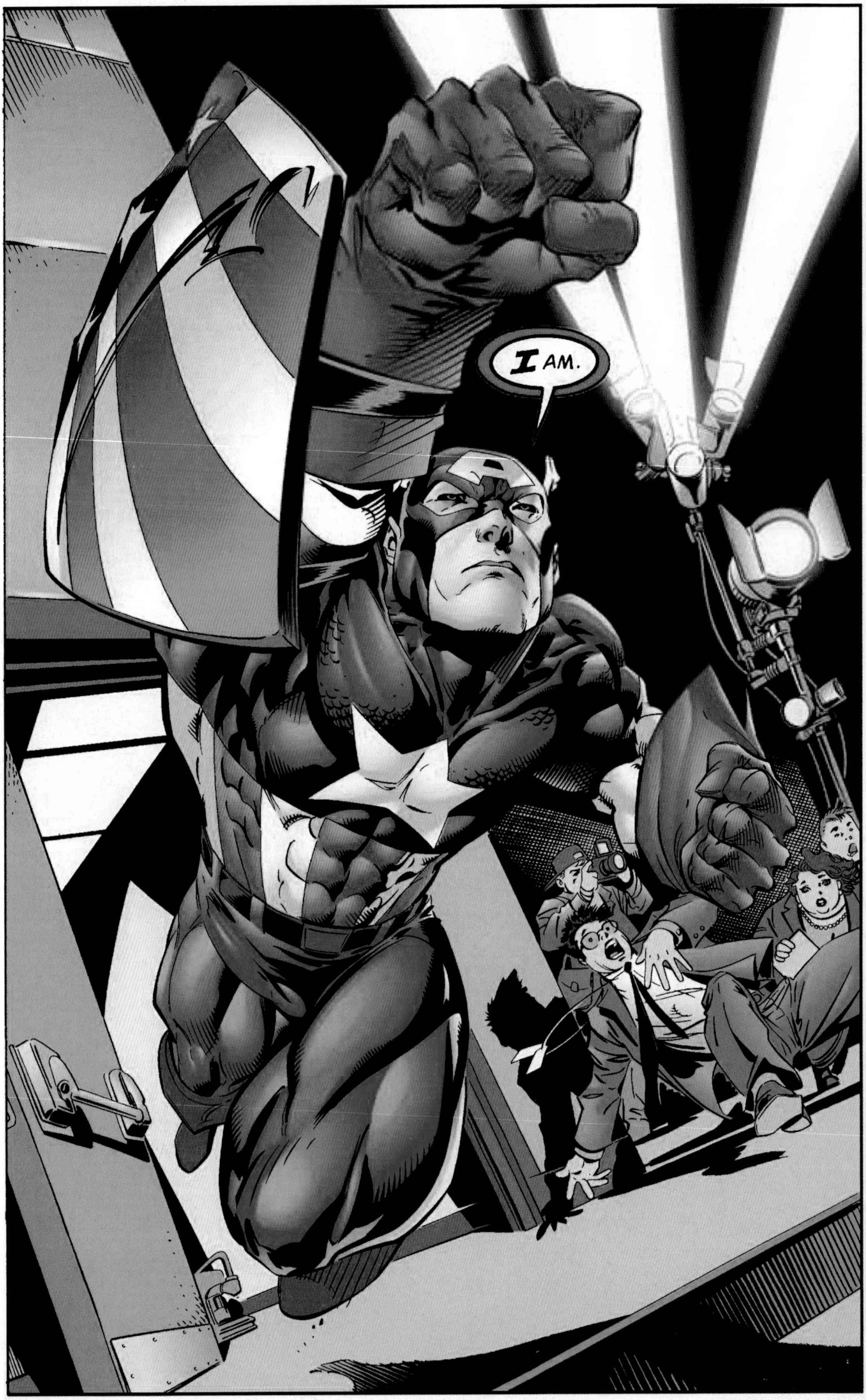
I AM.

YOU'RE A SKRULL--

--HIT WITH A *RAY* THAT REVERTED YOU TO YOUR *TRUE* FORM!

ONLY FOR A *MOMENT*, CAPTAIN!

CONGRATULATIONS! YOU'VE *EXPOSED* ME--BUT I'LL *STILL*--

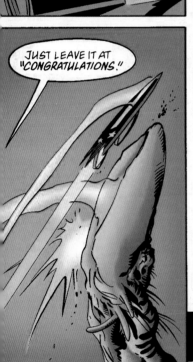

JUST LEAVE IT AT "CONGRATULATIONS."

NO. ON *SECOND* THOUGHT, DON'T SAY A *WORD*.

WE'VE HEARD *ENOUGH* FROM *YOU*.

I--I DON'T *UNDERSTAND*--!

THE *FIRST CAP*-- HE WAS A SKRULL ALL *ALONG?*

BUT *THAT* MEANS--

--THAT MEANS YOU HAVE TO GET *OUT* OF THERE AND BREAK THE *NEWS!*

THE *SKRULL THREAT*-- EVERY *WORD* OF IT-- WAS A *HOAX!*

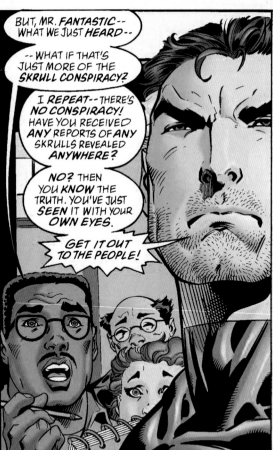

BUT, MR. *FANTASTIC*-- WHAT WE JUST *HEARD*--

-- WHAT IF THAT'S JUST MORE OF THE *SKRULL CONSPIRACY?*

I *REPEAT*-- THERE'S *NO CONSPIRACY!* HAVE YOU RECEIVED ANY REPORTS OF *ANY* SKRULLS REVEALED *ANYWHERE?*

NO? THEN YOU *KNOW* THE TRUTH. YOU'VE JUST *SEEN* IT WITH YOUR *OWN EYES.*

GET IT OUT TO THE PEOPLE!

NEXT TIME YOU WANT TO GET *BACK* AT A PLANET FOR CRIMES AGAINST *SKRULL-DOM*--

--PICK A WORLD WITHOUT *ME* ON IT.

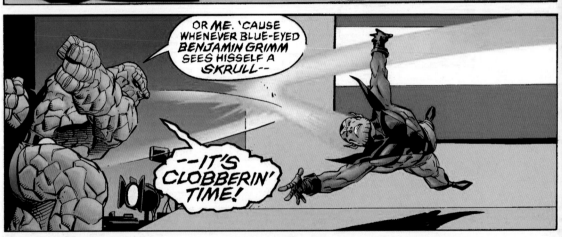

OR *ME.* 'CAUSE WHENEVER BLUE-EYED *BENJAMIN GRIMM* SEES HISSELF A *SKRULL*--

--IT'S *CLOBBERIN' TIME!*

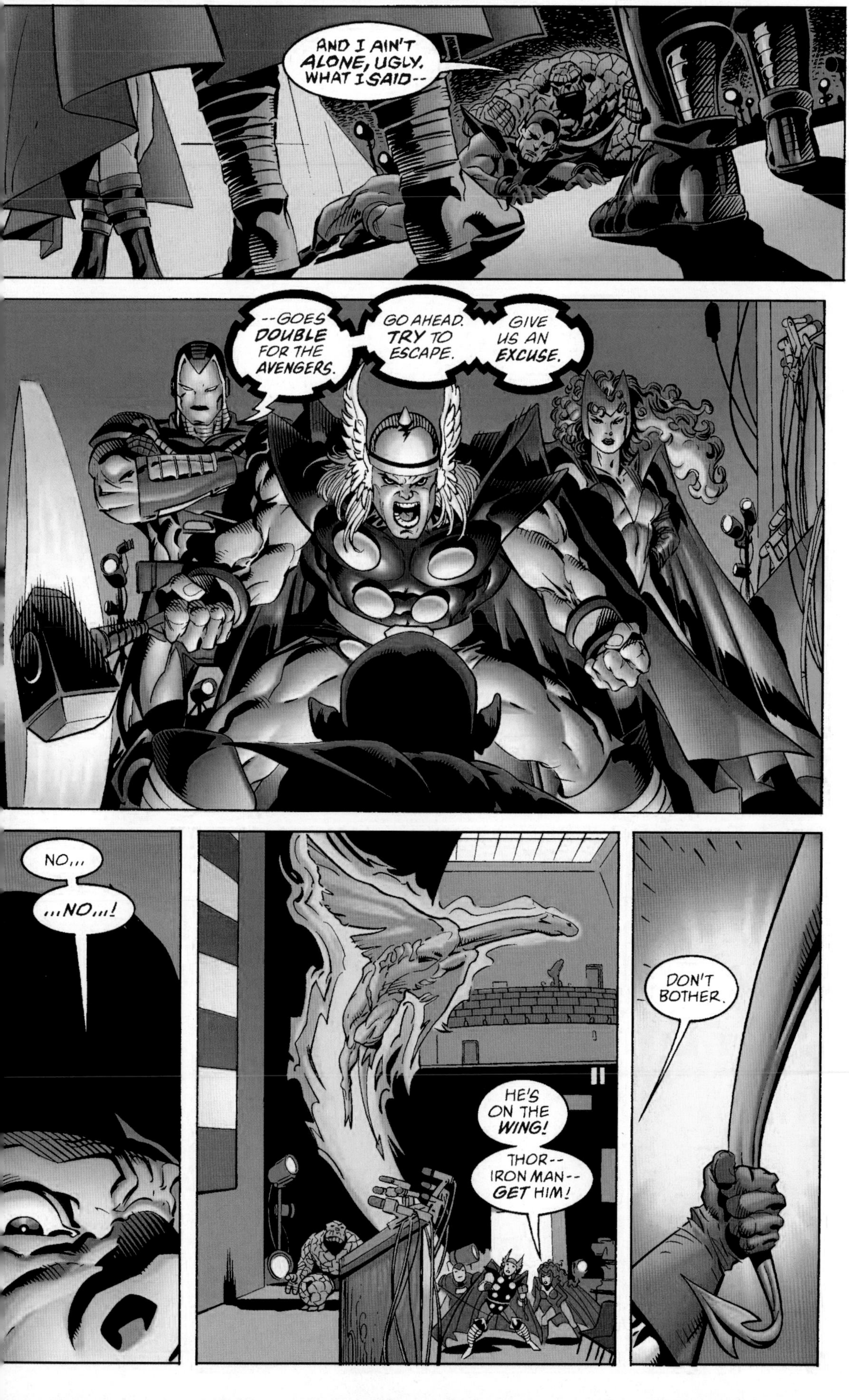
AND I AIN'T ALONE, UGLY. WHAT I SAID--
--GOES DOUBLE FOR THE AVENGERS.
GO AHEAD. TRY TO ESCAPE.
GIVE US AN EXCUSE.
NO...
...NO...!
HE'S ON THE WING!
THOR-- IRON MAN-- GET HIM!
DON'T BOTHER.

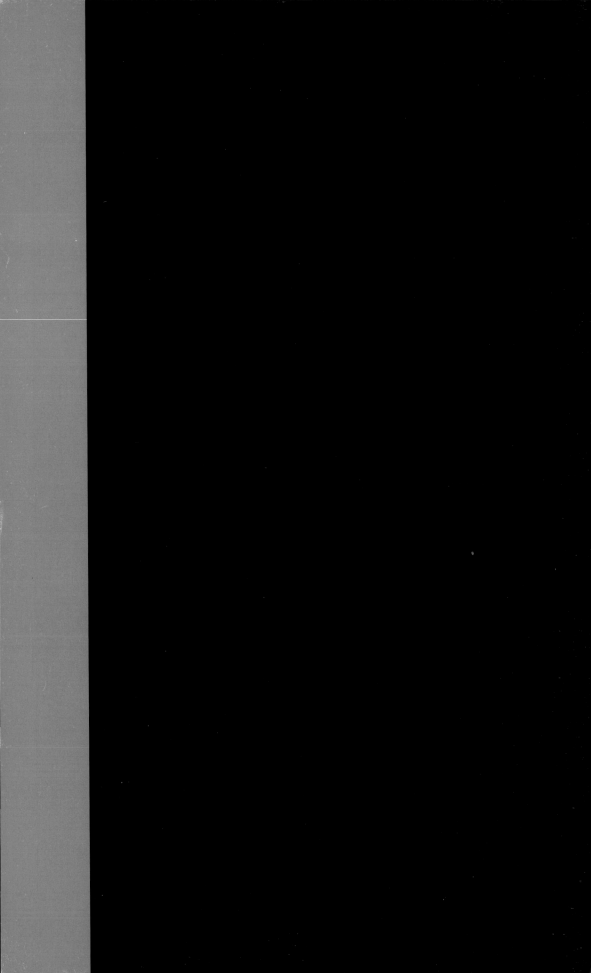

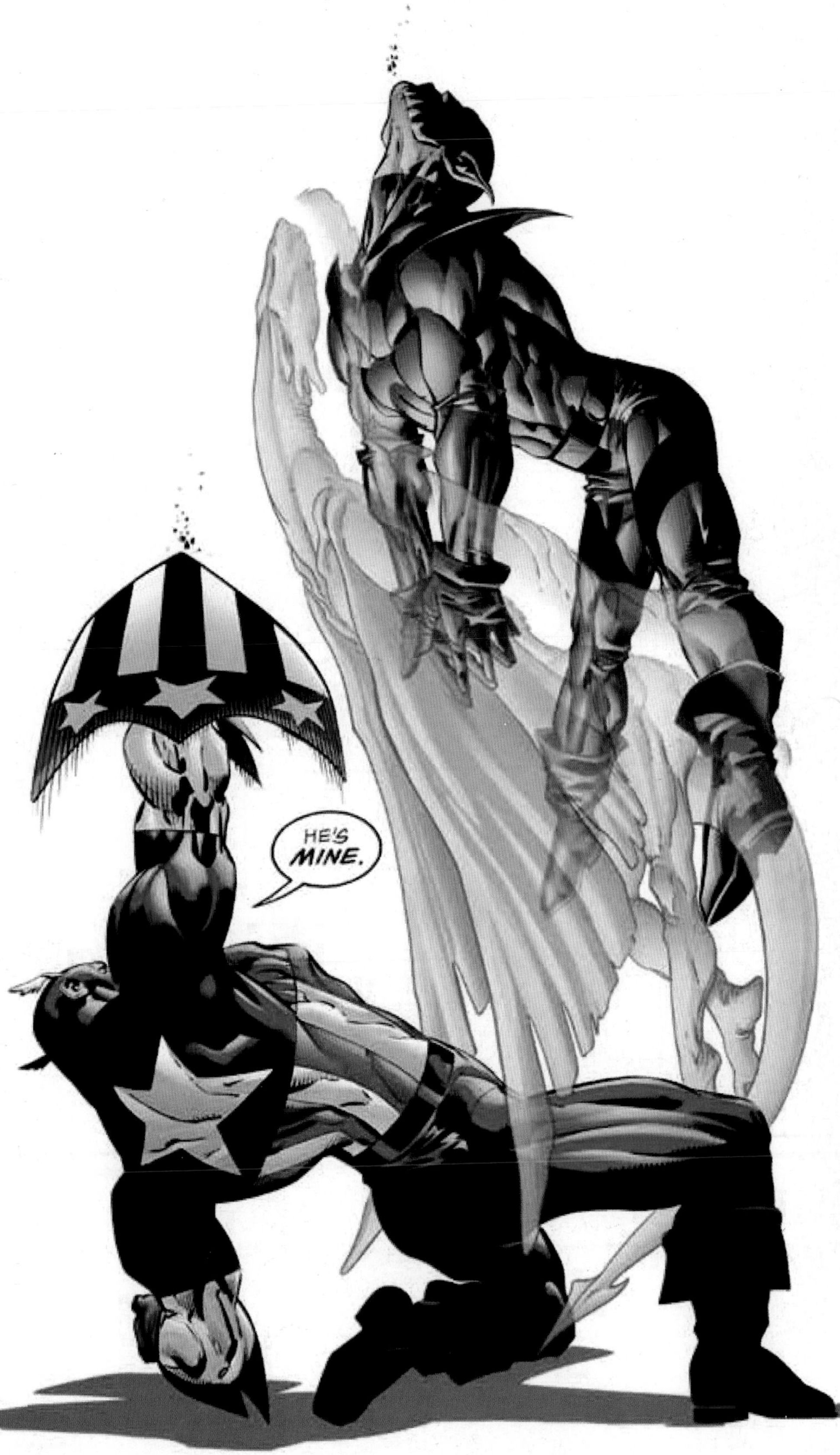
HE'S MINE.

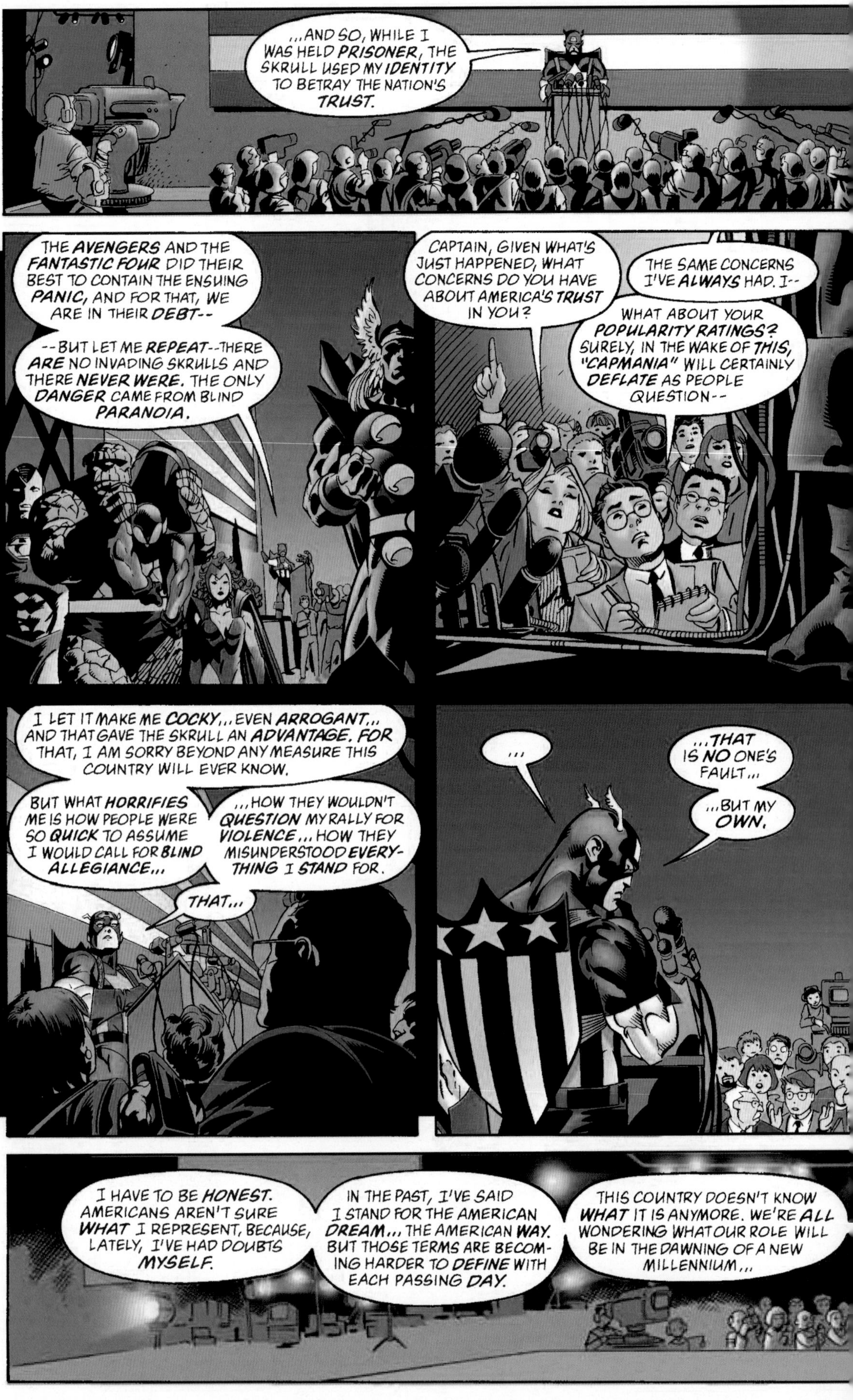
...AND SO, WHILE I WAS HELD PRISONER, THE SKRULL USED MY IDENTITY TO BETRAY THE NATION'S TRUST.
THE AVENGERS AND THE FANTASTIC FOUR DID THEIR BEST TO CONTAIN THE ENSUING PANIC, AND FOR THAT, WE ARE IN THEIR DEBT--
--BUT LET ME REPEAT--THERE ARE NO INVADING SKRULLS AND THERE NEVER WERE. THE ONLY DANGER CAME FROM BLIND PARANOIA.
CAPTAIN, GIVEN WHAT'S JUST HAPPENED, WHAT CONCERNS DO YOU HAVE ABOUT AMERICA'S TRUST IN YOU?
THE SAME CONCERNS I'VE ALWAYS HAD. I--
WHAT ABOUT YOUR POPULARITY RATINGS? SURELY, IN THE WAKE OF THIS, "CAPMANIA" WILL CERTAINLY DEFLATE AS PEOPLE QUESTION--
I LET IT MAKE ME COCKY... EVEN ARROGANT... AND THAT GAVE THE SKRULL AN ADVANTAGE. FOR THAT, I AM SORRY BEYOND ANY MEASURE THIS COUNTRY WILL EVER KNOW.
BUT WHAT HORRIFIES ME IS HOW PEOPLE WERE SO QUICK TO ASSUME I WOULD CALL FOR BLIND ALLEGIANCE...
...HOW THEY WOULDN'T QUESTION MY RALLY FOR VIOLENCE... HOW THEY MISUNDERSTOOD EVERY-THING I STAND FOR.
THAT...
...
...THAT IS NO ONE'S FAULT...
...BUT MY OWN.
I HAVE TO BE HONEST. AMERICANS AREN'T SURE WHAT I REPRESENT, BECAUSE, LATELY, I'VE HAD DOUBTS MYSELF.
IN THE PAST, I'VE SAID I STAND FOR THE AMERICAN DREAM... THE AMERICAN WAY. BUT THOSE TERMS ARE BECOM-ING HARDER TO DEFINE WITH EACH PASSING DAY.
THIS COUNTRY DOESN'T KNOW WHAT IT IS ANYMORE. WE'RE ALL WONDERING WHAT OUR ROLE WILL BE IN THE DAWNING OF A NEW MILLENNIUM...

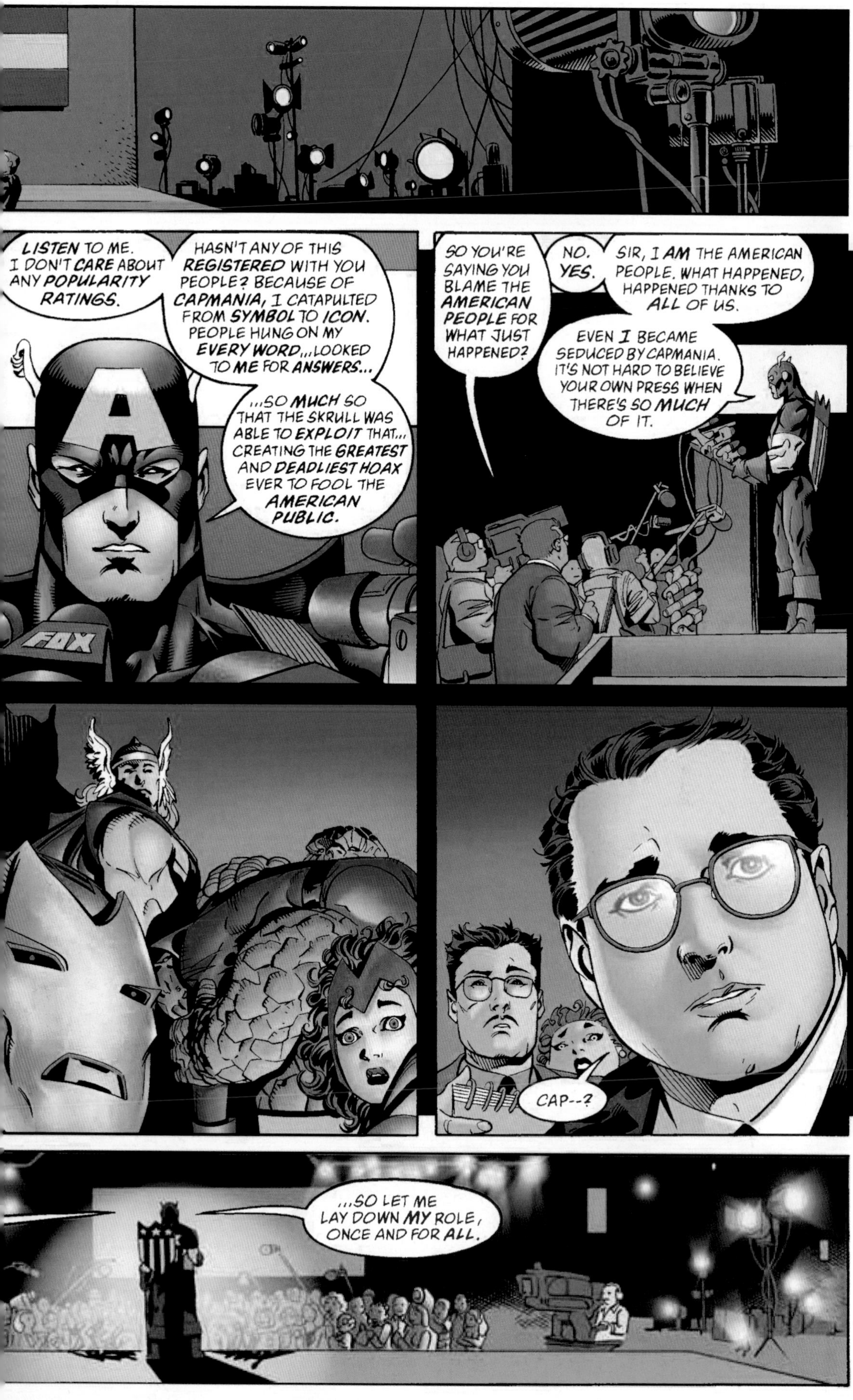
LISTEN TO ME. I DON'T CARE ABOUT ANY POPULARITY RATINGS.
HASN'T ANY OF THIS REGISTERED WITH YOU PEOPLE? BECAUSE OF CAPMANIA, I CATAPULTED FROM SYMBOL TO ICON. PEOPLE HUNG ON MY EVERY WORD,,,LOOKED TO ME FOR ANSWERS...
...SO MUCH SO THAT THE SKRULL WAS ABLE TO EXPLOIT THAT... CREATING THE GREATEST AND DEADLIEST HOAX EVER TO FOOL THE AMERICAN PUBLIC.
FOX
SO YOU'RE SAYING YOU BLAME THE AMERICAN PEOPLE FOR WHAT JUST HAPPENED?
NO. YES.
SIR, I AM THE AMERICAN PEOPLE. WHAT HAPPENED, HAPPENED THANKS TO ALL OF US.
EVEN I BECAME SEDUCED BY CAPMANIA. IT'S NOT HARD TO BELIEVE YOUR OWN PRESS WHEN THERE'S SO MUCH OF IT.
CAP--?
...SO LET ME LAY DOWN MY ROLE, ONCE AND FOR ALL.

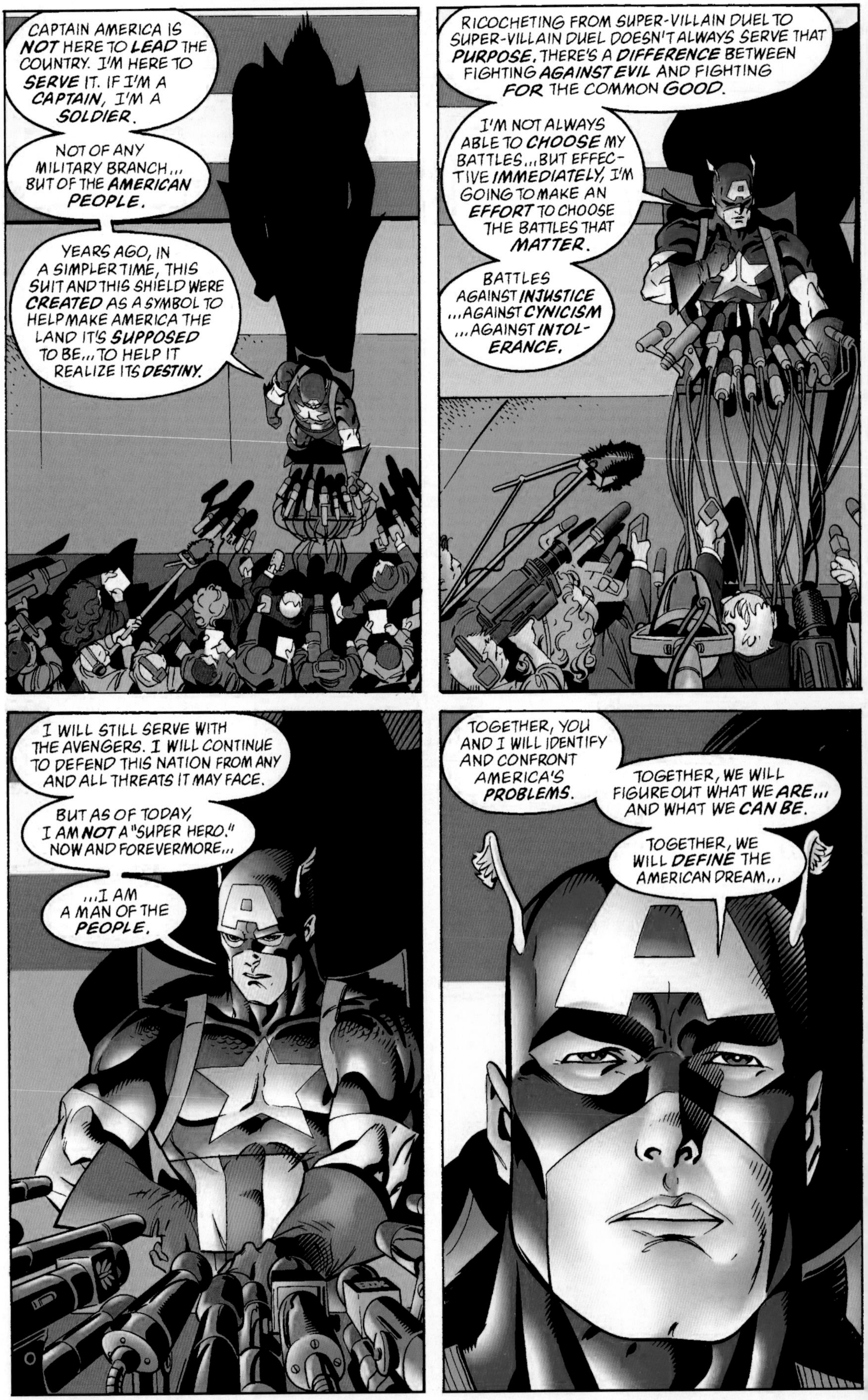
CAPTAIN AMERICA IS NOT HERE TO LEAD THE COUNTRY. I'M HERE TO SERVE IT. IF I'M A CAPTAIN, I'M A SOLDIER.
NOT OF ANY MILITARY BRANCH... BUT OF THE AMERICAN PEOPLE.
YEARS AGO, IN A SIMPLER TIME, THIS SUIT AND THIS SHIELD WERE CREATED AS A SYMBOL TO HELP MAKE AMERICA THE LAND IT'S SUPPOSED TO BE... TO HELP IT REALIZE ITS DESTINY.
RICOCHETING FROM SUPER-VILLAIN DUEL TO SUPER-VILLAIN DUEL DOESN'T ALWAYS SERVE THAT PURPOSE. THERE'S A DIFFERENCE BETWEEN FIGHTING AGAINST EVIL AND FIGHTING FOR THE COMMON GOOD.
I'M NOT ALWAYS ABLE TO CHOOSE MY BATTLES... BUT EFFECTIVE IMMEDIATELY, I'M GOING TO MAKE AN EFFORT TO CHOOSE THE BATTLES THAT MATTER.
BATTLES AGAINST INJUSTICE ...AGAINST CYNICISM ...AGAINST INTOLERANCE.
I WILL STILL SERVE WITH THE AVENGERS. I WILL CONTINUE TO DEFEND THIS NATION FROM ANY AND ALL THREATS IT MAY FACE.
BUT AS OF TODAY, I AM NOT A "SUPER HERO." NOW AND FOREVERMORE...
...I AM A MAN OF THE PEOPLE.
TOGETHER, YOU AND I WILL IDENTIFY AND CONFRONT AMERICA'S PROBLEMS.
TOGETHER, WE WILL FIGURE OUT WHAT WE ARE... AND WHAT WE CAN BE.
TOGETHER, WE WILL DEFINE THE AMERICAN DREAM...

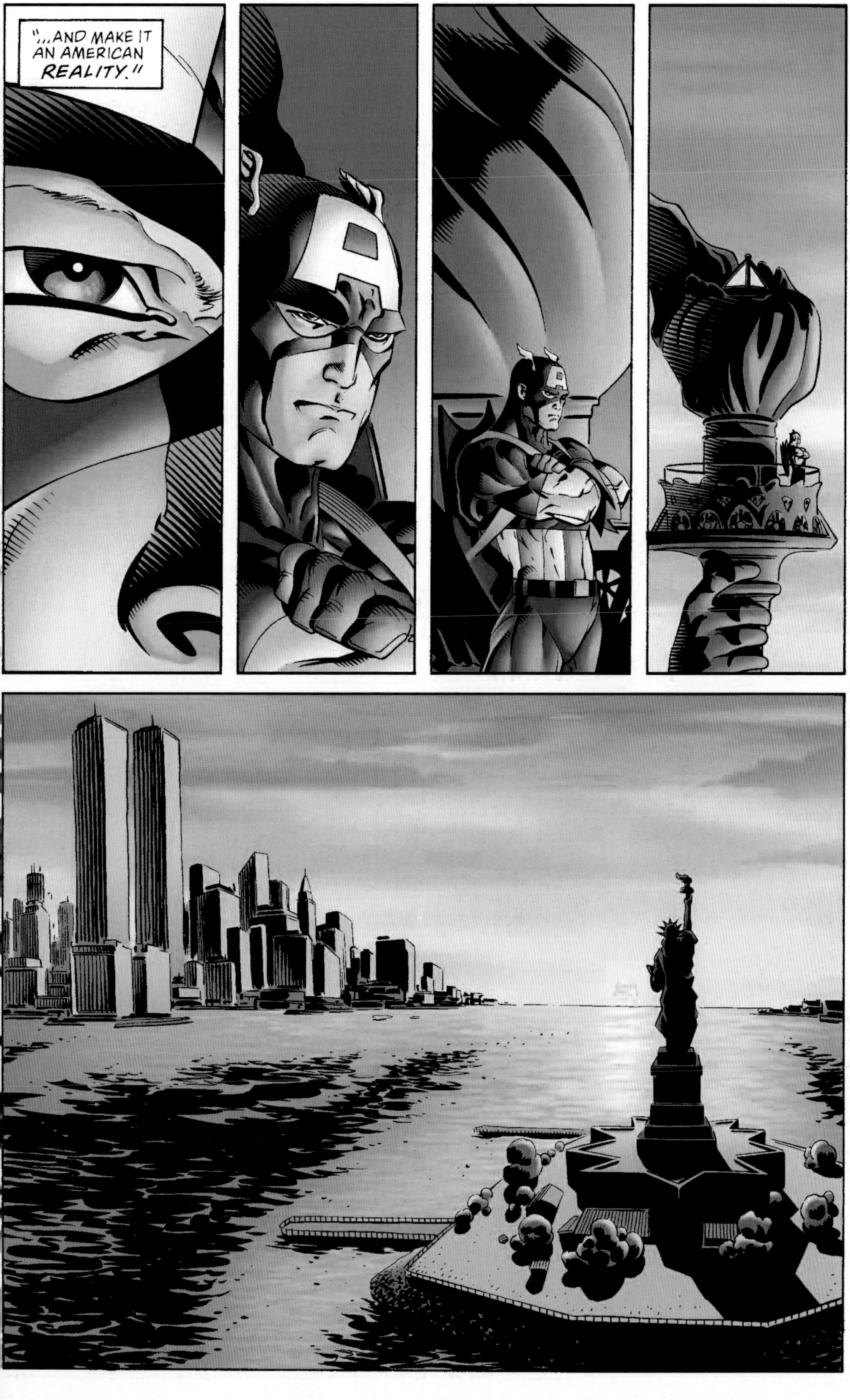
"...AND MAKE IT AN AMERICAN REALITY."

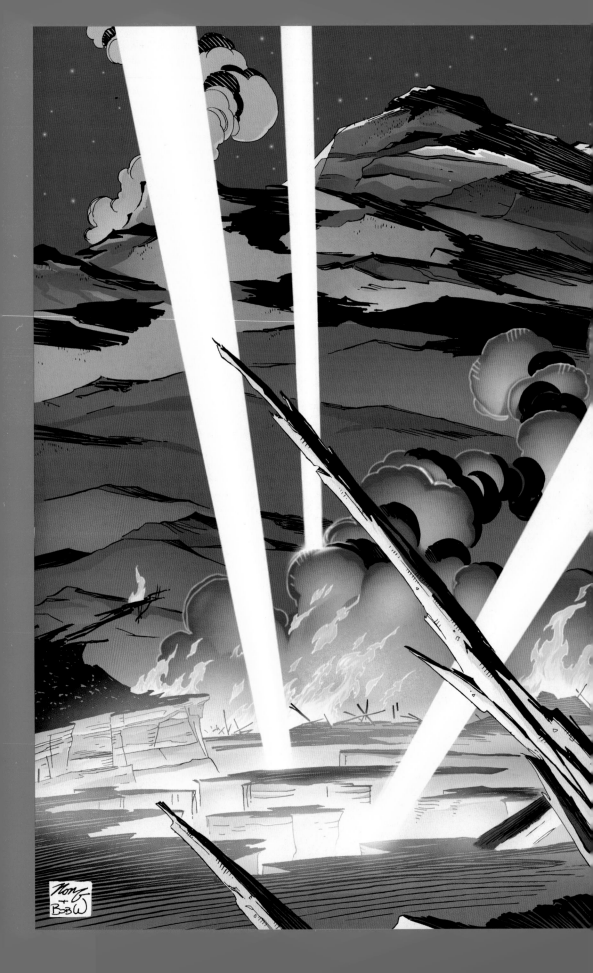

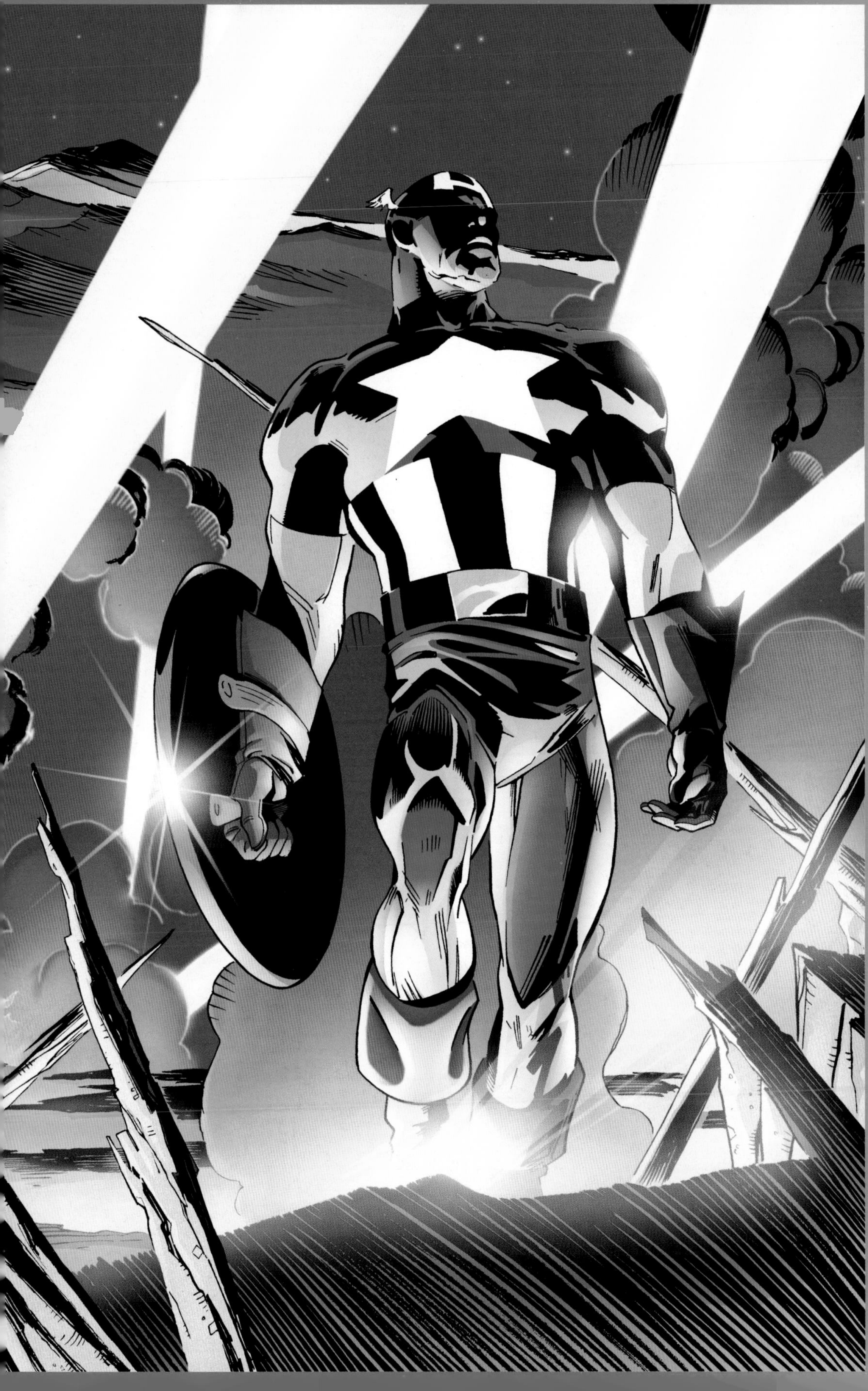

BEHIND THE SC

WITH RON GA

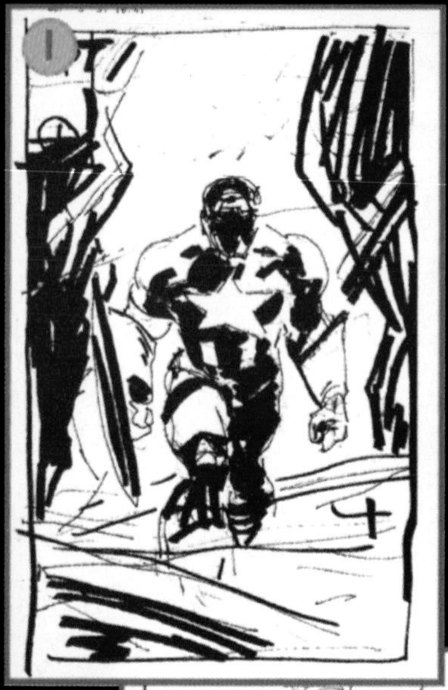

1

Hey, folks! Just to give you some insight into my twisted psyche, I thought I'd use this little forum to illustrate the steps it takes to get a cover I like. And so, let the games begin!

We decided very quickly to have a cover featuring Cap sort of walking out of the wreckage of his crash-landing after HEROES REBORN, since it isn't shown there or in our story. That was the easy part, getting a shot of Cap that we were happy with.

#1--This initial thumbnail sketch was no good. He's walking into darkness instead of out into the light. He's also a little too hunched over--it's more of a mysterious cover instead of some kind of rebirth. Which leads us to...

#2--This puppy. There's more light coming from behind Cap, which is a good thing. While I like the framing on the first thumbnail, I think framing the figure with light is more complimentary to Captain America's character in general. So far, so good.

#3--With the second thumbnail done, it was time to do a finished sketch of the whole cover. I knew I needed some kind of volcanic background with light from the crevasses, and we needed, on some

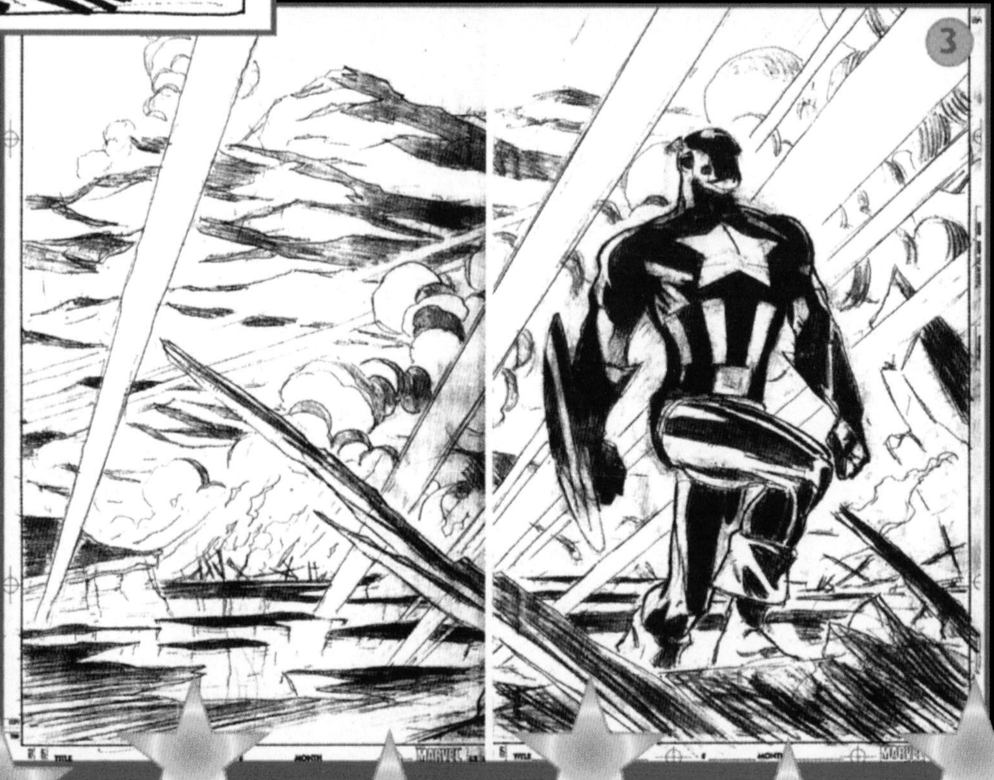

3

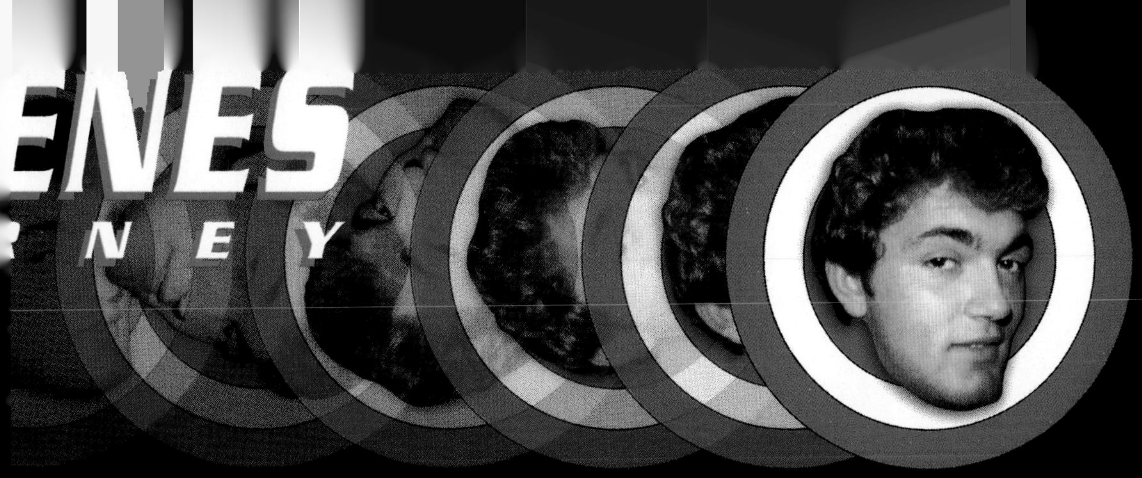
ENES
R N E Y

level, to illustrate something of Japan, with a Mount Fuji type mountain the background. As I said before, that's the easy part. Then I slave-labored over the figure. The biggest problems I had with this shot were with the leg and the twist of Cap's body. This final version of the cover was done, but it didn't quite work right, either. It didn't hit me until I went back and looked at it later how stiff I had drawn the figure. This particular figure looked too robotic. It didn't capture the presence of Captain America I was looking for. It's too moody, and it focuses too much on the debris itself instead of his relationship to the debris. So, back to the drawing board.

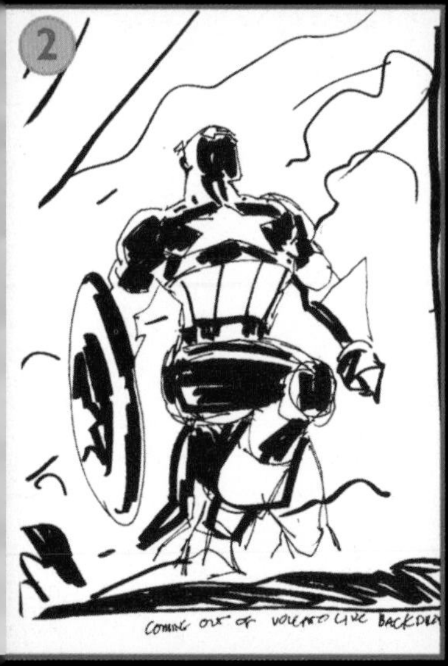
2
COMING OUT OF VOLCANO LIKE BACKDR

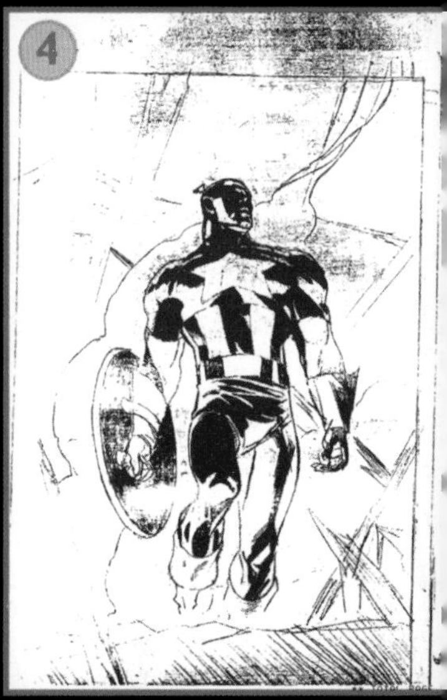
4

#4--After several discarded attempts, this one started to look like what I was going for. Again, having problems with the right leg coming forward--it was throwing him a little off balance. Plus getting him right with the lighting. The light coming over his trunks was creating a real problem. Not to mention the background--the smoke coming up over Captain America's right shoulder created too much of a tangent problem and didn't frame him well enough. The cover needed some kind of framing device with the debris to get the right point of focus.

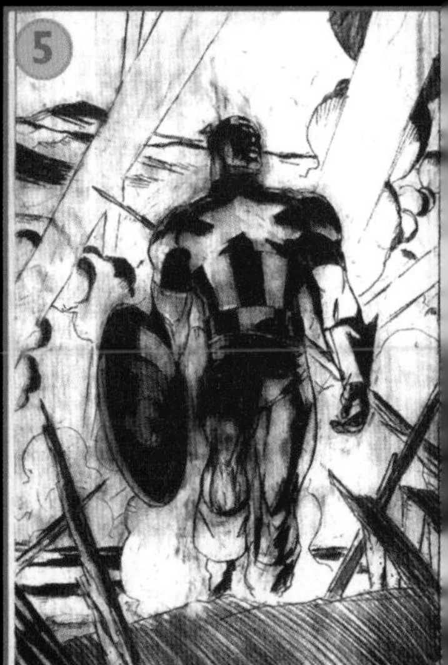
5

At this point it was time to go back and incorporate the things that worked so far. Another major problem with sketch **#3** was Cap's face; it was too much of a black glob--it needed to have more highlights underneath to suggest his features. Using the background of **#3** as a point of contrast, sketch **#1** didn't work, and **#2** had Cap going in the same direction as the debris. The lack of chaos around the figure created too much of a static feel, so I needed to rearrange the beams in more of a disorganized manner. This also worked well in helping me create the framing device I was looking for. Applying all these particular problems together led me to sketch **#5**.

There you go. Now you know why I'm insane, but at least the end result was worth the agony. After studying the final thumbnail **#5**, I think I really nailed it with all the principles I was trying to apply in the previous four sketches. Now excuse me while I cut off my left ear, and happy reading!

-- Ron Garney

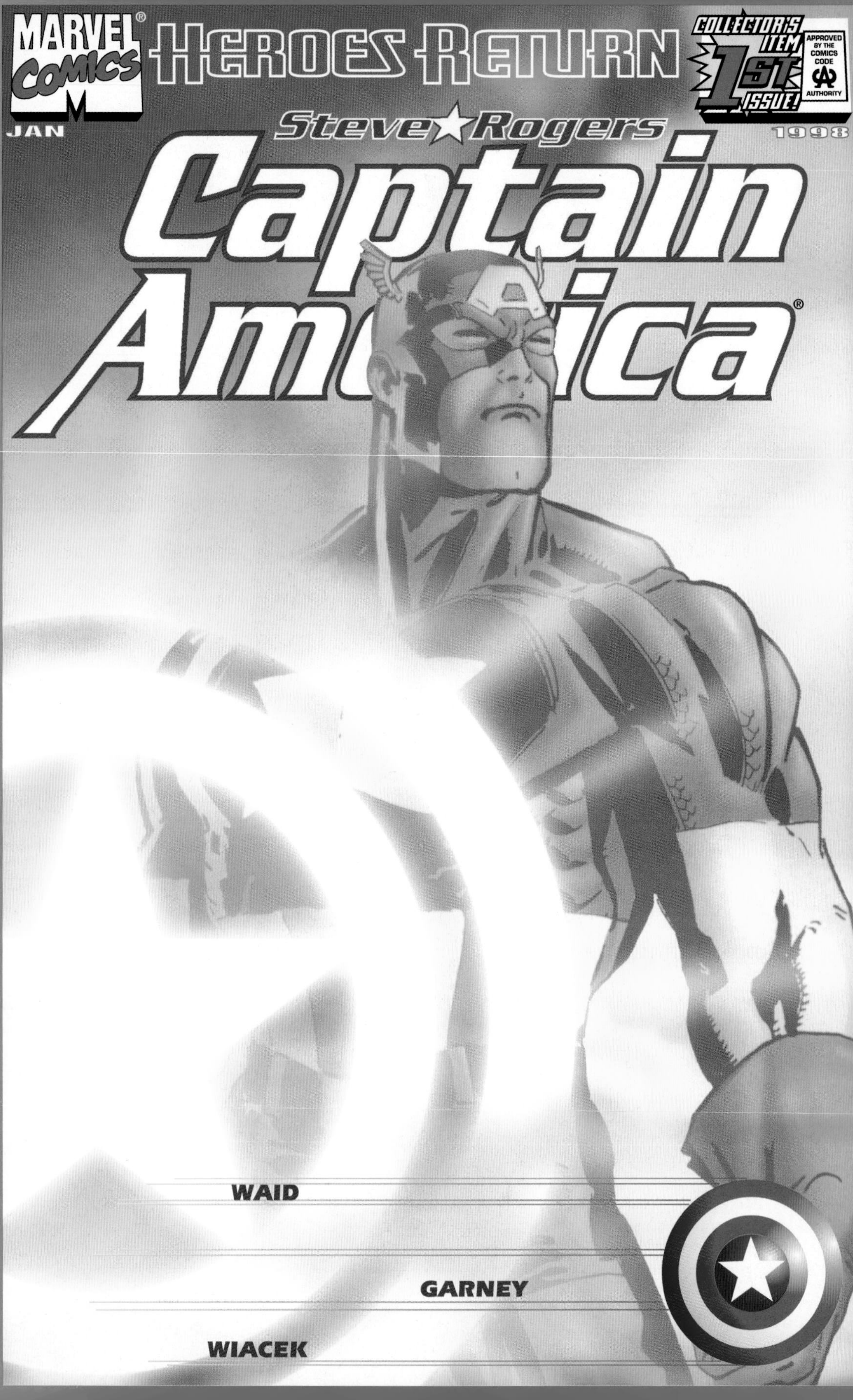
MARVEL COMICS
HEROES RETURN
COLLECTOR'S ITEM 1ST ISSUE!
APPROVED BY THE COMICS CODE AUTHORITY
JAN
Steve★Rogers
1998
Captain America
WAID
GARNEY
WIACEK